Creativity, Innovation and the Cultural Economy

What is creativity, and how can we understand innovation? Are they one and the same? Are cultural and creative industries the lodestone of the knowledge economy?

This edited collection discusses the interrelationship between creativity and innovation, and the cultural and creative industries. Working through a range of international industry specific case studies, the book examines the nature of a range of cultural and creative industries (such as film, new media, theatre, galleries, music, design and advertising) and the important similarities and differences between them. It raises the question of whether it is valid to see the cultural and creative industries as the 'leading edge' of innovation and creativity in the contemporary economy, and whether the cultural and creative industries are as innovative and creative as the rest of the economy.

The book highlights the role of particular cultural industries within the cultural economy, paying attention to the dynamics of context, organisation and labour process issues. It is particularly critical of the concept of innovation and creativity as a 'magic bullet' in the contemporary economy; the collection offers an alternative conception of the 'field of innovation and creativity' that is embedded in place, and in social and economic networks. This collection brings together international experts to consider key issues and debates from across this developing arena of the global knowledge economy.

The book will be useful to students and researchers in the cultural and creative industries, business organisation, management, labour markets and economic geography. It will be of particular interest to geographers, planners, economists and sociologists concerned with the localisation of cultural production.

Andy C. Pratt has been researching and writing about the cultural and creative economy for more than a decade. He has advised policy makers at urban, national and international levels: most recently UNCTAD and UNESCO. Andy is a Reader in Urban Cultural Economy in the Department of Geography and Environment, and Director of the Urban Research Centre at the London School of Economics.

Paul Jeffcutt is Professor of Management Knowledge and the Founding Director of Queen's University's interdisciplinary Centre for Creative Industry. He is a published poet and has been elected to the Academy of Social Sciences (AcSS) and elected Fellow of the Royal Society of Arts, (FRSA).

Routledge studies in global competition

Edited by John Cantwell
Rutgers, The State University of New Jersey
and
David Mowery
University of California, Berkeley, USA

1 **Japanese Firms in Europe**
Edited by Frédérique Sachwald

2 **Technological Innovation, Multinational Corporations and New International Competitiveness**
The case of intermediate countries
Edited by José Molero

3 **Global Competition and the Labour Market**
Nigel Driffield

4 **The Source of Capital Goods Innovation**
The role of user firms in Japan and Korea
Kong-Rae Lee

5 **Climates of Global Competition**
Maria Bengtsson

6 **Multinational Enterprises and Technological Spillovers**
Tommaso Perez

7 **Governance of International Strategic Alliances**
Technology and transaction costs
Joanne E. Oxley

8 **Strategy in Emerging Markets**
Telecommunications establishments in Europe
Anders Pehrsson

9 **Going Multinational**
The Korean experience of direct investment
Edited by Frédérique Sachwald

10 **Multinational Firms and Impacts on Employment, Trade and Technology**
New perspectives for a new century
Edited by Robert E. Lipsey and Jean-Louis Mucchielli

11 **Multinational Firms**
The global-local dilemma
Edited by John H. Dunning and Jean-Louis Mucchielli

12 **MIT and the Rise of Entrepreneurial Science**
Henry Etzkowitz

13 **Technological Resources and the Logic of Corporate Diversification**
Brian Silverman

14 **The Economics of Innovation, New Technologies and Structural Change**
Cristiano Antonelli

15 **European Union Direct Investment in China**
Characteristics, challenges and perspectives
Daniel Van Den Bulcke, Haiyan Zhang and Maria do Céu Esteves

16 **Biotechnology in Comparative Perspective**
Edited by Gerhard Fuchs

17 **Technological Change and Economic Performance**
Albert L. Link and Donald S. Siegel

18 **Multinational Corporations and European Regional Systems of Innovation**
John Cantwell and Simona Iammarino

19 **Knowledge and Innovation in Regional Industry**
An entrepreneurial coalition
Roel Rutten

20 **Local Industrial Clusters**
Existence, emergence and evolution
Thomas Brenner

21 **The Emerging Industrial Structure of the Wider Europe**
Edited by Francis McGowen, Slavo Radosevic and Nick Von Tunzelmann

22 **Entrepreneurship**
A new perspective
Thomas Grebel

23 **Evaluating Public Research Institutions**
The US advanced technology program's intramural research initiative
Albert N. Link and John T. Scott

24 **Location and Competition**
Edited by Steven Brakman and Harry Garretsen

25 **Entrepreneurship and Dynamics in the Knowledge Economy**
Edited by Charlie Karlsson, Börje Johansson and Roger R. Stough

26 **Evolution and Design of Institutions**
Edited by Christian Schubert and Georg von Wangenheim

27 **The Changing Economic Geography of Globalization**
Reinventing space
Edited by Giovanna Vertova

28 **Economics of the Firm**
Analysis, evolution and history
Edited by Michael Dietrich

29 **Innovation, Technology and Hypercompetition**
Hans Gottinger

30 **Mergers and Acquisitions in Asia**
A global perspective
Roger Y. W. Tang and Ali M. Metwalli

31 **Competitiveness of New Industries**
Institutional framework and learning in information technology in Japan, the US and Germany
Edited by Cornelia Storz and Andreas Moerke

32 **Entry and Post-Entry Performance of Newborn Firms**
Marco Vivarelli

33 **Changes in Regional Firm Founding Activities**
A theoretical explanation and empirical evidence
Dirk Fornahl

34 **Risk Appraisal and Venture Capital in High Technology New Ventures**
Gavin C. Reid and Julia A. Smith

35 **Competing for Knowledge**
Creating, connecting and growing
Robert Huggins and Hiro Izushi

36 **Corporate Governance, Finance and the Technological Advantage of Nations**
Andrew Tylecote and Francesca Visintin

37 **Dynamic Capabilities Between Firm Organisation and Local Systems of Production**
Edited by Riccardo Leoncini and Sandro Montresor

38 **Localised Technological Change**
Towards the economics of complexity
Cristiano Antonelli

39 **Knowledge Economies**
Innovation, organization and location
Wilfred Dolfsma

40 **Governance and Innovation**
Maria Brouwer

41 **Public Policy for Regional Development**
Edited by Jorge Martinez-Vazquez and François Vaillancourt

42 **Evolutionary Economic Geography**
Location of production and the European Union
Miroslav Jovanovic

43 **Broadband Economics**
Lessons from Japan
Takanori Ida

44 **Targeting Regional Economic Development**
Edited by Stephan J. Goetz, Steven C. Deller and Thomas R. Harris

45 **Innovation, Knowledge and Power**
Theodora Asimakou

46 **Creativity, Innovation and the Cultural Economy**
Edited by Andy C. Pratt and Paul Jeffcutt

Creativity, Innovation and the Cultural Economy

Edited by Andy C. Pratt and Paul Jeffcutt

Routledge
Taylor & Francis Group
LONDON AND NEW YORK

First published 2009
by Routledge
2 Park Square, Milton Park, Abingdon, Oxon, OX14 4RN

Simultaneously published in the USA and Canada
by Routledge
270 Madison Avenue, New York, NY 10016

Routledge is an imprint of the Taylor & Francis Group, an informa business

Typeset in Times New Roman by Swales & Willis Ltd, Exeter, Devon
Printed and bound in Great Britain by
TJ International Ltd, Padstow, Cornwall

British Library Cataloguing in Publication Data
A catalogue record for this book is available from the British Library

Library of Congress Cataloging in Publication Data
Creativity, innovation and the cultural economy/edited by
Andy C. Pratt and Paul Jeffcutt.
p. cm.
Includes bibliographical references and index.
1. Cultural industries. 2. Creative ability in business.
3. Knowledge management. I. Pratt, Andy C. II. Jeffcutt, Paul.
HD9999.C9472C74 2009
658.3′14—dc22
2008041888

ISBN10: 0–415–41975–1 (hbk)
ISBN10: 0–203–88001–3 (ebk)

ISBN13: 978–0–415–41975–8 (hbk)
ISBN13: 978–0–203–88001–2 (ebk)

Contents

List of illustrations

Boxes

Tables

Figures

List of contributors

Chris Bilton is director of the MA in Creative and Media Enterprises at the Centre for Cultural Policy Studies, Warwick University. He is the author of *Management and Creativity: from creative industries to creative management* (2007), and is currently working on a book on *Creative Strategy*, co-authored with Professor Stephen Cummings. Prior to his academic career, Chris worked in community arts, theatre and local arts development.

Doris Ruth Eikhof is Lecturer in Organization Studies at the Stirling Management School, University of Stirling, UK, and Research Associate at the Wirtschaftsuniversität Wien, Austria. Her research interests include creative industries, changing forms of work and organisation, organisational boundaries, organisations and lifestyles and social theories in organisation studies. She has published in international and German academic journals and books and is co-editor of *Work less, Live more? Critical Analysis of the Work-life Boundary* (2008).

Simon Frith is Tovey Professor of Music at the University of Edinburgh, **Martin Cloonan** is Senior Lecturer in Music at Glasgow University and **John Williamson** is a PhD student at Queen Margaret University, Edinburgh, and manager of Belle and Sebastian. They have worked together on various projects concerning the music industry in Scotland, and Frith and Cloonan are presently directing an AHRC funded research programme on the promotion of live music in the UK.

Rosalind Gill worked for 10 years in LSE's international and interdisciplinary Gender Institute. She recently moved to the Open University to take up a Chair in Social Psychology and Cultural Theory. She is author of *The Gender Technology Relation* (with Keith Grint; Taylor & Francis, 1995) and *Gender and the Media* (2007). She is conducting research on the experiences of people working in new media, and has recently completed a large study of workers in web design, digital special effects and the games industry with Andy Pratt and Volker Spelthann.

Galina Gornostaeva is an associate research fellow in the Department of Geography at LSE, she works on issues of film and television industry in

London, cultural clusters and quarters and night-time economy. She has participated in several research projects including the ESRC funded project on production chains in film and television industry, the INTERREG IIC funded project GEMACA II on functional urban regions in Europe, etc. She has also taught the course 'Information Technology and Society' at the University of Greenwich.

David Hesmondhalgh is Professor of Media and Music Industries in the Institute of Communications Studies at the University of Leeds. His publications include *The Media and Social Theory* (co-edited with Jason Toynbee, Routledge, 2008) and *The Cultural Industries* (2nd edition, 2007).

Tom Hutton is Professor in the Centre for Human Settlements at the School of Community and Regional Planning, University of British Columbia, Canada. His research agenda concerns processes and outcomes of industrial restructuring in the metropolis. He has conducted investigations of change in production systems, labour markets, and land use, with special emphasis on the cultural economy of the city. His recent work includes a series of articles in *Urban Geography, Urban Studies, Cities,* and *Environment and Planning A.*

Deborah Leslie is Associate Professor in the Department of Geography and Programme in Planning at the University of Toronto. Her research interests focus on cultural industries, urban-economic development policy, and commodity chains. She is co-author of a number of recent articles on the design sector in Montreal, and recently co-edited a special issue of *Environment and Planning A* on geographies of creativity. Her recent projects include work on Liberty Village, a creative quarter in inner city Toronto, the circus in Montréal, and the dynamics of talent attraction and retention in the art and fashion industries in Toronto.

Mark Lorenzen is Associate Professor in the Department of Innovation and Organizational Economics, Copenhagen Business School. In his research, Mark focuses upon economic organisation of the market, in e.g. networks, projects and clusters, currently within the cultural industries. Mark is Director of the *imagine Creative Industries Research Centre*, member of the executive committee of the Danish Research Unit on Industrial Dynamics (DRUID), and Executive Editor of *Industry and Innovation.*

Sean Nixon teaches media and cultural studies in the Department of Sociology at the University of Essex. He is author of *Hard Looks: masculinities, spectatorship & contemporary consumption* (1996) and *Advertising Cultures, gender, commerce, creativity* (2003). He is currently working on a book on post-war advertising practitioners provisionally titled *Entrepreneurs of Affluence*.

Dominic Power is Professor of Economic Geography at Uppsala University, Sweden. His research is concerned with regional and industrial competitiveness, consumption, branding, and innovation dynamics. His chief empirical focus has been the workings of the cultural industries: in particular the music, design and fashion industries. Dominic has worked as a policy advisor and consultant to various Nordic government ministries and innovation authorities.

Norma Rantisi is Associate Professor in the Department of Geography, Planning and Environment at Concordia University in Montreal, Canada. Her research interests focus on the restructuring of mature manufacturing industries, local innovation systems and the cultural economy of cities. She has authored several articles on the economic organisation of New York City's fashion industry and co-authored articles on the design economy of Montreal. She is presently researching the geography of design innovation for the Montreal fashion and fur industries and examining how Montreal's social and cultural characteristics contribute to the dynamism of its videogame industry.

Sara Selwood is Professor of Cultural Policy and Management at City University, London, and an independent cultural analyst. She was previously Head of the Cultural Programme at the independent think-tank, the Policy Studies Institute, and Quintin Hogg Research Fellow, University of Westminster. Much of her research focuses on cultural policy and the subsidised cultural sector. She has written extensively on the relationship between the expectations of policy, its implementation, funding and the publics' experience of cultural provision. She edits *Cultural Trends*, a journal which combines statistical evidence on the cultural sector with commentary and interpretation.

Acknowledgements

Andy would like to thank Ros Gill for supportive feedback, constructive criticism and patience with this book. Thanks also to Tom and Kat for being living reminders of the creativity and innovation that all humans possess.

Paul would like to thank David Hitchens, Michael MacBean, Elizabeth Sloss, Phil Morgan, John Clements, Gisela Lauschner, Peter Trimble, Maxine Orr and Nigel Rodden for their help and encouragement during what has been a difficult time.

Andy and Paul would like to thank ESRC and AHRC for having faith in their idea that a sound academic knowledge base needed to be constructed for the cultural economy; we both thank the hundreds of enthusiastic contributors and attendees at the programme of seminars that we organised across the UK over the four years of funding. The legacy of this series is a website which contains its archives and a live list serv: www.jiscmail.ac.uk/cgi-bin/webadmin?A0=cultural-industries.

Our sincere thanks to Terry Clague at Routledge for supporting the production of this book and to Tom Sutton for taking it though the final stages.

Thanks to Tarek Virani for final copy-editing and indexing.

Part 1

Introduction

1 Creativity, innovation and the cultural economy

Snake oil for the twenty-first century?

Andy C. Pratt and Paul Jeffcutt

Introduction: surveying the territory

Creativity has recently joined innovation and become a key term in debates about the knowledge economy. It is difficult to find a popular book on this topic at present without 'cultural' or 'creative' in the title. In one sense, this attention is obvious: which person, group, firm, city or region would aspire to be uncreative (and not innovative)? Put in this way, of course, nobody. But is this the right question to ask? Such characterisations of innovation and creativity present them as 'magic bullets': one shot solutions to problems. It is tempting to ask whether innovation and creativity might not be the new 'snake oils'. Certainly, no one has managed to bottle either. This is not to suggest that creativity and innovation are unimportant, rather that we have to be careful how we understand and work with them. In this chapter we argue that this recent enthusiasm for creativity needs to be placed in context and, in particular, connected to strategic responses to competitive and globalised challenges in the contemporary economy.

There are two main types of strategic response from those concerned with managing the economy. In the first response, it is believed that competitiveness can be maintained by downward pressure on costs that are either met by the substitution of labour by technology, or by cheaper labour (usually in a different region or nation state). In the second response, competitiveness can be maintained through innovation in products and services. The focus on 'price', which underpins the first response, has been termed 'old competition', whilst the focus on quality, innovation (and creativity) has been called 'new competition' (Best, 1990).

In 'new competition', innovation relies upon creativity in the generation of novel products and services. Indeed, in enterprises, it is creativity (or invention) that stimulates and supports the achievement of innovative outputs. Organisations may thus become configured to value creativity and innovation as sources of competitive advantage rather than as additional costs. Hence, the second cycle places emphasis upon loose networks of enterprises that can mix and match skills and expertise to produce short runs of new products and services of high quality at short notice.

With creativity and innovation at a premium in short product runs and rapidly changing product ranges, the key question that follows is how to maximise creativity and innovation in any individual, enterprise, region or economy. In order to respond effectively, one has to understand where creativity and innovation is 'located'. Obviously, individuals are a primary source of creativity (and invention), but it is somewhat short-sighted to simply seek to increase the 'creativity' quotient of each individual in the hope that this will make a significant difference. Whilst we acknowledge that all humans have the potential to be engaged in 'creative' activities we would reject a 'psychological pathology' of creativity which reduces it to some 'hard-wired' aspect of the brain. Likewise, we find the binary categorisation of activities – 'creative' or 'not' – unhelpful. Our emphasis here is on the mobilisation of creativity – in other words, how the 'creativity effect' is achieved. This effect, we argue, will always be socially and economically situated.

Are innovation and creativity one-and-the-same? Certainly, it is common usage that creativity is the 'ideas' part of innovation; innovation usually being characterised as the practice of implementing an idea (for example, see Amabile *et al.*, 1996). Others dispense with creativity altogether replacing it with stages of innovation (for example, see Van de Ven *et al.*, 1999). For others still, creativity is quite different from innovation. Creativity encompasses new knowledge, whereas innovation may not be creative and can be incremental (for example, see Bessant, 1998). On the other hand a common measure of innovation is the number of patents registered. As has been extensively discussed, such measures mis-identify innovation processes: a patent is only valorised when it is turned into a product. Despite their differences most points of view acknowledge that context is important for innovation and creativity.

New ideas certainly require a context in which they may be nurtured, developed and passed on, or made into something more generally useful. Some contexts and settings appear to enable creativity and innovation to flourish – but is creativity and innovation all context? Clearly, creativity and innovation do require both context and organisation – indeed, creativity and innovation do appear to be embedded in a complex interaction of the two. In other words, creativity and innovation need to be addressed as a *process* (requiring knowledge, networks and technologies) that enables the generation and translation of novel ideas into innovative goods and services. This key (but still poorly understood) process in the contemporary knowledge economy has been underlined by recent interest in creative industries and the cultural economy.

In Scott's (2007) view, the rising importance of the cultural economy signifies a phase of convergence and culturalisation of global capitalism. However, the debate about the cultural economy, whilst certainly important, may be distracting when mired in this binary discussion. What, if anything, is specific, or exceptional, about the cultural industries that comprise the cultural economy (as opposed the *culturalised* economy)? What is the relationship between the cultural economy and the knowledge economy? Is the cultural economy, as some authors claim, the leading edge of economic change that other industries will follow?

A better understanding of this cultural economy is thus crucial to understanding the global complexity of the contemporary knowledge economy. However, currently there is a lack of strategic knowledge about the relationships and networks that enable and sustain creativity and innovation in the cultural economy. Recent work on these problems, such as those identified in the papers collected in this volume, emphasises the significance of particular types of knowledge relationships in particular situations.

The aim of this book is to examine the formulation, relationships between and practices of creativity and innovation in the cultural economy. The collection comprises of six pairs of chapters that examine the issue from the perspective of different industries within the cultural economy. We have chosen to offer pairs of chapters in order to stress the importance of an openness to methodological variety in the analyses; this objective also results from our starting point, namely that both quantitative and qualitative methods are required, as well as a range of approaches, within and across both. The social sciences have been in the grip of a 'cultural turn' in recent years; namely, they have sought to develop a less functional or reductive approach to economy and society (Amin and Thrift, 2004). At present, we are far from a consensus as to what such a new 'approach' might be. However, there has been a lively exchange about the cultural and more broadly, social, aspects of economic life. The irony is that until now the cultural turn has not been matched by a similar focus on the cultural economy as an object of analysis. Consequentially, our approach has been to seek out the social and cultural dimensions of economic life of the cultural economy. Lest we back into another difficulty, we would immediately state that we reject any hard and fast distinction between the socio-cultural and the economic; we are working on the basis that they are co-constitutive (Pratt, 2004).

A second starting point is that the cultural economy is characterised by variety; obviously, collectively it may be argued that the cultural economy is distinguishable from the 'rest' of the economy in some important ways, but there are also significant variations across particular industries. In effect, this blurs the distinction between the cultural economy and the 'rest' by acknowledging commonalities as well as differences. There has been a sustained debate over the last decade about the naming and definition of the cultural economy. Labels such as creative industries, cultural industries, creative economy and cultural economy, or cultural and creative industries have all been used. Whilst academic cases can be made for a differentiation between them, the overwhelming policy discourse is one in which they are used interchangeably (see Pratt, 2005). This does not help clarify the concept, nor make it operational. Thus, the real struggle is to develop meaningful statistical definitions from the definition popularised by the UK Department of Culture, Media and Sport, which identifies 13 industries that comprise the 'creative industries' (see Box 1.1). This is significant because it has been copied extensively by many policy makers and academics. Despite the global popularity of this definition, it does have a number of significant shortcomings (see Jeffcutt, 2008): for example, it focuses on outputs but excludes the public sector, informal activities, and the 'production of culture'. A definition developed for UNESCO – the framework for cultural statistics (Box 1.2) – is far more useful in an analytic sense as it is based upon a 'production chain' model that exposes the dynamics that underlie the outputs; it is the one that we prefer to use here.

Box 1.1 The UK Department of Culture Media and Sport definition of the 'creative industries' (DCMS, 1998)

Advertising
Architecture
Arts and Antiques
Crafts Design
Designer Fashion
Film
Leisure Software
Music
Performing Arts
Publishing
Software
Television and Radio

Third, we point out that the cultural economy and the 'rest' of the economy is not static, nor universal. The cultural economy has emerged from being a relatively insignificant part of economic life to a major player in advanced economies. Moreover, some have argued that the rise of the cultural economy is part-and-parcel of a wider transformation of the whole economy: the culturalisation of the economy. From a cultural point of view many argue that the commodification of culture has led to its economisation, placing bias in favour of quantity and against quality

Box 1.2 The cultural industries production system, the example of music (see UNCTAD, 2008)

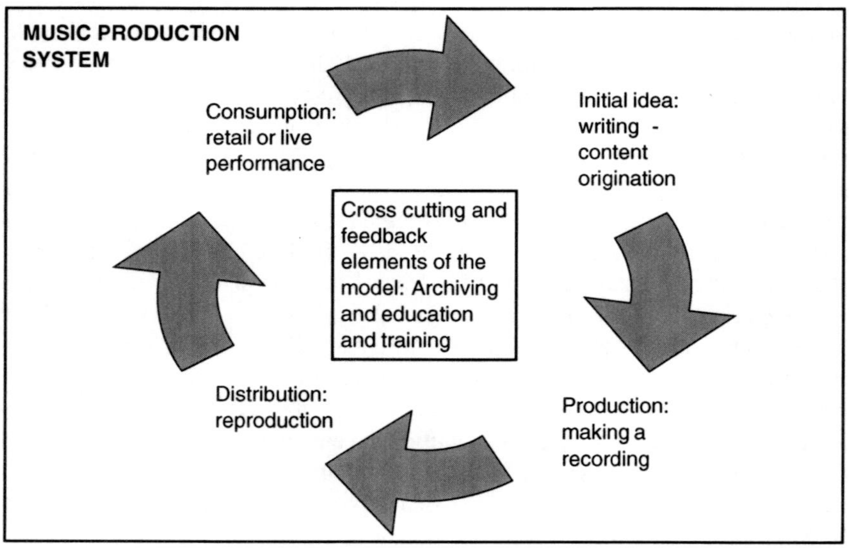

of cultural products and artefacts. Thus, it is increasingly difficult to disentangle the rise of the cultural economy from the transformation of the 'rest', and it is unclear what the causal direction and strength is. For many policy makers it is this innovation or creativity 'spill-over', and not the intrinsic or substantive economic and cultural value, that is the prize to be gained from the promotion of the cultural economy. Such a view rests on the assumption that culture and entertainment are necessarily inferior and dependent upon the 'real economy'.

Aside from the growth of the cultural economy, there has been discussion as to whether it might be different in organisational terms. Certainly, there appear to be some common characteristics of the cultural industries (See box 1.3), evidenced by many studies. The further dimension of this question is that the cultural economy does seem to operate variously in different industries, and it does not operate equally the world, or nation over. One of the distinctive points about the cultural economy is its unequal distribution, and asymmetric power/value-structure of the key organisations and networks, as well as its tendency to co-locate or cluster in a small number of places. Obviously, this has consequences for both economic and cultural development. Recent debates about cultural production chains have raised the issue as to whether the upgrading of activities in some locations to higher value activities is possible (for example, from production to design) (Pratt, 2008b). Critically, this organisational variation concerns the changing scale of operation of the cultural economy, and the variety of regulatory and governance contexts within which it operates. In a similar manner to which 'varieties of capitalism' have been identified (Hall and Soskice, 2001), we would expect to find 'varieties of cultural economy' *and* variations *within* the cultural economy.

Box 1.3 Characteristics of the cultural industries

- An industrial structure better characterised as an ecosystem
- Overlapping networks, mediated by intermediaries and facilitated by the movement of freelance workers and informal interaction
- A relative lack of middle-sized companies
- A preponderance of short life, project based companies with freelance workers
- Massive market uncertainty, coupled with very high risk of failure
- Very rapid turnover of innovation, fashion and the product cycle
- A 'winner takes all' system: massive differences between what it means to win and lose
- Tension between content regulation and competition regulation

Fourth, we want to highlight questions about the very notions of creativity and innovation, their relationship, and their character. We seek to challenge what we regard as a simplistic and superficial notion that creativity and innovation are separate and distinct 'things' that can act as inputs, or outputs, or are connected in a unilinear process. Our stress is upon the exploration of the relational nature of these ideas. As we will note, thinking about creativity and innovation in a relative manner opens up a fruitful line of investigation.

However, before we get to this point in our discussion it is necessary to distinguish our position in relation to some common, or taken for granted, assumptions. The 'big questions' that are often brought to the table in debates in this field are: What is the relationship between creativity and innovation?; Is innovation or creativity in the cultural economy the same, or different, to that found in the 'rest'?; and, What is the relationship between the cultural economy and the 'rest' of the economy (does it, in effect, act as a creative stimulus)? The main body of this chapter sketches out our position on, and relationship to, these questions. Our approach mobilises a multi-disciplinary background, drawing upon sociology, economics, geography and management studies.

Building a better mousetrap

What counts as innovation, and how might it be understood? The answer is either to 'build a better mousetrap', or to originate 'the very idea of a mousetrap'. That is, make something everyone will want, and no-one has thought of before. With mousetraps as with innovation more generally it is difficult to separate out the incremental from the revolutionary change. Thus, it is common to fall back on a proxy, something that is believed to be associated with innovation. Here, the common culprit is 'technology'. Of course, technology is another term for the application of a novel process or product innovation. However, as we will note below 'throwing technology at a problem' does not make an innovation, it merely offers a way in which a product or process can be modified. Whilst it is clear that there is significant investment in new technology, it is not so clear that this has directly led to comparable, or greater, increase in output. Many researchers argue that claims about the role of new technologies in economic growth have generally been based upon 'hope value' rather than fact (Jorgensen and Stiroh, 2000; Oliner and Sichel, 2000). Furthermore, it is not obvious whether new technologies *cause* things to be done differently, or are simply the exploitation of opportunistic changes. There are clear cases where the possibilities of new technology are deployed by managers to achieve reorganisation and cost savings, but such changes are not a necessary outcome of the application of technology. Classic examples of organisational change are the adoption of digital newspaper production in London in the 1980s, self-operated news reporting adopted by television companies, and the adoption of 'bi-media' strategies by both broadcasters and newspapers in the early 2000s. Interestingly, changes in film production appear less significant, with much of the attention being placed on the use of special effects for artistic expression; digitisation has not yet greatly impacted upon distribution and exhibition.

Generally, we can view innovation and creativity in at least two ways with particular respect to the cultural economy: first, related to content origination; second, associated with industrial production. If we consider content production, traditional ideas encapsulate the Romantic notion of 'the artist as genius' (Pratt, 2007). By this we simply mean that innovation and creativity are seen as being primarily located in an individual, for example 'the author' or 'the artist', the outputs of which are routinely put into standardised production (be it in the form of a book or a film). Significantly, this tradition of the primacy of the individual artist/author interconnects with the valorisation of longstanding separations between the arenas of culture and industry (for example, see Jeffcutt *et al.*, 2000). Of course, as has also been pointed out, copyright law has instituted these notions to such an extent that creative workers may resist copyright regulations *in order to be* creative (that is their process does not correspond to the individualistic model presumed by the legal concept of copyright). Moreover, we do not have to look far to find examples of large corporations who are copyright holders blocking the innovative use of ideas (see Lessig, 2004). This is not to suggest a 'free for all', simply that copyright controls always need balancing such that they actually protect and enable the processes that they were created to support.

These atomistic concepts of creativity and innovation are often linked with diffusion models to account for dissemination and change, such that a quantum of 'innovation' can be 'diffused' to a population. Lack of innovation is thus like a railway network, and can be considered a failure of the carrier (the diffusion system). Of course, this may also be a result of the failure of the technology. Criticisms of these notions come from those who stress the importance of context, that of organisations and institutions in shaping ideas (Hodgson, 1993). In our railway example it might be a lack of co-ordination of operating companies, or poorly integrated time-tabling. In an example drawn from the cultural economy we could consider the editorial function of a publishing house in the case of a book, or, the actors, director, camera operator, or the commissioner of the programme/film etc. in the case of film and television. Classic examples of this institutional or organisational effect have been discussed in relation to the role of genre, and of 'programming' and schedules, that provide the necessary pigeon holes for ideas, and thereby make 'boundaries of the possible' for creativity and innovation (Williams, 1990).

The same analytic tensions exist in conceptualisations of innovation in respect to industrial production. Traditional models of innovation characterise a linear, discrete, stepwise process, which begins with a 'bright idea' (an innovation), and proceeds via prototype and manufacture to market. Such a model makes implicit assumptions about causality and process, for example, that innovation is a discrete activity, or that it has a unidirectional causal relationship with manufacture and production. Moreover, linear innovation models are linked to two other narratives: first, the notion of diffusion of ideas through society and space; second, that of the external relationship of technology and organisation to economic processes. This ideal-type concept of innovation can be bent to either a methodological individualism or a structural functionalism.

Endogenous growth: the perpetual motion machine

Economists are prisoners of their own models, the assumption that everything that is not defined or assumed is 'exogenous' to the model, factory or region. A classic case is an import or export – the distinction seems plain enough, until one examines it in practice when it may be one and the same thing. Exogenous growth is seen as inferior to endogenous growth; the former requires inputs from outside, the latter develops its own inputs. This has often been characterised as 'learning by doing' (Arrow, 1962). As with imports and exports, the devil is in the detail of definition. For the general reader, it may be surprising to discover that technology is an exogenous factor for economists, as are innovation, creativity, knowledge and organisation. Thus, the focus is on how to manage, transfer (from where it is in surplus to where it is in demand), and efficiently use the scarce resource in question. Thus, the developing business or economy needs to source ideas, technologies, etc. from elsewhere; however, it is like a hamster on a wheel: running faster but going nowhere. The alternative – to undercut labour costs – seems to be even worse, to do more will result in less.

A new variant of exogenous growth masquerading as endogenous growth, based upon 'creativity' is found in Florida's (2002) notion of the creative class. In its simplest interpretations this idea has been used to argue for a new form of place marketing based on a cultural beauty contest. With cities seeking to out 'boho' the others and thus to become the 'coolest city to be'. Florida argues that the 'creative class' are a mobile labour force who are attracted to tolerant and culturally rich cities and neighbourhoods; therefore, a new downtown boho 'cultural magnet' needs to be created. Importantly, Florida argues that the creative class are important because high quality, hi-tech, employers will move to where they are. So, the city that attracts the creative class will benefit from the new technology that comes with the high-tech businesses. So, whilst this strategy looks superficially to be an endogenous story it is in fact an exogenous one. There is no attention to the development of sustainable cultural production, only to sites of cultural consumption (Peck, 2005; Pratt, 2008a).

Put in this way it becomes clearer that the scarce resource in question is knowledge itself. Not surprisingly, endogenous growth theories (Nelson and Phelps, 1966; Romer, 1994) seek to re-define terms (internalising, or substituting, some of the exogenous factors), thus creating new organisations, new labour processes, new labour contracts and a research and education system to sustain the flow of new ideas and people. As we noted earlier some strategists have argued that focusing on both 'quality' and 'knowledge' (or creativity) puts one in a favourable position – at the head of the pecking order, a leader in the information society. However, despite the enlightened race for the heights of knowledge, as opposed to the bargain basement of the sweatshop, these notions still rely upon a problematic conception of knowledge – its just that 'we' have it, rather than our competitors. It is not the purpose here to deny competition exists, but it is to point out that knowledge is not atomistic; it is relational and contextual, and can take on particular powers when combined in specific ways.

Building upon traditional notions of agglomeration economies, so-called constant returns to scale, the idea of industrial clustering has become popular with policy makers (DTI 2001). As numerous critiques have pointed out, the processes of interaction and their precise benefits have not been established for industries in general (Martin and Sunley, 2003), let alone for the cultural industries. However, this has not held back policy makers and politicians from recommending 'cultural clusters' as a solution to economic regeneration. As noted earlier, such policies commonly have an instrumental character to them associated with place marketing rather than the sustainability of cultural industries. Clearly, in order to form the latter, one would need a sophisticated understanding of the processes by which cultural industries benefited, or not, from co-location. As we will elaborate in this collection, the nuanced interplay of social and physical embedding in place and industry may produce the innovative effect. Clustering may be necessary, but it is not sufficient, for innovation. Clearly we regard as mistaken the presumption that converting an old building and branding it a cultural quarter will lead to either economic activity in the cultural economy, or urban regeneration.

Other approaches are emerging in the wake of the technologies and systems of the world wide web that illustrate the multi-dimensional character of knowledge and learning. We are not suggesting that this technology and organisation is intrinsically more 'innovative', only that it has yet to be normalised and proscribed and shaped as rigourously as previous technologies. What is commonly known as 'web 2.0' relates to an interactive and peer-to-peer networking process that is possible with this technology. It enables a reconfiguration of old norms. Two examples of which are 'the long tail' and the 'wisdom of crowds'. In the former (Anderson, 2006), the supply of cultural goods was previously limited by warehousing costs; moreover, the logical business model was to encourage consumers to have minimal choice and benefit from economies of scale in supply and manufacture. Thus cultural products for which there was a small audience lost out, it was too expensive to provide for them. The so-called long tail model points to the possibility with digital goods where storage and distribution are nearly zero, so that even goods for which there is a very small market may, over a very long time recoup investment. Time is no longer the penalty it was. In the latter case (Tapscott and Williams, 2006), it has been argued, most clearly in 'Wikinomics', that it is possible to develop new products and ideas using proprietary controls and secrecy, but in the end it is very expensive. The alternative is to have the R&D done by a large number of individuals (also termed 'democratised innovation', see von Hippel 2005); examples of this being the development of the Linux operating system and software, as well as the encyclopaedia Wikipedia.

The insight that these empirical examples point to, in relation to our prior discussion, is a simple one, but one that mainstream concepts deny, that knowledge can be advanced collectively and relationally. Perhaps the transformation of web 2.0 could suggest that previously it was not possible to develop sufficient 'critical mass' of interested parties in a project in one place at a time. At the same time several researchers in the field of intellectual property law have pointed out that the current configuration of intellectual property laws was based upon a materialist conception of property not on a relational nor virtual conception. Moreover, that the current regime may have the effect of undermining the very creativity that it was established to protect.

Re-conceptualisations

The linear and atomistic innovation model as discussed in the section before last, applied to content or to technology, still remains a common lay conception;

however, it is much criticised in academic writing (Simmie, 2004; 1997). Three categories of criticism can be identified: first, those that find fault with the unidirectional nature of the model; researchers have pointed to the importance of feedback mechanisms, and this agenda has obvious resonance with the work on innovation systems that have emerged from institutional and evolutionary economics (Hodgson, 1993). The second theme of criticism is one that seeks to substitute a network model in the place of a linear-feedback one. Broadly speaking, institutional approaches seek to internalise elements of organisation and of technology into the processes of production; in some analyses these also extend to the incorporation of governance or regulatory relationships. Third, the notion that ideas are autonomous, free standing, or that technical objects are 'self-defining'. The criticism here is that meaning and use are context dependent, as has been debated under the heading of the Social Shaping of Technology (SST) (MacKenzie and Wajcman, 1999; Pratt, 1996). SST studies take issue with the ontological and epistemic assumptions of atomistic and teleological perspectives that underpin many notions of innovation. SST is critical of the teleological and determinist inflection of technology and organisation in this work, as well as what it regards as the naïve empiricist assumptions of the constitution of objects. There is not space to elaborate on these debates here; however, we want to position ourselves to engage with the SST thematic. Perhaps one of the most striking and novel dimensions of SST work is the agency that it seeks to situate with 'users' and the 'objects of technology' (Cawson et al., 1995; Haddon, 1992; Woolgar, 1991). The emphasis is very much on the situated co-constitution of objects, products and effects. Very simply, such approaches direct our attention to the ways in which final users, or more generally markets, cannot be viewed as simple receptors of innovation, instead they might be better considered as constituting the utility of innovations.

A simple case, taken from another media, music, might be the design of the *Apple iPod* by Jonathan Ive. The design created a market and wove together technologies to create a new form of music distribution and potential revenue models. More specifically, it is interesting to see how a key site of struggle has been the 'chart' that previously mimicked distribution channels. In heterogeneous fashion markets (book, music, film, etc.) charts perform an important function of concentrating demand on a small number of products, and specifically, one product that gains near monopoly profits from being 'No 1'. The very fact of being 'No 1' means that, aside from the publicity engendered, distribution channels stock the item. The potential of download charts to dilute market concentration and hence monopoly is clear counter to the interests, and past organisation, of industries such as music, film and fashion (Jeffcutt and Pratt, 2002; David Hesmondhalgh's chapter elsewhere in this collection). An important point in such analyses is the deconstruction of notions of 'technology' and 'innovation' and their companion atomistic and romantic notions of artists that are otherwise mobilised in traditional analyses in an unproblematic way.

Discussion of the social shaping of technology seeks to reposition innovation and creativity as co-constructions and outcomes or effects. Researchers point to the temporary success of innovations when other conditions are stabilised, or held steady, or, all participants are encouraged to enable something to happen. It is apparent that this is as much of a political and management achievement as one of economics and technology, and of material things. Researchers examining the organisation of work in the cultural economy have highlighted a couple of aspects of work that are becoming more widespread. The first is the performative nature of work; it is not simply enough to perform the task, but it has to be done in a particular manner, in extreme cases almost as theatre. This performance extends to appearance and dress; Warhust (2001) terms it aesthetic labour. The second is the incorporative nature of management. Boltanski and Chaipello (2005), in an extensive study of changing management practices, have pointed to the way that employers seek to minimise the alienation of 'creatives' through 'soft' management techniques, we also see this in Chris Bilton's chapter in this collection. Elsewhere, Thrift (2005) extends this notion to suggest that new management discourses have come to characterise 'soft capitalism'. Writers such as Hardt and Negri (2004) have suggested that such means are doomed to failure, as in effect they are creating a new precarious army of labour (from cleaners to 'creatives') which will have common cause and will potentially reject the siren calls to give their labour 'free' and their ideas to employers. As Rosalind Gill shows in her chapter, the demands of aesthetic and emotional labour might be different in kind, but otherwise just as exhausting as those of physical labour (see Gill and Pratt 2008).

The core questions of this book

Pulling together the threads of the arguments and criticisms reviewed in this chapter we can now highlight what we feel are important questions concerning the relationship of creativity and innovation, and the cultural and creative industries (CCI). Whilst the field of the cultural and creative industries is marked by research and assertions that they are 'different' from the rest of the economy, there is little discussion about the variations between the different industries, nor amongst the same industry along its production chain. Hence, a central argument that we need to test is whether the cultural and creative industries are 'cut from the same cloth' or to what extent they are different from one another, and why.

Our main focus in this introduction has been both the conceptualisation of creativity and innovation, and to what extent may this be regarded as a characteristic (or differentiator) of the cultural and creative industries. The outcome of this concern is of considerable interest to policy makers, like that of the differences between and within the cultural and creative industries already referred to. The discussion in this chapter has sought to tease out a number of strands. First, we offered some criticisms of the ontology of innovation and creativity: was it a quality of an individual or a structure? We pointed to the inadequacies of both approaches, plus the related ways of measuring creativity and innovation in terms of outputs and inputs (which normative accounts suggested were open to manipulation via incentives based upon rational choice). Our point, a significant conceptual challenge to normative literature in the field, was that innovation and creativity are better conceived as 'emergent'; or to put it another way, they are constituted by the agent in a structural context, the outcome of which cannot be simply anticipated in advance and is subject to considerable feedback (and, one major source of uncertainty, the competence of agents to recognise, understand and act upon, such feedback).

We argued that such a perspective resonates with the strong critique of linear and unidirectional models of innovation and creativity. Once again we found that the potential for feedback and learning was constituted *in situ*, in places, and in an embodied fashion. Simply reading about it was not enough, you had to be there. This embodied nature of interaction was related to the subtlety and timeliness of information exchange, its often informal character, and its reliance upon (the swiftly shifting) reputation of the carrier. A useful representation of this process is characterised – after Bourdieu (1993) – as the 'field of innovation and creativity'. Finally, we draw another radical conclusion – one that is increasingly being suggested in empirical studies – that of the collapsing of the categories of production and consumption into one another; or, at the very least the creation of a significant and fluid relationship between them[1].

Given our argument for the importance of situated and embedded practice, we could not, nor have sought to, offer a detailed 'model' of innovation and creativity; instead we underline the importance of detailed and industry- and place-specific studies to bring out these issues. This approach should not be read as a rejection of any cross-locational or industrial process, rather that one should be able to identify some common processes; but also, that one can see how even similar processes, when mobilised under different conditions, produce a variety of outcomes[2].

Approach and structure

This section elaborates upon the method behind the structure of the collection, and how we have sought to use this to develop an interrogatory framework that tests and challenges some of the assumptions laid out in this introductory chapter. Our book is different from most that have been written about the cultural and creative industries; its main point of differentiation is the fact that we seek to highlight the role of particular cultural industries within the CCI sector, paying attention to organisation and to labour process issues. This is a point that has been made elliptically in the various creative industry mapping documents where cultural and creative industries are differentiated, for instance, in the classic UK version in 13 industries. However, whilst these reports use a taxonomic division of the cultural and creative industries, little further analysis is carried out into the possibility of different forms of organisation, innovation or creativity, or labour organisation or process that is to be found there. Such a lack of empirical investigation has led to a lack of questioning of the normative statements concerning the internal sameness of the cultural and creative industries (and their difference to non-cultural and creative industries). Hence, our desire in this collection is to examine differences as well as similarities within industries.

It was not our objective to provide a comprehensive and complete study of every industry, in particular the taxonomies of the creative industries; we sought to focus on a range of different industries that might point out salient issues. Our selection encompasses the traditional fields of the arts looking at galleries and museums; and extends all the way to the ultra-commercial field of advertising. We draw upon analyses of the design field, perhaps the most amorphous but emblematic area of the creative industries, particularly for politicians and lay people an expression of the 'creative' premium. We also examine the traditional and well recognised, but under-researched, stalwarts of film and television. Finally, we take in the range from the new to the old media form, notably those at the cutting-edge of digitisation: new media to music. We believe that our selection illustrates the range of activities in the cultural economy. We have also sought to draw upon a range of national contexts: primarily European, but including North America. These nation states are in an internationally controlling position regarding the political economy of the cultural economy. However, the impact and organisation of the cultural economy is global in its reach, and clearly there still remains a need for complementary analyses from the rest of the world. We recognise this as a weakness, and one that, given our emphasis upon the social, economic, cultural and political embedding of cultural production, is even more limiting. However, this collection is but a starting point and we hope that others will follow to pick up these themes (see Barrowclough and Kozul-Wright 2006; UNCTAD 2008; Kong and O'Connor 2008).

Given our comments about the conceptualisation of innovation and creativity, and the appropriateness or not of particular data, we pay particular stress on more qualitative methods of information gathering. A related problem for researchers is how to reach out beyond the narrow confines of traded and formal products and information; the role of trust and reputation suggests a rather complex 'terms of trade' between individuals and groups. Thus, our contributors steer clear for the most part of general measures and indicators in favour of trying to understand the processes and translation of information and ideas, as well as the socio-economic structures, networks and institutions that sustain them. As will be noted in the concluding chapter, we argue that this approach has yielded particular insight into the processes under which the cultural and creative industries operate, as well as the subtle differences between different industries as they constitute their local forms of innovation and creativity.

The industries/chapters covered

The aim of the chapters that constitute the body of this book is to look more closely at the process of innovation and creativity in the context of the cultural economy. As noted earlier, by pairing the chapters we have sought to bring out further dimensions of the range of processes involved, and point to appropriate means of information capture. Moreover, we have selected chapters from an illustrative range of industries that comprise a range of the cultural economy. Our objective here is to point out the salient differences, as well as similarities within these activities. We have chosen writers from a range of disciplines as we argue that a multi- and cross-disciplinary perspective is needed on these issues. Indeed, the papers originated in a programme of seminars we organised, funded by both the Social Science (ESRC) and Arts and Humanities (AHRC) research councils in the UK.[3] The objective of these seminars was twofold: to highlight and develop academic work in the field of the cultural economy, and to develop a language and forum for the interchange of knowledge about research on the cultural economy.

The 12 substantive chapters are paired into 6 industries; we use the pairing to play off different approaches and methodological insights as a strategy to highlight a variety of nuances of particular industries. We begin our illustrative journey across the breadth of the creative and cultural industries with advertising in London, perhaps the most obvious example of 'commercial' culture. However, as we can see in the chapters by Sean Nixon and Chris Bilton, a pure art/commodification dichotomy is not simply apparent, rather it is one of both a mixture of commercial *and* creative pressures, without a presumption of which will gain the upper hand. The issue is never simply a matter of cost, but of a particular quality. An intriguing point that arises from these chapters is how are such qualities instilled? In a complex manner both chapters examine different ways in which particular types of workers have been constituted by the industry through its organisational structure, its recruitment, and its office culture.

The next pair of chapters shifts our focus to music; here, again we have two contrasting perspectives that highlight significant complexities. Simon Frith, Martin Cloonan and John Williamson's paper on the music industry in Scotland discusses the instrumental use of music for economic development that fails to attend to the music form itself. David Hesmondhalgh examines the regulatory structure of copyright that, whilst so often presented as protection of the artist, may often as not undermine artists through a transfer of rights to a larger corporation. Both chapters illustrate how a nuanced understanding of music production is a foundation for unpicking the 'creative process' and beginning to consider effective interventions into it.

The third pairing illustrates very clearly the complex trade-off that occurs between creativity and profit in the film industry. Whilst Mark Lorenzen examines the framing of creativity at an industry and organisational level, the second paper by Andy Pratt and Galina Gornostaevas' on London's film industry shifts its emphasis to the governance of risk within the film making system. Both chapters highlight the local constitution of what constitutes creativity and risk – on the one hand the role of industrial organisation structures, and on the other regulatory structures, a point which echoes the chapters on advertising.

The fourth pairing examines the new media industry, predominantly the area of design for the World Wide Web. Tom Hutton's paper on Vancouver provides us with a clear example of the urban and physical co-location of this industry (a point that can be replicated in other cultural and creative industries); it is clear that such industries are embedded in place. Rosalind Gill's chapter on web designers in Amsterdam takes us inside the new media companies and workers' lives. She provides a stark and subtle illustration of the social and affective nature of work in this industry, and the ways in which 'new' work practices are embedded in identity and a particular form of sociality (again illustrating the corresponding existence of strong 'artistic', as well as 'commercial' values).

Our fifth pair of chapters examines the design industry, which is for many casual observers the archetypical 'creative' activity. Returning to the theme of policy-led attempts to promote 'creativity' as we saw in Simon Frith, Martin Cloonan and John Williamson's paper on music, Deborah Leslie and Norma Rattansi's work based in Montreal, examines the attempt to promote creativity more generally through the promotion of 'design'. Dominic Power's paper drawing upon a case study in Stockholm also pursues this theme, but – touching on some of the themes that the papers by Rosalind Gill, Andy Pratt and Galina Gornostaeva, and Sean Nixon raised – seeks to focus on the processes of clustering and affect.

Our final pairing locates us at the core of the traditionally defined 'arts' sector. Many might baulk at calling this an industry; however, the papers illustrate in contrasting ways that the melding of commodification and art are the everyday experience (as in the more commonly considered 'commercial' fields). Taking two contrasting nation states – Germany with a traditional well supported state system, and Britain with a 'middle way', state guided but one in which commercial support is vital – Sara Selwood's elaboration of the case of British galleries and museums, and Doris Eikhof's case study of German theatre, show how creativity is as much in the juggling of resources and institutional norms, as it is on stage or in the gallery. Again, this underlines the hybrid nature of cultural production, even in what is usually considered the 'pure art' sector.

Notes

1 See the work on pro-sumption (Tapscott and Williams 2006).
2 Our approach draws upon the ideas of critical realism for such an insight (see Pratt 2008c).
3 ERSC award number: RES-451–26–0090.

References

Amabile T, Conti R, Coon H, Lazenby J and Herron M, 1996, 'Assessing the work environment for creativity', *Academy of Management Journal* 39:5 pp. 1154–1184.

Amin A and Thrift N, 2004, *The Blackwell Cultural Economy Reader*, Blackwell, Oxford.

Anderson C, 2006, *The long tail: how endless choice is creating unlimited demand*, Random House Business, London.

Arrow K J, 1962, 'The economic implications of learning by doing', *The Review of Economic Studies* 29: pp. 155–173.

Bessant J, 1998, 'Developing continuous improvement capability', *International Journal of Innovation Management* 2: pp. 409–429.

Best M H, 1990, *The new competition: institutions of industrial restructuring*, Polity Press, Cambridge.

Boltanski L and Chiapello E, 2005, *The new spirit of capitalism*, Verso, London and New York.

Barrowclough D and Kozul-Wright Z, 2006, *Creative industries and developing countries: voice, choice and economic growth*, Routledge, London.

Bourdieu P, 1993, The field of cultural production, or The economic worlds reversed, in *The field of cultural production: essays on art and literature*, (ed.) R Johnson, Polity Press, Cambridge, pp. 29–72.

Cawson A, Haddon L and Miles I, 1995, *The shape of things to consume: delivering information technology into the home*, Avebury, Aldershot and Brookfield, USA.

DCMS, 1998, *Creative industries mapping document*, Department of Culture, Media and Sport, UK, London.

DTI, 2001, *Business clusters in the UK: a first assessment*, Report by Trends Business Research, Department of Trade and Industry, London.

Florida R L, 2002, *The rise of the creative class: and how it's transforming work, leisure, community and everyday life*, Basic Books, New York.

Gill R and Pratt A C, 2008, 'In the social factory? Immaterial labour, precariousness and cultural work', *Theory, Culture & Society*, 25: pp. 1–30.

Haddon L, 1992, 'Explaining ICT consumption: "The case of the home computer"', in *Consuming technologies: media and information in domestic spaces*, (eds) R Silverstone and E Hirsch, Routledge, London, pp. 87–92.

Hall P and Soskice D, 2001, *Varieties of capitalism*, Oxford University Press, Oxford.

Hardt M and Negri A, 2004, *Multitude: war and democracy in the age of Empire*, The Penguin Press, New York.

Hodgson G M, 1993, *Economics and institutions: a manifesto for a modern institutional economics*, Polity Press, Cambridge.

Jeffcutt P, 2008, 'Creativity and knowledge relationships in the creative industries, in *The Routledge Companion to Creativity*, (eds) T Rickards, M Runco and S Moger, Routledge, Abingdon, Oxon, pp. 88–98.

Jeffcutt P, Pick J and Protherough R, 2000, 'Culture and industry: exploring the debate', *Studies in Cultures, Organizations and Societies* 6:2 pp. 129–143.

Jeffcutt P and Pratt A C, 2002, 'Managing creativity in the cultural industries', *Creativity and Innovation Management* 11: pp. 225–233.

Jorgensen D and Stiroh K, 2000, 'Raising the speed limit: US economic growth in the information age', *Brookings Papers on Economic Activity* 31: pp. 125–211.

Kong L and O'Connor J (eds), 2008, *Creative economies, creative cities: Asian-European perspectives*, Springer, Berlin.

Lessig L, 2004, *Free culture: how big media uses technology and the law to lock down culture and control creativity*, Penguin, New York.

MacKenzie D A and Wajcman J, 1999, *The social shaping of technology*, Open University Press, Buckingham, England and Philadelphia.

Martin R and Sunley P, 2003, 'Deconstructing clusters: chaotic concept or policy panacea?', *Journal of Economic Geography* 3: pp. 5–35.

Nelson R R and Phelps E S, 1966, 'Investment in humans, technological diffusion, and economic growth', *The American Economic Review* 56: pp. 69–75.

Oliner S and Sichel D, 2000, 'The resurgence of growth in the late 1990s: is information technology the story?', *Journal of Economic Perspectives* 14: pp. 13–22.

Peck J, 2005, 'Struggling with the creative class', *International Journal of Urban and Regional Research* 29: pp. 740–770.

Pratt A C, 1996, 'The emerging shape and form of innovation networks and institutions', in *Innovation, networks and learning regions*, (ed.) J Simmie, Jessica Kingsley, London, pp. 124–136.

——, 2004, 'Retail Therapy', *Geoforum* 35: pp. 519–521.

——, 2005, 'Cultural industries and public policy: an oxymoron?' *International Journal of Cultural Policy* 11: pp. 31–44.

——, 2007, 'Innovation and creativity', in *The Sage Companion to the City*, (eds) J R Short, P Hubbard and T Hall, Sage, London, pp. 266–297.

——, 2008a, 'Creative cities: the cultural industries and the creative class', *Geografiska Annaler: Series B, Human Geography* 90: pp. 107–117.

——, 2008b, 'Cultural commodity chains, cultural clusters, or cultural production chains?', *Growth and Change* 39: pp. 95–103.

——, 2008c, 'Critical realism', in *International encylopedia of human geography*, (eds) R Kitchen and N Thrift, Elsevier, Oxford.

Romer P M, 1994, 'The origins of endogenous growth', *The Journal of Economic Perspectives* 8: pp. 3–22.

Scott A J, 2007, 'Capitalism and urbanization in a new key? The cognitive-cultural dimension', *Social Forces*, 85: pp. 1465–1482.

Simmie J, 2004, 'Innovation and clustering in the globalised international economy', *Urban Studies* 41: pp. 1095–1112.

Simmie J M, 1997, *Innovation, networks and learning regions?*, Jessica Kingsley and Regional Studies Association, London.

Tapscott D and Williams A D, 2006, *Wikinomics: how mass collaboration changes everything*, Portfolio, New York.

Thrift N J, 2005, *Knowing capitalism*, Sage, London and Thousand Oaks, CA.

UNCTAD, 2008, *The creative economy report*, UNCTAD/ UNDP, Geneva/New York.

UNESCO, 2008, *The 2009 UNESCO framework for cultural statistcis (Draft)*, UNESCO/ UIS, Montreal.

Warhurst C and Nickson D, 2001, *Looking good and sounding right: style counselling and the aesthetics of the new economy*, Industrial Society, London.

Van de Ven A, Polley D, Garud R and Venkataraman S, 1999, *The innovation journey*, Oxford University Press, Oxford.

Von Hippel E, 2005, *Democratising innovation*, MIT Press, Boston.

Williams R, 1990, *Television, technology and social form*, Routledge, London.

Woolgar S, 1991, 'Configuring the user: the case of usability trials', in *A sociology of monsters: essays on power, technology and domination*, (ed.) J Law, Routledge, London, pp. 57–102.

Part 2

Advertising

2a Relocating creativity in advertising

From aesthetic specialisation to strategic integration

Chris Bilton

The title of this book indicates the extent to which aesthetic creativity in the creative industries is being married to a process of managed innovation (Weisberg 2006). Twenty years ago, the concept of the 'cultural' industries located creativity in distinctive cultures, often with a specific cultural geography or an identifiable subcultural content and context. Today definitions of the 'creative' industries and the creative economy relocate and redefine creativity in the managerial rhetoric of value chains, knowledge management and innovation.

In the creative industries, the association of creativity with 'individual skill' and 'talent' (DCMS 1998) draws upon Western Romantic and psychological theories of individual creative genius (Weisberg 1986). At the same time the identification of the creative industries with 'the generation and exploitation of intellectual property' frames creativity in terms of a managed process of production and delivery of inputs and outputs (DCMS 1998). The creative economy takes us still further from notions of individual talent and aesthetic quality. Beyond the officially sanctioned 'core' creative industries, as defined by governments including Britain, the creative economy encompasses R&D, agriculture and 'creative technologies' (Howkins 2001; Bilton 2006). Creative occupations have extended to include everybody from footballers to accountants. The networks which underpin this emergent creative economy extend both horizontally into cultural and aesthetic communities, and vertically into managerial systems of implementation and distribution.

Just as the new rhetoric of creative industries and creative economy locates creativity within a process of managed innovation, today's managers and management gurus are increasingly likely to describe the processes of innovation and management as inherently 'creative' (Prichard 2002). Innovation in technology, management processes and new product development has always contained this element of 'creativity'. 'Innovation' describes a series of processes, including product testing, implementation, market testing, distribution and delivery, through which this raw creative idea is converted into an innovative product or service. Such a progression is not dissimilar to psychological theories of creativity as an incremental process involving multiple stages of development and styles of thinking (Weisberg 1986, Boden 1994, Sternberg 1988). As creative industries and creative processes take on the rhetoric of value chains, inputs and outputs, and vice versa, we should perhaps describe innovation as a variant or extension of the creative process rather than something distinct or separate from it.

Where once we might have described creativity in terms of idea origination, and innovation as a process of idea implementation, today that distinction looks increasingly untenable. What does 'creativity' mean in today's creative economy, and where do we find it? My argument is that creativity is no longer the sole preserve of the traditionally defined creative industry, occupation or department. Creative work and creative workers are having to take on managerial functions. At the same time, managers are beginning to seek recognition for their 'creative' contribution. Creativity is accordingly being relocated and redefined, first as something integral to the process of management, second as a brand value which managers and non-managers actively seek to promote to their clients.

This process of relocation and redefinition will be examined in the advertising industry. Traditionally, creative teams in advertising have been separated from the rest of the agency both structurally through the division of labour between 'creatives' and account managers, and culturally (as Nixon describes in his contribution to this book). In this chapter I argue that creativity in advertising is no longer the preserve of specialist functions and departments, but is used to refer to a broader range of strategic business services. This new emphasis is reflected in the growing importance of media planning and account planning in the organisational hierarchy, and in the prioritising of strategic analysis over creative execution in the industry's value chain.

I will chart these developments through a historical overview of the industry and a more detailed examination of one agency, Naked Communications[1]. The historical section covers three phases. The starting point is a belief in creativity as the core competence of the agency, identified with star copywriters and art directors from the 1960s onwards. Over the next twenty years, this belief has been replaced by a growing emphasis on management competences, in particular the functions of account planning and media planning and a more 'holistic' approach to the client's needs. This change in emphasis was reflected in new business models and structures responding to changing client priorities and a new media environment. Finally I will argue that whilst advertising agencies have redefined their role, from creative producer to strategy adviser, 'creativity' nevertheless remains an important residual reminder of the agency's unique competences and brand. Even if clients are being given a management solution rather than a creative one, the proposed strategy is still likely to be branded as 'creative'. The 'culture' of creativity in advertising, as described by Nixon in this book, is in any case too strong to be submerged in general consultancy services. In this third phase of development I argue that creativity in advertising functions primarily as a branding strategy rather than as a designated function or activity.

1960s to 1970s: creative specialisation

In the advertising industry small creative teams and networks coexist with global corporations. Culturally and structurally, the 'no-collar workplace' (Florida 2002) and 'project ecology' (Grabher 2002) of the creative agency are contained within hierarchical systems of control and accountability. These paradoxes are reflected in the ambiguous positioning of creativity within the business of advertising. David Ogilvy claimed to have banned his staff in his agency from using the word 'creative' to describe any of the functions of advertising (Ogilvy 1963, 91). Sergio Zyman, the former Head of Marketing at Coca Cola, is similarly dismissive, arguing that the business of advertising is about selling, not about creativity (Zyman 2002, 14–16). Historically there has existed a structural and functional division in advertising between the 'creative' work of copywriters and art directors and the management functions of account planning and strategy. Culturally these functional distinctions have been reinforced by the mutual suspicion between 'creatives' and 'suits' (Bilton, Cummings and Wilson 2003; Hughes 2007), based on gender, education and class (Nixon 2003).

When senior advertising professionals like Ogilvy and Zyman express their suspicion of creativity and creatives, they refer to a rather narrow, individualised and self-serving form of creativity which is disconnected from its strategic and commercial goals. Such a narrowly defined, purely aesthetic creativity is only one small part of the business of advertising; Ogilvy is warning that, freed from all constraint and accountability, personal creative goals might overtake the larger objectives of a campaign. To cite a more recent self-critic of creativity in advertising, Simon Clemmow of Clemmow Hornby Inge, 'the desired response to a great ad is not "What a great ad" but "What a great product"' (Clemmow 1999, 67).

This suspicion that creative processes and creative people might get in the way of the business of advertising is both cause and effect of the structural division between account executives and creative teams. The practice of 'buffering' the creative process insulates 'creatives' from direct contact with the client, on the assumption that either the client will undermine the integrity of the creative process, or the maverick creative will sabotage the client relationship (Bilton 2006). This view of the creative individual as a destructive narcissist, is rooted in western theories of creativity, from Plato's 'divine madness' to Weisberg's 'myth of genius' (Weisberg 1986). In management discourse, 'creative destruction' is a disruptive force which can produce positive (Schumpeter 1943) or negative (Levitt 1963) effects.

The narrow definition of creativity as the product of uniquely talented individuals, driven by ungovernable desires, tells only half of the story. Most contemporary theories of creativity insist that individual talents are embedded in social systems or creative teams (Czsikszentmhalyi 1988; Becker 1982), and that invention and inspiration are only possible in a context of more rational processes of logic, memory, expertise and revision (Weisberg 2006; Boden 1994, 75–117). Indeed one of the characteristics of creative people and processes seems to be an ability to switch from one frame of reference to another, between different styles of thinking (Sternberg 1988, Koestler 1964). According to this logic, isolating the creative individual is likely to inhibit the capacity for making unexpected connections; we should instead be exposing our creative teams to different experiences and scenarios. Far from being a delicate, introverted system in need of protection, one of the hallmarks of creative thinking is an ability to tolerate contradictions and encompass different styles of thinking, described by Barron as 'ego strength' (Barron 1968).

Implicit in cognitive theories of creativity and the sociological theories of cultural production referred to here is an assumption that what Margaret Boden calls 'mere novelty' (Boden 1994, 75–76) is inadequate as a definition of creativity. Ideas alone are only truly creative if they are both novel and valuable; this dualism is implicit in the creativity tests and exercises based on problem-solving (Adams 1979, Torrance 1988). Ideas become valuable as they are developed and applied, so theories of innovation and creativity encompass a series of different stages, processes and thinking styles.

In advertising, there is a growing recognition that creativity is no longer the preserve of the 'creative' functions such as art direction or copywriting. Market positioning, communication planning, branding and consumer research all demand forms of creative thinking. At the same time, agencies are responding to the increasingly complex demands of contemporary advertising and marketing. Clients are no longer satisfied by a 'creative' idea – the 30-second television advertisement – but want access to the strategic thinking which precedes and frames it. The 'integrated' approach to marketing communications in the 1990s responded to this demand by attempting to construct a business model in which clients were buying a strategic solution, not just a one-off product (Schulz and Kitchen, 2000).

This broader concept of advertising as a form of strategic consultancy can be seen as another step in the continuing evolution of advertising. In the early twentieth century, the function and business model of advertising were premised on selling space in publications – the creative design and concept of the advertisement were thrown in for free. With the advent of television advertising, the core of the business became the conception and design of original and memorable campaigns; here the creative product took centre stage, and strategic planning was concealed as a valuable 'extra' behind the core costs of producing and placing advertisements.

Creative advertising was made possible by a billing system which cross-subsidised creative work from discounts on media expenditure. These discounts (usually 15 per cent of media spend) were rebated by the media owners to the advertisers and passed on to the advertising agencies as fees. The billing system was dependent on the cost of media, not the value of advertising. There was an inbuilt tendency to prefer expensive mass media, especially television, over cheaper and possibly more effective alternatives. Television advertising in turn became the cornerstone of creative advertising in Britain.

By the 1970s the old business model was threatened by specialist media buying agencies and increased competition brought about as a result of an economic downturn in the industry and by legal challenges to anti-competitive practices (Pratt 2006, 1889–1890). The demise of the commission model has resulted in a structural transformation of the industry over the last 25 years, leading to vertical disintegration ('unbundling') of the full service agency and 'selective horizontal integration' of certain functions, as new alliances are formed between media buying agencies, account planning agencies and creative agencies. Pratt describes these structural changes as amounting to 'a tectonic shift in the advertising landscape' (Pratt 2006, 1890). As a result the creative function is no longer the dominant partner in the advertising process. There is a growing acceptance that media and creative disciplines must work together, based on an acknowledgement that 'media buying can be more creative too' (Pratt 2006, 1895).

Today most agencies bill according to a negotiated fee for services. This has had the effect of disconnecting fees from media spend and forcing a reassessment of what precisely the client is paying for. The fee-paying model makes possible a more strategic, integrated approach in which creative concepts take second place to the overall communication strategy. In effect, where before the core product was advertising and strategy was bundled in for free, today that situation has been reversed and the 'creative' component is often an ancillary product, outsourced to a third party. With the transition to a more complex media landscape, many professionals and commentators argue that the core of the advertising business is media planning (Taylor 2005, Collin 2003). It is argued that media planning, paid for by fees, provides a more valuable and trustworthy service to the client than media buying, paid for on commission.

In the remainder of this chapter, I will explore how definitions of creativity in advertising are changing, and how this in turn is reflected in structural changes in the roles and functions of the industry.

1970s to 1990s: from creative specialisation to strategic integration

Since the 1960s, creativity in advertising has been recognised as a significant asset. In the age of television advertising, a distinctive aesthetic was essential to effective branding. Through the 1960s and 1970s, the specifically 'creative' functions of copywriting and art direction took on a new importance within the organisational hierarchy. At the same time, the 'creative concept' of an advertising campaign was recognised as a significant step in the process of advertising, following on from the 'customer proposition' or 'unique selling proposition' (USP). Whereas the customer proposition required a rational, analytical mindset, the creative concept would draw on other types of thinking, in particular divergent or 'lateral' thinking processes. Stories of quixotic individuals and flashes of inspiration became part of the popular mythology of advertising, obscuring the equally important but less exciting processes of customer research and market analysis which preceded them.

The mythology of 'creative' advertising in the 1960s was closely allied to the mythology of individual genius in creativity. Alex Osborne, who popularised the notion of 'brainstorming' in the late 1950s, developed his approach in the advertising industry. The essence of Osborne's theory was that by removing or deferring the process of evaluation and criticism from the process of idea generation, a group would be empowered to produce more original and abundant ideas. Osborne was putting into practice a theoretical assumption that creative thinking is diametrically opposed to rational, critical judgement. As noted earlier in this chapter, in the light of most cognitive theories of creativity, such an account of the creative process is at best only partially true. Thus Weisberg argues that brainstorming, if it is to be genuinely productive of 'better' ideas (as opposed to simply producing 'more' ideas), needs to be framed by preparatory and evaluative phases which establish rules and precedents and filter the results (Weisberg 1986, 59–69).

What is apparent both in the theory of brainstorming and in the dynamics of twentieth century advertising is not a denial of rational thinking, but a desire to separate out the 'creative' or spontaneous elements in the process from the more deliberate phases of preparation and evaluation. This functional separation was applied both structurally to roles and relationships and dynamically to the process of developing a brief. Structurally, the creative team was to be kept at arm's length from the client and from the commercial realities of the brief. The role of the account executive was designated specifically to protect the creative team from the business of advertising and to provide an autonomous zone of unfettered creativity where ideas could be generated at their own pace and according to their own rules.

The value chain of advertising followed a similar logic of separate specialisms. In terms of process, it is typically followed a sequence of discrete steps, starting from the initial brief from the client. This brief would then be sharpened through research and analysis into a customer proposition. This proposition would in turn be interpreted and transformed into a creative concept. The creative concept would then be implemented and turned into media artefacts (television advertisements, posters, images, slogans, etc.). Finally each artefact would be delivered to the potential customer through the process of media buying. Each of these phases would draw upon different competences, either within the agency or outside it, and would be continually checked back against the explicit and implicit requirements of the client.

Despite the mythology of genius and Osborne's emphasis on unconstrained, free-flowing idea generation, it is clear that even in this model of advertising 'creativity' is more than mere innovation or inventiveness. The creative function is framed within the organisational hierarchy under the overall control of the account executive. 'Creative' employees are given specific roles and responsibilities within a larger system and other departments are needed to deal with other aspects of the work. The whole process draws upon different thinking styles, competences and people, sometimes from more than one organisation.

Nevertheless, the version of advertising described here was problematic on two counts. First of all, the multi-step process was relatively slow and expensive. As the baton passed from one division to the next, the process of converting a brief into a creative concept could take several months. In the meantime market conditions (and client priorities) could change. Costs on both sides were also high. The process of pitching for work required considerable agency input, with no guarantee of securing the account. For the client, the model was premised on the delivery of an artefact (the advertisement) and the intervening stages, however necessary, felt like an expensive preamble. With more sophisticated tools for measuring advertising effectiveness, clients and advertisers began to question 'value for money', and costs were placed under renewed scrutiny. Meanwhile market changes in the last quarter of the twentieth century have made speed to market a key competitive advantage. Advertising is no exception to the new 'post-Fordist' logic of quicker turnaround, just in time delivery and rapidly changing customer needs and wants. In the 1990s, the advertising model of the 1960s appeared slow and expensive.

The second pressure on the old model came from the perceived failure of the traditional 'one-shot' advertising campaign. As media fragmented, the available channels to reach the consumer expanded. The 30-second television spot was no longer the only or best way to reach the customer. The influx of new channels through cable and satellite in the 1980s, followed by the growth of digital and online media, undermined mass media. Given the choice, some clients decided that massive audience reach was not the prime or only objective, particularly in the case of niche products. The process of media planning and media buying thus became increasingly complex. Instead of being the final step in the chain, after all the creative decisions had been made, media planning was, according to some commentators and practitioners, the first step in the chain – the most important set of decisions was not around the creative content but around the methods of communication with the customer (Collin 2003). The ascendancy of media planning was partly at the expense of the creative functions of the agency; as media planners began to call the strategic shots, creative concepts and creative disciplines were relegated to operational status, increasingly delegated outwards from the strategic core of the campaign to other partners and contractors.

Finally the old divisional structure of advertising was threatened by its own success. Advertising functions and expertise became increasingly specialised in response to an increasingly complex market and an increasingly fragmented media environment. The unbundling of services following the demise of the commission system allowed new types of agency with new business models into the system. In the UK these included the new independent media agencies like PhD and Carat. Operational disintegration fuelled a need for strategic integration. Agencies promised a 'one-stop shop' to the client, but were only able to achieve this through a network of partners and relationships with other service providers. Advertising thus became a network business in which a designated 'lead agency' temporarily took centre stage for a given client and configured a supporting cast of appropriate service providers according to the varied needs of the job; next time the roles could just as easily be reversed. Agencies became floating brands for a wider network of individual talents. Integration was achieved by prioritising the strategic objectives of the client and outsourcing everything else.

The demand for faster turnaround and streamlined processes, the demand for more sophisticated media and communication planning, and the growing importance of strategic coordination across multiple agencies all challenged the old advertising model. Taken together these three trends pushed advertising away from a model based on the separation of managerial and creative functions towards their integration. This transformation was underpinned by the abandonment of commission as the basis for agency billing. The result was a restructuring and redefinition of agency functions and a growing recognition that 'creativity is not enough' (Levitt 1963) if it is not embedded in an integrated strategy. This takes us back to the arguments of Ogilvy, Zyman and Clemmow at the start of this chapter. What then are the consequences of these developments for the meaning and location of 'creativity' in advertising?

1990s to present: creativity as strategy, strategy as creativity

Creative thinking in advertising today has become more closely integrated with strategic thinking. This integration is reflected in job descriptions, organisational structures and the preoccupations of commentators in trade journals like *Campaign* and *Admap*. The core product of the industry is no longer creative content or 'great ads', and has become instead the development of a strategic (and creative, perhaps) approach to communications with the customer. This leads away from the free-flowing, self-consciously spontaneous creativity of Alex Osborne in the 1960s towards a definition of creativity based on problem-solving. In theory at least, the industry appears to have abandoned the old 'genius' myth of individual creativity in favour of a multidimensional, multi-perspective model, using multiple intelligences and thinking styles. In practice, as will be seen, the old charismatic mythology has proved difficult to cast off.

As a business, advertising has recognised the importance of strategic planning as a dominant partner and has relegated or outsourced many of its creative functions. At the same time, culturally and psychologically, most of those working in the industry still see advertising as a creative industry and regard themselves as creative thinkers. This impression is reinforced by a trade press which celebrates novelty, quirkiness and high profile 'creative' personalities. One way of squaring this circle has been to change the definition of creativity. In effect, 'creativity' has been redefined to apply not just to the copywriter and the art director but to the media planner, the strategist and the researcher. What does all of this mean for the status and definition of creativity in advertising? In particular, how have the roles and functions of agencies changed to reflect the rhetorical shifts outlined here?

The redefinition and repositioning of creativity in advertising is reflected in structural changes in response to changing market conditions and new business models. Agencies have sought to innovate along the whole value chain, from original customer insights through to branding and communication strategies. Structurally the business model is based on the total package of services, in particular the integration of media planning functions with creative content. As noted at the start of the chapter, advertising agencies have moved from a purely aesthetic, individual model of creativity towards a managerial model of product innovation. Yet they have not altogether abandoned the old rhetoric and culture of individual creative genius, now reapplied to brand the integrated, strategic model as itself inherently creative. Here I want to consider three related examples of a more 'integrated' approach to creativity in advertising: account planning, media planning and branding.

Account planning – reconfiguring the value chain

From its origins in the 1960s, account planning was popularised by agencies such as Chiat Day and Fallon during the 1980s and 1990s. At first account planning simply responded to the need for a more sophisticated integration of market research into the advertising process. Account planners were thus expected to provide 'consumer insight' and to act as 'the voice of the client' within the agency, mediating between client needs and creative process. In terms of the agency's internal value chain, account planning was located at the start of the process, close to the client's original brief.

This research function of account planning expanded to occupy a more strategic role within the agency. As markets and consumer behaviours became more diverse and unpredictable and brands more powerful, account planners played an increasingly important role on the creative side of the agency. Planners were expected to integrate an understanding of clients, consumers and brands and to condense these insights into a clear strategic proposition which would form the core of an agency's creative work. This strategic role also consolidated their creative function as 'midwives to creativity' (Hackley 2003).

Mike Sims at EHS Brann cites one of the truisms of account planning: 'a problem well defined is a problem half solved'.[2] According to Sims, if the client gets the briefing right, the job of the creative team is easy. If the initial brief is not right, it becomes extremely difficult for the creative department to salvage the situation. Winston Fletcher reinforces the point in his 'brief on briefing'; effective briefing, according to Fletcher, is an integral part of the creative process in advertising (Fletcher 1999, 83–90). The strategic role of the account planner thus became part of the creative process.

Michael Porter has pointed out that value chains are essentially hierarchical (Porter, 1985). Bargaining power is distributed unevenly between buyers, sellers and intermediaries. In terms of the advertising value chain, planners were upstream of the creative departments and their proximity to the client gave them a political advantage over the creative team. Working out the strategic proposition allowed the planner to pre-empt the creative decisions which occurred downstream of them. By taking ownership of the value chain, the account planner also takes ownership of the creative idea.

The value chain in advertising depends upon clear divisions of labour. Copywriters and art directors may well become resentful of account planners who attempt to intervene too directly in the creative execution of an idea; Kathy Slack, herself an account planner at Bartle Bogle Hegarty, warns planners not to 'follow the creative along the corridor'.[3] Nevertheless, the difference between account planning and market research is that a good planner will translate consumer insights and strategic propositions into a language designed to stimulate the creative process, not to inhibit it. The germ of the creative idea is already there, it is up to the creative team to bring it to life.

Media planning – redefining creative thinking

The pre-eminence of account planning in advertising has more recently been challenged by the emergent discipline of media planning. Media buying has always been the financial core of the industry, and media agencies have emerged as powerful players in the industry, able to call the shots over their creative counterparts because they effectively define their resources and priorities. This dominant industry position has been strengthened as a result of increasingly ambitious media strategies. With the expansion of media channels since the 1990s, agencies have struggled to provide clients with what Mike Sims calls a 'total customer solution', with different experiences of the brand in different media meshing together to form a composite whole for the consumer. For this to occur, the different media elements needed to be coordinated. Having outsourced much of their old expertise in media to external specialists, agencies now had to take back control over the process and did so by appointing communication specialists to take charge of media planning.

As with the account planner, the media planner took control of the value chain by asserting a strategic role which pre-empted other inputs and made other roles secondary. Where the account planner had achieved this by claiming proximity to the client, the media planner claimed proximity to the customer. Only by understanding the various ways in which consumers experience the product and the brand could an agency understand how to communicate with them. And only by establishing the most effective method or methods of communication could an agency select the most appropriate creative ideas.

Changes in the commission system had removed the special relationship between advertising agencies and the media, creating new economic opportunities for independent media buying agencies in the 1980s and 1990s. A new generation of media agencies set out to consolidate this advantage by presenting themselves as not just media buyers but communication and media planners. PhD was one of the first such agencies in the UK, and in 2000 staff from PhD helped to found a new agency called Naked Communications. Will Collin, one of Naked's founding partners, became one the most articulate proponents of media planning. Collin (2003) argued that the media planner is in the business of strategic communication. Beginning from customer research, the media planner analyses the available channels and comes up with a strategic proposition which can work across various media appropriate to the client. The creative execution of the advertising must work within these boundaries. As noted earlier, the relationship between creative concepts and media strategy was reversed – now media planning became the starting point, not the afterthought.

Naked was one of a handful of agencies which pioneered the idea of 'media neutrality' in advertising. The principle behind 'media neutrality' was that the approach to communication should not be wedded to any specific medium or even to a specific methodology. This approach aimed to correct the inherent bias in the old commission system by focusing on the relationship with the customer and selecting the most appropriate means of reaching them. Media decisions preceded and pre-empted creative decisions on content.

The strategic importance of media planning has been reinforced by the shift towards advertising in digital media. According to figures from Carat Group, television advertising revenues in the UK showed a fall of 4% from 2005 to 2006 and advertising revenues in digital media rose by 45% during the same period. Meanwhile Channel 4's chief executive Andy Duncan recently announced that he expected Google to overtake Channel 4 in extracting advertising revenues in the UK market for 2006 (Times, November 1st 2006). The evidence for such a shift is debatable,[4] but the fact that Duncan felt it politic to highlight the claims of a rival medium in this way is nevertheless revealing. Even mainstream advertisers have begun to exploit new media including email, websites and mobile, and to work with a roster of smaller agencies rather than a single 'one-stop shop'.[5]

The significance of these developments is qualitative rather than quantitative. Nobody is denying that mainstream television remains the best method of reaching a mass audience instantly, and despite percentage shifts, television still commands the majority share in advertising revenues. Most of the brands making creative use of digital media (BMW, Honda) continue to use television advertising as well. However, the qualitative difference is that digital media are more complex and require a more precise alignment of targeted consumers and niche products. Effectiveness can be tracked more accurately, for example by counting 'hits' on company websites; meanwhile the quality of attention given to television advertising is threatened by new technologies and changing consumer attitudes (Ritson 2003). Digital media allow consumers to 'pull' content according to their interests and needs by registering their preferences, participating in viral campaigns and uploading personal information to advertisers in exchange for customised offers. Digital media are part of a more complex, targeted and interactive media system where customer needs are more varied and individualised, and where customer relationships have replaced one-off transactions as the most valued commodity. To take advantage of these new media requires a more strategic approach to media and communication.

What this means in practice is that that the 'product' of the agency becomes a creative communication strategy rather than a creative execution. When Naked was hired to promote the UK telephone directory service 118 118 The Number, the creative concept (two long distance runners sporting retro running vests and moustaches) was chosen specifically because it would work across multiple media, not just on television. In order to reach the target market of busy, mobile professionals, a combination of viral advertising and street media was selected prior to roll-out of the television campaign. Having identified the appropriate media channels and communication concept, Naked was happy to hand over the creative reins to its partner agency, WCRS. But the key strategic decisions were already in place.

The founders of Naked have emphasised a commitment to communication in its purest 'naked' form and placed media planning at the centre of their creative work. The redefinition of creativity in terms of value for the client is carried over into the modus operandi, with detailed attention to planning and delivery at the point of consumption outweighing the grand creative concept; creativity in advertising is perhaps becoming more client-led. 'Creative' work in the older sense of devising striking combinations of words, ideas and images has to a large extent been outsourced to partner agencies, leaving staff free to concentrate on strategy and delivery. Of course these elements of planning and operational control have always been part of the agency offering, in the form of account planning and account handling. Naked's boldest innovation may not be in their attempt to talk up these elements as strategically important, but in their attempt to brand media planning as part of the 'creative' mix.

Brand consultancy – from hired gun to trusted partner

By moving functions like account planning and media planning from the back room of consumer research to frontline strategy, companies like Naked are challenging definitions of 'creativity' in advertising. Naked does not describe itself as an advertising agency, preferring to describe its role as 'creative problem solver' for the client. Creativity is now being used to describe a combination of brand and media consultancy, not in the specialised, functional sense referred to by Ogilvy and Zyman at the start of this chapter. As a theoretical model of creativity, this approach seems more convincing than the genius mythology surrounding a handful of great designers, copywriters and art directors. However, it does also produce some challenges for the advertising industry.

As noted at the start of this chapter, advertising is a network industry with a range of service agencies being connected together to provide an overall solution to the client. Increased complexity and sophistication of consumer behaviour, media channels and brand identities have combined with changes in the business model to 'unbundle' the full service agency. This has encouraged greater specialisation in the industry. It has also created a need for intermediaries who can manage these networks of specialists on the client's behalf and connect them together into an integrated strategy. This is the leading role sought by the major players in the advertising industry, whether they are communications specialists like Naked Communications or more traditionally structured 'creative' advertising agencies like BBH. As Mike Sims at EHS Brann notes, the aim of today's advertiser is to move from service provider to 'trusted friend' of the client.

Advertising is a competitive industry, particularly at the 'creative' end of the business; barriers to entry are low and the appeal of novelty and change is high in an industry which loves to hype the next big thing. Clients recognise the PR value of switching accounts, and career turnover among marketing directors on the client side encourages competitive 'churn' among agencies; every marketing director, especially if newly appointed, recognises the personal kudos of changing agencies. Small wonder then that agencies seek to consolidate their best friend relationship with their clients. Strategic partnership lifts the agency out of the choppy waters of inter-agency competition and allows them greater control instead of being on the receiving end of other people's decisions.

In order to take on this role of strategic consultant, today's advertising and communication agencies must claim to understand the client's brands better than the client. In the past this role might have been taken on by the client's own marketing department. The new intermediaries like Naked and PhD argue that because brands are entangled in complex relationships with consumers and media channels, an external agency with expertise in these fields is better placed to identify and develop the brand than is the client.

This is a bold claim. The problem with this position is that 'strategy' is an even less tangible product than was 'creativity' in the past. At least with 'creativity' the advertising agencies could lay claim to a specialism that lay outside the client's frames of reference. By offering 'strategic' solutions to the client's problems, they are moving onto the client's own turf. And it is much harder to build a mystique around business consultancy services than it was to glamourise the creative process.

Two recent episodes illustrate the problems in upholding the 'trusted friend' role. In July 2006 one of Naked's most prestigious clients, Honda, announced that it was parting company with the agency after four years. During that period Naked had been involved in some highly regarded campaigns including the 'cog' advertisement made by creative agency Wieden and Kennedy, showing a series of components from the Honda Accord rolling, bumping and tapping into each other to form an extraordinary chain reaction filmed in a single take (allegedly at the 606th attempt). Three months earlier Honda had appointed a new marketing director, Jeff Dodds. According to the trade journal *Campaign*, one possible explanation for Honda's decision was that Naked had been too successful. One of the risks in setting up an effective strategy is that there is little incentive to continue to hire the strategy consultant once the strategy has been agreed (*Campaign*, July 21st 2006). Despite claiming that Honda no longer had a 'requirement for a communications planning agency', Dodds retained the services of the creative agency, Wieden and Kennedy. In this case the need for strategy was temporary, but the creative partnership was continuing.

The second episode was the departure of Russell Davies, Head of Planning at Wieden and Kennedy, to work for Nike in February 2005. Davies was and still is regarded as one of the leading practitioners of account planning and had been in the business for 20 years. In choosing to work on the marketing of a global brand from the inside, rather than as its 'trusted friend' on the outside, perhaps Davies too, like Dodds, was sending a message to the advertising industry: however much the account and media planners would like to manage the process, strategy is still controlled by the client.

By attempting to include branding strategy in the mix of services they offer to their clients, agencies are beginning to take on the core business functions previously undertaken by their clients. The gradual merging of 'creative' and 'strategic' functions described here, from account planning and media planning to branding, completes the transition from creative specialisation to a broader definition of creativity as something integral to business, not separate from it. Advertising has always sat awkwardly among the core creative industries, combining aesthetic creativity with commercial realities. Yet the overlapping creative and strategic functions of advertising may be part of a more general shift in the creative industries, recognising that creativity depends on organisational innovation as much as it does on individual talent and skill.

So what is creativity in advertising?

I began this chapter by suggesting that definitions of creativity in the creative industries are being stretched to encompass a broader, more holistic approach to creativity, business and strategy. Along with their contemporaries and sometime collaborators at Mother and CHI, Naked Communications belongs to a new generation of UK advertising and media agencies which claim to challenge the existing structures and models of business in advertising. This is reflected in their rejection of traditional hierarchies and job titles, the use of open plan offices and 'hot-desking', the move away from the geographical hub of Soho towards less conventional locations and premises (Mother was at one time housed in a caravan, while Naked began life as a strategy shop floating on a boat on the Thames). All these innovations have been gleefully observed by a trade press which likes to highlight new trends and personalities. Yet behind the self-consciously quirky exterior, much of what these agencies do is far removed from the old stereotype of 'creative' advertising, firmly rooted in market research and planning – the kind of functions which a previous generation of creative advertisers would have consigned to a back room marked 'research', outsourced to a media agency, or left to the client's own marketing department. By labelling creativity as a form of strategy and vice versa, agencies like Naked are having it both ways – embracing a broader, more holistic definition of creativity at the same time as holding onto their roots as a maverick start-up staffed by 'brilliant misfits'.

Restructuring of the business of advertising has led to a more holistic approach, with account planning and media planning tightly integrated with the creative execution of a campaign. The functional specialisms are still there, but are increasingly being outsourced to external agencies. What emerges is a more integrated approach in which creative teams and creative ideas are expected to work within strategic objectives, and communication and branding strategies are expected to integrate with creative concepts. The approach is more collective and less dependent on the star creatives of the 1980s and 1990s who came up with memorable mass media campaigns. Today a great deal of creative advertising takes place below the line, in packaging, point of sale, direct marketing and online advertising – not in the 30-second mini-movie format of the past.

This relocating of creativity in advertising as a collective function is a more truthful reflection of how agencies actually work, particularly following the shift from a business model based on commission on advertising to one based on fees for advertising-related services. It is also a more accurate version of the creative process, in which multiple talents collaborate towards a shared goal (Bilton 2006). Finally too, it confirms one of the themes of this book, that the creativity of the creative industries is located in structures and systems, not in flashes of individual inspiration. As such, the more strategic, holistic approach to advertising noted in this chapter stands in stark contrast to the British government's continued policy emphasis on 'individual creativity, skill and talent' in the creative industries.

However, such a redefinition of advertising is not without risk. If creativity becomes just another way of describing strategic planning, if it becomes too much 'business as usual', there is a danger that everybody (including the client) will consider themselves to be part of the creative process. By demystifying the creative process, agencies might end up losing business; as in the case of Honda, clients will pay a one-off consultancy fee for a new strategy on branding or communication, then implement it for themselves. Agencies might find their strategic expertise becoming absorbed by the client, their status as trusted intermediaries usurped by the client's own marketing director.

There are further difficulties in sustaining a more holistic, interdisciplinary approach to creativity as agencies expand. The advertising industry has relied on the functional divisions between creatives and suits as a means of structuring the process of acquiring, developing and delivering advertising to clients, but also as a system of internal organisation and hierarchy. Smaller independent agencies like St Lukes, Naked Communications and Mother have attempted to blur the distinction between strategic proposition and creative execution and to avoid hierarchical and divisional distinctions between different parts of the agency. Instead, they promise to adapt their structures, processes and personnel to the needs of the client; as one staff member at Naked commented, 'everybody here has to know about strategy and everybody here has to be creative'.[6] When firms get bigger, such multifunctional roles tend to harden into distinct specialisms (McCrimmon 1995). Naked are struggling with that transition as they attempt to shift power and responsibility from the founding partners to the next generation of creative strategists or strategic creatives. It remains to be seen whether it is possible for everybody to be good at everything in an expanded organisation where personal ties between the company founders can no longer be relied upon to stitch the different mindsets and specialisms into a composite whole.

Finally there is the problem of measurement and accountability. As a media neutral agency, Naked Communications sees its approach as ideas-led rather than product-led; the aim is not to produce an artefact in a particular medium but to generate an idea which can work across many different media. This moves from an output-based model of creativity based on 'great advertising' to an input-based model based on the ideas which lie behind and precede great advertising. The output model made possible a business model which treated advertising as a form of cultural production with the value of the product, measured through media expenditure, used to calculate a fee. Today's model requires agencies to calculate the value of their strategic or creative input and to bill accordingly. There is no gold standard for measuring this input, other than by referring to actual results of the campaign – at which point it is extremely difficult to separate out the various inputs from multiple agencies and to attribute a value to each of them. Perhaps by emphasising the 'creative' aspects of these various inputs, agencies can persuade clients to pay a premium for their services.

Conclusion

Jeffcutt and Pratt (2002) have rightly warned against the perception that creativity in the creative industries acts as a kind of 'magic dust' which can turn base metal into gold. In many respects the advertising industry seems to be accepting this challenge. What some of the new generation of advertising and communications agencies offer to clients is no longer creativity, it is strategy. Yet they continue to sprinkle the 'pixie dust'[7] of creativity over what they do, perhaps in a recognition that this in the end is a language the client understands, values and is prepared to pay for. Quirky décor, pinball machines and pool tables in reception,[8] outlandish dress codes and behaviour may no longer be a real reflection of organisational culture, but they still provide a powerful signal to clients (Gardener 2004).

Despite significant structural changes in the advertising industry towards a more strategic, integrated definition of creativity, the organisational culture of advertising is still premised on the old-fashioned virtues of 'great ideas' and creative content. Brand consultancy, media strategy and consumer research have accordingly been placed under the 'creative' banner, and even if some of these services seem to relate to core management competences rather than creative processes, the culture around them is resolutely and resiliently 'creative'. This creative culture is manifest in the stories and personalities which dominate trade publications and award schemes and in the language of recruitment, company websites and job descriptions. Whilst other competences have always been important, 'creativity' has continued to be the industry's unique selling point not only to clients but to its own workforce. The mythology around creative talent underpins the self-belief and self-identity of those who work in advertising as well as the value perceptions of those who hire them.

From this perspective 'creativity' is no longer a description of the services performed by advertising agencies, it is a branding strategy. The 'creative' in advertising may have been relocated from a specific specialised function or role towards a general approach which cuts across a range of services including media planning, communications strategy, account planning and network coordination. Yet it is necessary to keep reminding the client of the agency's 'creative' credentials because this is the one source of competitive advantage which the agency enjoys over the client's own marketing department. Creativity is used as a descriptive term, spread approvingly across various functions and services delivered by the agency, not as nominal term designating a specific element. The myth of individual creative genius has become increasingly tangential to the business of advertising. Yet, like the discarded pinball machine, it is still part of the furniture and even if nobody plays with it, the client still needs to be reminded it is there.

Notes

1 The case study is based on interviews and correspondence with Matt Hardisty, Niku Banaie and Will Collin of Naked Communications between December 2005 and June 2006, as well as my own observations and published articles and information on the Naked website.
2 Interview with the author, 30th November 2006.
3 Interview with the author, 30th November 2006.
4 Google does not give figures by territory, although the aggregate figures did seem to confirm Duncan's estimates. Meanwhile Duncan was speaking at the time of a review of the channel's long term financial future by the industry regulator, Ofcom. Falling advertising revenues strengthened his argument that regulators needed to 'protect the fantastic legacy of UK broadcasting'.
5 For example, Boots the Chemist, one of Britain's biggest retail brands hired Naked Communications on its 2006 Christmas campaign. The government's Central Office of Information hires a range of small 'creative' agencies including CHI, Mother and

St Luke's to deliver government information through a range of digital media including online and mobile. Unilever (Lynx) and Random House (Thomas Harris's *Hannibal Rising*) have both opened promotional spaces on the social networking site MySpace.

6 Interview with the author, February 21st 2006.

7 Naked Communications website.

8 There is a pinball machine at Naked Communications, now gathering dust in an upstairs room following a recent refurbishment.

References

Adams, J L (1979) *Conceptual blockbusting: a guide to better ideas*, New York, London: WW Norton.

Barron, F (1968) *Creativity and personal freedom*, Princeton, NJ: Van Nostrand Company.

Becker, H (1982) *Art worlds*, Los Angeles: UCLA Press.

Bilton, C (2006) *Management and creativity: from creative industries to creative management*, Oxford: Blackwells.

Bilton, C, Cummings, S and Wilson, D (2003) 'Strategy as creativity' in S Cummings and D Wilson (eds) *Images of strategy*, Oxford: Blackwells, pp. 197–222.

Boden, Margaret A (1994) 'What is Creativity' in Margaret A Boden (ed.) *Dimensions of creativity*, Cambridge MA/London: MIT Press / Bradford Books, pp. 75–117.

Campaign (2006) 'Axed Naked to continue working for Honda', *Campaign*, 21st July 2006.

Clemmow, S (1999) 'Strategy development' in L Butterfield (ed.) *Excellence in advertising* (second edition). Oxford: IPA/Elsevier Butterworth-Heinemann, pp. 63–79.

Collin, W (2003) 'The interface between account planning and media planning: a practitioner perspective', *Marketing Intelligence and Planning* 21 (7), pp. 440–445.

Csikszentmihalyi, M (1988) 'Society, culture, and person: a systems view of creativity', in R J Sternberg (ed.) *The nature of creativity: contemporary psychological perspectives*, Cambridge: Cambridge University Press, pp. 325–339.

DCMS (1998) *Creative industries management*, London: Department of Culture, Media and Sport.

Fletcher, W (1999): *Tantrums and talent: how to get the best from creative people*, Henley-on-Thames: Admap.

Florida, R (2002) *The rise of the creative class: and how it's transforming work, leisure, community and everyday life*, New York: Basic Books.

Gardener, R (2004) 'First impressions' *Campaign* (30th July 2004), pp. 28–29.

Gladwell, M (2000) *The tipping point: how little things can make a big difference*, London: Little, Brown.

Grabher, G (2002) 'The project ecology of advertising: tasks, talents and teams', *Regional Studies* 36 (3), pp. 245–262.

Hackley, C (2003) 'From consumer insight to advertising strategy: the account planner's integrative role in creative advertising development', *Marketing Intelligence and Planning* 21 (7), pp. 446–452.

Howkins, J (2001) *The creative economy: how people make money from ideas*, London: Penguin.

Hughes, B (2007) '"Suits" and "creatives": managerial control, the expropriation of fun and the manufacture of consent' in U Haws (ed.) *The spark in the engine: creative workers in a global economy* (special edition of *Work organisation, labour and globalisation* 1 (1) Winter 2006–7), pp. 76–88.

Jeffcutt, P and Pratt, A C (2002) 'Managing creativity in the cultural industries', *Creativity and Innovation Management* 11 (4) (December 2002), pp. 225–233.

Koestler, A (1964) *The act of creation*, London: Hutchinson.

Levitt, T (1963) 'Creativity is not enough', *Harvard Business Review*, 80 (8) (August 2002), pp. 137–144.

McCrimmon, M (1995) 'Teams without roles: empowering teams for greater creativity' in *Journal of Management Development,* 14 (6), pp. 35–41.

Nixon, S (2003) *Advertising cultures, gender, commerce, creativity*, London: Sage.

Ogilvy, D (1963) *Confessions of an advertising man*, New York: Atheneum.

Pratt, A C (2006) 'Advertising and creativity: a governance approach. A case study of creative agencies in London', *Environment and Planning A* 38 (10), pp. 1883–1899.

Porter, M E (1985) *Competitive advantage: creating and sustaining superior performance*, New York: Free Press.

Prichard, C (2002) 'Creative selves? Critically reading "creativity", in management discourse', *Creativity and Innovation Management*, 11 (4) (December 2002), pp. 265–276.

Ritson, M (2003) 'It's the ad-break . . . and the viewers are talking, reading and snogging', *Financial Times Creative Business*, 4th February 2003, pp. 8–10.

Schultz, D E and Kitchen, P J (2000) *Communicating globally: an integrated marketing approach.* Basingstoke: Macmillan.

Schultz, D E, Tannenbaum, S I and Lauterborn, R F (1993) *Integrated marketing communication: putting it together and making it work*, Chicago: NTC Business Books.

Schumpeter, J (1943) *Capitalism, socialism and* democracy, London: Allen & Unwin.

Sheth, J and Sobel, A (2000) *Clients for life: evolving from an expert for hire to an extraordinary advisor*, New York: Simon & Schuster.

Steel, J (1998) *Truth, lies and advertising: the art of account planning*, Chichester: John Wiley.

Sternberg, R J (1988) 'A three-facet model of creativity' in R J Sternberg (ed.) *The nature of creativity: contemporary psychological* perspective, Cambridge: Cambridge University Press, (reprint 1997), pp. 125–147.

Taylor, J (2005) *Space race: an inside view of the future of communications planning*, Chichester: John Wiley.

Times (November 1st 2006) 'Google "to overtake C4" in ad revenues', *The Times*, 1st November 2006.

Torrance, E P (1988) 'The nature of creativity as manifest in its testing' in R J Sternberg (ed.) *The nature of creativity: contemporary psychological perspectives*, Cambridge: Cambridge University Press, (reprint 1997), pp. 43–75.

Weisberg, R W (1986) *Creativity: genius and other myths*, New York: W.H. Freeman.

—— (2006) *Creativity: understanding innovation in problem solving, science, invention and the arts*, Hoboken, NJ: John Wiley.

Zyman, S (2002) *The end of advertising as we know it*, Hoboken, NJ: John Wiley.

2b Provincial parvenus

The subaltern sensibility of London advertising creatives

Sean Nixon

Introduction

Reflecting on some of the problems that have dogged the study of advertising and consumer culture over a long period, Peter Miller and Nicholas Rose have suggested that advertising and the adjacent persuasion industries engage not so much in manipulating the consumer or simply responding to their needs, but rather act to mobilize the consumer; that is, attempt to form connections between human passions, hopes and desires and the world of commercial goods and services (Miller and Rose, 1997: 2). Taking some licence with Miller and Rose's argument, we might profitably turn their formulation around and reflect on the ways in which the creative people who are professionally engaged in mobilizing the passion of others, use the job they perform as the vehicle for the pursuit of their own consumerist desires and ambitions. In this sense, opening up advertising agency offices and the social networks which abut to them might reveal an emotional landscape of consumption every bit as vivid as that composed by agencies in the technical process of 'mobilizing' the consumer on behalf of their clients. In this chapter, I want to reflect on the forms of social longing for the world of goods which advertising people themselves express through the job they perform. It is these passions and desires that I explore. In developing this analysis, the chapter draws on a larger study of the workplace cultures of London-based advertising agencies and the subjective identities and motivations of a group of young male art directors and copywriters and their female colleagues. In documenting the working lives of these practitioners, it has a number of things to say about the links between gender, commerce and creativity within this sector of commercial endeavour.[1]

My argument here focuses upon the investment of these art directors and copywriters in the social rituals and forms of sociability that formed a significant part of their working lives. In fact, as I want to suggest later, for some of these practitioners a large part of the initial appeal of the job, as well as their subsequent experience of it, was the access it gave them to metropolitan consumption and what they saw as a world of glamour and style. The celebration of these consumerist pleasures was itself the product of particular class-and gender-specific sensibilities and desires and I suggest that we ought to understand the participation of creative people within these social rituals and fantasies of the good life within a longer history of metropolitan consumption by subaltern social actors. Specifically, the practitioners I interviewed shared much in common with their historical precursors – what Gareth Stedman-Jones has called 'those socially indeterminate young men' working in the service industries – who were increasingly visible in London from the mid-nineteenth century onwards (Stedman-Jones, 1989: 289–90). The participation of creative people within contemporary patterns of urban consumption and entertainment also brought them into contact with other participants within these metropolitan leisure cultures, and how the practitioners I discuss rubbed up against and negotiated their relationships with these other users of London's spaces of entertainment represents a further theme of the chapter.

There is good reason for such an excursion into the subjective and cultural dimensions of advertising production. Opening up the subjective motivations of these advertising people and the cultures of their workplaces is important because both these elements of agency life mediate the process of reaching out to and connecting with consumers that is at the heart of an agency's promotional work. This is particularly significant in those markets where art directors and copywriters are culturally close to the target consumer, but it applies more generally as well. In insisting on this point, I'm not suggesting that we reduce the commercial practices of advertising to the subjectivity of its key practitioners or the cultures of agencies. The process of commercial cultural production in which advertising agencies are engaged is highly structured and involves a range of practitioners deploying different kinds of formal knowledge and expertise, as well as the mobilization of a set of economic and cultural resources, in order to generate promotional materials and associated services for clients. This process, however, is clearly also shaped by more informal factors and judgements, including those bound up with the particular social make-up and subjectivities of key practitioners. It is clear, for example, that informal knowledge possessed by practitioners about the target consumer, which is not itself present in the market research or planning documentation, can be important in helping agencies to manage the relationship between their clients and consumers. Furthermore, the cultural identifications of practitioners and the wider occupational culture in which they move will both provide resources for and set certain limits to the process of cultural production in which they are engaged. In this sense, the social longings and consumerist desires of art directors and copywriters matter.

There is also a broader significance to be gained from exploring these aspects of the social and cultural formation of these practitioners. Driving the argument that I develop in the chapter is the ambition to contest the more reified or synthetic conceptions of the 'creative worker' which dominate both the prescriptions of policy makers and the pronouncements of management and organizational studies textbooks. Certainly, the ideal of the creative, 'self-expressive' worker that recurs so strongly in prescriptive and normative accounts of the 'creative industries' is a social type in need of more concrete rendering. As Durkheim suggested in relation to the concept of 'economic man' within political economy, it is an ideal in need of fleshing out and grounding within a time, a place and social relations. It is, in short, an ideal in need of the injection of the life that the abstract agent lacks (see Callon, 1998: 51).

In the first part of the chapter, I detail the educational and social backgrounds of art directors and copywriters and reflect on the distinctive social composition of this cadre of 'creative workers'. In part two, I move on to document the social rituals and forms of sociability in which these practitioners participated, developing an account of the spatially concentrated character of the London advertising industry's informal recreational culture and its appeal to these provincial parvenus. I conclude by suggesting that the account of advertising creatives that I have developed offers us some clues about the distinctive creativity of British-based advertising. Echoing arguments about the distinctiveness of British pop music, the subaltern and provincial make-up of advertising's creative people and their exposure to an art school ethos hint at some of the reasons for the characteristic look and feel of British advertising over the last 30 years.

Declasse and parvenus

The art directors and copywriters employed by London agencies represent a distinct social grouping within the industry. For a start, against the drift of gender equality in most areas of advertising employment, their jobs remain overwhelmingly male-dominated with 80 per cent of art directors and copywriters being men (Baxter, 1990; Klein, 2000). This distinctiveness is further enhanced by the typical social backgrounds and educational experiences of creative people. Whereas most of the professional jobs in advertising are dominated by graduates from middle-class backgrounds, the social make-up of creative jobs is more clearly skewed towards individuals from subaltern backgrounds with generally lower levels of certificated education (Nixon, 2003: 57–73). The contrast between the educational trajectories of creative people and account handlers brings these differences out particularly well.[2] Whereas account handling is defined as a graduate career and account handlers tend to be drawn even more exclusively from old, established universities and to hold generalist degrees, art directors and copywriters are less solidly graduate in their make-up and hold specialist degrees or qualifications (IPA, 1998a; 2000). Amongst the practitioners I interviewed, the majority had honours degrees, but a significant minority counted HNDs as their highest educational qualification (Nixon, 2003: 59–65). The subjects they studied were also markedly different from their professional colleagues. While the holding of generalist degrees was common, they were more likely to have studied either art or graphic design courses. In fact, they were five times more likely to have studied a degree or HND in art or graphic design than any other subject. Those who had studied generalist degrees typically had additionally taken a further post-graduate diploma in art direction and copywriting or else been through the D&AD's creative workshop that offered technical training in the same skills (D&AD, 1997). These different educational routes were clearly bound up with assumptions within the advertising industry about the kinds of technical or craft skills required to perform these jobs. It is clear, however, that the educational experiences of creative people, together with their generally more subaltern backgrounds, combine to socially distinguish them from their colleagues working in the other core jobs. Equipped with more technical and quasi-vocational training and more likely to come from lower middle class or working class backgrounds, they formed a distinct social grouping within the industry. As Paul Holt, the executive creative director at Klein & Hart, romantically put it, 'I tell people in my department that we're the C1s, we're the skilled workers, the skilled artisans' (Nixon, 1997).

It was also noticeable that creative people were overwhelmingly provincial in their origins and hailed from towns and cities like Norwich, Warrington, Loughton, Ware and greater Manchester. Only a small minority came from metropolitan London. For example, Teresa Walsh, a 36-year-old art director, came from a lower middle class background. Her father had run his own small business, while her mother was a care-worker. She went to the local secondary school, leaving after completing her 'A' levels. After initially training as a nurse, she eventually went to a northern polytechnic to study animation and left with a degree in graphic design. Phil Chantler, a 31-year-old art director, came from a skilled working class family, where his father was an electrician working on the North Sea oil rigs and his mother was a hairdresser. He too went to the local comprehensive and took 'A' levels. He then spent 4 years at the local art college, doing first a graphic design course and then an HND in advertising. Chris Bradshaw, a 35-year-old art director, too came from a lower-middle class family. His father worked in the motor-trade as a salesman and his mother was a housewife. He took 'A' levels, before completing a degree in graphic design at St. Martin's School of Art. Murray Wright, a 35-year-old copywriter, was from a working class Norwich family. His father was a school caretaker and his mother had done a variety of ancillary jobs, including cleaning and kitchen work. He won a scholarship to the local grammar school, before reading Modern and Medieval Languages at Jesus College, Cambridge.

Taken together, the educational and social mix of art directors and copywriters meant that these practitioners brought to the job a particular set of dispositions and sensibilities. These were sensibilities that were subaltern, provincial and informed by an art school ethos. These generated patterns of social longing that shaped in important ways their investment in the job of being an advertising creative. This was particularly clear in relation to the social rituals and forms of sociability that were an integral part of their jobs.

A world of glamour and excess

Unlike the not-dissimilar world of financial services concentrated in the City of London, the London-based advertising industry lacks the kind of large-scale, corporate provision of leisure and recreational facilities for its key workers (McDowell, 1997). The leisure and entertainment culture associated with the industry has a far more informal character and is generally serviced by a plethora of commercial restaurants, bars and clubs. At the heart of this recreational culture is the liberal consumption of alcohol. Many of the larger agencies support this activity by running their own bars (see, for example, *Campaign*, 21/4/00: 30–1). Others put agency money into subsidizing drinking, as well as underwriting day, and sometimes weekend, excursions for staff in which alcohol figures prominently.

The industry's main social events, including the prestigious annual creative awards ceremonies hosted by D&AD and the Advertising Creative Circle, are celebrated for the drinking that takes place. Drinking with colleagues after work in the local pub on Friday nights, as well as frequently in the week, forms a more regular social ritual. For more senior agency staff – notably creative directors and other agency managers – dining out at restaurants or enjoying the benefits of socializing at one of a number of private clubs is also an important part of their professional lives. Access to these clubs is determined by rank and seniority and they are generally well beyond the means of younger practitioners.

Perhaps the most striking feature of much of this industry related social activity – and something that is most readily noted upon by a range of commentators – is its strong concentration within one particular quarter of London – Soho (*Campaign*, 29/4/89: 55–6; 13/12/91: 22–3; *Creative Review*, August 1997: 29–31; Mort, 1996: 170–182). Certainly those establishments that are heavily used by advertising people and most associated with the industry are geographically concentrated in this area of London's West End. The Ivy (West Street, WC2, off Long Acre), Coast (Albermerle Street, W1), Soho House (Greek Street, W1), The Groucho Club (Dean Street, W1) and The Union (W1) are all within shouting distance of each other in and around Soho. There are notable exceptions to this picture. The prestigious advertising clubs are found in the more rarefied atmosphere of Clariges (The 30 Club of London), The Dorchester (The Solus Club) and The Savoy (WACL) (see *Campaign*, 27/5/94: 26–8). This spatial differentiation is not without its significance. These clubs formed part of the industry's inner court and are a place where the social elite of British advertising mixes with other business leaders and politicians. Modelled on gentlemen's clubs, they are within or adjacent to the networks of established business and political culture, and are notably distanced from the more polymorphous space of Soho. It is this feature of Soho that is important in shaping the character of the industry's more informal social rituals. As Frank Mort has argued, Soho has a long history as the recipient of avant-garde and bohemian culture. It is this history, laid down in the fabric of the district, which has helped to shape its continuing association with transgressive and bohemian social scripts. The more recent influx of social actors, including advertising and media people, whilst transforming the area through their economic and social presence, continue to draw on and be formed in relation to this sedimented history (see Mort, 1996:170–182). For advertising practitioners – including creative people – these associations were often expressed through a valorization of Soho as a centre of cultural provision and innovation, a place of stimulating energy. Paul Davenport, a creative at Klein & Hart, for example, was enthusiastic about the industry life centred upon the district. Reflecting on the nature of his working life at Klein & Hart, which was based in London Docklands, at the eastern edges of the city, he suggested:

> Soho is where the industry is really based. We miss it big time . . . massively. Mind you, the distractions are immense in Soho. You do get a lot more work done here, because there's bugger all else to do. There's an energy in Soho . . .

> because you've got everything there. You've got cinemas, you've got libraries, you've got restaurants, you've got odd little things, you've got Foyles.
>
> (Nixon, 1997)

Ben Langdon, Managing Director of CDP, was also reverential towards Soho. In an interview in Campaign he gushed about the pleasure of returning to work in the district. CDP had long been exiled on the Euston Road and for Langdon returning to Soho produced in him a state of near reverie. As he put it, 'we did miss the stimulation of Soho and are delighted to be back. It has made us feel vibrant again' (*Campaign* 11/8/95: 26–7). Even those agencies that had taken the positive decision to relocate from Soho in the mid–late 1990s – in large part because of the limited availability of suitable office accommodation – acknowledged its symbolic power. Thus, Steve Gatfield, Chief Executive of Leo Burnett, an agency which had moved to Kensington, spoke of the wrench of moving from Soho and the pull of its 'buzz', while Lance Smith, Director of UK operations of DMB&B, which had moved to Victoria, confessed to the 'strong emotional' appeal of the district (ibid.). These comments hint at a strong sense of ownership of the district and of feeling centred through an assertion that the advertising industry was now a part of the heritage of Soho. As another of the young creatives I talked to earnestly put it, 'Soho is the spiritual centre of the industry'.

The location of so much of the informal work-based and work-related entertainment and recreation participated in by advertising people in and around Soho gives these forms of sociability a strongly metropolitan character. Precisely what this meant for these practitioners and how they inhabited these social relations is very difficult to gauge. At issue here is the complex cultural heritage of Soho that I noted earlier and the contemporary diversity of social actors that populated its social spaces. As Frank Mort has argued, the expansion of legitimate commercial developments in Soho through the 1980s and 1990s (including the increasing presence of media companies and advertising agencies) interacted in complex ways with the bohemian and avant-garde culture formed in Soho over the preceding century. One form this took was the updating of older forms of bohemianism into contemporary style culture by some of the newer commercial arrivistes. *Midweek*, the free magazine for office workers, for example, celebrated this new vision of Soho bohemianism:

> Cosmopolitan, bohemian and wildly trendy [. . .] the land of the brasserie lunch and the after-hours watering hole, the land of accessories and attitude, where fashion relentlessly struggles to become style and image is simply everything; the glittering heart of medialand where the worlds of art, journalism, film, advertising and theatre blend into one glamorous heady cocktail.
>
> (Midweek, 20/2/92, quoted in Mort, 1996:157–8)

The relations between old and new habitués of Soho were not always smooth, however. The journalist Jeffrey Barnard, himself a member of a post-war circle of artists, actors and literary types (including the artist Francis Bacon) who frequented the famous Colony Room in Dean Street, was scathing about the new media interlopers. Clearly feeling his version of Soho bohemianism was under threat, he railed against the new inhabitants of Soho. Writing in the early 1980s, he melodramatically claimed that:

> Soho is dead. Massive injections of advertising executives with pocket bleepers and a taste for cheap wine [. . .] have finally killed off what was just about the best part of London for anyone who never saw virtue in work for its own sake.
>
> (Taki and Bernard, 1981:16, quoted in Mort, 1996:162)

Elsewhere he castigated these new players as 'tight assessed nancy boys' and offered a withering parody of the dispositions of advertising creatives in his diatribe against these interlopers:

> The TV commercial boys sat there plucking there croissants and saying 'Yes, I know love, but if we cut it then – bang, bang – like that, we wouldn't have to hold the long shot coming down those stairs [. . .] Let's face it, loves, we're basically trying to sell wretched stuff' [. . .] By this time my coffee was cold and my mouth locked in open-jawed disbelief.
>
> (Taki and Bernard, 1981:23)

Soho's history had also been shaped by a long tradition of tolerance to sexual dissidence and transgression, including both a long tradition of male homosexual culture (itself increasingly visible and expanded through the 1980s and 90s) and the licensed sex industry of cinemas, bars and clubs (Mort, 1996:157–182). The relationship between advertising people and these other Soho constituents is hard to unpack. Certainly – Barnard's insinuations notwithstanding – the relations with gay male culture were particularly difficult to read, and the accounts generated by the advertising trade press and by my interviewees were notable for occluding these relationships in their valorization of Soho life. It is possible, however, to get some clues as to the character of the informal cultures participated in by advertising people. *Campaign*, in its limited coverage of the industry's social life, certainly gave tantalizing glimpses of the place, most notably, of an entrenched masculine culture of excess within the industry's social rituals. For example, in December 1991, the paper reported the drama of that year's D&AD award ceremony held not in Soho, but in the more rarified setting of the Grosvenor House hotel in Park Lane, Mayfair. The event had been marred by what *Campaign* described as an 'outbreak of drunken vandalism' in which thousands of pounds of damage was done to the hotel (*Campaign*, 20/12/91: 7). Detailing the event, the paper claimed that 'a bunch of cretinous creatives high on booze and drugs left a trail of destruction' (ibid.). *Campaign* also reported how in August 1996, staff from the agency APL, had caused considerable damage to a hotel by squashing food and drink into the venue's carpet and indulged in playing games such as pouring water over each other (*Campaign*, 16/8/96:11). In March of the preceding year, the paper's regular diary page further documented the emergence of a new game practiced in nightclubs by a group of enterprising young admen. Known as 'hotlegging', it involved urinating down the leg of a colleague if you caught them 'chatting up a girl' (*Campaign*, 24/3/95: backpage).

Negotiating these cultures of excess and juvenility was an especially pressing issue for the few young women creatives. One response was to embrace them, though this could be nuanced in rather different ways. Samantha Jones and Miranda Harris, for instance, appeared relatively at ease inside these forms of sociability. As Samantha Jones revealed:

> It used to be [that we went drinking] every single Friday at the Crown, and it got to a point where there were actually quite a few nights during the week to the extent that we had to knock it on the head because we were drinking too much.
>
> (Nixon, 1997)

Miranda Harris continued: 'if you're not careful, when your agency's going through a period of having a good social life, you find you're having several [drinks] every night, maybe more'. Teresa Walsh also confessed to youthful excesses. She recalled:

> I used to drink a lot. I remember one year I went to an industry event – and I used to wear the most ridiculous clothes like a tutu and things like that to work. And I remember once going to the creative ball and dancing on the table in my tutu and the table collapsing. And next morning I was so embarrassed. The following year, they ran an ad for the event and there I am stood on the table screaming as it collapsed. I was a bit of a wild one in those days.
>
> (Nixon, 1997)

Walsh's former antics belonged within a distinct tradition of feminine excess associated with the 'unattached female hedonist' (Mort, 1996: 173) and formed part of a flamboyant public persona. Her self-presentation hinted at a fundamental problem for women creatives concerning how they should behave in the strongly masculine worlds they were forced to inhabit. In Walsh's case, being as wild as the men represented one way of holding her own in this context. Jones and Harris took a rather different root and became 'one of the lads'. They were, in fact, explicit about appropriating these codes of masculinity. Reflecting on their departure from a previous agency they suggested, 'we were the wrong type of women . . . The creative director liked young, quiet, very pretty, tall women, and we didn't fit into that category. We were a bit loud and brash and rude, a bit laddish'. When I quizzed them on what they meant by that they confessed, 'Well, we swear, and burp and fart and muck about and we have a good sense of humour.'

For the men I interviewed, their accounts of the industry social life in which they participated pointed to a smoother, less self-conscious passage into work related cultures of drinking. In fact, for some of the men, gaining access to this world was a central part of the declared appeal of the job. Both Steve Dempsey and his partner Chris Bradshaw, creatives at Knight & Stewart, for example, became very animated when recalling the levels of social drinking that opened up to them during summer placements in an advertising agency when they were students. For Steve Dempsey, in particular, access to subsidized drinking stood as a defining feature of his experience of the placement and set it apart from his experience in the adjacent field of graphic design. He recalled:

> I spent a couple of weeks at Michael Peters and Partners, and they had tea and cakes in the afternoon, which was very 'nice'. There was one girl there who was very 'nice', and she spent three weeks drawing a little sheaf of corn, and she drew it about fifty times, in different ways. And for me, it was a sheaf of corn when I arrived, and it was a sheaf of corn when I left [...] On the last day, we went down the pub. And I had a pint and everyone else had halves. And as soon as the drinks were drunk, people went. And then we went to the ad agency, and I think pretty much the first day we were there, they won a new piece of business and at 4'o clock in the afternoon, it was 'right, everyone downstairs', to this big room, and there was basically beer and Champagne and we got hammered.
>
> (Nixon, 1997)

Dempsey's commentary is noteworthy in terms of the way he dramatizes the appeal of agency life next to a denigration of graphic design work. Thus, he conjures an image of graphic design as a quaint and genteel world, with its rituals of afternoon tea and quiet civility and a careful, almost studious approach to work. Against this he sets up his identification with the more exuberant culture of the ad agency, with heavy drinking spilling over into the hours of the working day and extending beyond it.

Its association with memories of youthful hedonism undoubtedly heightened the drama of Dempsey's account and he was keen elsewhere in his comments to demarcate the excesses of life as a junior from the more serious and sober character of his contemporary working life. Nonetheless, as he relives the excitement of the placement, he reveals his investment in conventionally gendered forms of socializing and definitions of enjoyment. A similar identification with these masculine scripts was also evident in the comments of other practitioners I interviewed when they too reflected on the initial appeal of the job. For Dave Cantelo and Jack Chantler, however, it was not so much the possibility of heavy drinking that they emphasized, but rather the access to a world of glamour and style. Dave Cantelo recalled:

> My Dad used to have a restaurant, and a lot of advertising people used to go and eat there ... And I remember, I was probably 14, I remember seeing all these really good looking blokes coming in, surrounded by good looking, beautiful women, driving these amazing cars, and they'd park them on the pavement, and then just chuck the waiter the keys, and say 'when the warden comes round, just move it'. And I thought, fucking hell, that looks good.
>
> (Nixon, 1997)

Cantelo's testimony is shot through with desire for the kind of social confidence and glamour embodied by the ad people who were customers in his Dad's restaurant. It conjures an evocative image of a lower middle class boy dreaming of access to a world of privilege beyond his current social horizon; a world of glamour that gave you access to style and beautiful women. Jack Chantler's comments revealed the same subaltern aspirations. Recalling the placements he went on as an aspiring creative, he said:

> I just loved sitting in the foyer at BBH and JWT and just thinking 'Wow!' All the receptionists are really beautiful and glamorous and everyone was so confident. We sat out here [at Serendipity] and a stream of gorgeous girls came in and out and we were like 'Ah' [breathless]. And we were just as scruffy as this really.
>
> (Nixon, 1997)

There is a strong line of self-deprecation in Chantler's comments, together, perhaps, with an overplaying of his ordinariness. Nonetheless, like the comments of Dempsey and Cantelo, they suggest a similar formation of heterosexual masculinity, one shaped through specific forms of heterosociability and ideas of what constitutes the good life. We might profitably suggest, in fact, that these men – particularly Chantler and Cantelo – exhibited an investment in what Peter Bailey has described as 'parasexuality', the form of 'framed liminality' that he associates with 'glamour' and the development of modern sexualized consumerism in the mid-nineteenth century. Parasexuality for Bailey, which he explores through the venerable figure of the Victorian barmaid, represented a distinctive kind of display marked by the incitement but careful containment of sexuality. Moreover, it is also a regime characterized by gendered divisions between the feminine object of glamour and its desiring masculine subject (Bailey, 1998). One might provocatively suggest that we should understand the 'framed liminality' associated with these desires for a world of glamour as itself the product of a form of banal social fantasy; a social fantasy that in turn tells us much about the subaltern status of those individuals who mobilized its tropes. In fact, there is good reason for attempting to socially place the forms of heterosociability with which these admen identified. The relationship that they had with the metropolitan leisure culture that so attracted them placed them squarely within a tradition of social longing pursued by subaltern migrants to the metropolis. Their historical precursors have been well documented by both Gareth Stedman-Jones and Peter Bailey. These were the 'socially indeterminate single young men', the 'linen drapers assistants', 'counter-jumpers', 'city clerks' or 'penniless swells' who became the principle audience for the London music halls of the late nineteenth century and who found their own 'sham genteel patterns of conspicuous consumption' celebrated by music hall figures like Champagne Charlie (Stedman-Jones, 1989: 289–90; Bailey, 1999). As I have noted, the overwhelming majority of the men I interviewed were from provincial backgrounds, and often from lower-middle class provincial or suburban backgrounds to boot. As such they shared similar social fantasies about the delights of metropolitan culture as their historical precursors, those earlier provincial parvenus. Their provincial and subaltern origins were certainly evident to practitioners from more securely middle-class and established metropolitan backgrounds. Ian Harding, for example, a creative director at XYZ, who came from what he described as an 'intellectual bohemian background' in London – he had grown up in Earls Court and Putney before being dispatched to a minor public school – suggested that he was constantly surprised by the frenetic embrace of the delights of metropolitan life by the young creatives he worked with and by their desire to be part of a more established metropolitan culture. He suggested:

> I'm a Londoner. Not many of us are. Born and bred Londoner, so this is my patch. Simon, my ex-creative partner, came from Belfast and his life, because he'd up sticks, centred much more around the creative business. My life was up and running and in fine shape before I came anywhere near advertising. So I have a separate social life. Agencies have always been much more a place to work for me.
>
> (Nixon, 1997)

Testimonies of this sort suggest important differences between the social aspirations expressed by the men I interviewed and that of differently constituted practitioners.

Conclusion

Where has this account taken us? I have argued that amongst young male advertising creatives a central part of the appeal of their job was the access that it offered to the delights of metropolitan life and its circuits of drinking and heterosociability. Their investment in these forms of hedonism revealed an avowedly consumerist conception of enjoyment and of what constituted the good life, which tells us much about these men. Just as revealing were the clear limit positions that framed the forms of gendered sociability in which they participated. These were established partly through the differentiation from more transgressive social actors, especially the diverse forms of urban gay male culture. Advertising people were generally silent on their relationship with these social actors and their silence hinted at the robustly heterosexual nature of both their identifications and the occupational culture they inhabited.

Their accounts and experiences were telling in other ways. They confirmed the particularly permeable boundaries of 'creative work' and the way, notably, that it blurs established understandings of the division between 'work' and 'leisure' in its organization and performance. Whilst the apparent hybridity of creative jobs in advertising is neither unique to this cadre of advertising practitioners or this sector as a whole, it does reveal the particular ways in which the encroachment of work into the world of leisure time is organized within advertising and the way that this can be experienced as pleasurable by the young creatives, even as they are required to invest more of themselves and their free-time in the performance of their jobs.

Running as a central theme through the chapter has been a reflection on the subaltern and provincial character of these advertising people. Migrants to the metropolis from all corners of Britain and Ireland, they were drawn to the mythical delights of big city life. In this regard, they shared something with the 'suburban sensibility' identified by Simon Frith in his comments on British rock and pop performers over the last 40 years (Frith, 1997). For Frith, British pop has 'articulated suburban pretension, suburban claustrophobia, suburban discontent' (Frith, 1997: 271). Central to this suburban sensibility has been the pull of the city as the site of sophistication and the place of escape from suburban conformity. In this narrative of suburban desire, the city becomes the mythical backdrop for adventure, danger and transgression. At the same time, as Frith notes, certain British pop performers have combined suburban pretension with a paradoxical nostalgia for and affection towards the ordinary, the suburban and provincial. As he puts it,

> there's a distinctly nostalgic strain to the music (from the Kinks to Blur), an oblique longing for some kind of lost innocence (the village green, the Ford Cortina) which in emotional practice seems to stand for childhood, for an idealized neighbourly life, for home.
>
> (Frith, 1997: 277)

The parallels between the suburban sensibility of British pop and the sensibilities of the advertising people I have been describing are suggestive, despite Frith's desire to draw a clear line between British pop's suburban pretension and the 'bloodless forms' of the suburbanism of television advertising (Frith, 1997: 271). Both groups of creative people are linked by the transformative experience of art school. For Frith it is the art school influence on British pop which is key to inflecting the suburban longings of its performers (Frith and Horne, 1987). Understanding how it might shape similar sensibilities amongst advertising's creative people is ripe for further investigation, as it hints at some of the reasons for the oft-quoted peculiarities, distinctiveness and creativity of British advertising. Fully unravelling these connections, however, is another story.

Notes

1 The research was based on interviews with 26 male and 6 female art directors and copywriters working for London-based advertising agencies. They formed a distinctive age cohort of 25–38 year olds. The interviews were conducted in the summer and autumn of 1997. The names of the practitioners, together with those of their agencies, have been changed to ensure anonymity. See Nixon, 2003.

2 Account handlers liaise between the client and the agency in the running of a client account.

References

Bailey, P, 1998, *Popular Culture and Performance in the Victorian City*, Polity, Cambridge.

Baxter, M, 1990, *Women in Advertising*, IPA, London.

Callon, M, 1998, *The Laws of the Markets*, Blackwell, London.
Campaign, 1990–2001, Haymarket Publications, London.
Creative Review, 1983–2000, Centaur Media: London.
Design and Art Directors Association, 1997, *D&AD Advertising Workshop*, London.
Fletcher, W, 1990, *Creative People: How to Manage Them and Maximize Their Creativity*, Hutchinson, London.
Forrester, M, 1987, *Everything You Always Suspected was True About Advertising, But Were too Legal, Decent and Honest to Ask*, Roger Houghton, London.
Frith, S and Horne, H, 1987, *Art into Pop*, Routledge, London.
Frith, S, 1997, 'The Suburban Sensibility of British Rock and Pop', in Silverstone, R (ed.) *Visions of Suburbia*, Routledge, London.
Institute of Practitioners in Advertising, 1995, *Graduate Careers in Advertising*, IPA, London.
——, 1998a, *IPA Census*, IPA, London.
——, 1998b, *Information Pack*, IPA, London.
——, 2000, *Portfolio People*, IPA, London.
Klein, D, 2000, *Women in Advertising, Ten Years On*, IPA, London.
McDowell, L, 1997, *Capital Culture, Gender at Work in the City*, Blackwell, Oxford.
Miller, P and Rose, N, 1997, 'Mobilizing the Consumer: Assembling the Subject of Consumption', *Theory, Culture & Society* 14 (1):1–36.
Mort, F, 1996, *Cultures of Consumption, Masculinities and Social Space in Late Twentieth Century Britain*, Routledge, London.
Nixon, S, 1997, Interview conducted with informant.
——, 2003, *Advertising Cultures, Gender, Commerce, Creativity*, Sage, London.
Scase, R and Brown, P, 1994, *Higher Education and Corporate Realities, Class Culture and the Decline of Graduate Careers*, UCL Press, London.
Stedman-Jones, G, 1989, 'The "Cockney" and the nation, 1780–1988', in G Stedman-Jones and D Feldman (eds) *Metropolis-London, Histories and Representations Since 1800*, Routledge, London.
Taki and Bernard, J, 1981, *High Life, Low Life*, Unwin, London.

Part 3

Music

3a The digitalisation of music

David Hesmondhalgh

Like all cultural industries, the music industries attempt to make profit out of producing and circulating goods and services based on acts of symbolic creativity. They do so under risky conditions, and one major source of this risk is that recordings of films, songs, television programmes etc are experienced via devices designed, manufactured and distributed by a very different set of interests – notably the telecommunications, consumer electronics, computer and software industries. While some parts of the cultural industries try to innovate in the realm of symbols – new sounds, new ways of telling stories, new types of performance – these other industries innovate by introducing new devices and processes, and some of these involve new ways of experiencing culture.

Threaded through the history of the music business[1] has been a series of key technological innovations – the pianoforte, the gramophone, and the CD player to name but three – developed mainly by companies that have been at most only tangentially involved in the production of music itself. The latest and probably the most complex of this series of technological innovations around music is digitalisation. (Some accounts would stress the internet, but this is only part of the problem.) And as most people will be aware, the digitalisation of music has caused major problems for the music business over the last decade. Indeed, the 'music industry' is widely referred to as a paradigmatic case of a business caught on the hop by technological innovations. A number of commentators have discussed the decline or even the death of the music industry (for example, Mann, 2000; Barfe, 2003). Many media accounts have portrayed the major recording companies as flat-footed bureaucratic behemoths, as 'an industry struggling to maintain control and remain relevant' in the face of digitalisation (Alderman, 2001, pp. 1–2). The prophets of technocapitalism in outlets such as *Wired* magazine have celebrated the creativity and innovation brought about by the supposedly more nimble entrepreneurs of web-based music. The problems of the music industry were often presented in such accounts as though they reflected a shift to an era of greater abundance and choice for consumers. Those on the left had their own versions of such hopes. It has been common for left-leaning musicians and their managers in the 2000s, for example, to speak of a more democratised set of production relations emerging from the chaos of digitalisation, wherein artists would be able to market and sell their products directly to audiences via the web, without the need for the mediation of entertainment corporations. Often such dreams represent a naïve vision of social creativity unfettered by big capital – though, as I shall discuss in due course, there have been interesting developments that offer new forms of relationship between audiences and producers.

My perspective in this chapter is somewhat different from those of market utopians and musical dreamers. I see digitalisation as an important form of technological innovation but my assumption in what follows is that analysis of such technologies needs to be combined with analysis of a matrix of other economic, political and cultural processes – including legal and regulatory frameworks, and the internal dynamics of businesses and organisations (see Hesmondhalgh, 2007a). My core argument is that analysis of the impact of digitalisation in the music industries requires an understanding of contradictions between different sectors of capital, each of which has its own specific interests, its own notions of innovation and creativity, and its own capacities in terms of lobbying government. And against those journalistic accounts and managerial perspectives that emphasise short-term transformation, I look at the events of the first decade of the twenty-first century in the context of a long-term analysis of the recording industry, and of the cultural industries as a whole, one which stresses continuity as well as the change that more easily makes media headlines. The way that recorded music is disseminated is undergoing huge transformation (and this may or may not be usefully thought of as 'innovation'), but certain familiar features of the global recorded-music industry – notably the dominance of oligopolies of vertically integrated corporations, based on systems of copyright ownership and exploitation – are likely to remain intact. In my view, the rise of digitalisation is unlikely in the medium and long term to lead to any profound democratisation of musical creativity and innovation without transformation of broader economic and social conditions. However, this does not imply pessimistic resignation to the inevitability of corporate power. On the contrary, I argue that the digitalisation of music has helped to expose contradictions in the strategies of the recording industry, an exposure which could pave the way for criticism and activism which recognise the central importance of copyright in contemporary cultural industries.

These arguments should be of relevance not only to those with an interest in music, but also to anyone concerned with questions of innovation and creativity in contemporary culture. The music business is the first major sector of cultural production to confront the challenges and opportunities offered by the internet. The music industries have their own distinctive dynamics, but the last decade has seen specific manifestations of more general phenomena, as transnational media corporations come to terms with digitalisation. And as I outline below, the issue of copyright is central to developments in the music industries and in the cultural industries more generally. The main aim of this chapter then is to examine the implications of digitalisation for musical production, distribution and consumption, as a particular and distinct case of the dynamics of digitalisation in the cultural industries.

Meeting the digital challenge: copying, file-sharing and DRM systems

The major challenge presented by digitalisation to the recording industry stems from the relative accuracy and ease with which digital recordings can be copied and circulated. Profit-making in the cultural industries depends on, amongst other factors, the production of artificial scarcity. Digitalisation makes copying of any information relatively easy, thus threatening that scarcity. Music takes up less disk space and bandwidth than other non-print media such as film. Musical consumption has for a long time been a relatively mobile affair, via devices such as transistor radios, car cassette players, 'ghetto blasters', the Sony Walkman and so on. Digitalisation allows further mobility, by allowing relatively easy transfer between multiple sites – including iPods, MP3 players and mobile phones. This is why the recording industry has been the first to face head-on the threat posed by digitalisation.

In all cultural industries, the spread of the personal computer and the internet have made digitalisation a major issue. But four inter-related technological innovations have been involved in shaping the particular forms that digitalisation has taken in the recording industry. Bakker (2005) has helpfully broken these down as follows:

- The development of the MP3 compression standard in the late 1980s and early 1990s, which allowed the vast amounts of digital audio information to be compressed into manageable sizes.
- The spread of flat rate, high bandwidth connections, such as ISDN, ASDL and cable. Even where such connections were not available domestically in the late 1990s and early 2000s, they were accessible via workplaces, places of study etc.
- The introduction of multi-media computers with increased storage capacity, soundcards, CD players and speakers.
- The development of usually free and relatively easy-to-use software that could 'rip' CDs into MP3 and other digital files and that could find and download these files.

Here, though, we need immediately to refer back to the methodological issues discussed in the introduction to this chapter. These technological developments cannot be understood independently of their economic, social and organisational contexts. A key context here is that such innovations have been primarily driven by the telecommunications and software industries. These represent rival sectors of capital to the cultural industries, who are involved in the production of primarily symbolic, aesthetic, less utilitarian 'content'. While the cultural industries would have liked serious restrictions to be placed upon the facilitation of copying on computers, the US software and telecommunications industries inevitably campaigned to prevent such restrictive measures, as this would limit the dissemination of the myriad new technologies and devices involved. And it needs to be remembered that the telecommunications and software industries were, even more than the cultural or 'creative' industries, central to government visions of future prosperity and comparative international advantage in 'the information society', in global 'knowledge economies' (see Galperin, 2004). While the cultural industries are powerful lobbyists, and have close relations to governments, they simply could not contain the developments listed above, given the information society agenda. This imbalance was even more pronounced in Europe than in the USA. As we shall see, the creative or cultural industries were, however, able to lobby for stronger copyright measures, to balance losses incurred as a result of the success of the new digital technologies.

Besides copyright, two major problems preoccupied the record companies in the first decade of the twenty-first century: file-sharing; and finding a means to make money out of 'legitimate' digital distribution. I will deal with each of them in turn.

File-sharing

By 2000, users were sharing digital music files over peer-to-peer (P2P) networks, the most famous and widely-used of which was Napster. Napster was soon closed down by a lawsuit brought by various US record companies, but was supplanted by other P2P networks which in effect merely provided software allowing users to search each other's computers for musical files (and which therefore made prosecution more difficult), such as Grokster and Kazaa. It is sometimes forgotten, in a rush to portray these companies as radical challenges to corporate power, that these networks were commercial enterprises, supported by advertising, and usually backed by venture capital.

An analysis of the divergent and sometimes contradictory economic interests of different sectors of capital (information technology and software, telecommunications, the cultural and creative industries) helps to go beyond a simplistic technological determinism in understanding digitalisation in the recording industry, but we need to go further still, and understand prevailing sets of values and beliefs concerning technologies, on the part of both consumers and producers. File-sharing takes place in a number of ways, such as lodging copies of recordings in chat rooms to make them available for recording, and also local area network sharing. For users of these networks, a kind of *gift economy* is at work (Leyshon, 2003). Files are exchanged for free, and reciprocation is understood to be an important part of appropriate behaviour. Underlying file-sharing, in many cases, is an ethic which Don Slater, in an analysis of some of the internet relay chat networks that preceded such sites, characterised as employing 'a version of freedom located in an anti-commercial anarchism of the "property is theft" variety' (Slater, 2000, p. 128). This is extremely significant for understanding changes in the music industry, and to attribute changes to technology-in-itself is to miss this.

The recording industry took various actions in the early 2000s in an attempt to limit the effects of such developments. After successfully closing down Napster (though this then became the name of a 'legal' downloading site, providing files to subscribers), recording industry associations and their allies in other cultural industries pursued litigation against the second-generation file-sharing companies operating such services. In June 2005, the US Supreme Court delivered its verdict on the case brought by MGM and twenty-seven other major entertainment companies against the developers of file-sharing software products, including Grokster and Morpheus. The unanimous verdict was widely reported as a crucial victory for Hollywood and the music industries, but of course this in no way signalled the end of file-sharing. The internet after all makes exchange of files and information very easy. The victory can be seen as a sign of the continuing legal and regulatory power of the oligopoly of corporations that dominate global music circulation and rights ownership, but this was no final victory against technology and telecommunications sectors.

The other response to file-sharing by the recording industry (carried out by the trade associations that represent the interests of the largest music recording companies and publishers, under its international arm, IFPI – the International Federation of Phonographic Industries) was a public relations disaster. In a series of actions in 2003–05, hundreds of cases were brought by these trade associations against private individuals who had downloaded music from peer-to-peer sites. Most famously, in September 2003, the Recording Industry Association of America (the RIAA) settled a copyright infringement lawsuit against a 12-year-old New York girl for $2,000. The same wave of lawsuits included a Yale University photography professor and a 71-year-old Texan grandfather (Teather, 2003). All this added grist to the mill of digital libertarians arguing against the idea of cultural property in general.

For all the media coverage of the phenomenon, file-sharing has in fact been the preserve of a committed niche of users (see Bakker, 2005) – a very significant and growing niche, but one that has grown too slowly to be the basis of a revolutionary transformation in musical production. At least for a few years to come, the views of many music consumers may well echo the novelist John Lanchester's pithy summary of his reasons for not using the file-sharing sites: 'because I don't quite trust them to work or to be uncontaminated by viruses; because I feel shifty about taking things without paying for them; and because I can't be arsed' (Lanchester, 2002, p.5). This is not to deny that 'illegal' file-sharing is here to stay and is spreading fast to other cultural forms such as film and television. But it is important to realise that the music business has always had to fight over the boundaries between 'legitimate' forms of musical consumption – those involving income flows to them – and 'illegitimate' ones. The rise of copying technologies has made this battle more intense, but file-sharing is extremely unlikely to lead to a collapse of the idea that huge amounts of money can be made through music. In general, across the world over the last hundred years, there have been steady increases in the amounts of time and money that consumers spend on entertainment and leisure goods such as music (Hesmondhalgh, 2007a). So while global recorded-music sales have certainly suffered over the last few years, the long-term prospects for music as a cultural industry are not nearly as bleak as one would believe from some of the more excitable journalistic commentary. Rather than the outright collapse of the music business, the big issue facing capital seeking to invest in culture over the next decade is how to find new ways of making money from music.

The search for 'legitimate' digital distribution

File-sharing networks have caused real problems for the multinational entertainment corporations that dominate the music business, but it needs to be remembered that the digital downloading of music offers considerable opportunities too. Collectively, the companies involved in the sale of recordings would welcome new platforms on which to sell music. An ideal medium-term future for the major recording companies over the next ten years would involve consumers purchasing tangible recorded-music commodities such as the CD (or some future format) *and* digital files on new formats such as mobile phones. While CD sales have fallen gradually in many leading markets, in many developing markets, they have been growing, however temporarily. The record companies have in the past done extremely well out of selling music to consumers in parallel formats: the single and the LP in the 1960s and 1970s, the CD and the audio-cassette (and vinyl too for many customers) in the 1980s and 1990s. In addition, digital distribution offers the chance to monitor the tastes and preferences of consumers, in order to gain market information which, however problematic its reliability and validity, can be sold on to other agents.

It is undoubtedly true though that the quest for a 'legitimate' digital distribution market presents considerable challenges too. There are two main ones at present: finding a way to prevent customers from simply reproducing infinite copies of digital files of music; and finding a method of payment that consumers feel happy with. But all industries under capitalism face rapidly changing conditions, and have to be engaged in a constant process of readjustment – often resulting in immiseration for workers, their families and communities (no-one seems to be writing about the closure of the plants that manufacture CDs for example). How have the music industries attempted to confront the challenges of creating new digital markets?

For many years, most music-industry effort went into the development, alongside the software industries, of digital rights management (DRM) systems: security measures that are embedded in computers, electronic devices and digital files to prevent copying and other unauthorised uses. But the successful implementation of DRM systems has encountered major problems. Here again the rivalries among the various hardware, software and telecommunications companies involved were significant (see Burkart and McCourt, 2006, pp. 101–119 for a detailed discussion). By 2007, however, cultural-industry companies were abandoning DRM. Instead, a shift was under way to developing fingerprinting technologies, which would be reactive rather than proactive in chasing down people posting copyrighted material on internet-related sites. These allow networks to examine an audio (or other digital) file, and determine its identity by looking up a mathematical fingerprint in a database. The network can then either forbid usage, or allow it under specified conditions. Even relatively successful implementation would involve the integration of peer-to-peer networks into the legitimate online music and entertainment markets, in large part as an alternative means of promotion and distribution.

What has happened over the last decade is that technology companies such as Google and Apple have become powerful new entrants into cultural markets, alongside the vertically-integrated companies who dominated these markets in the 1980s and 1990s (Disney, News Corporation, Time Warner, and so on). Some of these companies have responded by making expensive acquisitions of these new 'platforms' (most notably News Corporation's purchase of MySpace). The music sharing and social exchange involved in subcultural peer-to-peer sharing is now becoming part of everyday media experience, via sites such as MySpace, Bebo and YouTube (the latter owned by Google), and yet these sites still residually draw upon the countercultural associations of the earlier forms of networking.

Yet, at the same time that the 'older' cultural-industry corporations and the newer technology giants represent different sectors, they also share an interest in forging strategic alliances. Together, they are involved in a battle to enclose the provisional and semi-legal commons afforded by file-sharing technologies, and while their actions will never be fully successful, they will ward off a catastrophic collapse of the possibilities of making money through music. This can be seen in the steady rise of digital musical markets. By 2005, digital sales accounted for $1.1 billion of total recorded-music sales, the equivalent of 5.5 per cent of the global trade value of recorded-music sales (*Music and Copyright*, 27 September 2006). An interesting difference that emerged was that in Europe and North America, most of these digital sales were online, but in Asia distribution by mobile telephony was dominant. Some industry analysts were, as a result of this, predicting that the growth of mobile distribution would outstrip that of online models, even in Europe and North America, but at the time of this writing (March 2008) it is too soon to be sure. It is also too early to be clear about how quickly digital sales will erode 'physical' sales of CDs, music DVDs, cassettes and vinyl. What is not in doubt though is that digital sales of music will increase rapidly in the years ahead. Sales of portable digital players have boomed and the iconic portable player, the iPod (which plays AAC files rather than MP3s) has been one of the most seductive consumer objects of the new century. While digital music players have not automatically led yet to big increases in online digital music purchases, such sales are likely to increase further with time.

With the DRM model fading, the majors began in 2007 to shift to new models of digital distribution, long discussed and occasionally experimented with, based on subscription and advertising. Subscription models are based on consumers paying a weekly or monthly charge for access, either by mobile phone or broadband internet or both, to banks of music. Advertising models are based on selling advertising for the site in general, or for the particular songs being downloaded – models derived from internet publishing and social network sites. On the surface, such advertising-supported options may seem to be the dream solution, providing 'free' music to the consumer and revenue to musicians and content owners. However, critical analysts of media economics have drawn attention to some potentially very important limitations of advertising-supported media, based on studies of existing markets of this kind, such as television, radio, newspapers and magazines (I draw on Baker, 2002, pp. 24–30 here). Advertisers have exerted influence consistently on media enterprises and their content – and the public will often be unaware of such influence. In some cases, this will be direct influence – where advertisers will put pressure on newspapers to withdraw certain stories for example. But many of the most important effects of advertising are indirect. In certain media, advertising has the effect of increasing the prevalence of media content relevant to favoured audiences, away from content valued by the poor. In other situations, it can encourage content that has a broad but shallow appeal. Baker shows that the effects of advertising are complex, but they certainly cannot be thought of as responding to the needs or wants of consumers (his arguments about advertising are part of a broader argument that capitalist media in general do not 'give the audience what they want', as naïve business arguments often claim).

Questioning the crisis: internationalisation, copyright and business cycles

I now want to probe further the assumption, prevalent in many media accounts, that music capitalism's fortunes in the first years of the twenty-first century were in irreversible decline and, in so doing, draw attention to three important features of the cultural industries neglected in much of the coverage: internationalisation, the importance of copyright, and the cyclical nature of business under capitalism.

Reports of decline were based on sales statistics collected by national recording industry trade associations affiliated with IFPI, a global trade association which strongly represents the interests of the multinational entertainment corporations that dominate the world music business. IFPI has done a very effective job of publicising the problems facing the record companies over the early years of the twenty-first century. Its website and various publications have given great prominence to various statistics showing declines in sales and revenues. It has worked tirelessly to attribute these declines to file-sharing and to more traditional forms of 'piracy' such as the large-scale copying of CDs and audio cassettes. IFPI have been involved in campaigns against these more traditional forms of piracy for decades, and there are signs that its campaigns are being taken increasingly seriously, with major crackdowns by authorities in Russia and China in 2006.

There is no reason to believe that IFPI is being dishonest about the decline in sales that it reports. But we should pause for a moment to consider why IFPI, on its website, in its various publications and in its dealings with general and business media, might want to trumpet its members' poor figures. The reason is that such rhetoric can help the lobbying power of the recording industry, by strengthening arguments that domestic industries need government support in shaping legislation, in carrying out successful litigation, and in gaining regulatory clearance for mergers, such as that between Sony and BMG's recorded-music divisions in 2004, or between Universal and BMG's music publishing arms in 2006.

A second reason for questioning the notion of a terminal crisis in the music industries is that, while sales figures have undoubtedly been poor in recent years, the music business does not consist entirely of the sale of commodities such as CDs to consumers by record companies. The music industries are based not so much around the manufacture of things, as the creation of rights (see Frith, 1987, p. 57). The opportunities to exploit the ownership of various rights in musical works have expanded consistently over the last century, as the mass media have proliferated and grown; and these opportunities continue to expand. The development of new media technologies has led to the extension of rights in musical works into new realms, beginning with 'author's rights' in the authorship of a musical work, then extending into 'mechanical rights' involving the incorporation of musical works into a whole series of new technological forms, including gramophone records, tapes and CDs; then expanding further to cover 'neighbouring rights' assignable to the *performers* of musical recordings, and 'synch rights' when music is used in films, adverts and TV programmes (for greater detail on these expanding rights, see Hesmondhalgh, 2007b and Laing, 2003).

It is essential to understand that in the vast majority of cases where such rights are in any way valuable, they are assigned to music companies – to music publishers as part of a publishing contract and to record companies as part of a recording contract. Most successful writers and performers are signed to a publishing and recording deal with a music publisher and a record company, each of which is usually part of a multinational entertainment corporation (sometimes both companies will be part of the same corporation, but not always). It is these companies which essentially 'own' the rights to the musical work. Contracts between composers and music publishers, and between performers and record companies, determine for how long the ownership of musical compositions and recordings (respectively) will stay in the hands of the companies to which they are assigned, and when, if at all, they will 'revert' to the composers or performers. These contracts are, with some rare exceptions, quite asymmetrical, in that publishing and record companies have a great deal more experience, expertise and power than the composers and performers they are signing. Reversion will usually happen when the copyrights are low in value. Meanwhile, the scope and duration of the actual rights (that is, when they cease to exist, as opposed to the assignment of them in contracts) are determined by statute. As we shall see, this has become a key battleground in the contemporary cultural industries. Because the cultural industries are businesses increasingly reliant on the value of rights (and this fact is now thoroughly recognised by institutional investors) the major corporations are involved in constant struggles to extend the scope and duration of these rights. What is more, the collection agencies that, on behalf of copyright owners, monitor the use of songs and recordings by broadcasters, shops, restaurants, airlines, cinemas, dance clubs, and hotels, are increasingly assiduous, and this is leading to increasing income from public performance licences. The music business is currently exerting considerable pressure on agencies (especially non-western ones) to improve their collections further. As non-western countries are integrated into such 'western' copyright practices, there is no doubt that rights incomes will rise. They already constitute an equivalent of 3 per cent of global recorded-music sales, but in some countries (such as the Netherlands and Denmark) this is now as high as 15 per cent (*Music and Copyright*, 13 September 2006).

The crucial point here is that the fate of the music business should not be understood in terms of sales alone. The music business is founded on rights, and the possibilities for exploiting these rights have grown steadily over time, and continue to grow. As Simon Frith has put it, in an analysis of the relationship of music to other media:

> Providing sounds for radio and television, for films and advertisements, for computer games and mobile phones, for public spaces generally, is nowadays as commercially important as directly pleasing the public. The 'music industry' describes a complex network of rights-owners and licensed users, a continual flow of rights income which seems inexhaustible and sometimes, indeed, quite random.
>
> (Frith, 2004, p. 176)

The main lesson for the current analysis is that we must not mistake reports of declining sales of CDs in the face of the impending rise of digital distribution as a reliable sign *in itself* of an out-and-out crisis amongst the music groups of major multinational entertainment corporations. While the revenues of the music publishing divisions of the multinational entertainment companies are not as formidable as the revenues of the recorded music arms, the profit margins are considerably higher. *Music and Copyright* estimates a return on sales of 20 per cent for music publishing, as compared with 10 per cent for recorded music (24 November, 2004). While the major companies do not dominate music publishing to quite the same degree as they do recorded music, the late 1990s saw big acquisitions of catalogues. The five major music publishers (Universal, Warner, Sony, BMG and EMI) in the early 2000s accounted for about 65 per cent of the global gross revenue of publishing (as opposed to about 70 per cent of the recorded music revenues).[2]

This consideration of rights raises another reason to treat ominous warnings about the death of the music business in the era of digital distribution with scepticism. These industries have been extremely successful in lobbying governments for changes in copyright law, changes which are decidedly favourable to the major corporations that dominate rights ownership. The supposed threat offered by digital technologies, in particular the internet, has brought about a legislative response which has 'vastly increased the scope of copyright but also has done so in a way which benefits corporate interests at the expense of those of both artists and consumers' (Frith and Marshall, 2004, p. 4). The first major response to the rise of the internet came with the World Intellectual Property Organisation conference in Geneva in 1996. Signatories agreed to update their national laws to allow rights holders to extend their rights into the internet and other computer networks. The result was the Digital Millennium Copyright Act in the USA in 1998, and the EU Copyright Directive of 2001, with various European countries making this Directive a law in their respective countries in subsequent years. Such an extension of copyright law into digital terrain was to be expected, but these acts also contained clauses which made illegal the development of software which could counter the DRM systems which are being used by cultural-industry corporations to protect their content (see previous section). This was a sign that the digital environment was being fruitfully presented by the copyright industries, such as the recording industry, as a threat, one against which legislation was needed to protect them. It was in this environment that the Sonny Bono Copyright Term Extension Act was passed by the US Congress in 1998. This extended the term of protection for works copyrighted after 1 January 1923 from the date of the death of the author plus 50 years, to the date of author's death plus 70 years. In addition, the 'protection' granted to works made by corporations, including films and most popular music recordings, since 1978, was extended from 75 years to 95 years.

Such acts of legislation suggest that the original stated purpose of copyright, to stimulate creativity within a society, is being sidelined in favour of the protection of corporate interests. This can be seen as part of a broader shift in the status of the cultural industries in economic and employment policy in the advanced industrial countries. Nicholas Garnham (2005) has shown how various strands of Information Society thinking have helped to sustain a very problematic view that the cultural sector is a key area of economic growth within the global economy, and how this in turn has led to an alliance between various business interests and the state around the extension of intellectual property rights. Garnham makes the further, related claim that the popularity of the notion of the 'creative industries' (as opposed to the term 'cultural industries', which has tended to be associated with more critical appraisals of media and cultural policy) derives precisely from its appropriation as part of Information Society rhetoric (see also Hesmondhalgh 2007a). Government reports echo the grandiose claims made about the economic value of intellectual property in (less than independent) research, claims which are in turn used by the 'creative' or 'copyright' industries to exert influence on policy-makers. The successful creation of such a coalition of interests around the value of the creative industries in many countries is another sign that we should take claims about the vulnerability of the recording industry (as opposed to the specific companies currently charged with managing the transition to a new form of making capital out of music) with a heavy flavouring of salt.

The digitalisation crisis in long-term context

I've been arguing that the crisis in the recording industry, often attributed to digitalisation, has been exaggerated, and while this exaggeration may not have been deliberately cultivated by the recording industry, it has favoured their interests in arguing, and powerfully lobbying, for policy change. Nevertheless, it cannot be denied that the early twenty-first century saw a downturn in the fortunes of this particular cultural industry. I now want to put this downturn in long-term context.

Many accounts treat crises of profitability and investor confidence in the cultural industries as if they depended on the diversity and quality of artistic creativity. According to this view, the problems faced by the recording industry have come about because the world lacks a Madonna, a Michael Jackson, or a Beatles – performers who can generate massive global sales across a series of releases. (There is an echo here of how popular accounts of cinema's re-emergence from its 1960s doldrums attributed its recovery to the artistic brilliance and/or commercial savvy of a new generation of young film directors). While such considerations are not irrelevant, it is hard to believe that there will ever be a serious lack of talented performers and composers in the world of music as a whole; what matters is how artistic creativity is framed, developed and understood. Two other factors have been much more important in the cyclical history of the ups and downs of the recording industry than supposed problems with talent: one is the level of demand in economies as a whole (which obviously affects all industries, though to different degrees – sales of a non-essential item such as music are obviously likely to suffer more than, say, those of soap in general conditions of falling demand); the other is the relationship of musical recording to changing technologies of storage and retrieval (gramophones and shellac 78 RPM discs, hi-fis and LPs, Walkmans and audio cassettes, CDs and CD players, to today's iPods, MP3 players and digital files).

The importance of these factors – general demand and technologies of storage and retrieval – can be examined by looking at the history of the recording industry, which has experienced three major periods of sustained growth, and three shorter periods of downturn, of differing degrees of seriousness. Major periods of growth have been marked by a synergistic relationship between increasing consumer demand for recorded-music commodities and for new playback technologies, as well as general economic growth. This was the case in the 1920s, when gramophones, phonographs and other devices fell in price and rose in quality. It was true of the 1960s and 1970s, when stereo records, audio cassettes and hi-fi helped to fuel further demand for rock, soul and other genres around the world. And it was especially true of the 1980s and early 1990s, the era of the CD and the Walkman. The successful marketing of the CD (on the basis of its supposedly better sound and undoubted playback convenience) meant that consumers accepted very high charges for the CD, and, as vinyl records and record players were increasingly hard to come by, paid to replace their old vinyl with new CDs.

The first period of downturn took place from 1929 to the mid-1930s, when worldwide economic depression sent sales of records and sheet music plummeting. The second came in the late 1970s and early 1980s, when global recession was again a major factor, compounded by high oil prices, which made vinyl records extremely expensive, and by increasing competition from new forms of leisure expenditure and, in the USA, the world's biggest entertainment market, new audio-visual technologies such as cable television.

The period from the late 1990s to the present can be seen as a third period of downturn. Like the earlier downturns, it derives partly from general economic patterns: the post-millennial, post-dot.com-boom recessions in the United States and financial collapses in Asia and Latin America set the first shock waves through the industry. The peaking and decline of demand for CD players and CDs was a major factor too, as was increasing uncertainty about what new form of distribution, storage and retrieval might ultimately come to replace it, as consumers read reports of new types of delivery systems on the horizon, but were unable to get any clear sense of what system might prevail – or, in many cases, of how the different systems worked.

My suggestion then is that the crisis and chaos in the music industry of the early 2000s was by no means unprecedented, and that digitalisation is just one of a series of technological innovations which have had impacts on the business of music over the last century. The difference is that the money to be made from the music industries is much bigger now than it has ever been, for reasons discussed earlier – the growth in leisure time and expenditure in western countries, and the increasing focus on the cultural sector for economic expansion – on the part of businesses and governments.

Concluding comments: 'Fuck you Lars, the music belongs to us too'

Throughout this chapter, I've emphasised the complex intermingling of a number of factors in understanding recent changes in the music business: not just technological innovations, but also general economic conditions, political values, lobbying powers, copyright law and practice. In this same spirit of stressing a multiplicity of causes and effects, let me now try to summarise – inevitably with a degree of speculation – the implications of recent developments for the industrial production, distribution and consumption of music, and for the analysis of the music industries and the cultural industries more generally.

The recording industry

Significant changes in the structure and strategy of the major corporations are taking place, and are likely to intensify. There has been withdrawal or partial withdrawal from manufacturing and distribution, with these operations being sold off to third parties. This should not be read as disintegration, however (this was the mistake that analysts of post-Fordism made in the 1980s in interpreting earlier developments in the film industry – see Hesmondhalgh, 1996). Nor is it a sign of the 'disintermediation' we heard so much about during the dot.com boom. For, the major corporations retain crucial control over the marketing and promotion that largely determine what music most consumers get to hear and know about. The signs are that such marketing is being centralised, in order to produce blockbuster hits, whereby key albums by key stars make an immediate and very big impact on public consciousness. A parallel here is with the increasing emphasis in the film industry on massive publicity to generate big revenues on opening weekends. Meanwhile, the size of record company rosters has been drastically cut – especially non-English rosters in the overseas divisions of the multinational corporations (*Music and Copyright*, 23 June 2004).[3] As already mentioned, there has been further consolidation of an already highly-concentrated business. A new development after the Sony BMG merger of 2004 was that the four majors divided (no doubt temporarily, for very little is stable in capitalism) into two tiers, with Universal and Sony BMG accounting for nearly a quarter of global music revenues, and EMI and Warner Music Group (no longer part of AOL Time Warner, but in the hands of an investment company) for about an eighth each. Small and medium-sized companies have generally not been able to reap the rewards of the new opportunities for promotion and marketing afforded by the internet and the world wide web in spite of some euphoric predictions in the late 1990s. Such companies have been able to develop key acts in certain genres, notably alternative rock and rap, but nearly always in conjunction with the financing and marketing expertise of the majors. A band such as the Arctic Monkeys can achieve great success within a particular territory, via 'independent' means, including at least in part their fans' use of the internet, but when it comes to moving beyond the UK, it was necessary to use bigger companies; and the band were signed to EMI Publishing early in their career. The interdependence of 'independents' and majors continues.

Consumption

Digitalisation and other recent developments have brought about a further proliferation of ways in which wealthier and time-rich consumers can experience music: on the computer while sending emails, choosing from vast databases of music while using digital music devices, and so on. This has led some commentators to speak, with awed reverence towards the efficacy of digital cultural markets, of a new era where consumers purchase an extraordinarily diverse set of products, and where even the least popular recordings are still purchased by *someone*. Perhaps the high ware mark of this hype was the huge attention given to the idea of 'the long tail' (Anderson, 2006). In effect, this is a market-oriented celebration of the diversity supposedly brought about by digitalisation. The problem however remains inequality of access, for example to broadband, and to knowledge about how to use these technologies. Wealthier and time-richer audiences are undoubtedly able to access great diversity. However, even those who can afford broadband and a variety of regularly updated playing devices, a considerable investment of time is still needed – uploading CD collections on to computer and then on to iPods and other MP3 players can take hundreds of hours. Even amidst the hype of the early 2000s, it was still the case that only the most committed downloaders were able to find their way effectively around the 'free' file-sharing world. Nevertheless, I don't want to deny some of the exciting possibilities that have opened up on the web, as thousands and thousands of musicians and intermediaries make their work available. This can be seen as a partial decommodification of music, and that is important and exciting.

Rights and critique

The record companies have been in the process of redefining themselves 'as creators and exploiters of intellectual property rights' (*Music and Copyright*, 1 September 2004) for many years. It seems highly likely that the high returns and low costs of music publishing and the constantly expanding opportunities for rights exploitation, both of which I've stressed above, will make copyright more and more central to the music business in the years to come – and similar trends are at work in the cultural industries more generally. This may well intensify the efforts of the 'creative industries', including the major record companies, to lobby governments in favour of copyright law and practice which will further threaten the public domain and which will favour private, corporate interests. This makes the struggles over digitalisation of music in the early twenty-first century particularly interesting, because of the tension between producers and consumers so beautifully crystallised in the music industry lawsuits against music downloaders. The attitude of consumers is not necessarily based on a fully worked-out critique of cultural-industry practice. It is often founded on romantic anarchism, rather than a commitment to the redistribution of wealth. Nevertheless, its affiliation to a notion of the public domain is ultimately critical of the privatising, individualising tendencies of contemporary capitalism. Mann (2000), for example, quotes one fan, addressing the drummer of the heavy metal band Metallica, who took Napster to court in 2000 and thereby instantly destroyed their subcultural credibility: 'Fuck you Lars, the music belongs to us too'.

While I have been sceptical about accounts of the death of the music business, this should not be read as a pessimistic dismissal of recent developments. For discursive struggles over copyright and the digitalisation of music have, I think, helped to reinforce amongst many ordinary music fans a strong sense that the current social relations of musical production should not and need not be as they are. This interpretation should not in any way be confused with the idea that digitalisation increases innovation, creativity or consumer choice. If my analysis is right, a long-term shift of control from the entertainment corporations to audiences is highly unlikely. But there are important countervailing elements in cultural attitudes towards music and towards creativity in general that continue to challenge corporate domination of musical production and circulation. There is a real opportunity in the present conjuncture to build on these romantic and anarchistic elements to spread a more coherent critique. In academia, a spate of recent critical work on these and related issues has helped to put questions of copyright at the top of the agenda of modern cultural criticism (notably Boyle, 1996, Lessig, 2001 and Vaidhyanathan, 2001).[4] The case of the music industries suggests that digital dynamics of creativity and innovation in the cultural industries simply cannot be understood without a critical analysis of copyright.

Notes

1 A brief note on terminology. I use the term 'music industries' here to differentiate between different industries centred on the cultural form that is music. These industries are principally those based on recording, publishing, live entertainment and musical instruments and software. Distinguishing between the first two of these is, as we shall see, particularly important in the present context. At times I use the term 'music business' to refer to these industries collectively – especially the first two.

2 The reason that I speak of five major music publishers and four major record companies in the early 2000s is that when Sony and BMG merged their recorded-music divisions in 2004 they did not merge their publishing. In September 2006, Universal's parent company Vivendi bought BMG Music Publishing, reducing the number of major music publishers from five to four.

3 This process is of course reversible, and the major companies may well revert to their strategy of spreading risk across a wider repertoire.

4 In this respect, the response of work in the political economy of culture tradition has been disappointing. The index of one otherwise impressive volume on the political economy

of culture (Calabrese and Sparks, 2004) contains no reference to copyright, and one reference to intellectual property rights. This remarkable lacuna is not untypical.

References

Alderman, J, (2001) *Sonic Boom: Napster, MP3 and the New Pioneers of Music*, London, Fourth Estate.

Anderson, C, (2006) *The Long Tail: How Endless Choice is Creating Unlimited Demand*, London, Business Books.

Baker, E C, (2002) *Media, Markets and Democracy*, Cambridge, Cambridge University Press.

Bakker, P, (2005) 'File-sharing – fight, ignore or compete: paid download services vs. P2P networks', *Telematics and Informatics*, vol. 22, no.1–2, pp. 41–55.

Barfe, L, (2003) *Where Have all the Good Times Gone? The Rise and Fall of the Music Industry*, London, Atlantic Books.

BBC (2006) *Kazaa site becomes legal service*, news.bbc.co.uk, 27 July 2006, accessed 2 August 2006.

Boyle, J, (1996) *Shamans, Software and Spleens*, Cambridge, Harvard University Press.

Burkart, P and T McCourt, (2006) *Digital Music Wars: Ownership and Control of the Celestial Jukebox*, Lanham, MD, Rowman & Littlefield.

Calabrese, A and C Sparks, (eds) (2004) *Toward a Political Economy of Culture*, Lanham, Maryland and Oxford, Rowman & Littlefield.

Frith, S, (1987) 'Copyright and the music business', *Popular Music*, vol. 7, no. 1, pp. 57–75.

Frith, S, (2004) 'Music and the media', in S Frith and L Marshall (eds), *Music and Copyright*, 2nd edn, Edinburgh, Edinburgh University Press, pp. 171–88.

Frith, S and L Marshall, (2004) 'Making sense of copyright', in S Frith and L Marshall (eds), *Music and Copyright*, 2nd edn, Edinburgh, Edinburgh University Press, pp. 1–18.

Galperin, H, (2004) *New Television, Old Politics*, Cambridge, Cambridge University Press.

Garnham, N, (2005) 'From cultural to creative industries: an analysis of the implications of the "creative industries" approach to arts and media policy making in the UK', *International Journal of Cultural Policy*, vol. 10, no. 1, pp.15–30.

Hesmondhalgh, D, (1996) 'Post-Fordism, flexibility and the music industries', *Media, Culture and Society* vol.18, no. 3, pp. 468–488.

Hesmondhalgh, D, (2007a) *The Cultural Industries*, 2nd edn, London, Sage.

Hesmondhalgh, D, (2007b) 'Digitalisation, music and copyright', ESRC Centre for Research on Socio-Cultural Change, working paper no. 30.

Laing, D, (2003) 'Copyright', in J Shepherd, D Horn, D Laing, P Oliver and P Wicke (eds), *Continuum Encyclopedia of Popular Music of the World*, Volume I: Media, Industry and Society, London and New York, Continuum, pp. 480–93.

Lanchester, J, (2002) 'Online goodies', *London Review of Books*, 25 April.

Lessig, L, (2001) *The Future of Ideas: The Fate of the Commons in a Connected World*, New York, Random House.

Leyshon, A, (2003) 'Scary monsters? Software formats, peer-to-peer networks, and the spectre of the gift', *Environment and Planning D: Society and Space*, vol. 21, pp. 533–558.

Mann, C C, (2000) 'The Heavenly Jukebox', *Atlantic Monthly*, vol. 286, no. 3, pp. 39–73.

Music and Copyright (various dates), London, Informa Telecoms & Media.

Slater, D, (2000) 'Consumption without scarcity: exchange and normativity in an Internet setting', in P Jackson, M Lowe, D Miller and F Mort (eds), *Commercial Cultures: Economies, Practices, Spaces*, Oxford, Berg.

Teather, D, (2003) 'Mother settles piracy case', *The Guardian*, 11 September. http://www.guardian.co.uk/technology/2003/sep/11/business.netmusic, accessed 15 January 2009.

Vaidhyanathan, S, (2001) *Copyrights and Copywrongs: The Rise of Intellectual Property and How it Threatens Creativity*, New York and London, NYU Press.

3b On music as a creative industry

Simon Frith, Martin Cloonan and John Williamson

This paper is concerned with a longstanding policy issue: the relationship between music as culture and music as industry. Music clearly is a significant part of the British economy – in terms of the income it generates, the employment it provides, its export earnings, the inward investment it attracts, and so on. But music making is not, in itself, an industrial activity; it is not something primarily brought about by market forces or moneymaking opportunities. Music is a human activity, something that happens in all societies regardless of their social or economic organisation. Even in the UK today there is a vast amount of music that is made and listened to in our everyday lives that is not made for profit (and is not profitable).

In considering music policy, then, we need to remember that most musicians don't make a living from their music, that most people who make music don't do so for a living. Even within the industrial sector most records/CDs released don't cover their costs, the great majority of songwriters and composers registered with the Performing Right Society don't make a living income from their rights earnings and a significant proportion of graduates from 'vocational' music courses (whether from conservatories or the FE/HE sectors) are unlikely to have long-term careers as professional musicians, or in the music sector.

Our point here is that we can still make a distinction between music making, something done for all sorts of reasons, in all sort of circumstances, and music exploiting, the ways in which money can be made out of music's cultural and social significance. Effective music policy needs to understand and take account of both processes and it is our contention that in treating music as a 'creative industry' policy makers have, rather, confused the two kinds of activity. We begin with a brief history of the way in which British state policy has changed emphasis in the last fifty years, from music as culture to music as cultural industry, focusing discussion on the way this policy shift has played out in Scotland.[1] Two related concepts have been important in the development of music policy: 'creativity' and 'locality'. In the second part of the paper we consider why this is so, and examine the conditions that allow local musical activity to flourish. We conclude that what matters here is, first, the nature of the local music culture (in which there is no clear demarcation between music amateurs and professionals, between people making music for love or for money) rather than its industrial infrastructure, and, second, the axes between local music making and global music exploitation rather than local attempts to replicate global industry institutions on a smaller scale. Policies for music as industry, that is to say, still need to be rooted in policies for music as culture.

From culture to cultural industry

In his book, *Popular Music and the State in the UK: Culture, Trade or Industry?* (2007), Martin Cloonan documents in detail the changes in the British government's interest in music over the last half century. One could summarise this as a shift from cultural policy to cultural industry policy but these terms need a little unpicking. Initially, post-1945, music was of interest to the state primarily as an aspect of high culture, to be supported along with the other arts through Arts Councils. The emergence of youth culture in the 1950s meant that music – popular music – also came to be understood, used and regulated as an aspect of youth policy. By the 1990s, though, and particularly following the Labour Party's electoral victory in 1997, the state's primary interest in music had become its economic potential, as a source of export earnings, inward investment and employment.

How does one account for this change? The answer lies, first of all, in changes within the music industry itself, both locally and globally.[2] Up to the late 1970s and the abrupt end (an effect of the oil crisis and the increased cost of vinyl) of the remarkable growth rate in record sales following the introduction of the long playing record in the early 1950s, the UK music industry had rarely looked to the state for explicit support (and had, indeed, prided itself on its free-market image).[3] From the 1980s, though, industry attitudes changed, on the one hand in response to the digital challenge to established ways of making money (pre-figured by the battle against home taping and the unsuccessful attempt to have a blank tape levy included in the 1988 Copyright Act) and on the other hand in response to globalisation and the changing nature of the international music market.

In looking to the government for support (initially in terms of amendments to copyright laws and regulations, subsequently with regard to piracy and international trade conditions) the music industry came up against its own less than respectable reputation. Indeed, the roots of national popular music initiatives could perhaps be traced back to the House of Commons National Heritage Committee 1993 investigation of CD prices, which followed and gave media publicity to a variety of claims by consumer organisations and MPs of record company profiteering. The Commons report led, in turn, to a Monopolies and Mergers Commission (MMC) investigation and, although the industry was formally cleared of over-pricing (MMC 1994), both the House of Commons hearings and MMC submissions showed that it had a major image-building job to do. It now set out to show politicians how important the sector was for the UK economy.

Moves to promote the industry to politicians included courting and lobbying them at industry events such as the annual Brits Awards (which was increasingly used to sell the industry as a whole as well as the featured artists and albums). As leader of the opposition, Tony Blair was invited to address the industry's umbrella organisation, the British Phonographic Industry (BPI), in July 1995 (he promised stricter copyright laws). He had been preceded in previous years by both the (Tory) Chancellor of Exchequer and Minister for National Heritage.

One result of this new conversation between industry and politicians was the launch of an employee exchange scheme between record companies and government departments as part of an attempt by the Department of Trade and Industry (DTI) to better understand the creative industries, and especially the music industry. The DTI established a Music Industries Unit whose remit was to deal with all aspects of creating and marketing music, and progress was such that by 1998 the BPI was able to report that since the 1993 House of Commons investigation of CD prices the industry 'has encountered much greater understanding of the industry in Whitehall.' The new Labour Government, the BPI was pleased to say, understood 'Britain's role as a world leader in music' (BPI 1998: 8, 1).

A key component of the industry's political strategy had been the provision of statistics, beginning with a commissioned report, *The Overseas Earnings of The Music Industry* (British Invisibles 1995), which suggested that the music industry created a trade surplus of £571 million a year. Thenceforth such reports became central to the way in which the music industry – and music industry policy – was understood. The 1997 Labour government thus flagged up its commitment to the newly christened 'creative industries' by carrying out its own mapping exercise to determine their economic value (DCMS 1998), and further reports on the economic value of music have followed at regular intervals (Dane *et al.* 1996, 1999, 2002). Such reports provide the 'evidence base' that policy now requires, but from an academic perspective the statistics are problematic. On the one hand, they describe 'the music industry' in essentially conservative terms even while drawing attention to the 'challenges' it faces in changing times; on the other hand, the numbers have to serve contradictory purposes, providing governments with measures of both the music business's success and the income crises it faces without state support.

These issues became apparent to us when we got involved in one such statistical exercise. This report was not the first attempt to map the Scottish music industry. *The List* magazine began publishing an annual special supplement, *The Rock Report*, 'The Essential Guide to the Music Business in Scotland', in 1987 and the most comprehensive of its reports, published in 1990, provided basic information on Scottish-based music companies under 16 headings: music shops, practice rooms, venues, pa hire, studios, video, tape duplication, promoters, management, labels, radio, press, music organisations, production companies, agents, miscellaneous. The report only covered the four major cities of Edinburgh, Glasgow, Dundee and Aberdeen but it did provide an early statement of what became recurring issues for Scottish music policy makers in the 1990s: the failure of local bands to make the move from Scottish to UK-wide or international success; the lack of independent Scottish record companies with any kind of sustained financial success; and the absence of an entrepreneurial infrastructure – specialist lawyers, accountants, etc. In 1994 (with support from Tennents Live!) MIST, Music in Scotland Trust (which was launched by the Princes Trust in 1989 to fund unemployed young people with 'an idea for a business in the music industry in Scotland that stands a reasonable chance of success'), published *The Scottish Music Guide*, 'a comprehensive guide to the Music industry in Scotland', which covered jazz and traditional music as well as rock and pop. While it was rather more upbeat than *The List* reports, here too Scotland's music industry problem was seen to be its inability to produce acts and performers who could sustain commercial success, and this was blamed on the talent flowing south and the lack of a music business infrastructure. At this point Scotland was still a 'stateless nation'. It was only with devolution in 1999 that a policy-making structure developed that could address these issues by looking to copy initiatives taken in other small European countries and even here the terms of devolution constrained the new Executive's powers (Symon and Cloonan 2002).

The Scottish Parliament has power over much of Scottish life but significant areas such as international relations, broadcasting, taxation, and employment laws are reserved to the UK Government in Westminster. The Parliament, for example, cannot impose radio content quotas nor levies on blank CDs.[4] It does, though, have control over cultural policy, economic development and education, and in August 2000 the new Scottish Executive published its cultural strategy document, *Creating Our Future . . . Minding Our Past* (Scottish Executive 2000). This was an oddly old-fashioned document – popular music was only mentioned (on page 52) as a means of countering social exclusion – and was soon overtaken by events. In terms of music policy there have been three main players engaged in determining what the state's involvement should be: Scottish Enterprise (SE), the Scottish Arts Council (SAC) and the Cross Party Group on the Scottish Contemporary Music Industry (CPG).

Scottish Enterprise is the lead organisation in Scotland's economic development strategy. (Scotland has a number of publicly owned economic development agencies, Local Enterprise Companies, LECs, which are brought together under two main bodies, Scottish Enterprise and Highlands and Islands Enterprise.) In 2001 it set up a new budget line of £25 million for 'the development of Scotland's creative industries to exploit the wealth of talent, skills and expertise in the sector'. In order to inform its popular music policies, SE commissioned a report from the Glasgow-based consultancy, New Media Partners (2001), having previously funded research on the creative industries in Scotland generally (Pratt 1999) and on the value of the music sector (Laing 2000). SE also part-sponsored the Go North festival in Aberdeen (and the accompanying promotional CD cover mounted on the UK music trade paper, *Music Week*), and helped to finance Music Works, an international music industry convention which took place in Glasgow annually from 2002–2005.

The Scottish Arts Council, meanwhile, had also been re-appraising its approach to the funding of music. In March 2001 it launched a new policy on Contemporary Popular Music (SAC 2001) which committed the SAC to supporting popular music and to providing the sector with additional resources. Funding priority was given to the support of touring, promotion and recording, and research and consultation within the sector were promised as key means of taking the programme forward (SAC 2001: 5). In 2002 the SAC described its future vision as one of 'equity of opportunity . . . across musical styles and musical interests' (SAC 2002: 2) and produced a report with Visit Scotland which examined ways of exploiting the potential of traditional music for promoting tourism. Even within the SAC, one could say, culture policy was now inflected with a cultural industry strategy.

The Cross Party Group on the Scottish Contemporary Music Industry followed the establishment in the new Scottish Parliament of a number of Cross-Party Groups, which are effectively means by which members of the Scottish Parliament (MSPs) can pursue their particular hobby-horses. Such Cross-Party Groups (there are others on Culture and the Media and Scottish Traditional Arts) have no legislative or policy-making powers, but act as lobbying groups with sometimes ready access to Ministers. The Contemporary Music CPG is made up of MSPs, musicians, managers, assorted industry folk and representatives from the educational sector. While it is essentially a talking shop, it has given some focus to the disparate music industry in Scotland and has acted effectively as a scrutineer of policy developments.[5] The CPG was thus vocal in its critique of, first, the Executive's initial cultural strategy and then of Scottish Enterprise's approach to music as a creative industry, twice summoning SE employees to appear before it to explain their plans.

This was the political context in which SE announced a tender for a mapping of the music industry in Scotland in order to provide an accurate picture of its economic state and to pinpoint the areas in which an economic development agency might be able to assist. It was also the political context in which we came to understand that 'mapping the music industry' is not a straightforward task. We have written elsewhere about the less than enthusiastic response of both SE and sectors of the music industry in Scotland to our findings (Cloonan *et al.* 2004). Some of these responses reflect the essentially contradictory nature of such mapping exercises that we have already mentioned. Thus we were criticised for how we defined the music sector, for what we included or excluded as economically relevant music activities (there were objections, for example, to our treating the record retail sector as part of the Scottish music industry).[6] And we were accused of being unduly pessimistic, of underestimating both the music sector's economic value to Scotland and the possible effects of state investment (this cut across both the Cross Party Group's attempts to make SE take the sector more seriously and the SE's justification for existing policies). From our own perspective we were most struck in our interviews by the quite different ways in which music entrepreneurs, on the one hand, and officials of the various state funded music agencies and trade bodies, on the other, understood and talked about music as a 'creative' business. And it is on this issue that we now focus this paper.

Local creativity

Music industry policy in the UK (as in most other Western countries) is these days focused on three issues: the definition, management and enforcement of digital and other rights; skill shortages and training; and export support. (See, for example, Gowers 2006; Creative and Cultural Skills 2005; D'Arcy and Brindley 2002.) But lurking within all these policy areas are assumptions about the nature of 'creativity'

– as the thing that drives the creative industries – and arguments about the role of the state in ensuring that national conditions are right for creativity to be called forth, nurtured, exploited and rewarded. And what is striking about music policy in this respect is the significance in the understanding of how creativity works with the concept of 'the local'.

There are a number of reasons for this. The first lies in the origins of cultural industries policy, which was not simply a response to industry lobbying. In the UK, music policy became a significant aspect of local authority economic and employment strategies in the 1980s (Frith 1993). Cities such as Sheffield, Manchester, Newcastle, Liverpool and Glasgow pioneered four kinds of municipal musical investment: in recording studios, in venues, in concert promotion, and in training schemes (Street 1993). In Scotland, the Scottish Development Agency (the precursor to Scottish Enterprise) had its own interest in music as an economic sector, funding the creation of a Scottish Record Industry Association and a Scottish record sales chart, and supporting the first Scottish attempt at an independent music business event, New Music World, in 1990.

These local initiatives often looked to Europe for policy models. At a time when successive UK governments were still content to leave the development of the music sector to market forces, many small European countries were investing in the state music agencies that continue to be central players in their cultural industry policies. Holland's Stichting Pomuziek Nederland (SPN) and Denmark's Dansk Rock Samråd (ROSA) thus pioneered the use of state funds to provide local music making with resources and venues and to give touring, recording and promotional support to established bands. These models were followed and developed in different ways by other European countries, such as France and Finland, which used money from blank tape levies to fund information offices, export drives and national musical showcases (Frith 1993; Rutten 1993). Such European initiatives continue to provide ideas to British politicians. Following his launch of the first All Party Music Group in the House of Commons in February 2002, Pete Wishart (a Scottish Nationalist MP and ex-member of Run Rig) told readers of *Holyrood*, the magazine of the Scottish parliament, that 'we only need to look across the North sea to Denmark to see how an indigenous industry can be built' (Wishart 2002).

The point here is that in a global industry like music the national becomes the local. Or, to put this the other way round, theories of local creativity become central to the ways in which concepts such as 'national talent' are understood. Hence the remarkably wide-ranging influence of 'cluster theory' on policy makers' approach to what makes creative industries creative. And this issue became of particular interest to us in the debate that followed the publication of our Mapping report.

Cluster theory, like historical materialism, is an entirely convincing post facto analysis – a successful cultural industry must, of course, have a locale – but rather more problematic as a predictive or diagnostic tool, as a guide to what needs to be done to produce a successful cultural sector, to turn a locality into a locale. Take as an example of the issues here the 2004 success of the Glasgow-based bands Snow Patrol, Franz Ferdinand, and Belle and Sebastian – the first two with million-selling albums, and all three being short-listed for the 2004 Mercury Music Prize.

Just a year after the press coverage of our Mapping report had highlighted our 'negative' findings, notably our observation that fewer Scottish acts than ever were signed to major labels and our analysis of the difficulties of sustaining record labels in Scotland, three out of the twelve Mercury short-listed acts came from one city and publications from *The Scotsman* to *Time* were hailing Scotland in general and Glasgow in particular as centres of both music and music business excellence. Following Franz Ferdinand's Mercury victory, Leon McDermott wrote in the *Sunday Herald* that their award was 'vindication of the idea that Scotland – and more specifically, Glasgow – can support a music scene all of its own.' He quoted BBC Scotland presenter Vic Galloway's remark that 'there's definitely a brilliant infrastructure for music in Scotland right now' (McDermott 2004). What we have here, one might say, is a kind of common sense retrospective cluster theory, and a number of politicians and policy makers (such as the SAC, which had put money into their appearance at the US trade fair, South by South West) were quick to take credit for Franz Ferdinand's success.

But had the condition of the music industry in Scotland really changed beyond all recognition in just over eighteen months? Had this really been the result of state policies? Can these bands' commercial earnings and newfound national and international status really be described as a local 'Scottish success'? The problem here lies in the stories the media didn't tell. Belle and Sebastian's higher market profile followed their signing to Rough Trade (London-based, part of the Sanctuary Group) and enhanced marketing/promotion after years of being labelled as a 'local band'; Franz Ferdinand signed to Domino, a London-based then independent label, and to a London-based management after the group's members had spent years in a variety of relatively unsuccessful local bands; Snow Patrol's breakthrough as an international act (even more commercially successful in the long run than Franz Ferdinand), clearly followed their deal with a large, London-based management company, Big Life, which signed the group to a major label, Polydor/Universal. The significant 'cluster' for these groups' success was, rather, an axis: Glasgow/London.[7]

Our own view, having followed or been involved in various attempts by Scottish policy makers to establish various strategies for encouraging the development of the Scottish music industry even before we did the research for Mapping the Music Industry in Scotland, is that the success of these contemporary bands is not in any clear way an effect of such policies nor a result of national or urban creative 'clusters' as they are usually described. Instead, the success of these bands could be said to reflect the strength of a particular local music culture, a culture on display in two events that preceded what happened in 2004: Belle and Sebastian's Glasgow launch of their Mercury nominated album, *Dear Catastrophe Waitress*, a 'karaoke' gig featuring performances from several generations of local musicians (including Franz Ferdinand's Alex Kapranos) and an earlier Glasgow show by Reindeer Section, an ad hoc band featuring members of Snow Patrol and numerous other Scottish groups. In both cases what was being celebrated was a particular kind of musicians' community.

What the Glasgow experience suggests is that it is a healthy musical culture that leads to a flourishing music industry and not an investment in music industry infrastructure that creates a flourishing musical culture. Music lawyers, PR companies and managers make money because their clients make effective music; musicians don't make good music because they've got good lawyers, PR companies and managers (even if much cultural industry policy seems to adopt the latter view). The question then becomes: what makes for a healthy local music culture, a culture, that is to say, which enables, encourages, nurtures and sustains a particular kind of creative music making?

Musician biographies and studies of music scenes in Britain and elsewhere (see, for example, Cohen 1991 and 2007 on Liverpool, Shank 1994 on Austin, Texas, and Robson 2006 on Sheffield) as well as our own research in Scotland suggest a number of answers.

First, musical resources: we would include under this heading free or affordable music lessons and instrumental tuition from an early age in all kinds of music;[8] the passing down of musical values and ambitions from parents, older siblings, and other family members and friends; ready access to local musicians as performers, teachers, models and mentors; locally available record shops and record collections.

Second, musical spaces: we would include here the variety of places to play, rehearse and see all kinds of music – rooms, venues, clubs, colleges, universities. Variety is the key term here, variety in terms of size, genre, time of opening, kind of audience, etc. (Recording spaces – studios – are less significant than they used to be since the development of cheap domestic digital recording technology – but remain important as a source of job opportunities and session work.)

Third, musical time: musicians need time to learn an instrument, time to practice, time to rehearse, time to write. Hence the importance of schools, colleges and universities, on the one hand, unemployment benefits, on the other. While it's possible to point to the particular significance of music courses here (the RSAMD for Scotland's classical and traditional performers, for example, or Stow College for Belle and Sebastian), it's the general rhythm of higher education that matters. Being a student is a social role particularly compatible with being a musician, as is being unemployed even if, these days, that may mean signing up to the New Deal for Musicians. (See Cloonan 2002) And there's another kind of time significant here: time to develop, time not to get signed up, time to gain experience before being pulled fully into the commercial system.

Our argument here is that it is the availability of sufficient musical resources, space and time that makes possible a particular kind of musical community or, as one might say, cluster. The dynamic of this kind of cluster is provided by musicians and their relationship to each other and following our research into music making in Scotland there are two further points we can make about this. First, as Nod Knowles, then Music Officer of the Scottish Arts Council, put it to us in his interview, 'A healthy pool of freelance musicians is really important for a healthy music scene. People who can turn their hand . . .' (interview). In other words a healthy music culture does indeed depend on employment opportunities but not necessarily on a local record industry infrastructure. Knowles' argument was that to retain musicians in a locality there must be performing work available, in orchestras and ceilidh bands, in sessions for advertisements, for business videos, for film makers, for the games industry, etc. In this sense musicians do rely on a cultural cluster, reasonable access to a more or less local network of musical activities and opportunities.

But such activities are a reminder, our second point, that the musicians' community is essentially mobile. People change bands and line-ups, go off (touring, gigging) and come back; move into the locality and out again (as university students, for example). But they also cross genres (from dance to rock and vice versa; from the 'high' culture of a conservatory or university music course to the 'low' culture of a pop or rock band and back again) and cultures (class cultures, ethnic cultures, taste cultures). To analyse local musical activity, then, and its creative potential, we need to apply a number of analytic concepts:

- Tradition: to what extent do musicians place themselves in a local music history? (Looking beyond cities there are clearly musical communities in Scotland which have thrived through the continuous regeneration of local instrumental practices – fiddlers in Shetland, accordion players in Tiree.)
- Taste: what kind of shared values do musicians' communities need as to good or bad music-making practices?
- Models: what is the role of particular bands or musicians as inspirations (the significance of the Pastels for the Glasgow musical community is far greater than one might conclude from their record sales)?
- Sociability: how do musicians relate to each other, what are the relative creative effects of collaboration and competition?
- Geography: how does the movement of musicians around venues map onto the organisation of city leisure and transport?
- Demography: what is the effect on local music making of patterns of ageing and migration?
- Soundscapes: what does a locality sound like?

We list such questions here (familiar to ethnomusicologists) simply to make the point that such matters are not usually the concern of music policy makers (nor of statistical reports on the 'value' of local musical activities). And if many of the factors that make for a healthy music culture seem of little interest to people trying to establish music as a healthy cultural industry, so, we would argue, much of activity taken to be necessary to establish a local music industry is not really relevant to what makes a local scene successful. We would argue this in two ways.

First, a flourishing musical community calls forth other activities rather than depending on them (hence the emergence of fanzines, promoters, club nights, deejays, managers, and even labels and radio shows).[9] This is to go against orthodox cultural industries thinking but there is little evidence that a local scene is dependent on an industrial infrastructure; rather industrial infrastructure develops to support it. Musicians don't flock to a scene because of its commercial expertise (except to major corporate centres like London) but because there are people that they want to play with and places to play with them in. We're sceptical, in short, about the efficacy of local government cluster policies designed to encourage local music industries. The most significant state policies for the making and unmaking of local music culture are not music policies at all but involve such issues as licensing and planning laws (which effect the distribution and regulation of venues), housing and education policies (which determine the shape of student populations) and employment laws (which affect musicians' working conditions and use of time).[10] In our interviews with musicians it became clear that that one of the most important aspects of a successful music locality is that it is a place where they want to live or come back to. From this perspective 'cultural' policies designed to make city areas attractive to tourists, affluent incomers and inward investors can effectively destroy their original bohemian appeal to music makers (for an example see Cohen 2007 on Liverpool).

Second, the paradox of the music sector (as became clear to us in our Mapping research) is that commercial success depends on the activities of people who make music for its own sake, without any economic concerns at all. It's always worth remembering when listening to music industry discussions that the biggest risks (and biggest proportionate investments) are carried by musicians who have usually been working for years before they get any sort of return commensurate with their outlay. And there's a broader point to be made here. In music, perhaps more than in any other cultural area (and in spite of the significance of market forces for musical tastes and practices), there is a significant blurring and overlap between the amateur (the music lover) and the professional (the music worker), between those musicians whose careers and livelihood depend on music making and those for whom it is a leisure activity, a hobby, something done for its own sake.

To put this another way, while there may, in the long run, be clear differences between the musical amateur and professional in terms of career commitment, self-definition and, of course, playing skills, there is a less clear distinction in what might be called the musical commitment involved. An amateur musician must also practice, be disciplined, take on something difficult that needs work, take part in performance practices in which self-expression is subordinated to collective ends. Much 'amateur' performance involves professionals too – to provide accompaniment or soloists, as part of the way in which a folk or traditional music night is organised or a jazz ensemble put together. In the rock world being a professional often describes a moment in a longer career that begins and ends and is interspersed with life as a musical amateur. A vibrant local musical culture, in other words, describes not just commercially successful or would-be commercially successful musicians but a much broader network of players, performances and audiences, one in which conventional distinctions between culture and commerce, art and pop, high and low culture, don't necessarily hold.

From cultural industry to culture

At the end of February 2007 Nicol Stephen, then Scotland's Deputy First Minister, announced that

> Scotland's music industry is to benefit from extra and better co-ordinated support from the country's enterprise network. A key element of this will be a new £500,000 fund – the Scottish Music Futures Fund – to support the music stars of tomorrow.
>
> (Scottish Executive 2007)

Further,

> the industry asked us to support the proposed new Scottish Music Industry Association. Scottish Enterprise and Highland and Islands Enterprise will now contribute to the creation of the new association [matching the commitment already made by the SAC] . . . The enterprise networks will also work alongside the Scottish Arts Council and industry representatives to support the industry to develop its strategy for contemporary music. The Scottish contemporary music industry is making its mark internationally and is something of which we should be proud.
>
> (Scottish Executive 2007)

Indeed, as the Cross Party Group on Contemporary Music puts it even more bullishly in the same press release, 'Scotland has the potential to be a world leader in the creation and marketing of contemporary music, and has a big contribution to make to the Scottish economy.'

While (at time of writing) it remains to be decided how the Scottish Music Futures Fund will be spent, Nicol Stephen's announcement can be said to mark a decisive moment for the music sector in Scotland in the shift from culture to cultural industries policy. (And we should note that a bill is also presently before the Scottish Parliament that would merge the Scottish Arts Council and Scottish Screen in a new body, Creative Scotland, while hiving off 'national' arts companies like Scottish Opera and the Royal Scottish National Orchestra for direct Executive funding. One implication of these changes is again a blurring of the distinctions between culture and cultural industry policy.)

There are two elements of the policy thinking here, revealed in Nicol Stephen's statement, that are worth examining. The first concerns the relationship of the local and the global: what is Scotland's musical place in the world? The second concerns the definition of the culture sector being deployed: what is meant by contemporary Scottish music?

One recurring tendency of music industry policy is to assume that a local music industry is best understood – should aspire to be – as a mini version of the global music industry, with the same structure of labels, publishers, managers, lawyers, producers, etc. (One can see this assumption shaping most mapping exercises.) One problem here we've already noted: this makes for policy decisions that are essentially behind the times, referring to a model of 'the music industry' that no longer exists. This is often apparent, for example, in the funding of local music business courses. As Philip Tagg puts it, 'I don't know how many students have followed relatively recent music business courses whose "practicalities" were based on observing industry structures from the phonogram era (c1900–c2000): fantastic if you wanted to join the industry in the 1980s!'[11]

But the broader point is that the argument by local/global analogy is misleading: as we've already argued, a local music scene doesn't necessarily need a local music industry. Rather, it needs a way of dealing with the overarching – global – business flows and networks directly. Local intermediaries may or may not be helpful; their value shouldn't be taken for granted. A couple of recurring issues in Scottish music policy debates reveal some of the problems here.

First, it has long been argued that Scottish musicians 'need' local radio outlets, that is programmes dedicated to local performers and performances on existing Scottish radio stations or a new dedicated Scottish music station.[12] But in practice local programmes are not usually the most significant radio-play factor in reaching a potential audience or developing a career. Historically local bands have looked, rather, to a John Peel play (Peel's support was crucial in Belle and Sebastian's early career and for breaking other Scottish acts, such as the Delgados), just as Scottish contemporary composers and jazz instrumentalists establish their reputations through Radio 3 rather than Radio Scotland. What such musicians 'need', in other words, is not sympathetic local radio but access to a national station with a sense of Britain as a network of localities. And the point here can be generalised to cover the other recurring Scottish music business problem: how to stop Scottish artists leaving the country to 'make it'. Of course they leave – this is what 'making it' means, having a presence in musical worlds which are organised globally, which involve playing, recording, selling, appearing, and often living in different countries at different times for different commercial and musical reasons. Successful Scottish jazz and classical musicians need commissions from German radio and appearances at Japanese music festivals, just as much as rock and pop musicians need to sign to London-based labels or agents, and film music and video game composers need to work with Los Angeles-based film producers and Californian game companies. This is how one makes a musical living.

The issue, then, is not how to avoid such deals but how to fit a local into such a global network. Again this is often discussed in monetary terms: how to ensure that money paid to a successful Scottish act or creator flows back into the Scottish economy (as if musicians could be understood as migrant workers, going off to richer countries and sending remissions home). Our argument, in contrast, is that a successful local musical culture depends on the circulation of ideas and experiences rather than money as such. The evidence is that in flourishing local scenes musicians go away and come back, use their resources to develop new projects in familiar surroundings, work with old musical collaborators but draw new ones in too. Doubtless certain kinds of state support can help here – investment to develop music businesses as promised by the Music Futures Fund – but what matters most is the belief among musicians who have made it and those who haven't that this is a good place to be creative.

And this leads us to the final point we want to make here, the continuing need even if we accept the importance of the concept of cultural industries for a policy on culture. We can best approach this by focusing on one of Nicol Stephens' key terms

– 'contemporary music'. What is meant here by the term 'contemporary'? 'Contemporary music' has long been the label applied to contemporary art music (for which the term 'classical' is clearly inappropriate) – hence, in the UK, the Contemporary Music Network, or in Scotland, the Edinburgh Contemporary Arts Trust (a contemporary music promoter). For the Scottish Executive, by contrast it seems, contemporary is defined against traditional music, on the one hand, but also against art music, however contemporary, on the other. The lead on this was clearly taken by the Cross Party Group on the Contemporary Scottish Music Industry. Traditional Scottish music has its own Cross Party Group, while complaints about the level of state funding for Scottish Opera, the Royal Scottish National Orchestra and other classical and art music companies have long been commonplace at CPG meetings.

What is being played out here is an implicit set of distinctions between folk music, art music and commercial music such that the shift from culture to cultural industry policy becomes, in effect, a shift from supporting (subsidising) 'high' culture (or art) to supporting (investing in) 'low' culture (or the commercial sector). One can trace this in the changing discourse of cultural bureaucrats, for example, or in the often thinly disguised class arguments of cultural politicians, or in the changing ways in which applicants for state support must now justify artistic activity, not for its own sake but in terms of various kinds of 'value added'. It would certainly be an interesting piece of sociological research to show how one network of influence in Scottish music policy making (rooted in the academic and classical worlds) has been replaced at the Scottish Arts Council by another network of influence, rooted in the world of music industry trade bodies and consultants. One narrow view of the musical world, that is to say, has been replaced by another.

In trying to make sense of the conditions for creativity such art/commerce distinctions make no sense. Artists respond to commercial constraints and opportunities (as well as looking to various sorts of state support) just as 'commercial' musicians have their own kinds of artistic ambition. All musicians have to take account of market conditions and devise ways to work with them; nearly all musicians have a sense of their musical value independent of their market value. And in the most creative musical places and times (variously since the 1960s, in Liverpool, San Francisco, New York, London) the distinctions between high and low musicians, artists and popular musicians, bohemia and the market place are blurred – in terms of who plays with whom, takes ideas from whom, makes money out of whom. The object of culture policy is to encourage such activity as a necessary form of experimentation; experimentation with new technologies, media, genres, audiences and, indeed, business models. Culture can be understood in this context as a kind of R&D, an exploration of what music (and making money out of music) could be, while cultural industry policy is dealing with the music business as it is – risk-avoiding, routinised, accountable. And just as in science 'blue sky' thinking is encouraged because research driven by intellectual curiosity, without economic or social purpose, is the most likely to come up with the new ideas and discoveries that will, in the future, have profound economic and social consequences, so music for music's sake provides the creative dynamic on which music as a cultural industry depends.

Acknowledgements

This paper is the result of ongoing collaborative research between the three authors but has also benefited greatly from the lead author's participation in the AHRC funded project, *Creativity: policy and practice. A study of the UK government, the BBC and UK Film Council*, ID No. 112152. Thanks also to Philip Schlesinger (principal investigator on that project) for inviting Simon Frith to the seminar on Public Support for the Creative Industries in Scotland, organised by the Centre for Cultural Policy Research, Glasgow University, for the Scottish Arts Council, at which some of the arguments made here were first rehearsed and usefully discussed.

Notes

1 While our discussion is drawn primarily from Scotland, the arguments we raise have general application. There are suggestive and perhaps surprising comparisons, for example, to be made between Scotland and Senegal – see Pratt 2007.
2 Two of the authors, Cloonan and Williamson, query the use of the single term, 'music industry' to describe the range of economic activities involved – see Williamson and Cloonan 2007. The term is employed in this paper as a matter of convenience but it should be stressed that 'the music industry' describes not just the recording industry but the live sector, retail, management, etc.
3 And following the success of the Beatles and the global success of rock as an Anglo-American form, the British industry, unlike those elsewhere in Europe saw no need for any kind of cultural protectionism.
4 In fact the law is a little unclear here. It may be that such levies could be treated as an allowable aspect of the Scottish Parliament's tax-raising powers but they would also challenge UK-wide copyright arrangements. It has always been unclear whether such levies should count as taxes or a form of rights income. These are ongoing matters of argument in the EU.
5 The Executive's 2007 announcement of an annual £500,000 investment in a Scottish Music Futures Fund was clearly the result of CPG lobbying activities. We discuss this further on.
6 We don't have the space to explore these definitional disputes further here but as an example of the problems involved consider coffee shops. Should Starbucks (having released the latest Paul McCartney CD on its own label) now be regarded as part of the music industry? Or, to stick to the Scottish case, should Beanscene? This successful chain of 15 coffee shops, in the words of its founder, sells 'an environment' (rather than simply coffee or food) of which music is the key part – it has a music director who programmes live performances and sells an exclusive range of CDs. Certainly, from the local musicians' point of view, it has become a significant feature in the live music scene.
7 Actually the most significant cluster here might have been among the Mercury Music Prize Judges. This wasn't noticed by journalists covering this story but in 2004, unusually, 4 of the 10 judges (including two of the authors of this article) were recently from or still based in Scotland. As John Williamson noted later about the media coverage of Scotland that followed the announcement of the Mercury shortlist, 'on a personal level, I would consider that my involvement as one of the judges for the Mercury Music Prize

last year had a far greater impact in terms of drip-down economics on those operating in the margins of the music industry in Scotland than the report I had worked on the year previously.' (quote taken from an unpublished paper for a seminar on European music policy held at Stirling University in 2005).

8 In 2003 a Youth Music Initiative was launched in Scotland (under the aegis of the SAC) following a Scottish Executive pledge that 'by 2006 all school children should have access to one year's free music tuition by the time they reach P6'. The SAC's 2007 Report on Local Authority Attainment over Three Years of the Youth Music Initiative suggests that while the policy has had some success in putting music back on the primary school curriculum, for most children in most authorities to pursue instrumental tuition still means paying for out-of-school lessons.

9 Long before their bands were successful Alex Kapranos and Stuart Murdoch (from Belle and Sebastian) had played an important role in the Glasgow scene as (unsubsidised) promoters.

10 The Musicians Union in Scotland is thus increasingly concerned about promoters' use of 'pay for play' deals. Music policies designed to support promoters need to take account of the kinds of deals they do with performers.

11 Tagg made this comment to the International Association for the Study of Popular Music discussion board.

12 Such proposals were put to the Cultural Commission, for example, the body set up by the Scottish Executive to generate proposals for Scottish cultural policy in the lead up to the decision to create Creative Scotland. They fell foul of the fact that broadcasting in Scotland is not a devolved area of policy.

References

British Invisibles (1995), *The Overseas Earnings of the Music Industry*, London: British Invisibles.

BPI (British Phonogram Industry) (1998), *1998 Handbook*, London: BPI

Cloonan, M. (2002), 'Hitting the right note? The New Deal for musicians', *Journal of Vocational Education and Training* 54(1), pp. 51–66.

—— (2007), *Popular Music and the State in the UK: Culture, Trade or Industry?*, Aldershot: Ashgate.

Cloonan, M., Williamson, J. and Frith, S. (2004), 'What is music worth? Some reflections on the Scottish experience', *Popular Music* 23(2), pp. 205–212.

Cohen, S. (1991), *Rock Culture in Liverpool: Popular Music in the Making*, Oxford: Oxford University Press.

—— (2007), *Beyond the Beatles: Decline, Renewal and the City in Popular Music Culture*, Aldershot: Ashgate.

Creative and Cultural Skills (2005), *Skills for Creativity: Strategic Plan 2005–2010*, London: Creative and Cultural Skills.

Dane, C. and Manton, K. (2002), *Counting the Notes*, London: National Music Council.

Dane, C., Feist, A. and Laing, D. (1996), *The Value of Music*, London: National Music Council.

Dane, C., Feist, A. and Manton, K. (1999), *A Sound Performance*, London: National Music Council.

D'Arcy, D. and Brindley, P. (2002), *Make or Break: Supporting UK Music in the USA*, London: British Council.

Department of Culture, Media and Sport (1998), *Creative Industries Mapping Document 1998*, London: DCMS.

Frith, S. (1993), 'Popular music and the local state', in Bennett, T. *et al.* (eds), *Rock and Popular Music: Politics, Policies and Institutions*, London: Routledge, pp. 14–24.
Gowers, A. (2006), *Review of Intellectual Property*, London: The Treasury.
Laing, D. (2000), *The Value of Music in Scotland: A Report for Scottish Enterprise*, Glasgow: Scottish Enterprise.
McDermott, L. (2004), 'Prize Guys', *Sunday Herald*, September 12.
Monopolies and Mergers Commission (1994), *The Supply of Recorded Music*, London: HMSO.
New Media Partners (2001), *Business Development Initiative – The Music Industry*, Kilmarnock: Scottish Enterprise.
Pratt, A. C. (1999), *Employment in the Creative Industries in Scotland: A Report to Scottish Enterprise*, London: LSE.
—— (2007), 'The music industry and its potential role in local and economic development: the case of Senegal', in Barrowclough, D. and Kozul-Wright, Z. (eds) *Creative Industries and Developing Countries: Voice, Choice and Economic Growth*, London: Routledge.
Robson, J. (2006), 'Finding the female fan: a feminist ethnography of popular music in Sheffield', PhD thesis, Sheffield Hallam University.
Rutten, P. (1993), 'Popular music policy: a contested area – the Dutch experience' in Bennett, T. *et al.* (eds) *Rock and Popular Music: Politics, Policies, Institutions*, London: Routledge, pp. 37–51.
Scottish Arts Council (2001), *Contemporary Popular Music*, Edinburgh: SAC.
—— (2002), Music Strategy 2002–2007, Edinburgh: SAC.
Scottish Executive (2000), *Creating our Future . . . Minding our Past: Scotland's National Cultural Strategy*, Edinburgh: Scottish Executive.
—— (2007), 'Support for Scottish Music Industry', Scottish Executive News Release, 27 February.
Shank, B. (1994), *Dissonant Identities: The Rock'n'Roll Scene in Austin, Texas*, Hanover, NH: University Press of New England.
Street, J. (1993), 'Local differences? Popular music and the local state', *Popular Music* 12(1), pp. 43–55.
Symon, P. and Cloonan, M. (2002), 'Playing away: popular music, policy and devolution in Scotland', *Scottish Affairs* 40, pp. 99–122.
Williamson, J. and Cloonan, M. (2007), 'Rethinking "the music industry"', *Popular Music* 26(2), pp. 305–322.
Williamson, J., Cloonan, M. and Frith, S. (2003), *Mapping the Music Industry in Scotland: A Report*, Glasgow: Scottish Enterprise.
Wishart, P. (2002), 'Hitting the right notes', *Holyrood Magazine*, February 4.

Part 4

Film and TV

4a Creativity in context

Content, cost, chance and collection in the organization of the film industry

Mark Lorenzen

This chapter combines theoretical literatures with empirical literature on the film industry, in order to analyze creativity at the industry level. The analytical framework presented in the chapter may not only be used to understand different national and regional "models" of filmmaking, but may also help to analyze creativity in other cultural industries.

The issue of creativity is not just at the heart of research on cultural industries (e.g. Caves, 2000; Hesmondhalgh, 2002), it is also becoming part of a broader agenda related to technological innovation, the rise of "the knowledge economy", and labor market dynamics (e.g. Florida, 2002). It is a common theme in these literatures that the issue at stake is not really the creativity of single individuals, because this is a raw material in quite some abundance. The core issue is how firms, industries, and the society at large organize for creativity, and the challenge is for managers and policymakers to opt for the most efficient organization in order to profit from the creativity of labor and citizens. In the case of cultural industries, the key problem is, therefore, how firms, labor markets, and industries are built around the raw material constituted by "creatives", i.e. individuals with cultural (as well as technical) skills. However, as noted by Richard Florida (2002), firms and industries do not just organize for creativity; a range of other concerns – for example, of control – is always balanced against creativity. Strategies and organizational forms reflect how this balance is made and unmade. Arguably, this is also true for cultural industries; contrary to popular belief, cultural industries are not only organized to maximize creativity, creativity is very often balanced with other factors. Hence, in order to understand the organization of cultural industries we must study creativity in context. By taking this into account, the study of cultural industries may well become inspirational to the study of creativity in other industries.

This chapter seeks to do just this. It picks a case of a cultural industry where creativity is indeed balanced with other concerns: the film industry. In the organization of this industry, creativity is traded off against contextual issues – even to the extent that creativity is often subsumed under other concerns. Through analyzing creativity and its context in the film industry, the chapter explains the industry's organization, and opens up for understanding its significant national and regional differences.

The chapter is hence conceptual, and it seeks to fill a gap in existing literature: there is currently very little focus upon the problem of creativity in the empirical film literature, nor in theoretical literatures, for example, the innovation studies literature. This chapter takes steps toward building a new analytical framework for analyzing creativity at the industry level through combining economic, socioeconomic and economic geography literature on the film industry, analyzing the importance of creativity, cost, chance and collection in the film industry, and exemplifying how these issues are balanced differently in different contexts. Hence, the chapter develops an analytical framework that may be used for understanding different "models" of filmmaking in future comparative work on the film industry, but also serves as inspiration for other work on cultural industries.

The chapter is structured as follows. Section 2 presents the film industry, and sketches out how different film clusters of the world perform very differently in economic terms. Section 3 introduces the problems of organization and of creativity in context, in order to understand these persistent performance differences of the film industry. Section 4 presents the first part of the analysis of what drives organization in the film industry: the balancing of creativity by concerns of cost. Section 5 discusses how creativity is also balanced by concerns of compensating for chance elements in the demand for films, and section 6 presents the last part of the analysis, discussing the balance of creativity by concerns of collection. A short section 7 summarizes the analytical framework and concludes the chapter.

Economic development and performance measures in the film industry

The film industry is, measured by its annual turnover of more than USD 25 billion in 2006 (MPAA, 2007), the largest of the sectors in the cultural economy, and, in terms of global penetration and shaping of identities, the most prolific (Hesmondhalgh, 2002; Scott, 2005). The film industry can be viewed as a paradigmatic case for a broader understanding of the development of cultural economy. On one hand, it shares its maturity and the nature of its product development processes – dominated by variety more than innovation (Caves, 2000; Lorenzen and Frederiksen, 2007) – with many other cultural industries, such as music, publishing, and arts. On the other hand, it is undergoing changes that may point to the future for other cultural industries, with increasing rates of product development, including stylistic and product innovations, as well as globalization, the performance growth of new clusters, and the growth of global corporations. Hence, the need for understanding the film industry is more acute than ever.

The film industry is ubiquitous, but very diverse. At the beginning of the 1900s, countries as different as France, Denmark, India, and the USA undertook film production and sales on a large scale, but with the growing importance of mass marketing during the latter half of the 1900s, US film production underwent significant organizational changes and became the most commercially successful. With a few notable exceptions in the UK (which is highly intertwined with US film production) and Asia, film production outside the USA is today small-scale. At this point, we should note that even if national policies – in the guise of, for example, tariffs, trade policy, tax, education, censorship and subsidies – greatly impact the film industry (Moran, 1996; Segrave, 1997; de Turégano, 2006; Flew, 2007), the film industry has a distinct geography in which sub-national *clustering* i.e. geographical agglomeration in localities such as cities (Storper and Christopherson, 1987; Maskell and Lorenzen, 2004; Scott, 2005) plays an important role. Vogel (1998), Wasko (2003) and Eliashberg *et al.* (2006) present more thorough accounts for the value chain activities in the film industry, but for our purpose they may be simplified thus:

- *Production*: preproduction (scripting, budgeting, casting, art design, etc), production (shooting), and postproduction (editing, effects, scoring and sound);
- *Marketing*;
- *Distribution*: sales and physical transport to cinemas and video, plus other sales channels;
- *Exhibition*: cinemas, video retail, TV, etc.

Exhibition is localized where consumers are, but firms undertaking production, marketing and distribution are to a wide extent clustered in major cities, and there are huge and consistent differences in output as well as in organization between these urban film clusters. Even if analysis of the national film industries of, for example, India, USA, Japan, France, UK, Italy and Denmark is interesting, more insights are yielded by analyzing clusters in Bollywood (Mumbai), Hyderabad, Chennai, Hollywood (Los Angeles), New York, Kyoto, Tokyo, Paris, London, Rome, Copenhagen, and so on.

A global mass medium, film continues to not only have a huge cultural impact, but also to be an industry with a notable potential for economic development. There are, as mentioned, notable differences between the performance and organization of the world's film clusters. How do we, then, measure a cluster's potential for economic development?

Revenues

Measuring the revenues of film firms is a direct way of measuring national or regional economic performance. With USA accounting for almost half of the world's box office (*Screen Digest*, 2007) and with the film production companies with the highest revenues (such as Universal, 20th Century Fox, Paramount, Columbia, MGM, Warner Bros., and Walt Disney) located in Hollywood, this cluster is the undisputed world top performer in terms of revenue collections. Kyoto/Tokyo (Japan) and London (UK) follow. Unfortunately, even if organizations such as the *Motion Pictures Producers' Association of America* and *European Audiovisual Observatory* seek to collect comparable statistics from national statistical offices and consultancy agencies (such as *Screen Digest* and *Nielsen EDI*), statistics are poor and difficult to compare across countries and regions (and the measurement of revenues is further complicated by the fact that media corporations and distributors register their turnover in other countries than where film revenues are produced).[1]

Employment

While the number of jobs in the film industry captures economic performance in terms of economic activity, it does not necessarily indicate it in terms of growth, as employment is not necessarily a sign of revenue collection. While Hollywood, Bollywood and other Asian film clusters are biggest in terms of size of their labor pool and number of jobs, a range of film clusters undertaking runaway production tasks (Wasko, 2003), typically outsourced from Hollywood, now experience booming employment. Examples are Vancouver (Canada), the Gold Cost (Australia) and Wellington (New Zealand), all undertaking the late stages in pre-production and shooting (Coe, 2001; Coe and Johns, 2004; Scott, 2005; Flew, 2007), and Manila (Philippines) and Bangalore (India) undertaking animation, special effects and postproduction. However, these clusters typically release few or no films themselves, and the outsourcing production companies, typically in Hollywood, London, or Bollywood, capture the rights to, and hence the revenues from, the finished products.

Releases

The total number of films released first and foremost reflects market size in terms of exhibition infrastructure (number of screens), cinema attendance, and purchase power. With huge home markets, clusters in India, USA, Japan, and China release most films annually (see table 4a. 1). The clusters with the biggest markets have typically bifurcated their film releases: in addition to the many films produced for niche audiences (e.g. art house or religious films, documentaries, or more mainstream films failing to reach mass audiences for reasons we shall discuss later), these clusters also release a lower number of films targeting mass audiences. Even if fewer in number, these films account for the bulk of revenues. The hugely successful mass-market segments of Hollywood and Bollywood films are best known, but we see bifurcation into niche vs. mass-market mainstream films in most clusters with a high number of releases.

However, a large number of film releases does not necessarily indicate that a cluster has developed a commercially successful mass-market segment, nor does it point to performance in terms of competitiveness or revenue collection. Due to state subsidies, clusters in some small European countries release an impressive number of films – in fact, Iceland, Denmark, Switzerland and Sweden release many more films per capita than non-subsidized and commercial clusters elsewhere.[2] Hong Kong is a rare example of a hitherto non-subsidized film cluster releasing many films per capita (in 2005, only Iceland released more per capita) (see table 4a.1).

Home market share

Releasing many films per capita does not necessarily entail capturing large home market shares (often measured as domestic films' share of gross box office revenues at the home market, and also called "self-sufficiency ratio"). Home market share measures economic performance in terms of different kinds of competitiveness.

Table 4a.1 Film releases

Number of films released 2005	*Number of films released per million capita 2005*
1 India (1,041)	1 Iceland (10.17)
2 USA (699)	2 Hong Kong (7.98)
3 Japan (356)	3 Denmark (7.58)
4 China (260)	4 Switzerland (6.48)
5 France (240)	5 Sweden (5.99)
6 Russia (160)	6 Slovenia (5.04)
7 Spain (142)	7 Luxembourg (4.39)
8 UK (124)	8 Norway (4.18)
9 Germany (103)	9 France (3.96)
10 Bangladesh (102)	10 Spain (3.28)
13 Korea (82)	14 Japan (2.79)
16 Hong Kong (55)	19 USA (2.36)
21 Denmark (41)	22 UK (2.06)
	24 Korea (1.70)
	38 India (0.93)
	64 China (0.20)

Source: *Screen Digest* (2006)

- First, competitiveness in terms of the experience value (see section 4) of the content of films can be important for winning the home market. State subsidies and high-value content of films have allowed French, Danish, and Italian clusters to successfully compete against imports, capturing notable shares of their home markets (see table 4a.2).
- Second, competitiveness in terms of a protected position through trade policies or language barriers may also lead to large home market shares, as is the case for film clusters in India and China and the Seoul (Korea) cluster.
- Third, a large home market share may also be a sign of competitiveness in terms of marketing and distribution capabilities. The unmatched home market share of Hollywood has been achieved through a combination of home market protection, high production values of Hollywood mass-market films, and Hollywood firms' unparalleled marketing and distribution capabilities.

Whether big home market shares result in notable economic development depends upon the purchase power of the home market. The wealth of the US home market compared to markets in India and China explains why the high home market shares and many releases of Indian and Chinese clusters do not translate into an economic growth comparable to Hollywood's.

Exports

Arguably, a film cluster's exports have a notable economic development potential, as exports capture revenue and prolong windows of earning beyond the home market (for a discussion of the differences between export, internationalization, and globalization in the film industry, see Lorenzen, 2007). Of course, the economic

Table 4a.2 Home market shares

Share of home market 2005
1 India (94.1%)
2 USA (93.4%)
3 China (60%)
4 Korea (57%)
5 Turkey (41.4%)
6 Japan (41.3%)
7 France (37.7%)
8 Thailand (35%)
9 UK (34%)
10 Hong Kong (31.4%)
11 Denmark (30.1%)

Source: *Screen Digest* (2006)

potential of exports depends upon the ratio of the purchase power of home vs. export markets: a cluster with a poor home market may increase its revenues notably by a modest increase in exports to rich markets, whereas a cluster with a rich home market exporting to poorer markets needs a sizeable increase of exports (and possible an increase in the number of export markets) in order to increase revenues significantly (Hoskins and Mirus, 1988; Hoskins *et al.*, 1997; Vogel, 1998). For example, Bollywood's recent export growth may be modest, but aiming at a few rich Western markets, it causes a revenue boom. By contrast, Hollywood's export revenues were built up over many years and entailed a lot of investments in many markets, because purchase power outside the USA is relatively low.

Exports indicate competitiveness of a film cluster in several dimensions.

- First, export may indicate a competitive content of films. This is reflected in the list of major exporters to the combined EU–US markets in 1999 where Belgium, Brazil and Denmark are featured prominently (see table 4a.3). However, exports based on film content alone may fluctuate a lot from year to year. For clusters with a low number of releases, export rates are highly influenced by single, successful films (as was exactly the case in 1999 for Belgium, Brazil and Denmark, in table 4a.3).
- Second, exports may also reflect a cluster's cultural competitiveness, or the preferences of consumers for particular film narratives, aesthetics, or, more simply, language (Hoskins and Mirus, 1988; Papandrea, 1998; Oh, 2001). A look at the EU market in 2004 indicates that while USA still has the undisputed highest market share (71.4 per cent), France (9.5 per cent), UK (6.1 per cent), Germany (4.5 per cent), Italy (2.2 per cent) and Spain (2.1 per cent) capture audiences with preferences other than English language and Hollywood-type narratives (Newman-Baudais, 2005). However, 1999 figures (table 4a.3) show that outside the home market, UK is a stronger European exporter than France: cleansed for home market sales, big-budget, English-language films produced in USA and UK capture the greatest shares of the combined EU–US market.

Table 4a.3 Exports

Admissions (cleansed for home market admissions) on the combined US–EU markets 1999
1 USA (536,7 million)
2 UK (103,5 million)
3 France (27,8 million)
4 Italy (24 million)
5 Japan (18 million)
6 Canada (7,5 million)
7 Spain (6,5 million)
8 Hong Kong (4,8 million)
9 Germany (4,3 million)
10 Denmark (3,1 million)
11 Brazil (2,4 million)
12 Belgium (1,7 million)
13 Russia (1,4 million)
14 India (1,3 million)

Source: European Audiovisual Observatory (2006)

Note: Apart from USA, UK, France and India, size of exports was determined mainly by the success of one film.

- Third, exports of course also reflect a cluster's competitiveness in terms of capabilities. As any cluster typically exports only a fraction of its releases, a strong global distribution network is essential to match indigenous films on various markets, and good marketing is important to overpower them.

However, a high export rate (typically measured as the percentage of revenues stemming from export markets) does not unequivocally indicate that a cluster has developed content-based, cultural preference-based, or capability-based export capabilities. This is because many film clusters enjoy state subsidies, not just for production, but also for export activities. In the EU, there is governmental export support at EU level, for both smaller and larger film clusters (de Turégano, 2006), and in Asia, Hong Kong is also beginning to attract government export support. Even if the world's most exporting film cluster, Hollywood, produces without government subsidies, its export success has been positively influenced by government policies. Because exports would boost domestic scale economies, the US State Department, the Department of Commerce, and various US embassies have traded strategically in film and paved the way for US film exports to Europe through the Marshall aid and EU disputes, and to Asia through GATT (the General Agreement on Tariffs and Trade) (Segrave, 1997; Ulff-Møller, 2001; Scott, 2005).

Organization and performance

Performance differences

Not surprisingly, Hollywood stands out as the top performing film cluster in most of the dimensions mentioned above. Even if several Asian clusters employ more people and the clusters in India release more films, Hollywood has many releases on not just a wealthy home market where it completely dominates, but also on all global markets, including those with highest purchase power, Japan and the EU (Segrave, 1997). This translates into revenue. As mentioned, clusters in Kyoto/Tokyo (Japan) and London (UK) are next best performing with respect to revenues, but because of the distribution of two other performance measures, the position of these clusters may be eroding now. First, the rapidly growing purchase power on the home markets for Indian and Chinese clusters is in the process of raising the revenues of these clusters. Second, the rapidly increasing export rates of a range of European as well as Asian clusters is stealing market shares from London as well as Hollywood. Given the modest number of releases of Hong Kong and Seoul (Hong Kong had 55 and Korea 82 in 2005 [*Screen Digest*, 2006]), the recent export boom of these clusters hardly threatens London or Hollywood. However, the slow but steady export rise of the hugely productive Bollywood cluster, moving beyond its traditional Asian and African export markets and successfully targeting EU and North America, may turn this cluster into a future major player with respect to economic development (Lorenzen and Täube, 2007).

What is the cause for the performance differences of film clusters? As hinted earlier, four factors *external* to the clusters play a role:

- First, in some cases, FDI influences employment;
- Second, cinema attendance and purchase power on home markets precondition the number of film releases;
- Third, cultural consumer preferences on foreign markets influence exports;
- And fourth, public policy plays a role for the home market share and exports of many, if not all, film clusters.

However, external factors alone cannot explain performance differences. Concerning the first external factor, FDI, what determines if a cluster receives or makes it? Why is Manila a recipient of FDI and Bollywood an investor, when both clusters have sizeable labor pools and low labor costs? Second, concerning home market size, what determines whether a cluster takes advantage of it? Why have Indian film clusters invested more in exhibition infrastructure (cinemas) than Chinese when India has fewer inhabitants with lower purchase power; and why does Bollywood release more films than Hollywood when USA's cinema attendance and purchase power is much higher than India's? Third, what determines consumer preferences for imported films? Why do consumers in Korea prefer Hollywood films to films from Asia or France, with whom Korea has much more trade and interaction, and, by the same logic, why do consumers in Finland prefer Hollywood films to Swedish or Russian? And finally, why do some countries, like Denmark and Korea, seem to benefit so much more from public subsidies and promotion than others?

Integration and market organization

We shall argue that internal *organization* of film clusters explains many of their performance differences. Even if there may be external preconditions for employment, the number of releases, home market shares, and exports, it is the internal organization of the film clusters that determines if they benefit from advantageous external conditions, or even invest in slowly changing them. Furthermore, organization greatly influences the major determinants of home market share and exports: the content (experience value) of films, and the marketing and distribution capabilities used for selling films.

"Organization" is a wide notion: it encompasses both how the "visible Chandlerian hand" (i.e. corporations), and the "invisible Smithian hand" (i.e. market institutions) coordinate economic activities.

- Concerning the former, the issue of *integration* – whether firms choose to internalize particular tasks and transactions through ownership and long-term employment contracts – is classic in the economics of organization (Coase, 1937; Williamson, 1975; 2000). According to Wildman and Siwek (1988) and Wildman (1995), it was the *horizontal integration* and scale economies in Hollywood's production activities that made this cluster win large home market shares and export so much. Hoskins *et al.* (1997), on the other hand, suggest that it was Hollywood's *vertical integration* of production, distribution, and exhibition, which was the key driver of US dominance on world film markets. This dominance may become self-reinforcing through cultural advantages. Gradually, if a powerful horizontally and vertically integrated film industry sinks sufficient investments into marketing and distribution over a sufficiently long time, it may change consumer preferences on foreign markets (Hoskins and Mirus, 1988; Vogel, 1998; Elberse and Eliashberg, 2003). The preferences on many national markets for English language films over other foreign language films (Oh, 2001), and for Hollywood-type narratives and aesthetics, have been created by Hollywood itself. The greater cultural differences there are among the world's other exporting film clusters, the greater the cultural advantages of Hollywood (Papandrea, 1998).
- Concerning the latter kind of organization, economic coordination is not just a question of where the boundaries of firms (hierarchies) go; it is also about how, in the absence of integration, firms "organize the market" instead (Richardson, 1972; Langlois, 1986; Maskell and Lorenzen, 2004). *Market organization* encompasses the institutions other than ownership that may coordinate and manage tasks and transactions among firms, such as projects, alliances, and social networks.

Even if home market size, policy, and so on, also play important roles for performance differences between clusters, the clusters' differences in terms of the extent and nature of horizontal integration (scale), vertical integration (joint ownership of several activities in the value chain), as well as the extent and nature of transactions among firms and people in projects, alliances, and networks (for example, recurrence, collusion, and whether they are strategic or short-term), take center stage.

Creativity and its context in organization

So, what drives organization? Why are different clusters organized differently? In the sections that follow, we analyze the factors behind organization in the film industry. Recently, scholars have dedicated growing attention to the role of *creativity* in cultural industries – the current volume being an example of this research strand (see also Caves, 2000; Hesmondhalgh, 2002). Creativity is also controversial among cultural industry observers, some arguing for the growing importance of the role of creativity ("content is king"), some arguing in the opposite vein that in the organization of mass-consumer cultural industries, creativity has long been subsumed under other concerns.

The following analysis of the film industry suggests a middle way. It argues that creativity plays a necessary role for the organization of the film industry, but that there are different ways of trading creativity off against its context. We shall focus upon the logics of *cost*, *chance* and *collection* and sketch out how the film industry organizes for, around, and some times against, creativity. Strategies – current and historical – of how to balance creativity, cost, chance, and collection shape the different organization, and ultimately performance, of the world's film clusters.

Creativity vs. cost

Creativity: Project organization of production

Cultural consumer industries (such as film, music, games, publishing and arts) produce *experience goods* (Nelson, 1970), in the sense that even if products are often developed with much involvement, dedication and integrity of creative labor or even artists, their market value ultimately hinges upon how their content is experienced by consumers (Pine and Gilmore, 1999; Cowen, 2000). The film industry is no exception, as the market value in cinemas, TV, and video of its core product, the feature film[3], depends on how the audience judges the narrative and aesthetic content of the film. This judgment, and hence the market value, of a film is related to the degree by which the aesthetics and narrative of its content *differentiate* themselves (Burke, 1996) to incumbent films on the market. To have experience value, a film need not differentiate its content in terms of both narrative and aesthetics; a differentiated aesthetics, obtained through a particularly high production value or a stylistic innovation, applied to a well-known narrative, has often proved valuable in itself.

The film industry produces differentiated content by differentiating creative inputs. A film is an immensely complex product, integrating numerous art forms (such as writing, design, and performing arts), and the scope for combining the inputs in order to achieve new content *varieties* are, in Caves' (2000) words, "infinite" (see also Eliashberg, 2006). Most content development of films is in reality the production of variety through recombining inputs (and proper innovations in the guise of new styles or whole new ways of marketing or distribution are rare [Lorenzen, 2007]). In order to thus recombine inputs, films productions are organized as *projects* – temporary and flexible groupings of skills and other inputs with given budgets and deadlines (Lundin and Söderholm, 1995; Hobday, 2000; Lorenzen and Frederiksen, 2005) and the end goal of producing a feature film.

The necessary skills for a film project are often so specialized and structured into narrow creative, technical, and managerial realms that they are held by individual experts: creatives (e.g. writers, designers, choreographers, actors, directors), technicians (e.g. editors, cinematographers, lighting technicians) and managers (e.g. producers, line producers, controllers, accountants, financiers, and marketers), working concurrently and successively on a film (Wasko, 2003; Eliashberg *et al.*, 2006). A film project is typically set up and controlled by a production company where the producers, marketers, and sometimes the financiers, are long-term employed.

Creativity: Horizontal disintegration of production

In the pre-World War II period, cost concerns typically overrode creativity in the organization of film projects. As a result, not just managers, but also creatives and technicians, were employed long-term in large "studios" – a somewhat misleading term, as these production firms integrated all aspects of production, not just studio facilities. Prior to World War II, there were integrated film producers in many different clusters, including Copenhagen (the integrated film company Nordisk Film), Paris (the companies Gaumont and Pathé), Bollywood (Prabhat, Wadia, Bombay Talkies and other companies), and of course Hollywood (the "seven sisters" Columbia, Walt Disney, 20th Century Fox, MGM, Paramount, Universal and Warner Bros.). The advantages of this horizontal integration of production was mostly in terms of planning of resource use with parallel film projects, and Hollywood, with the biggest home market and number of release of all clusters, was able to make the most out of such scale economies (Wildman, 1995). Scale of production also encompassed re-use of concepts and brands in successive projects: the integrated film companies had huge success with producing low-budget films and serials (for example, Bollywood's *Fearless Nadia* and Hollywood's *Kings of Comedy* series [Chisholm, 2003]).

TV, which was introduced on a large scale in the US in the 1950s, in Europe in the 1960s, and in most parts of Asia in the 1980s, quickly took over the market for low-budget films and serials (Chisholm, 1993; De Vany and Eckert, 1991; De Vany and Walls, 1999). In addition, the increasing purchase power and heterogeneity of markets in the US and Europe since World War II changed the demand for films: film audiences now wanted high production value and high product variety. This demand for variety, and hence for more varied inputs to projects, undermined the internal economies of planning and carrying them out in-house (Lorenzen and Frederiksen, 2005). The profits of the integrated production companies in Europe and Bollywood had already been eroded by World War II,

Bollywood's incumbent production companies faced a huge entry of competitors after Indian independence, and the business model of Hollywood's integrated production companies – combining horizontal integration of production with vertical integration of distribution and exhibition (see the next section) – was punctuated by an anti-trust High Court ruling in 1948. As a result of these combined pressures, after World War II, production disintegrated in many of the world's film clusters, into a flexibly specialized production model of small-scale independent production firms and numerous specialized suppliers (Robins, 1993; Storper, 1989), and a labor market of freelancing creatives and technicians (Faulkner and Anderson, 1987; Storper and Christopherson, 1987; Blair, 2001). This model allowed for much higher variety of film aesthetics and narratives, and in Hollywood, the growing skill levels of specialized suppliers also raised production values.

The horizontal disintegration of production was also spurred by the integrated production companies' problems of motivating labor in long-term employment. New small production companies and a thickening labor market offered both creatives and technicians attractive freelance alternatives to long-term contracts: freelance work, or the option to start up own companies. The tendency to go freelance was most prominent for star actors, and from the 1950s, they broke out of their long-term contracts with production firms in many clusters, including Hollywood and Bollywood. The disintegration of production hence was the beginning of an era where star actors became independent, as well as (as shall be discussed in the next section) powerful.

According to classic economic logic (Smith, 1776), the horizontally disintegrated system of production should make those world's film clusters with the largest labor pools, such as Hollywood, Paris, London and the clusters in India, particularly competitive with respect to creativity. The size of their internal market for projects and labor should, in principle, allow for high specialization of firms and labor, and hence deepening of firm competences and labor skills. Even if it may be subject to controversy whether all clusters take due advantage of the potential for creativity offered by the size of their labor pool, it is true that the film clusters that perform well in terms of number of releases have sufficient reputation to create significant backwash effects for talent. Hollywood, Bollywood, Paris and London remain magnets for film talent from a regional or even global hinterland, constantly adding to these clusters' stock of specialized firms and the density of their labor markets. However, with targeted (often public) investments in education, some clusters that are smaller in terms of both employment and number of releases are able to boost skill levels beyond what their size would allow for in a pure market logic. For example, public education in the Copenhagen and Rome clusters has made skills in scriptwriting and direction at least at par with the huge market-driven cluster of Bollywood, where investments in public film education are very modest.

Cost: Horizontal ecologies and small world networks of production

A disintegrated organization of production is beneficial to creativity in the film industry, but also raises the question of how production companies may manage film projects that cross the companies' boundaries, using more freelancers than long-term employees. In the design of projects "on the market", there seems to be a trade-off between maximizing creativity and minimizing transaction costs (Lorenzen and Frederiksen, 2005). The optimal design in terms of variety and differentiation vis à vis earlier projects would be to use as many *new* creative (and possibly also technical) skill holders as possible. However, the creative benefits of using new skill holders must be balanced against the costs of using strangers who may shirk or cheat (Williamson, 1975; 2000). To minimize such transaction costs, it is more efficient if the producer signs creatives and technicians with whom he has a relation because they have worked with him before.

Social networks allow for working with new people with low transaction costs, and hence facilitate the balance between creativity and cost. Using social networks, producers typically choose to sign people who are easily identified and contacted, and the past performance of whom is easily checked, not necessarily because the producers have worked directly with these people before, but because it is very likely that they have worked with people who have. This network-based way of hiring, checking and controlling new people is possible because of the geographical clustering of film production and labor markets. Film clusters are project *ecologies* (Grabher, 2002) of skill holders who are constantly combined and recombined in new film projects. Because of this constant recombination of people, ecologies get socially structured into dense and ever-growing social networks constituted by friendships and acquaintanceships made in earlier film projects. In such networks, reputation effects and sharing of information may allow participants to a new project to achieve swift trust (Meyerson *et al.*, 1996), even if none of them have worked together before. There is evidence for how film projects are thus based on social networks in Hollywood (Baker and Faulkner, 1991; Sorenson and Waguespack, 2006), Rome (Soda *et al.*, 2004; Delmistri *et al.*, 2005), and Bollywood (Lorenzen and Täube, 2007).

We argued earlier that film clusters with big labor pools have particular creative potentials, by virtue of the size of their internal markets for labor and projects. We can now see that whether a film cluster realizes its potential for taking advantage of its variety of local competencies and skills, depends upon the social structure of its project ecology. If the social networks of the cluster are colluded, there is much re-use of skill holders, and less variety of film aesthetics and narratives. If the social networks, on the other hand, provide access to many new skill holders in each new film project, creativity may blossom. The bifurcation of clusters with many film releases into a segment of niche films and a segment of mainstream films also typically means social bifurcation – the rise of one network of skill holders who mainly participate in the productions of niche films, and another network of skill holders who mainly participate in mainstream film productions.[4] If these two social networks are cut off from each other, bifurcation entails a division of a cluster's project ecology into smaller and less varied markets for labor and projects. If, on the other hand, the social networks centered around niche and mainstream film segments respectively, are coupled to each other by a few central people who work in both film segments, such as eclectic actors or directors, the cluster's ecology is socially structured so that it allows for higher creativity. The coupling of different internally densely knit social networks to each other through a few crucial social relations is called a *small world network* (Milgram, 1967; Watts *et al.*, 2002). In a film cluster, such a social structure allows for minimizing transaction costs in the majority of project relations (which are carried out internally in dense networks where people know about each other and can easily build trust), while boosting creativity in a few crucial project relations that cross over to other networks and access the information and skills found here (Granovetter, 2005; Uzzi and Spiro, 2005). While Bollywood has historically been more of a collusion than Hollywood, as its mainstream network was relatively closed to the niche networks, Hollywood is now moving towards more collusion while Bollywood's mainstream network is opening up. Thus, Bollywood may be moving towards greater creativity and Hollywood towards less (Lorenzen and Täube, 2007).

Cost: Outsourcing

While transaction costs may be kept at bay through social networks, even with horizontal disintegration, production costs of most film projects have exploded over the last decades, due to the demand for ever more production value and the salaries of star actors, in combination with the lack of scale economies of planning after the horizontal disintegration of production. Several of the clusters with big-budget productions, including Hollywood, London, and Bollywood, are now outsourcing labor-intensive production tasks to clusters with lower labor costs, such as Vancouver, Australia's Gold Cost, and Wellington. This "runaway" mode of organization (Wasko, 2003) mostly concerns the technical aspects of production, leaving creative tasks in the home cluster. While this growing aspect of the organization of the film industry thus influences creativity of the outsourcing clusters only little, it, as mentioned in section 2, also bears only modest development potential for those clusters receiving runaway production tasks (Coe, 2001; Chaminade and Vang, 2007).

Creativity vs. chance

Chance: Horizontal network collusion and integration of production

Like other cultural products, films have a highly uncertain demand. In film clusters as different as German (Jansen, 2005), Indian (Kohli-Khandekar, 2006; Lorenzen and Täube, 2007), and US (Vogel, 1998; De Vany and Walls, 1997; De Vany, 2004; Eliashberg *et al.*, 2006), less than 20 per cent of films break even, and much fewer make notable revenues. The demand for art house or other niche films is limited, but it varies on a relatively predictable scale (Cameron, 2003). It is mass-markets that are really uncertain. Growth, globalization, and increased consumer spending on experience goods since World War II have created global mass-markets for feature films with potential huge revenues, and this has facilitated the rise of mass-market film segments in the clusters with most releases. However, mass-markets are also characterized by unforeseeable – and rapidly changing – consumer tastes and infinite variance of revenue distribution (De Vany and Walls, 1997; Sawhney and Eliashberg, 1996; Walls, 2005). Hence, on mass-markets for films, "nobody knows anything" about demand (a phrase coined by the scriptwriter Goldman (1983) and empirically addressed by a range of scholars, for example in a 2005 special issue of *Journal of Cultural Economics*).

Economists of an evolutionary stance (e.g. Nelson and Winter, 1982; Rosenberg, 1992) often associate demand uncertainty to the firm-level process of *experimentation*: developing new products without whether they will sell or not, and subsequently testing them on consumers over limited (if often flexible) test periods (Raubitschek, 1988; Kerke and Srinivasan, 1990). Such experimentation with producing mass-market films can be costly. With life cycles of mass-market films shortening (the dramatic shortening of a film's life span in movie theatres has not yet been compensated for by the prolongation of windows of earning on TV and video), there is significant pressure on production companies within the mass-market segments to develop new films at a rapid pace, which further increases the potential costs of experimentation. Consequently, the incentives for production companies in the mass-market segment for *compensating* for the aspect of chance are great. This impacts upon the organization of not just the mass-market segment, but also the entire film industry.

One means of compensating for chance is the use of *stars* – that is, creatives with proven consumer appeal and high brand value – in the production and marketing of mass-market feature films. Worldwide, the most prominent stars are actors, but to some extent, directors (and, in Bollywood, composers) are also gaining star status. Contrary to common belief among film producers and marketers, there is little evidence that star actors systematically increase the likelihood of box office performance (De Vany and Walls, 1996; 1999; De Vany, 2004). However, their brand value for attracting investments remains huge in Hollywood as well as Bollywood (De Vany and Walls, 1996; 1999; Elberse, 2007; Lorenzen and Täube, 2007), and their salaries have increased to constitute half of some mass-market films' budgets. A disproportional number of film projects centers around the most branded star actors and directors (some stars are even in a position to fund and produce their own film projects). However, this centering does not necessarily inhibit creativity. Quite the opposite, the use of stars may reinforce the small world properties of a cluster's social network. For example, in both Hollywood and Bollywood, some star actors or directors who are highly paid in the mass-market segment occasionally work for much less in more artistically satisfying projects in the niche segment, thus coupling the skill holders in the two segments who are otherwise segregated, into a small world network.[5]

Another means to compensate for the element of chance in demand for mainstream films is producing *sequels*. Whereas stars are used in both mass-market and niche films, the production of sequels is a strategy used almost exclusively in mass-market films. As mentioned, the use of stars alone does not efficiently compensate for chance. However, the re-use of a star cast in combination with the brand value of a previous box office hit has proved a much more successful formula

(Elberse and Eliashberg, 2003). Today's serials do not resemble the low budget productions of Hollywood and Bollywood 50 years ago: *Pirates of the Caribbean 2*, *Dhoom: 2* or, *Umizaru 2* are top of the range productions, with the most expensive stars, lavish production value, and often technical virtuosity. Their box office success notwithstanding, as sequels prioritize brand value over novelty, they also prioritize compensating for chance over creativity. They encompass not only the re-use of star cast but also writers, directors, producers, and sometimes also designers and some technical staff, thus lowering the variety of narratives and aesthetics.

Chance: Horizontal integration of marketing – and vertical integration of production into marketing

The box office collections of niche films depend mainly upon the films' content, and this content often encompasses widely varied narratives and novel aesthetics. Due to the limited budgets for advertising, niche films typically need to signal the experience value of their content at film festivals, through critical reviews (Caves, 2000; De Vany, 2004), and at award shows (awards being important for niche films on both big and small markets [De Vany, 2004; Jansen, 2005]). The ultimate aim for a niche film is to create sufficient word-of-mouth publicity and reputation to convince theater owners and other exhibitors to take the film in. This slow and cheap mode of marketing of niche films corresponds to their long windows of earning and low collections.

The collections of mass-market films, on the other hand, depend primarily on good targeting of particular audience segments (age, class, race, sometimes also religion), and good timing of release (as these films often target moviegoers at particular holidays and coordinate their timing to competitors' releases). The experience value of mass-market films often encompasses high production value and/or formulaic narratives. Huge marketing campaigns signal this experience value of new releases to target audiences, aiming at creating hoarding effects (Caves, 2000; De Vany, 2004). Large-scale marketing also serves to achieve nominations for major commercial awards (but not necessarily winning them [Deuchert *et al.*, 2005]), and ultimately convincing theater owners of the market potential of new releases, paving the way for exhibition at just the right time. In sum, large-scale marketing is an efficient means of compensating for chance (Prag and Casavant, 1994; Eliashberg *et al.*, 2006), and its value grows with market size (Lee and Waterman, 2006).

There are notable scale economies in marketing, as the marginal costs of e.g. promotion campaigns decrease rapidly (Caves, 2000; Chisholm, 2003). The larger the market, the larger the importance of endogenous sunk costs represented by marketing (Sutton, 1991; Bakker, 2005) and the more prominent the scale advantages: for example, Elberse and Eliashberg (2003) argue that Hollywood's large-scale marketing on the huge US home market forms a necessary platform for the global marketing of Hollywood films.

Due to these scale economies and importance of sunk costs, the film industry often sees notable horizontal integration in marketing – the dominance of a few, powerful, marketing firms. With respect to scale economies and horizontal integration, film marketing is very different from film production, which, as discussed earlier, is organized in disintegrated projects due to concerns of creativity. Hence, in many film clusters, production firms and marketing firms stay separate, the former employing the latter. However, in a few clusters with a big commercial segment, such as Hollywood and London, producers of mass-market films have integrated mass marketing. The Hollywood pre-World War II major production companies did not just integrate production horizontally; they also integrated marketing, distribution, and exhibition vertically, boasting large-scale marketing departments, distribution networks, and theater ownership. As mentioned, demand developments and creative concerns after the 1950s led to the horizontal disintegration of production, and the 1948 US High Court ruling forced vertical disintegration of exhibition, but the major Hollywood film companies remained powerful in marketing and distribution (for a discussion of the latter, see next section). They developed core competencies in finance, marketing, and distribution – outsourcing production to specialized subsidiaries or even to "independent" production companies, occasionally buying and marketing niche films with potential mass appeal. Such vertical integration of production with marketing is a costly, but also efficient response of a few powerful firms to the high demand uncertainty on mass-markets, and as pointed out by Hoskins *et al.* (1997), this organization of Hollywood's mass-market segment is a key explanation for the export success of this film cluster.

Ever since World War II, the growing marketing power and the gradual development into media conglomerates of these major Hollywood film companies has shaped the development of not just Hollywood, but the entire film industry. For the mass-market segment, it represents a further compromise regarding creativity for the sake of compensating for chance: producers of mass-market films in, for example, Hollywood or the UK, who are also, and first and foremost, marketing firms, focus increasingly upon marketing and are gradually less prone to experiment with variety. In the niche market segments, creativity is not compromised by this organization of the mass-market segment, but, as will be outlined below, the competition for exhibition – and ultimately survival – in *all* of the film industry is significantly stiffened by the organization in the few large clusters' mass-market segments.

Chance: Horizontal integration of distribution – and vertical integration of production and marketing into distribution

Distribution of niche films and mass-market films function quite differently. Because the main selling point of niche films is their content, they are often long in production and postproduction, and can take long after completion to find distributors targeting the right niche markets. The success of mass-market films, on the other hand, is hugely dependent upon scale of exhibition and timing of release (which sometimes leads mass-market films to be rushed through postproduction): opening in many screens simultaneously – "block booking" – is a way of propagating hoarding effects while crowding out competing films (Donahue, 1987; Caves,

2000). This means that efficient, large-scale distribution is immensely important to take advantage of mass marketing.

As in marketing, there are also large scale advantages of distribution, given the decreasing marginal costs of, for example, physically transporting prints, and keeping in contact with theater owners (Caves, 2000; Chisholm, 2003). Scale – spreading risk over a large number of films – is also a means by which distributors can compensate for chance (Cameron, 2003). Scale economies have driven integrated organization of distribution in smaller clusters, such as Denmark or Korea. Here, a few large distribution firms distribute for all production companies. The sunk costs represented by distribution are, like marketing, also endogenous, so in principle, larger markets should render horizontal integration efficient (Sutton, 1991; Bakker, 2005). However, this is not the case for all clusters with big home markets; whereas a few powerful distributors of mass-market films dominate Hollywood, Bollywood is still disintegrated, with hundreds of small-scale independent distributors.

One explanation for the horizontally integrated organization of distribution in Hollywood is that the media conglomerates which integrate both production and marketing have also vertically integrated into distribution, driven firm sizes up here, and raised entry barriers against newcomer distributors (Caves, 2000). The reason for this vertical integration of production and marketing into distribution is simple – it is the ultimate way of compensating for chance. Controlling distribution, integrated production and marketing companies can ensure preferential treatment of their own films in the best (first-run) theaters (Vogel, 1998) and systematically use block booking as a competitive strategy (Hanssen, 2000). The Hollywood media conglomerates have used these effects to a wide extent during the last two decades of the last century. As these conglomerates now also re-invest in exhibition (buying theaters, TV channels, and Internet services), hence compensating even more for chance while appropriating residual earnings from successful films (Chisholm, 2003), scholars such as Schatz (1997) refer to "the return of the Hollywood studio system" of the pre-World War II period. Through their unique control over marketing and distribution, these new conglomerates are able to completely finance their own film productions, as well as ensuring them large-scale exhibition.

To the extent that media conglomerates also facilitate the distribution of niche films, horizontal integration of distribution and vertical integration of production and marketing into distribution do not necessarily negatively influence creativity. However, if niche films are denied distribution for strategic reasons, this organization of a film cluster adversely influences the diffusion of niche films produced with a comparatively high emphasis on variety of inputs, narratives and aesthetics – and ultimately threatens the survival of firms in the niche film segment. As we shall see in the next section, in some film clusters, collaborations between niche producers and media conglomerates are becoming rarer still.

Chance: Horizontal integration of production

With a scale sufficient to finance, market, and distribute own film productions (as well as the occasional "independent" film), the major Hollywood media conglomerates of the late twentieth century pursued a strategy of releasing different types of films simultaneously, compensating for chance by spreading risk across different films. While the high horizontal as well as vertical integration in the mass-market segment of Hollywood put some competitive pressure on niche producers, there was, as mentioned, some collaboration between the segments, allowing for finance, marketing and wider distribution of the occasional niche film, and the maintenance of a small world social network coupling creatives across segments.

However, there are recent signs that the mass-market segment in Hollywood and other big commercial clusters, such as London, is moving towards an organization that further prioritizes compensating for chance over creativity. As mentioned earlier, mass-market segments in many clusters currently produce a rising number of sequels, in an attempt to compensate for chance. Many sequels are also examples of a third recent strategy for mainstream films, *flagpole productions.* Earlier, managers and economists (e.g. De Vany, 2004) agreed that budget size did not necessarily increase chances of box office success, but some of today's films with more than double the average production and marketing budget have proven able to sweep the tables because they create brand value for use in subsequent TV shows, video games, music, books, and so forth.[6] Given the size of their production budgets, as well as their necessary scale of marketing, distribution, and collection (see further), flagpole productions are only undertaken by the biggest film production companies that are a part of large media conglomerates. Over the last five years, the strategy of flagpole productions has added to the horizontal integration of production in Hollywood and the UK, because the big production companies tend to finance fewer, but larger productions. As flagpole productions are designed to minimize experimentation, and as they imply the integration of production, they clearly represent a strategy that prioritizes compensating for chance over creativity. As documented by Scott (2005), in Hollywood, this results in collusion and still less coupling between the parts of the bifurcated cluster, with fewer films – and more of them own productions – financed, marketed and distributed by major conglomerates. This leaves niche producers with still more difficulties in achieving finance, marketing, and distribution. However, Bollywood looks a bit different: even if flagpole productions are now also seen here, the cluster's disintegrated industry structure means that this strategy does not lead to noteworthy changes in how creativity is balanced with compensation for chance in the cluster as a whole.

Creativity vs. collection

Collection: Cross-industry integration

The basic value of feature films lie in the *property rights* to them, and the *collection* of the payment for using such rights has always been a part activity in film distribution. However, such rights, and collection on the basis of them, are becoming an increasingly complex and much growing business in itself (for discussions, see Caves, 2000; and Andersen et al, 2007). Whereas for the first century of the film industry, copyrights – the use of rights to copies of the feature film – were central to earnings, a range of auxiliary revenue streams is now arising from further rights. The rights to parts of the feature film product are now also sold and re-sold. A classic example is soundtracks, but to an increasing extent, other parts of successful mass-market films, such as the scripts (and re-make rights), characters, and art design, are also sold separately. This has created specialized firms in the guise of publishing houses, which typically administer, sell, and collect fees based on rights.

There are notable scale economies (diminishing marginal costs) in trading with and collecting fees from rights, and quite similarly to marketing and distribution activities, these scale advantages grow with market size. There are also synergies of selling use rights in bundles, and of targeting multiple outlets with bundles of rights. For instance, the rights to the storyline and character of *Spiderman* can be sold to TV production companies wanting to produce a show based on the feature film, toy and (computer) game producers, book publishers, and so on. Consequently, publishing houses are often big, they often administer rights not just in films, but also in music, plays, books, and more, and they have often grown to spanning globally.

Not surprisingly, the integrated media corporations in Hollywood and other large film clusters are also integrating into publishing. As the media conglomerates focus more and more on how they can collect from existing successful films (such as sequels and flagpole productions), they also focus upon the efficient administration of property rights to these films, creating and capturing as many auxiliary revenue streams as possible. Investing in the media industries where synergies of rights are most profound, US, UK, German, French and Japanese media conglomerates are now turning into *multi*-media conglomerates, integrating the production, marketing, distribution (and to some extent also exhibition) of films, TV, music, computer games, book publishing, and more (Litman, 1998). The "return of the studios" (Schatz, 1997) is in reality the rise of a new breed of global multi-media conglomerates, organized around rights and collection.

This increasing focus upon collection in the mass-market segments of Hollywood and other of the big commercial clusters complements their increased focus upon sequels, flagpole productions, and brand value. As mentioned above, this also represents a shift in the balance away from creativity, since the result is fewer mass-market films with less variety, as well as higher entry barriers for niche films to marketing and distribution.

Summary and conclusion

The sections above were based on a novel combination of literatures, many of which are rarely applied to the study of the film industry. This analytical framework allowed the chapter to sketch out the main drivers of organization in the film industry. The basic argument is that different clusters' different economic performance in the film industry is related to how these clusters organize as a means of balancing concerns for creativity, cost, chance, and collection. As far space has allowed, the sections have also exemplified how different clusters balance these concerns:

- The concern for *creativity* – consumer demand for differentiation of content (aesthetics and narrative) – drives *project organization.* Arguably, this type of organization is ubiquitous in all film clusters.
- The concern for *creativity* – variety of inputs – drives *disintegration of production activities and use of shifting and varied freelancers and firms.* Whereas all clusters have functionally disintegrated production activities, the major production companies in some of the biggest clusters maintain a relatively higher level of control over production than many other clusters, owning or writing multi-film contracts with suppliers.
- The concern for lowering transaction *costs* drives the emergence of *social networks* among producers, directors, and creatives in film project ecologies. But whereas the various filmmaking segments in some clusters are well coupled internally in *small worlds*, others are more colluded, to some extent hampering creativity.
- The concern for lowering labor *costs* drives *outsourcing* from some clusters in high-wage countries to new peripheral clusters, but this impacts creativity little.
- The concern for compensating for *chance* in demand drives the increasing use of stars in most clusters, but as this may *strengthen small world network structures*, this has not per se an adverse effect on creativity.
- The concern for compensating for *chance* drives the increasing number of sequels in most clusters with mass-market segments, and this leads to *network collusion*, impacting adversely upon creativity.
- The concern for compensating for *chance* drives *horizontal and vertical integration of marketing* in Hollywood, and until recently, this has not hugely counteracted creativity.
- The concern for compensating for *chance* drives *horizontal and vertical integration of distribution* in Hollywood, and until recently, this has not had any major adverse effect on creativity either.
- The concern for compensating for *chance* drives the increasing number of flagpole productions in some clusters with mass-market segments and hence increased *horizontal integration of production*, compromising creativity to some extent.
- The concern for *collection* of auxiliary revenues from multiple rights in different industries has created *cross-industry integration* and multi-media conglomerations in some of the world's biggest clusters, with potential negative impacts on creativity.

While film as a cultural endeavor is recognized as a global phenomenon, many film scholars have equated film as an industry with Hollywood. However, there is clearly not just a Hollywood industrial model of commercial filmmaking; there are other models. Even if all commercial filmmaking models balance creativity, cost, chance and collection issues, they do so in different ways. We have briefly exemplified how clusters in, for example, Bollywood, Hollywood, Kyoto/Tokyo, Paris, London, Rome, and Copenhagen have developed differently; even if the drivers of organization are the same, chance and local historical events have set these clusters on different paths, and future comparative work should take on the challenge of systematically comparing them.

The analysis presented in this chapter is, hopefully, a useful tool for such cross-cluster comparisons in the film industry. In its first sections, the chapter argued that in general, focusing upon organization is a fruitful way of analyzing creativity and its context. The analysis of the film industry presented in the chapter provided examples of how organization, the historical development of such organization, and ultimately creativity, can be studied. Hence, the chapter can be seen as a step towards developing a broader analytical framework, giving hints as to how studies of creativity in the different industries in the cultural economy can be conducted in the future.

Notes

1 The poor availability of statistics for the film industry also encompasses figures of e.g. marketing, collections, and FDI, rendering it difficult to discuss these phenomena in a quantitative sense.

2 Munich (Germany) is another subsidized cluster that has also been releasing an increasing number of films per capita during the last decade (Kaiser and Liecke, 2007).

3 Definitions of "feature film" vary, but the US Academy of Motion Picture Arts and Sciences define it as a film longer than 40 minutes.

4 In Hollywood, there is even evidence that there is a third network of skill holders related to porn films, clearly distinguishable from the networks of skill holders involved in mainstream and niche non-porn films.

5 Folklore often describes Kevin Bacon as "the centre of the Hollywood universe", but actually, Rod Steiger has highest centrality in Hollywood's small world network, according to University of Virginia Computer Science Department's *Oracle of Bacon*, www.oracleofbacon.org/center_list.html.

6 The average combined production and marketing costs of a Hollywood film was 100.3 million USD in 2006 (MPAA, 2007). *Spiderman 2* cost an estimated 200 million USD and collected 784 million USD worldwide. *Pirates of the Caribbean 2* cost an estimated 225 million USD and collected over a billion USD worldwide www.imdb.com (accessed October 30, 2008).

References

Andersen, B, R Kozul-Wright and Z Kozul-Wright (2007), Rents, rights n'rhythm: cooperation, conflict and capabilities in the music industry, *Industry and Innovation*, 14(5): 513–540.

Baker, W and R R Faulkner (1991), Role as resource in the Hollywood film industry, *American Journal of Sociology* 97(2): 279–309.

Bakker, G (2005), The decline and fall of the European film industry: sunk costs, market size and market structure, 1895–1926, *Economic History Review*, 58(2): 310–351.

Blair, H (2001), You're only as good as your last job: the labour process and labour market in the British film industry, *Work, Employment, and Society*, 15(1): 149–169.

Burke, A E (1996), The dynamics of product differentiation in the British record industry, *Journal of Cultural Economics*, 20: 145–164.

Cameron, S (2003), Cinema, in R Towse (ed.) *A handbook of cultural economics*, Cheltenham: Edward Elgar, 114–118.

Caves, R E (2000), *Creative industries: contracts between art and commerce*, Cambridge, MA: Harvard University Press.

Chaminade, C and J Vang (2007), Global–local linkages, spillovers and cultural clusters: theoretical and empirical insights from an exploratory study of Toronto's film cluster, *Industry and Innovation*, 14(3): 401–420.

Chisholm, D (1993), Asset specificity and long-term contracts: the case of the motion-picture industry, *Eastern Economic Journal*, 19(2): 143–155.

—— (2003), Motion pictures, in R Towse (ed.) *A handbook of cultural economics*, Cheltenham: Edward Elgar, 306–313.

Coase, R (1937), The nature of the firm, *Economica*, 4(16), 386–405.

Coe, N M (2001), A hybrid agglomeration? The development of a satellite-Marshallian industrial district in Vancouver's film industry, *Urban Studies*, 38(10): 1753–1775.

Coe, N M and J Johns (2004), Beyond production clusters: towards a critical political economy of networks in the film and television industries, in D Power and A Scott (eds) *The cultural industries and the production of culture*, London: Routledge, 188–204.

Cowen, T (2000), *In praise of commercial culture*, Cambridge, MA: Harvard University Press.

Delmestri, G, F Montanari and A Usai (2005), Reputation and strength of ties in predicting commercial success and artistic merit of independents in the Italian feature film industry, *Journal of Management Studies*, 42(5): 975–1002.

Deuchert, E, K Adjamah and F Pauly (2005), For Oscar glory or Oscar money? Academy awards and movie success, *Journal of Cultural Economics*, 29: 159–176.

de Turégano, T H (2006), *Public support for the international promotion of European films*, Strasbourg: European Audiovisional Observatory.

De Vany, A (2004), *Hollywood economics: how extreme uncertainty shapes the film industry*, London and New York: Routledge.

De Vany, A and R D Eckert (1991), Motion pictures antitrust: the Paramount cases revisited, *Research and Law and Economics*, 14: 51–112.

De Vany, A and W D Walls (1997), The market for motion pictures: rank, revenue, and survival, *Economic Enquiry*, 35(4): 783–797.

—— (1999), Uncertainty in the movie industry: does star power reduce the terror of the box office? *Journal of Cultural Economics*, 23(4): 285–319.

Donahue, S M (1987), *American film distribution: the changing marketplace*, Ann Arbor: University of Michigan Press.

Elberse, A (2007), The power of stars: do star actors drive the success of movies? *Journal of Marketing*, 71(4): 102–120.

Elberse, A and J Eliashberg (2003), Demand and supply dynamics for sequentially released products in international markets: the case of motion pictures, *Marketing Science*, 22 (3): 329–354.

Eliashberg, J, A Elberse and M Leenders (2006), The Motion Picture Industry: critical issues in practice, current research and new research directions, *Marketing Science*, 25 (6): 638–661.

European Audiovisual Observatory, 2006, website statistics: http://lumiere.obs.coe.int/web/sources/analyse.html.

Faulkner, R R and A B Anderson (1987), Short-term projects and emergent careers: evidence from Hollywood, *American Journal of Sociology*, 92(4): 879–909.

Flew, T (2007), *Understanding global media*, New York: Palgrave Macmillan.

Florida, R (2002), *The rise of the creative class: and how it's transforming work, leisure, community and everyday life*, New York: Basic Books.

Foss, K and N J Foss (2002), 'Organizing economic experimentation', *Review of Austrian Economics*, 15(4): 297–312.

Goldman, W (1983), *Adventures in the screen trade*, New York: Warner Books.

Grabher, G (2002), Cool projects, boring institutions: temporary collaboration in social context, *Regional Studies*, 36(3): 205–214.

Granovetter, M (2005), Business group and social organization, in N Smelser and R Swedberg (eds) *Handbook of Economic Sociology*, Princeton, NJ: Princeton University Press, 429–450.

Hanssen, F A (2000), The block booking of films reexamined, *Journal of Law and Economics* 43(2): 395–426.

Hesmondhalgh, D (2002), *The cultural industries*, London: Sage.

Hobday, M. (2000), The project-based organization: an ideal form for managing complex product and systems? *Research Policy*, 29: 871–893.

Hoskins, C and Mirus R (1988), Reasons for US dominance in the international trade in television programmes, *Media, Culture and Society*, 70: 499–515.

Hoskins, C, S McFadyen and A Finn (1997), *Global television and film: an introduction to the economics of the business*, Oxford, England: Clarendon.

Jansen, C (2005), The performance of German motion pictures, profits and subsidies: some empirical evidence, *Journal of Cultural Economics*, 29(3): 191–212.

Kaiser, R and M Liecke (2007), The Munich feature film cluster: its degree of global integration and explanations for its relative success, *Industry and Innovation*, 14(3): 385–399.

Kerke, S and K Srinivasan (1990), Broader product line: a necessity of achieving success? *Management Science*, 36: 1216–1231.

Kohli-Khandekar, V (2006), *The Indian media business* 'Second edition', New Delhi: Response Books.

Langlois, R N (1986), *Economics as process: essays in the new institutional economics*, Cambridge, UK: Cambridge University Press.

Lee, S-W and D Waterman (2006), Theatrical feature film trade in the United States, Europe, and Japan since the1950s: an empirical study of the home market effect, working paper, Department of Telecommunications, Indiana University.

Litman, B R (1998), *The motion picture mega-industry*, Boston: Allyn and Bacon.

Lorenzen, M (2007), Internationalization vs. globalization of the film industry, *Industry and Innovation*, 14(4): 349–357.

Lorenzen, M and L Frederiksen (2005), The management of projects and product experimentation: examples from the music industry, *European Management Review*, 2(3): 198–211.

—— (2008), Why do cultural industries cluster? Localization, urbanization, products and projects, in P Cooke and R Lazzeretti (eds) *Creative cities, cultural clusters, and local economic development*, Cheltenham: Edward Elgar, 155–79.

Lorenzen, M and F A Täube (2008), Breakout from Bollywood? The roles of social networks and regulation in the evolution of Indian film industry, *Journal of International Management*, 14(3): 286–299.

Lundin, R and Söderholm, A (1995), A theory of the temporary organization, *Scandinavian Journal of Management*, 11(4): 437–455.

Maskell, P and M Lorenzen (2004) The cluster as market organization, *Urban Studies*, 41(5/6): 975–993.

Meyerson, D, K E Weick and R M Kramer (1996), Swift trust and temporary groups, in R M Kramer and T R Tyler (eds) *Trust in organizations: frontiers of theory and research*, Thousand Oaks, CA: Sage, 166–195.

Milgram, S (1967), The small-world problem *Psychology Today*, 1 (1): 61–67.

Moran, A (ed.) (1996), *Film policy: international, national and regional perspectives*, London: Routledge.

MPAA (2007), 2006 US theatrical market statistics, Los Angeles: MPAA, http://www.mpaa.org/2006-US-Theatrical-Market-Statistics-Report.pdf.

Nelson, P (1970), Information and consumer behavior, *Journal of Political Economy*, 78(2): 311–329.

Nelson, R R and S G Winter (1982), *An evolutionary theory of economic change*, Cambridge, MA: The Belknap Press of Harvard University Press.

Newman-Baudais, S (2005), *Access to the European market for non-European films: a statistical analysis*, Strasbourg: European Audiovisual Observatory, http://www.obs.coe.int/online_publication/expert/filmdistribution_mif2005.pdf.en

Oh, J (2001), International trade in film and the self-sufficiency ratio, *Journal of Media Economics*, 14(1): 31–44.

Papandrea, F (1998), Protection of domestic TV programming, *Journal of Media Economics*, 11 (4): 3–15.

Pine, J B and J H Gilmore (1999), *The experience economy: work is theatre & every business a stage*. Boston, MA: Harvard Business School Press.

Prag, J and J Casavant (1994), An empirical study of the determinants of revenues and marketing expenditures in the motion picture industry, *Journal of Cultural Economics*, 18(3): 217–235.

Raubitschek, R S (1988), Hitting the jackpot: product proliferation by multiproduct firms under uncertainty, *International Journal of Industrial Organization*, 6: 469–488.

Richardson, G B (1972), The organisation of industry, *Economic Journal*, 82: 883–896.

Robins, J (1993), Organization as strategy: restructuring production in the film industry, *Strategic Management Journal*, 14(Summer): 103–18.

Rosenberg, N (1992), Economic experiments, *Industrial and Corporate Change*, 1: 181–203.

Sawhney, M and J Eliashberg (1996), A parsimonious model for forecasting gross box-office revenues of motion pictures, *Marketing Science*, 15(2): 113–131.

Scott, A J (2005), *On Hollywood: the place, the industry*, Oxford: Princeton University Press.

Schatz, A (1997), The return of the Hollywood system, in P Aufderheide (ed.) *Conglomerates and the Media*, New York: New York Press.

Screen Digest (2006), no. 417, June: 205.

—— (2007), no. 425, February: 38.

Segrave, K (1997), *American films abroad: Hollywood's domination of the world's movie screens*. Jefferson, NC: McFarland.

Smith, A (1776), *An inquiry into the nature and causes of the wealth of nations* 'The Modern Library', reprinted 1937, New York: Random House.

Soda, G, A Usai and A Zaheer (2004), Network memory: the effect of past and current networks on performance, *Academy of Management Journal*, 47(6): 893–906.

Sorenson, O and D Waguespack (2006), Social structure and exchange: self-confirming dynamics in Hollywood, *Administrative Science Quarterly*, 51(4): 560–589.

Storper, M (1989), The transition to flexible specialization in the US film industry: external economies, the division of labour, and the crossing of industrial divides. *Cambridge Journal of Economics*, 13: 273–305.

Storper, M and S Christopherson (1987), Flexible specialization and regional industrial agglomerations: the US film industry, *Annals of the Associations of American Geographers*, 77(1): 104–117.

Sutton, J (1991), *Sunk cost and market structure: price competition, advertising, and the evolution of concentration*, Cambridge: MIT Press.

Ulff-Møller, J (2001), *Hollywood's film wars with France: film-trade diplomacy and the emergence of the french film quota policy*, New York: University of Rochester Press.

Uzzi, B and J Spiro (2005), Collaboration and creativity: the small world problem, *American Journal of Sociology*, 111:447–504.

Vogel, H L (1998), *Entertainment industry economics: a guide for financial analysis*, New York: Cambridge University Press.

Walls, W D (2005), Modeling movie success when 'nobody knows anything': conditional stable-distribution analysis of film returns, *Journal of Cultural Economics*, 29(3): 177–190.

Wasko, J (2003), *How Hollywood works*, London: Sage.

Watts, D J, P S Dodds and M E J Newman (2002), Identity and search in social networks, *Science*, 296: 1302–1305.

Wildman, S S (1995), Trade liberalization and policy for media industries: a theoretical examination of media flows, *Canadian Journal of Communication* 20: 367–388.

Wildman, S S and S E Siwek (1988), *International trade in films and television programs*, Cambridge. MA: Ballinger.

Williamson, O E (1975) *Markets and hierarchies: analysis and antitrust implications*, The Free Press: New York.

—— (2000), The new institutional economics: taking stock, looking ahead, *Journal of Economic Literature*, Vol. XXXVIII: 595–613.

4b The governance of innovation in the film and television industry

A case study of London, UK

Andy C. Pratt and Galina Gornostaeva

The focus of this chapter is innovation and creativity in the film and television industries in London. In the case of film and television industries one may expect to find some of the most enthusiastic adopters of digital technologies and hence a clear case of the impact of digitisation on innovation. This chapter adopts a cautious analysis of the role of technology stressing the co-constitutive role of technology, organisation and regulation that is situated in industries, places and times.

In principle, it is possible to make a film, or a TV programme, on a laptop or a mobile phone, however, in practice this is unusual. Where such practices are adopted their use is commonly strategic, in order to achieve other organisational aims such as simple cost reduction or novelty. In many respects the film and television industries are 'poster children' for digitisation and innovation; the question is, whether such changes produced are superficial, in the sense of new delivery systems for the same old production model, or, if they represent a substantial transformation of the process. In this chapter we argue that complex regulatory structures and market structures mean that innovation is a more organic and systemic process rather than a technological 'big bang' that it is commonly represented as. In this chapter we argue for the need to account for the complex inter-relationship of technologies, organisation and regulation. Moreover, that the roles of technology (digitisation), organisation (the fragmented small firms), and governance (deregulation) cannot be generalised and will be resolved, necessarily, in particular spaces and times resulting in unique locational outcomes.

If one examines the UK FTV at a macro-scale considerable success of both TV sales and film production (receipts) can be identified both relative to the size of the UK economy, and by comparison with other economies (DCMS, 1999). How do we begin to understand this relative success? One answer might be innovation or improved competitiveness (Porter, 1998); however, arguably such 'catch-alls' disguise as much as they reveal (Pratt, 1996; 2008). This chapter approaches the problem by shifting analytic attention to the micro-scale and to organisational concerns in order to explore ways in which similar technologies or innovations may produce quite different industry outcomes in terms of practice. The chapter is structured around this argument; we begin by prefacing this with a discussion of innovation and creativity and next elaborating how this is worked through in the case of the film and television industries.

Innovation and creativity

In order to sidestep some of the problems associated with technological, or economic, reductionism we have sought to take a radical position. This chapter treats innovation and creativity as 'effects', or emergent properties, rather than externalities or inputs (see for example the discussion of Hodgson, 1993). Our concern here is to explore systemic effects situated within and produced by networks of activities. Additionally, we are less concerned with the semantics of innovation versus creativity, for our purposes we elide the terms; but we view them both in a socialised manner and seek to frame them in a broader process of transformation.

More generally, we can usefully consider what might be termed the 'governance' of the film and television industries: a notion that incorporates organisation and regulation in relation to particular industries and technologies (Pratt, 1997; 2005; 2006a). In the field of television we can note the shifts of ownership and control from public to private, to regulation of content, and regulation of monopolies. The point being that these products, processes and concepts are inter-related. The concept of innovation that we want to propose has four parts: technology, regulation, organisation, (regulation and markets are considered in particular relationship to individual industries and their particular markets) and situatedness in time/space (location).

First, technology; this seeks to highlight the range of possible technologies, the emergent empirical forms of action, organisation and output are deemed creative or innovative relative to past products, and against competing products in the market. Second, the relationship between (and within) market and state is the field of regulation. A critical point here is the degree to which power relations are skewed to the interests of consumers or producer(s). The outcome of which is commonly referred to as 'the market'. Third, all of these relationships are situated within the particular production practices and forms of industries/products, and they are embedded in space and time. A fourth, and final, dimension is organisation, the situated character of film and television and the fact that they operate, and are institutionally configured, in different, although sometimes overlapping, markets. Quite clearly they have different distribution and exhibition systems, they have different production cycles and budgets, not surprisingly these all shape the ways in which film or TV responds to changing technologies or regulation.

These four parts might be conceived of, with the aim of avoiding linearity, or hierarchy of cause, by representing the process as an intersection of a four circle Venn diagram (see Figure 4b.1). The figure represents innovation/creativity as a field *not* as the intersection of the elements per se. It is possible to generate innovations in any of the interactions; for example, organisational innovation, regulatory innovation etc. Hence, we can refer to it as a 'field' of innovation (like an electrical force field).

By seeking to describe this process as the governance of innovation we seek to draw parallels with the usage of the term 'field' by Bourdieu (1993) in relation to cultural production – the conjunction of forces that generates production and innovation – we are seeking to avoid the a priori prioritisation of one or other 'factors'.

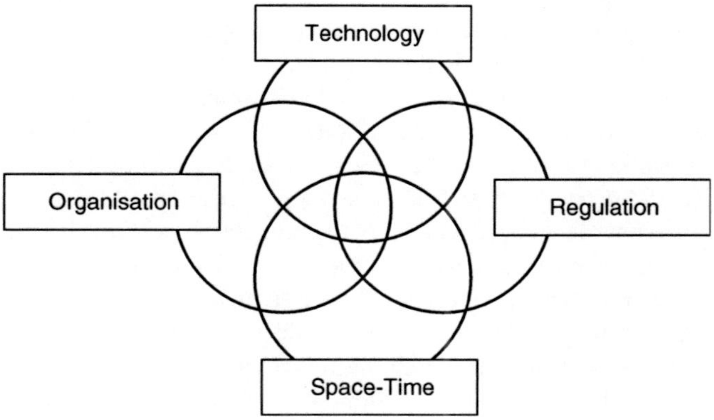

Figure 4b.1 The field of innovation

Instead, we are proposing that these are examined *in situ*. The innovation that we seek to examine is not simply an increase in the volume or turnover of new products or patents as is normal in industry studies; rather, it is concerned with how the field of production is organised within the context of a particular set of constraints. For this reason we avoid a preparatory general historical narrative to the following section: we are more interested in how the threads of this process are woven. This chapter is divided along the lines suggested above by the four main dimensions of technology, regulation, organisation and location; consistent with our approach we examine, in turn, the film and television industries.

The film and television industries

Technology

In essence, the task of making either a film or a TV programme is the same; in fact hybrid 'made for TV' films are common. Moreover, there are complex co-funding relationships for films 'made by' some TV companies. However, the essential difference is the technical quality of the product; films are generally more expensive, and require higher technical and artistic qualities in their making. The primary recording medium for film was film, and for TV was videotape. The editing process was similar, although different, as was the recording. Film has to be developed (like a domestic photograph), whereas TV on tape can be instantly played back. Digitisation has first allowed the quality of image found on film to be saved first on tape, and then on a hard drive. Consequently, data files of images and sound can be easily copied, transported, and edited and re-edited, without quality loss. Editing, does still come down to the selection and ordering of images, and matching with sounds, in order to convey a message. Technology may speed up the physical process, but the deliberative processes are more or less the same.

Film

Digitisation has actually had relatively little impact on filmmaking. There is the potential to use cheaper recording media, and use cheaper, and more mobile, cameras and lighting. This has reduced costs and the number of people 'on set/location', and technology has generally been grafted on to previous production forms with little change. Location shooting has become more attractive in cost terms as a result. Additionally, the proportions of frames per film that are digitally enhanced have increased; in recent cases approaching 80% (Pratt, 2006b). Editing has become digital (rather than physical), special effects have become more on-line creations than physical deceptions; special effects or effects treatments have come to impact upon a significant percentage of total frames of films, rather than on a few discrete inserts. This expansion of editing and digital enhancement activity has led to the growth of the post-production side of filmmaking (Culkin *et al.*, 2005). Due to the scale of production, and the volume of CGI (Computer Generated Images), several companies and locations may be involved. In London a privately financed high-capacity broadband network, Sohonet (Nachum and Keeble, 2003), was established in 1995 to route part-finished CGI work around Soho (Sohonet, 2007), and a link was also provided to Burbank, California (the location for much film making in Los Angeles). This latter link allowed CGI to be added 'overnight' so that the Burbank next day rushes could have CGI added.

However, for all its uptake of innovative technical content film has remained very similar in terms of its distribution and exhibition. The technical possibility exists for digital distribution and exhibition of film to be revolutionised (like the music industry). However, the distribution companies have sought to retain control over film by maintaining analogue distribution and exhibition, or at least the analogue structures. Even where digital exhibition is available, the movie is projected directly from physical film stock that has to be developed and physically transported; and of which there are a finite number of copies. There has been much effort to avoid downloading film, either direct to cinemas, or to the home. It is important to contrast the film industry where there is a separation of distribution and exhibition from production, and music where it is the same organisation; hence, in the latter case digitisation poses less of a threat (if it can be retained within the music company).

Film financing is structured in dualistic manner where studios seek to recoup investment via a portfolio of films that they seek to sell on to distributors and exhibitors (who are separate organisations and industries). Filmmakers commonly seek to attach extra rights through merchandising or licensing deals. Exhibitors make money via ticket sales, but increasingly through confectionery at the point of sale where profit margins are astronomical (Epstein, 2005). Clearly, there is a potential possibility that downloading could put the exhibitors out of business.

TV

The same digital technologies have had a far deeper impact on TV production where there are different organisational and regulatory contexts. As with film digital editing is used, however, this was not such a big shift from videotape. Because the timescales are shorter in TV the possibility of distribution of part-edited material and its re-combination in a new location is used to an advantage (in the real time transfer of programmes to meet the tight temporal constraints of TV). Generally TV quality thresholds, and budgets, are much lower than those in film. In recent years the field of TV distribution and exhibition has changed radically. Until the 1990s most TV was distributed via radio signals that required a TV and aerial to receive broadcasts; however, the bandwidth expansion (and the number of possible channels) that came with the development of cable and satellite systems created the potential for a 'multi-channel' environment. At the same time new funding arrangements were developed and, along with traditional advertiser paid TV and public service provision, there emerged a subscription service[1]. Inevitably, this multi-channel system diluted audiences per channel; in response broadcasters such as Sky set about aggressively to draw new customers with pre-pay premier sport broadcasting. The marginal cost of a new channel to the distributor is very small, but the potential returns are high. In the case of sport, the high costs work as a 'loss leader' to drive the positioning of the channel. It has been argued that such tactics have been used to drive down prices and quality of news television (BBC, 2003; Lambert, 2002). Downloading has not been constructed as such a threat to TV as the product is rapidly changing and the distributors can still retain control of the revenue stream. In fact, pod-casts and downloads are being encouraged. Another form of innovation has been the emergence of programme formats that are based upon telephone voting; the receipts from such interactive services contribute a massive 22% of *all* TV industry revenues (which total £743m) (Ictis, 2006).

Regulation

By regulation we mean any way in which markets are shaped by state policy, except, through direct investment (which is dealt with in the section on organisation). Thus, it includes a range of legal statutes that fall into two categories. First, those that regulate content and are the more traditional site of debates about quality and 'good taste'. The system has evolved from an informal and fragmented one to its recent collective and formal manifestation – Ofcom – that regulates amongst other things advertising and a significant dimension of commercial television. In film there is a film classification system that regulates who can view films. Second, those concerned with issues of competition and monopoly, and more recently about licensing new technologies (such as cable and satellite systems.) To this should be added the BBC, which is funded by the licence fee and, initially, solely regulated by Charter; some of its regulation now falls within the purview of Ofcom (GB, 2003). Our main concern in this chapter is with the second category of regulation.

Film

The history of regulation in film industry before 1980 represented a contradictory mixture of protectionist measures focused on support for indigenous productions against US dominance on the market and policies directed on attracting foreign investment (Pratten and Deakin, 2000). Examples of the former are 'quotas' introduced by The Cinematograph Films Act 1927 requiring that UK cinemas show a certain percentage of British films in order to boost local production, or the 'Dalton Duty' implemented a 75% tax on US films in 1947. In the UK the Palache Committee's report (Baillieu and Goodchild, 2002) emphasised a necessity of anti-monopolistic intervention in the UK film industry of 1944 which tried to stop the attempts of British businesses in film to follow the Hollywood model of aggregating in one company production, distribution and exhibition (much as the Paramount agreement in the US also sought in 1947). The introduction of Eady Tax in 1957 added an attraction for US companies as it gave subsidies for films registered as British, even where the finance came from abroad. The long decline of the British film industry can be dated from this time; during 1950–60s the number of studios reduced from 21 to only 7 (Kempton, 2007). The 1980s decade began with the worst recession the British film industry had ever seen. In that year only 31 UK films were made, down 50% on the previous year, and the lowest output since 1914 (Baillieu and Goodchild, 2002). Admissions in early 1980s had fallen below 100 million (BFI, 2007). In 1984 national Film Finance Corporation was privatised causing producers to securing distribution and seek finance from multiple sources.

Film finance in the UK has always depended upon private capital; regulators have sought to manage the margins via direct (subsidy), and indirect (tax relief), interventions. The Eady tax concession was also abolished in 1984, as a result several film studios owned or leased by major US companies closed or re-directed their activities to television. In 1985, the first multiplex was built in Milton Keynes and, as the new cinema chains built the new complexes, audiences were revived. In 1999 month-on-month admissions were the highest since 1971 (Hicks and Allen, 1999). Interest of US companies in British productions recovered by mid-1990s, when new incentives were introduced in the UK for foreign companies and when the US freed up the monopoly roles; cinema chains in Britain as a result belong mainly to US majors (Dyja, 2005). Recovery started in 1992 with the introduction of the tax incentive ('Section 42'), which allowed British qualifying films[2] with budgets in excess of £15 million to deduct expenditure, on completion of the film, over three years (however, by 2005 the cost of the average US film shoot in the US was $34.1 million [Katz, 2006]). This incentive strongly encouraged – or rather, continued the practice of – Hollywood investment in the UK film industry. US companies managed to use other advantages of UK incentives for film industry. In 1997 'Section 48 relief' was introduced allowing 100 per cent write-off of costs on completion of the film, designed to help low budget British productions to start up; however this system was also exploited by US companies seeking to promote offshore production. In 2005 there was an additional concern expressed by the industry when budgetary rules were again changed, prompting filmmakers to suggest that they would move offshore from the UK. At the same time the DCMS developed a more complex set of rules for defining what a British film is for the purposes of subsidy and tax relief (DCMS, 2006).

TV

As noted above, the BBC is regulated by Charter and has dominated TV in the UK. One element of the BBC Charter has been a commitment to broadcast 'significant' national sporting events. Definition of the events, and the competition from Sky in relation to sporting events in particular, opened up commercial competition for sporting events (which resulted in a huge cash injection into the British football industry); as noted above, a similar process has had a negative impact on news production at the BBC. Moreover, in the 1990s the BBC tended to take an overtly commercial tack, a significant innovation was 'producer choice' (see Born, 2004 for details of the organisational implications). A significant, although under reported dimension of this process has been the establishment of a system that requires broadcasters to choose a percentage of content from independent production companies. This has, in effect, led to the BBC outsourcing a large proportion of its programmes, and consequently significant expansion of the programme market; and the precise proportion has been changed several times. As early as 1986 The Peacock Committee recommended 40% independent quota on BBC and ITV, in the event a 25% quota was introduced by the Broadcasting Act 1990 for terrestrial broadcasters. A 10% quota on DTT (Digital Terrestrial Television) channels was introduced by the Broadcasting Act in 1996. Most recently, the 2003 Communications Act set the 25% independent quota for all public service channels, including BBC digital channels (Ofcom, 2006).

Commercial broadcasting in the UK began with the establishment of ITV funded by advertising revenue, in 1955. However, only with establishment of Channel 4 in 1982 and especially after deregulation was confirmed by the broadcasting act in 1990 that influence of commercial television became prominent; in particular, the new model of broadcaster as publisher (which was echoed at the BBC with producer choice). A franchise system in TV started in 1983 with TV-am. Channel 5 came on air in 1997. The final shift in terrestrial television has been the merging of the previously regionally-based ITV network. The significance of this regulatory relaxation is that it has allowed consolidation and the creation of large and dominant company. Whilst local cable networks had existed for years as a parallel to terrestrial broadcasts in areas of poor reception, cable and satellite broadcast opened up multi-channel broadcasting for the UK. After considerable organisational flux Sky was the net winner in the satellite business, and Virgin Media (NTL-Telewest) in cable. The analogue broadcasting infrastructure was also privatised, and is set to become digital only around 2010. Both the regional allocation of cable licenses and the 'digital switch off' have been driven by Government seeking to promote a digital TV platform and 'hoped for' innovation related to it.

The first cross-border television channels were also launched in Europe in the 1980s with developments in satellite broadcasting. Two decades on, there are more than 100 trans-national channels operating across Europe and approximately 80 of them hold a license from the British Independent Television Commission. The ITC is a popular regulator because licenses are cheap (£250) and simple to obtain. One of the main conditions is that broadcasters must be based in the

UK, making London the European centre for trans-national television. (Chalaby, 2002).

Organisation

The organisational response to new technologies and the shifting regulatory environment, as well as the changing structure and organisation of the market, is the focus of this section. There is no 'essential' form of organisation for any particular set technology, industry or regulation; there are simply numerous fixes. The film and television industries are good examples of the possibility (and an historical example) of large-scale mass production and its transformation into a fragmented flexible production system, and everything in between. This transition cannot be reduced to a simple 'technology fix'. Each particular configuration represents a different balance of risks, from one extreme of within the corporation, to the other of outsourced individuals. As we have already noted, the regulatory regimes and take up of technologies have not been parallel in film and TV, and the market for film and television are quite different.

Film

As has already been noted, the British film industry has never been able to echo Hollywood's 'film factories'. The few examples of larger studios and a significant throughput of films existed in the 1920s and 1950s but they were never sustained. In the 1960s when film once again had an upturn the industry had already been dominated by US investment. The pattern has been a large number of small film production companies, often referred to as a cottage industry, some of which have had limited success, but none able to grow or to sustain large scale production. US majors dominate distribution, and exhibition, despite once being under major British control, has shifted to French and US major chains that have undertaken a huge re-investment in infrastructure, out of town multiplexes, in the last 20 years (UKFC, 2006).

Film finance is another story; historically the US has had major investments in film companies and film making in the UK, the highpoint was undoubtedly the 1960s. However, the UK film industry continues to be a significant source for US investment, and partnership funding with European funded filmmaking. A minor, although significant source of film finance does originate from UK private sources, and London is still a draw for those seeking to make a deal.

The UK film industry had a limited success in the 1980s (e.g. Goldcrest, Handmade Films and Merchant Ivory Productions) with the growing audience for film, and Hollywood's turn to blockbusters. By the late 1980s decline was the rule once again: first, the majority of attempts to develop large film companies failed as US majors and other foreign companies controlled distribution and exhibition. Second, there were difficulties in obtaining funds for a 'slate' of films. Third, intellectual property rights were transferred to the distribution company, so that film libraries were then concentrated in the hands of distributors allowing them control of the (intellectual property rights) residuals from the further exploitation of the product (on television, as a DVD, etc.)

In 1990s film companies became smaller and single project oriented, responding to a regulatory system which encouraged a separation of income streams for production (including fees for creative staff) and profits going to distributors. In 1996 UK National Lottery money was first invested into the film industry. The scheme required a number of consortia to be formed comprising film production, distribution and sales companies to bid for lottery money on a franchise basis. This initiative was focused on creation of mini-studios (Baillieu and Goodchild, 2002) in order to remedy one of the common problems for publicly funded filmmaking (distribution); previously, this had led to the embarrassment of films being subsidised and made, but never exhibited. Even worse, those that were exhibited did not do well at the box office.[3] The 30 films financed by the Lottery accounted for only 1% of box office takings (Le Breton, 2000). Distribution rights of those newly created mini-studios were attached to US distribution companies, such as Universal and the 20th Century Fox or French Pathé (Baillieu and Goodchild, 2002). The intention was to create a small but sustainable film industry, and for mini-studios to be able to create a slate or portfolio so that successes could be countered by failures.

In film, as in television, production has been organised around projects (programmes/films). In the classic Hollywood system projects were internalised within one company and workers re-allocated to another project at the end of the one that they were working in; the BBC worked in a similar way. With fragmentation came project firms, but also project labour. Whilst there had always been a residual freelance component to film and television production, in effect outsourcing of programme and film production made freelancing and short term working a norm. Traditionally, the strong unionisation and high pay of these industries had sought to counterbalance this risk. However, the repealing of union laws in the UK has tipped the balance seriously in favour of project companies. (Blair and Rainne, 2000; Blair, 2001; Blair *et al.*, 2001; Blair, 2003). It is for this reason that there has been such concern about working conditions. Whereas previously part of a career was extensive training freelancers do not get trained, or they train themselves. Arguably, the British film and broadcasting industries are trading on a legacy of past training provision; this is one of the reasons for the intervention of Skills Investment Fund that has recently introduced a training levy on companies.[4]

TV

Independent producers and a freelance labour force started to become significant in the 1950s as a result of restrictions of trade unions in film and television industry on new employees in the industry. Many of those first independent production companies and freelancers were used by the mainstream (BBC and ITV) television even at a time when strict regulations by the trade unions were in operation. Another source of the origin of the present independent production companies in television – spin offs from ITV and BBC after deregulation began. BBC was oriented to Oxbridge graduates with specific cultural capital. Many producers that we spoke to complained that the BBC suffocated their ideas, and they celebrated an ability to be independent, seeing it as a great advantage for creativity. Our interviewees mentioned that they stopped working for the BBC because their programmes were no longer needed or were politically unacceptable (Darlow, 2004). Some of the more 'rebellious' independents tried to challenge the older channels with newer contexts and formats. Others, however, as our interviewees put it, were 'good boys and girls' taking with them not only well established reputations but also stable contracts with former employers.

Organisational change in the TV industry in the UK has two distinctive phases. First, the appearance and flourishing of a large number of small independent production companies related to processes of deregulation and commercialisation of needs and structures of TV and creation of 'quasi' markets (Deakin and Pratten, 2000). At this stage independent production companies had a chance to establish their reputation and relationship to the commissioning body: public or private, indigenous or foreign, broadcaster, channel, distributor or sales agent and funding bodies. At that time, as one of interviewees mentioned, 'the BBC came to us to see what we were doing, not another way around'.[5] With the passage of time the situation changed (1990s). The main broadcasters work with 300 or so independent production companies in total but only a handful of them produce the majority of output hours (Mcgown, 2005). Total number of independent production companies involved in television is more than a thousand according to the UKFC database.

In contrast to the experience of film, independent production companies in TV have expanded their scale of production, internalised in many cases post-production, diversified markets via diversification of products (e.g. entertainment programmes in combination with serious documentary) and sales territories, independent production companies combine production and distribution and acquire small companies representing expertise in particular products. The 2003 Communications Act introduced a new code of practice whereby the terms of trade between public broadcasters and production companies were changed giving producers greater control over intellectual property rights in their programmes, which helped them in accumulating finance for the development of the next programme, and in the building up of libraries of their products, which can be later sold or rented thereby producing another income stream (Channel 4, 2005; Pact, 2002; 2003). Film companies couldn't achieve the same result, which was another reason for not being able to accumulate capital and to retain film libraries. The film libraries were sold, together with the property rights, to privately owned distributors.

Television has also become a player in film, Channel 4 had set up a film fund, and the BBC has expanded its operations. In 1998 the Arts Council for the first time awarded £1million of lottery money to the US major (Miramax) for its £6.4 million adaptation of Jane Austen's *Mansfield Park* (1999), and, as a result, the film was distributed by Miramax in the US market, with the film's television rights going to one of the film's co-financiers, the BBC (Kim, 2003). The BBC has undoubtedly provided a vital training ground for generations of workers. One of our interviewees described with admiration the BBC training system where for several weeks a person moved between departments and watched and learned special skills, e.g. production, directing, documentary work, etc. and then this person could choose the work he was most interested in. Work was concentrated on creativity; trainees had to produce 'an idea', 'to generate the story' and to develop it. This type of career and skill development does not equate with the new independent sector where projects are so tightly costed, and time scales do not allow for, training (see Christopherson, 2003 for a US example). The Government and industry have also invested in the National Film School[6] in response to training issues, plus a recent agreement has placed a levy on ITV companies for freelancers' training (Ofcom, 2005).

Location

The film and television industries are concentrated in London in terms of the number of firms, workers and turnover. This pattern has not changed significantly in the last 100 years. However, such a gross generalisation does cover up a more complex geography. In the early years film and television might be best described as co-incident, there is evidence that in recent years this relationship has developed into a closer dependency. At the same time as commercial pressures seem to have favoured concentration, there has been growing political pressure to disperse television production, and to a lesser extent film production (Cornford and Robins, 1991; 1992).

Film

The historic focus of the film industry is Soho, London – to be precise Wardour Street. It was really in the 1920s that Wardour Street was redeveloped with significant investment from US film companies seeking to secure a foothold in the UK. The primary activities in these locations were business and administration; film making proper, that is the sound stages, were located on the outskirts of London. Over time the ailing fortunes of the British film industry reduced capacity and led to the closure of many studios. Some were converted to television use (Elstree, for example) in the 1960s, others were closed altogether, and a few merged. The US investment of the 1960s, and the positive exchange rate in the 1980s gave UK studios a temporary competitive edge. At the current time there are 10 studios remaining in Greater London region operating across 13 locations; the locations of these are in the Central, North and West of London and outside the M25 (see Figure 4b.2).

Initially, filming and editing were carried out at the studio (sound stage); however, as these services have become more specialised and expensive they have relocated to Soho. A good example is film special effects; initially the UK gained pre-eminence in this area with films such the James Bond and Star Wars franchises, and *2001: A Space Odyssey*. The transition from physical effects and models to digital effects was echoed by relocation to central London where there had been already existing expertise in video and sound editing; activities which overlapped with those requirements of TV. In the twenty-first century Soho has become one of

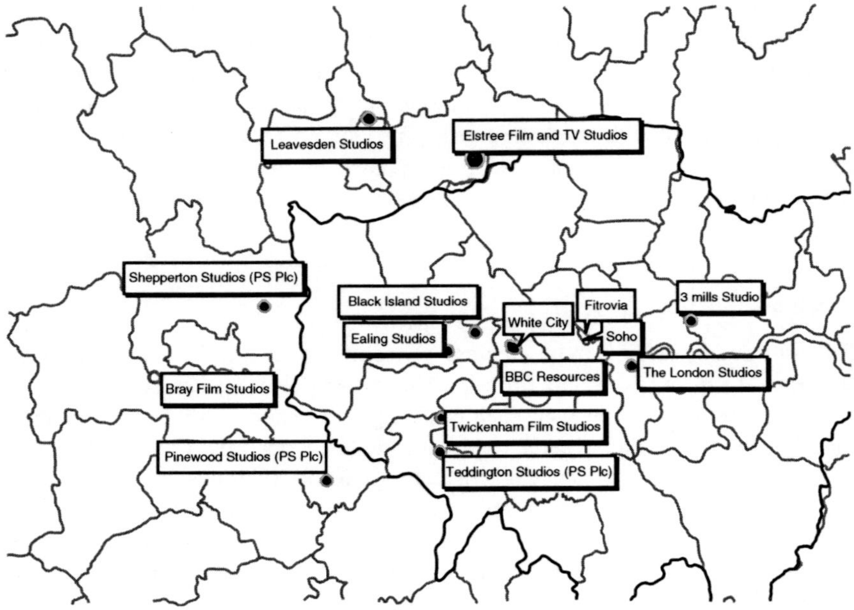

Figure 4b.2 Film and TV production spaces in London

the global nodes of special effects work. However, one of the problems with this work is that it is very labour intensive and irregular. The Mill, a pioneer company in this field, has recently announced that it will withdraw from film special effects and concentrate on the more balanced market of TV and advertising (Kemp, 2007).

Soho provides a number of critical services for filmmakers. First, it offers a vast source of industry knowledge and informal information exchange through serendipitous interactions ‘on the street’ and in the restaurant. In 1985 Groucho Club was established in Soho, this and a number of other clubs serve as an important networking space for the TV industry. Second, there is access to film funders, and to distributors (who are also located there), and to the international TV market. Third, it is a hub of a large and very specialised labour market (technical and artistic) that facilitates the diverse possible skillset combinations that are necessary for varied film output. Undoubtedly, a Soho address is prestigious; we have noted that many smaller production companies have a ‘Soho address’ in name only; the fact that this is deemed necessary is indicative of its import. In fact, a number of smaller production companies are to be found on the edges of inner North London (Camden, Kentish Town); here, locations are cheaper, and occasional access to Soho is possible. More established companies seem to require a permanent presence in Soho.

A recent change to this pattern has been the establishment of a new studio in Glasgow; devolution has created a significant economic and administrative unit of Scotland. In recent years Scotland has attracted location shooting, and the development of a sound stage has been pushed to sustain such ambitions.

TV

There was not really a significant independent television production scene before 1982. There were independent producers but they worked for the BBC or ITV (Darlow, 2004). The establishment of Channel 4 called into being a number of small companies (many of these were ex-BBC, a trickle that became a tide with producer choice). Initially, these companies clustered around Channel 4's commissioning HQ just north of Soho. Soho was attractive in terms of relatively low rents and proximity to the advertising industry (who used their services as well). As the sector grew and Soho was regenerated with other investment, prices became high. However, Soho remained the epicentre of post-production for TV, and the site of many independent producers. In 1986 Framestore was established to serve the needs of advertising first, and later of film animation, and animation in TV. A sub-cluster also emerged around the BBC TV centre in Shepherd's Bush/White City, West London. A number of sound stages and theatres are used by TV located in central London; however, Soho remains convenient, especially with the development of Sohonet, to relay part-finished programme materials for editing and post-production work.

In the 1960s and 1970s television had a pronounced regional dimension; the BBC had a number of regional broadcasting studios, and ITV had a parallel network. For the BBC, London was still 'the centre', and in the commercial sector Manchester became a significant centre based around Granada TV. The development of 'producer choice' in the BBC pulled the focus back to London and the new independents needed to be close to the 'commissioners' to get the right pitch to gain work. The merging of ITV has meant that Manchester and Glasgow remain significant players in TV. Two other factors have led to a counter-London shift for the BBC. First, a later manifestation of producer choice has created a quota for 'outside M25' programming (Ofcom, 2006); this had been introduced in 1998 by the Channel 4 'Nations and Regions' initiative, which required to spend 30% out of London, which has resulted in a focus on Glasgow as well as London. Channel 5 agreed to a 10% 'outside of London' target in 2001, and in 2002 the ITV Charter committed ITV1 to an out of London spend of at least 50% including both regional and network programmes. In 2005 public sector broadcasting review increased ITV's out of London (OOL) quota; second, the BBC had plans to relocate Children's TV and Sport to Manchester (Breen, 2004). This move has yet to materialise. In fact, the success or otherwise of the initiative will reveal much about the critical mass and attraction of London to TV.

Conclusions

On first impression, film and television appear to be very creative industries, and, moreover, industries that are at the forefront of the use of new technologies in the form of digitisation. We have outlined a conception of creativity and innovation that was about interconnected systemic changes in networks of firms. The chapter was structured around the idea that production process (which may or may not be 'inside' a firm) is best viewed as a 'field of innovation' that is articulated around the four 'moments': regulation, technology, organisation and location. We argued that creativity and innovation are an effect of particular configurations of the 'moments' in relation to particular industries. This is why we argued for the need to examine film and television separately.

It might be attractive to point to the role of new technologies in change: to be sure technologies used in production have changed the best example being digitisation. However, the chapter shows that there is more of a question as to the ways in which this has changed the organisation of production. It is clear that a raft of regulatory changes have enabled, although not determined, significant organisation change – predominantly the creation of an independent sector in TV; and less positively, the maintenance of a 'cottage industry' in film. Finally, markets and means of distribution have changed, especially in TV. In a multi-channel environment the audience is re-constituted and re-segmented; moreover as funding shifts to income generation via secondary sources (phones, or merchandising) this also has an impact. In short, there has been a shift away from a centralised productivist forms, not to complete fragmentation and niches but rather to a more dispersed/fragmented and hybrid form (production and consumption, niche and core). It is the outcome, the effect, of these tensions that produce and value a particular spatial form: prioritising more networking, regard networks, niche competition, cartels; at the same time the particularity of spatial form enables certain types of social and economic interaction.

We have shown that the re-constitution of the field has led to the production process being re-articulated in quite different ways due to the particular capacities of firms associated with capitalisation and access to markets; these factors in turn are filtered through regulatory structures, local organisational arrangements and shifting market structures. We noted that both film and TV industries have been through significant changes, but that they have responded in different ways. One of the physical expressions of these shifts has been location. Whilst we noted that London, and Soho, has been the core location over a number of years, the precise patterns (and functions performed there) and reasons for this preference have changed.

This analysis points us to a number of issues regarding innovation and creativity – the context and setting of innovation and creativity. An issue pointed to in this chapter and expanded elsewhere concerns the physical co-presence that is needed to produce film and TV programmes to sustain the labour market, and the information system upon which both rely. In our view their underlines the importance of reputation for workers and companies engaged in competition with others in the same industry and locale. Second, we also have argued that we need to look outside *and* across firms to see the network within which they are embedded. At least two can be identified. The first comprising of the shifting production chains of film and TV that link sound stages, post-production, commissioning and financing, and selling on product. Second, the international production networks that London is embedded in both as a global city and an international node of image production (film, theatre, fine art, new media, and advertising). The wider intersection of these local and global flows is critical to understanding the growth and sustainability of London's film and TV competitiveness.

The next few years may prove to be interesting as the BBC seeks to develop a stronger presence in Manchester, and Glasgow seeks to develop its support for film and TV. Whilst these shifts are based to a major extent on the supply of infrastructure, the real question will be if they achieve to sustain a critical mass in the labour market to sustain and grow the skill set that the industry depends upon. In addition, as we have noted, there is a systemic problem with training in both industries, especially in TV. The challenge is for agencies such as Skillset to create a training levy that will match the past solution that was the BBC training; and understand where the new skills for cross-media working will come from.

Acknowledgements

This research was funded through ESRC Award 'The Role of Production Chains in the London Film & Television Industry Cluster.' Reference Number: RES-000–23–0653.

Notes

1 Sky Television plc was a four-channel satellite television service launched by Rupert Murdoch's News International on February 5, 1989. Sky Television merged with collapsed rival British Satellite Broadcasting in 1990 to form British Sky Broadcasting (BSkyB). The merger was effectively a takeover of BSB by Sky, although the latter was also suffering massive losses (Wikipedia, 2007).
2 There is a long debate about what a 'British qualifying' film is; see http://www.culture.gov.uk/Reference_library/Publications/archive_2006/culturaltestguidance.htm (accessed March 24 2007).
3 In film, marketing is critical to success, so this failure is as much to do with marketing and distribution issues as with 'quality' per se.
4 See http://www.skillset.org/skillset/press/2003/article_2555_1.asp (accessed March 24 2007).
5 Interview carried out for the project. 'The Role of Production Chains in the London Film and Television Industry Cluster', funded by ESRC, upon which this paper is based.
6 See http://www.skillset.org/film/training_and_events/screen_academies/article_4190_1.asp (accessed March 24 2007).

References

Blair, H. (2001) 'You're only as good as your last job': the labour process and labour market in the British film industry, *Work, Employment and Society* 15(1), pp. 149–169.

—— (2003) Winning and losing in flexible labour markets: the formation and operation of networks of interdependence in the UK film industry, *Sociology – the Journal of the British Sociological Association* 37(4), pp. 677–694.

Blair, H. and Rainne, A. (2000) Flexible firms, *Media Culture & Society* 22(2), pp. 187–204.

Blair, H., Grey, S. and Randle, K. (2001) Working in film – employment in a project based industry, *Personnel Review* 30(1–2), pp. 170–185.

Baillieu, B. and Goodchild, J. (2002) *The British film business*. London: John Wiley & Sons.

BBC (2003) The BBC's response to the DCMS' independent review of News 24 in 2002 (the Lambert report), dated 20 February 2003. BBC.

BFI (2007) Cinema admissions in the UK. BFI.

Born, G. (2004) *Uncertain vision: Birt, Dyke and the reinvention of the BBC*. London: Vintage.

Bourdieu, P. (1993) The field of cultural production, or: The economic worlds reversed, in Johnson, R. (ed.) *The field of cultural production: essays on art and literature*, pp. 29–72. Cambridge: Polity Press.

Breen, R. (2004) BBC plans for Manchester move, BBC News, Manchester.

Cawson, A., Haddon, L. and Miles, I. (1995) *The shape of things to consume: delivering information technology into the home*. Aldershot; Brookfield, USA: Avebury.

Channel 4 (2005) Code of practice for commissioning programmes from independent producers. Channel Four, London.

Chalaby, J. K. (2002) Transnational television in Europe – The role of pan-European channels, *European Journal of Communication* 17(2), pp. 183–203.

Christopherson, S. (2003) The limits to 'New Regionalism'– (Re)Learning from the media industries, *Geoforum* 34(4), pp. 413–415.

Cornford, J. and Robins, K. (1991) Spatial implications of the reorganization of the British television industry, *Regional Studies* 25(6), pp. 555–562.

—— (1992) Development strategies in the audiovisual industries – the case of North-East England, *Regional Studies* 26(5), pp. 421–435.

Culkin, N., Morawetz, N. and Randle, K. (2005) *Facing the digital future: digital technology and the Film Industry* (2nd edition). Film Industry Research Group, University of Hertfordshire Business School, Harlow.

Darlow, M. (2004) *Independents struggle*. London: Quartet.

DCMS (1999) Creative industries: UK television export inquiry. The report of the creative industries task force inquiry into television exports. Department for Culture, Media and Sport, London.

—— (2006) Revised cultural test for British film. http://www.culture.gov.uk.

Deakin, S. and Pratten, S. (2000) Quasi markets, transaction costs and trust: the uncertain effects of market reforms in British television production, *Television & New Media* 1, pp. 321–354.

Dyja, E. (ed.) (2005) *BFI film handbook*. London: British Film Institute.

Epstein, E. J. (2005) *The big picture: the new logic of money and power in Hollywood*. New York: Random House.

GB, S. O. (2003) Communications Act 2003 Elizabeth II. Chapter 21, Stationery Office.

Haddon, L. (1992) Explaining ICT consumption: the case of the home computer, in Silverstone, R. and Hirsch, E. (eds) *Consuming Technologies: Media and Information in Domestic Spaces*, pp. 87–92. London: Routledge.

Hicks, J. and Allen, G. (1999) A century of change: trends in UK statistics since 1900. House of Commons, Social and General Statistics Section, London.

Hodgson, G. M. (1993) *Economics and institutions : a manifesto for a modern institutional economics*. Cambridge: Polity Press.

ICTIS (2006) Trends in the communications sector relevant to the scope and nature of ICTIS regulation. London: ICTIS.

Jeffcutt, P. and Pratt, A. C. (2002) Managing creativity in the cultural industries, *Creativity and Innovation Management* 11, pp. 225–233.

Jorgensen, D. and Stiroh, K. (2000) Raising the speed limit: US economic growth in the information age, *Brookings Papers on Economic Activity* 31(1), pp. 125–211.

Katz, S. M. (2006) The global success of production tax incentives and the migration of feature film production from the US to the world, in Rosenthal, M. A. (ed.) *Year 2005 Production Report*. The Centre for Entertainment Industry Data and Research (CEIDR), Encino, CA.

Kemp, S. (2007) Mill turns on management buyout, The Hollywood Reporter.

Kempton, M. (2007) An incomplete history of London's television studios. http://www.tv-studiohistory.co.uk.

Kim, J. (2003) The funding and distribution structure of the British film industry in the 1990s: localization and commercialization of British cinema towards a global audience, *Media, Culture & Society* 25(3), pp. 405–423.

Lambert, R. (2002) Independent Review of BBC News 24. DCMS.

Le Breton, J. -M. (2000) The film industry in Britain and France–strategies for success, Seminar of the Franco-British Council. Franco-British Council.

MacKenzie, D. A. and Wajcman, J. (1999) *The social shaping of technology*. Buckingham, England; Philadelphia: Open University Press.

McGown, A. D. (ed.) (2005) BFI *television handbook*. BFI.

Nachum, L. and Keeble, D. (2003) Neo-Marshallian clusters and global networks – the linkages of media firms in Central London, *Long Range Planning* 36(5), pp. 459–480.

Ofcom (2005) Memorandum of Understanding. Office of Communications, London.

—— (2006) Review of the television production sector. Consultation document. Office of Communications.

Oliner, S. and Sichel, D. (2000) The resurgence of growth in the late 1990s: is information technology the story?, *Journal of Economic Perspectives* 14(4), pp. 13–22.

Pact (2002) Response to consultation on media ownership, London.

—— (2003) Pact submission to the review of the television without frontiers directive, London.

Porter, M. E. (1998) *The competitive advantage of nations*. London: Collier Macmillan.

Pratt, A. C. (1996) The emerging shape and form of innovation networks and institutions., in Simmie, J. (ed.) *Innovation, networks and learning regions*, pp. 124–136. London: Jessica Kingsley.

—— (1997) Production values: from cultural industries to the governance of culture, *Environment and Planning A* 29(11), pp. 1911–1917.

—— (2005) Cultural industries and public policy: an oxymoron?, *International Journal of Cultural Policy* 11(1), pp. 31–44.

—— (2006a) Advertising and creativity, a governance approach: a case study of creative agencies in London, *Environment and Planning A* 38(10), pp. 1883–1899.

—— (2006b) 'Imagination can be a damned curse in this country' : material geographies of filmmaking and the rural, in Fish, R. (ed.) *Cinematic countrysides*. Manchester: Manchester University Press.

—— (2008) Creativity, innovation and urbanisation, in Short, J. R., Hubbard, P. and Hall, T. (eds.) *The SAGE Companion to the City*. London: Sage.

Pratten, S. and Deakin, S. (2000) Competitiveness policy and economic organisation: the case of the British Film Industry, *Screen* 41(2), pp. 217–237.

Simmie, J. M. (1997) *Innovation, networks and learning regions?* London: Jessica Kingsley and the Regional Studies Association.

—— (2004) Innovation and clustering in the globalised international economy, *Urban Studies* 41(5–6), pp. 1095–1112.

Sohonet (2007) Company website, http://www.sohonet.com. Sohonet.

UKFC (2006) Statistical Yearbook 2005/06. UK Film Council, London.

Wikipedia (2007) Sky Television plc. http://en.wikipedia.org/wiki/sky_Television_plc (accessed October 28, 2008).

Williams, R. (1990) *Television, technology and social form*. London: Routledge.

Woolgar, S. (1991) Configuring the user: the case of usability trials, in Law, J. (ed.) *A sociology of monsters: essays on power, technology and domination*, pp. 57–102. London: Routledge.

Part 5

New Media

5a Cultural production in the transnational city

A study of new media in Vancouver

Tom Hutton

Introduction: new media in context

New media has been widely acknowledged as a key industrial aggregate within advanced urban-regional economies. The origins of new media can be traced to experimentation in modern (and postmodern) arts and media production in the 1980s. New media was subsequently recast as a defining sector of the technology-intensive New Economy over the 1990s (Bauman 1997), and, following the tech-crash of 2000, has been reconstituted as a key industry group of the cultural economy of the city (Christopherson and Jaaresveld 2005). Other classifications position new media as an essential feature of the 'information economy' or the 'knowledge-based economy', acknowledging the critical roles of applied design and information as production inputs, and the application of new systems of transmission for images and information in a digital age.

This elusive industrial positioning of new media poses definitional problems, both for research and policy purposes. The dot.com crash of 2000 burst the New Economy bubble (although this euphoria has seemingly been transferred to the 'creative economy', itself a vigorously contested concept; see for example Peck 2005), forcing a more penetrating approach to the 'real' or tangible structures of production in the advanced economy – firms, labour, production networks, industrial districts, and markets, i.e. the normal stock-in-trade of industrial investigation.

This task has been hampered by the shifting boundaries of function, evolving technical divisions of labour, and emergent product sectors associated with new media. As Crosbie has noted, too, there is also a tendency to confuse 'media' and 'the medium': personal computers, the Internet and magazines are vehicles situated within a medium – not 'media' themselves (as cited in Pratt 2005). One fruitful approach has been to take a more incisive look at the composition of industries and labour task specializations in new media and other New Economy activities, exemplified by the work of Andy Pratt, Anne Markusen and others. Britton, Smith and Tremblay acknowledge that the emergence of new media can be traced to computer graphics and specialized services associated with film production, advertising and television; further,

> [w]hile much of this activity normally is viewed as part of the entertainment sector, over the last decade much of its expanded product range has taken the

> form of producer services enabling businesses in all sectors to use the Internet for a variety of commercial purposes.
>
> (Britton *et al.* 2005: 1)

This working definition has its uses but for analytical purposes the new media sector has proven to be a slippery concept. New media is in some respects the successor to the earlier construct of multimedia, a term deployed during the apogee of the information- and technology-driven New Economy over the last years of the twentieth century, a sector described by Pratt as an industry constantly 'in the making' (Pratt 2000). The relentless search for new software and for new synergies between technology and creative practices tends to shift the boundaries of new media practices, product sectors and occupational skill sets, stretching the capacity of scholars to position new media activity within conventional or discrete industry categories. The literature on new media is replete with discursive treatments of 'moments' in the evolution of new media, emphasizing the value of interviews, anecdotes and storylines as means of explication. These contributions generate insights into the commingling of the social and economic worlds which characterize new media industries and occupations, as well as the distinctive practices of new media work which tend to feature extensive subcontracting, intense competition, and irregular hours (see Gill, this volume).

Situating new media development in 'space' and 'place'

Within the burgeoning literature on new media as a process of industrial innovation we can identify as a distinctive genre case studies of specific cities and sites. These treatments offer a means of investigating the experience of new media as a place-situated process of industrial innovation, the significance of relational geographies in specialized production industries, and the influence of local conditions in shaping new industry formation. There are salient differences in the experiences of new industry development, not only between cities, but also among particular sites within the metropolis (Hutton 2004a). Prominent examples of research within this genre include Andy Pratt's study of multimedia and new media in San Francisco (Pratt 2000), Michael Indergaard's investigation of 'Silicon Alley' in New York (Indergaard 2004), and K. C. Ho's profile of multimedia film production in the 'unruly spaces' of Singapore's Little India (Ho forthcoming). New media development, as for other cultural industries, is manifestly about 'place' as well as 'space'.

In this paper I propose to contribute to this genre of case studies by developing a profile of new media industries in Vancouver, framed within a context of recurrent restructuring in the metropolitan core. Vancouver has served as an exemplary site for studies of contemporary urbanism (see for example Ley 1996; Olds 2001), as well as for industrial innovation and restructuring (Barnes *et al.* 1992; Coe 2000; Hutton 2006). To an extent experiences of restructuring in Vancouver follow the familiar patterns of postindustrialism, tertiarization and the ascendancy of a hegemonic new middle class, replicating on a smaller scale the patterns of redefining socioeconomic change in London (Hamnett 2003) and Singapore (Ho 2005). But in other respects the Vancouver story is quite distinctive, shaped by local conditions for new industry formation in Vancouver's metropolitan core. These include the effects of a post-staples development trajectory and deepening transnationalism across Vancouver's economy and society; the distinctive spatiality and built form of the metropolitan core; the extraordinary 'social density' of the inner city shaped by local policies for land use and housing; and new institutional arrangements which influence the configuration of cultural production.

My purpose in this essay is to develop an incisive account of new media development in Vancouver, informed both by structural and more locally-contingent features acknowledged above. The specific objectives are first, to depict the evolving spatiality of new media activity within the metropolitan core, demonstrating in a particularly vivid way Scott's dictum concerning the ongoing internal specialization of the metropolitan space-economy; second, to present a survey of the penetration of new media across a representative sampling of creative economy industries; and, third, to offer insights into the role of new media spaces in the re-establishment of the inner city as a primary zone of industrial experimentation and innovation in the advanced urban economy. Data sources for this exercise include (1) a program of field surveys and interview panels with new media firms in Vancouver, undertaken by the author and graduate student RAs over the period 2003–2005;[1] (2) a continuing program of empirical research conducted by City of Vancouver planning staff, as part of the Metropolitan Core Jobs, Economy and Land Use project;[2] (3) preliminary findings from research conducted by Trevor Barnes and I on new industries and innovation in the city-region, part of a national project directed by Meric Gertler and David Wolfe at the University of Toronto;[3] (4) insights generated from a national survey of new media industries, published by Britton *et al.* (2005);[4] and (5) thesis work undertaken by students at the University of British Columbia.[5]

Organization of the chapter

Following this introduction a concise outline of developmental conditions for new media development in Vancouver will be presented, as a means of illustrating the saliency of local contingency in the mediation of global economic processes. Next, the chapter offers a sketch of the geography of cultural production in Vancouver's core, including three linked but imperfectly articulated ensembles of new media production (Sacco 2006): (1) the East End Artists' District, (2) 'core' new media firms and proximate production networks, and (3) advertising and architecture. Each of these industries demonstrates, in different ways, the incorporation of new media technologies and practices across the key sectors of the creative economy. Over the past decade and a half concentrations of firms within each of these industry sectors have established (or in some cases relocated) within Vancouver's inner city, contributing to the formation of new production districts in the core, and to the inner city's re-emergence as critical zone of industrial experimentation and innovation. These place-based production ensembles appear robust for the moment. But tensions between the attraction of the core for new media and other creative industries, and the force of social reconstruction as represented by rampant condominium development and social class reformation, are acknowledged as destabilizing tendencies, following in some important respects the experience of London. A concluding section seeks to draw both specific observations about the Vancouver experience and its potentially broader applications and implications, in light of the 'precarious reindustrialization' syndrome characteristic of the inner city economy.

Development conditions for Vancouver's New Economy

The broad pathway of Vancouver's economic development follows the familiar lines of urban restructuring over the last 25 years, including a marked postindustrial trajectory, comprising (first) the contraction of traditional manufacturing and ancillary industries, and (second) a corresponding growth of services, notably intermediate service industries and specialized labour. Further, Fordist industries and labour in all sectors have borne the brunt of restructuring and decline, while a diverse array of post-Fordist industries and employment, including high-value manufacturing as well as advanced services, has been in the ascendant since the 1970s. The defining spatial imprints of these processes, as elsewhere, include the formation of a high-rise corporate office complex within the Central Business District (CBD) (Ley and Hutton 1987), coupled with industrial disinvestment and decline in the CBD fringe and inner city, and waves of gentrification which have transformed the social morphologies of inner city neighbourhoods (Ley 1996). In socioeconomic terms the growth of advanced service industries and employment is expressed in a dominant professionalization tendency within the workforce, although the (somewhat less rapid) expansion of low-level service workers suggests a parallel polarization experience (Table 5a.1).

While the postindustrial economy and social morphology shape the basic framework of Vancouver's metropolitan core, new processes (or adaptations of established ones) have shaped a phase of urban development which marks a break with the past (Hutton 2004b). In Vancouver, as in many other cities, this most recent stage of the city's development has included the reassertion of production industries and labour in the inner city, including a sequence of mostly small firms

Table 5a.1 Vancouver workforce employed as professionals and low-level service workers, 1971 and 2001

	1971	*2001*	*Change*
Professionals			
As % of workforce	17	30	+13
Number of workers	81,190	320,695	239,505
Low-level service workers			
As % of workforce	13.1	14.5	+1.4
Number of workers	57,845	156,190	98,345

Source: Table constructed by Markus Moos, UBC Department of Geography, from Statistics Canada census data (occupational categories)

engaged in the production of 'cultural goods', comprising a mix of products and services. Again, as in other cities, the specific mix of industries within the reconstructed production spaces of the core have evolved according to abbreviated restructuring cycles since the late 1980s, including, initially, artists and crafts production, 'outlier' business services (such as lawyers, accountants, and management consultants), the 'New Economy' of the late 1990s with its proliferation of dot.coms, and the recent emergence of an apparently more durable 'recombinant economy' of creative industries, institutions, and labour, characterized by dense linkages with proximate consumption amenities and housing.

Local contingency and new media production in Vancouver

The broad strokes of Vancouver's new inner city economy outlined in the previous section suggest a familiar profile of inner city industries, location, and relational geographies of production, commonly found in cities which figure among Richard Florida's 'core creative' places – Vancouver is widely acknowledged as one of the winners in the cultural economy league tables, at least for now (Gertler 2006). That said, local conditions have the power to influence (and at times decisively transform) pervasive global processes, and in the Vancouver case we can readily identify local contingencies which have shaped the industries and production sites of the inner city. First, Vancouver's restructuring trajectory has been influenced by 'post-staples', as well as postindustrial, forces. Vancouver's inner city industrial zones were dominated for most of the twentieth century by resource processing and manufacturing, as well as the transportation and distributional roles associated with the western terminus of the national rail system and the functions of Canada's largest port. While the core processing industries in particular have long gone, the associated warehousing and distributional activities produced a distinctive built form within Vancouver's inner city which has increasingly been recycled over the past decade and a half for new media and other creative industries, as well as for housing.

Second, Vancouver's central city is increasingly 'post-corporate', as the rounds of globalization and reconcentration of control since the 1980s have effectively stripped the city of most of its head office functions, as well as much of the intermediary financial and support services encompassed within the CBD. This process vitiated the city's corporate 'throw-weight' and international projection, but also freed up a substantial volume of office space for other uses. These activities include new media and other creative industries which have recolonized the vacant office space of the downtown, notably on the CBD fringe and in the northern crescent of the CBD proper. At the same time, the multiple connections (control, finance, services, and production) between Vancouver and an expanding staple hinterland, which underpinned the growth of the CBD office complex, have been largely supplanted by other economic and social linkage systems. These are varied, and include ties of kinship, trade and capital between Vancouver and Asia-Pacific societies and markets (Asia Pacific Foundation of Canada 2007); but these also incorporate a recent history of subcontracting relations between Los Angeles film and video corporations and new media firms in Vancouver. As observed in the histories of other Vancouver-region companies and head offices, notably in resource sectors and in advanced-technology industries, these new media firms tend to be vulnerable to foreign takeover once a certain scale threshold is reached, a syndrome characteristic of 'periphery' regional economies subject to the controlling power and capital resources of the corporations domiciled within the global 'core', situated in cities such as Los Angeles.

Third, the space-economy of the central area has been reconfigured by local policy initiatives, notably the urban structure and land use tenets of the *Central Area Plan*, approved by City Council in 1991. The underlying policy values and far-reaching outcomes of this strategic policy plan have been evaluated in detail elsewhere (see Hutton 2004b), but the most salient economic implications concerned the consolidation of the CBD's corporate complex within a distinctly smaller territory, while privileging high-density residential communities in the urban core beyond this tightly bounded CBD. At the same time, the *Central Area Plan* avoided an overly-prescriptive approach to land use in many of the older industrial, mixed-use and heritage districts in the inner city, instead allowing the market to explore possibilities of industrial experimentation and innovation, facilitating the emergence of new ensembles of creative industries beyond the consolidated CBD (Figure 5a.1). The *Central Area Plan* was followed by the release of City documents which underscored the need for special land use policies and building regulation adjustments for new media and other New Economy industries (City of Vancouver 1995), as well as a special-purpose land use and zoning (I-3 High

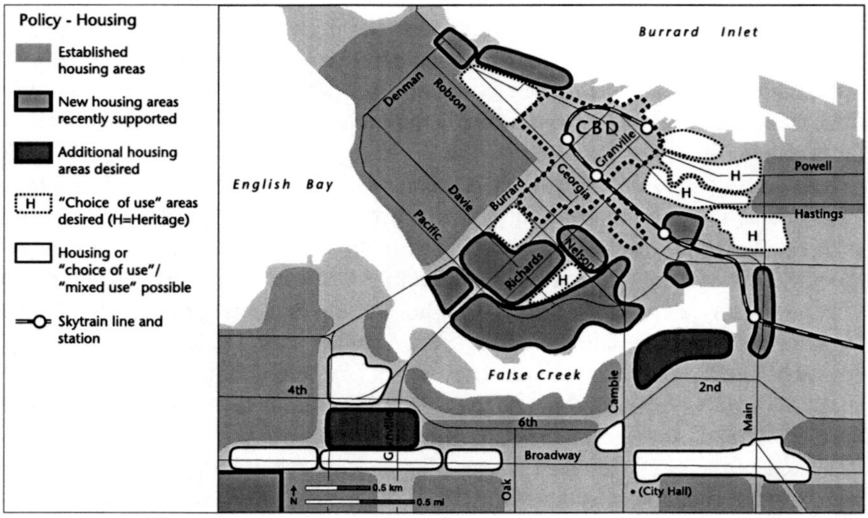

Figure 5a.1 Designation of new housing, mixed use and 'choice of use' districts for Vancouver's central area in the *Central Area Plan*

Source: (City of Vancouver 1991)

Technology) schedule for the False Creek Flats on the eastern margins of the inner city. The latter (City of Vancouver 1999) was introduced at the height of the tech-boom, and was designed to facilitate the development of a propulsive-scale New Economy site. The development vision of the False Creek Flats I-3 site as a New Economy platform was compromised by the dot.com crash of 2000 and its aftermath. But False Creek Flats is now apparently experiencing a more organic and diverse development as a precinct for biotech industries, higher education and the knowledge sector, and for cultural production, as well as for new media enterprises, including digital media and video game production.

Fourth, the development of new residential communities on the CBD fringe and inner city, taking the form mostly of point tower condominiums mounted on podiums, but also including live-work conversions and adaptive reuse, has facilitated the comprehensive social reconstruction of Vancouver's metropolitan core. This rapid expansion of the downtown residential population, with target thresholds reached far in advance of schedule, has generated mixed influences on new media and other creative and knowledge-intensive industries in the core. On the positive side, the greatly increased social density of the core has created a large proximate labour market for new media firms, as well as opportunities for social interaction widely acknowledged as key to industrial innovation and creativity in the knowledge economy. The new public spaces, consumption amenities and sites of spectacle in Vancouver's core, financed both by the City and by developers and other private sector firms, have also contributed to attractive conditions for amenity-seeking New Economy firms and workers, a fact cited by interviewees encompassed in field surveys conducted by the author in London, Singapore, San Francisco and Vancouver (Hutton 2008). At the same time, the rapid growth of an affluent residential population in the downtown, coupled with the wealth of amenities provided *in situ*, has generated an insistent revalorization of property on the CBD fringe and inner city, destabilizing firms and promoting accelerated succession processes, analogous to those documented within certain of London's City Fringe districts.

Finally, in addition to these distinctive market, social and policy influences, the structure of new media enterprise and production in Vancouver is shaped by the local 'cultural bases of production'. These constitute an ever-evolving mélange of attributes, but in the Vancouver case manifestly include the sites of artistic production within the East Side especially, articulated imperfectly (but in some cases effectively) within new media production systems and businesses. Then there is the recurrent relayering of cultural values, motifs and practice shaped by Vancouver's evolving *transnational* character, expressed most emphatically in the city's connections with the societies of the Asia-Pacific, which underpin Vancouver's status as a centre of inter-cultural production, exchange and transmission.

The space-economy of new media production in Vancouver

The spatial dimensions of new media industry development in Vancouver tend to follow the familiar template of clustering within central and inner city precincts and

Table 5a.2 Central Area concentration of new media for Canada's largest cities, 2004

	Firms (%)	*Employment (%)*
Vancouver	46	54
Toronto	43	58
Montreal	51	71

Source: Britton *et al.* 2005

'cultural quarters', typically highly textured postindustrial landscapes in old manufacturing and warehouse districts. There is a substantial literature which elucidates the attractions of the inner city as a terrain of new industry formation (Short *et al.* 1993; Hutton 2000; Pratt 2000; Costa 2004), comprising a unique mix of environmental, social, cultural and institutional attributes. These together constitute the 'relational geographies' of specialized production which support in many ways innovation processes for creative, contact-intensive industries (Gertler 2003). Certain districts of the inner city generate what Marshall described as the 'atmosphere' of an industrial district, a precursor to the contemporary 'buzz' of innovation sites in the city.

What we find in the Vancouver case are clusters of creative industries concentrated within multiple sites of the metropolitan core, following a pattern observed in other large Canadian cities (Table 5a.2), each comprising a range of 'new' (and 'old') industries as well as an element of specialization, together with distinctive labour ensembles and production system relations. A number of important firms have been attracted to the inner suburbs because of space requirements or institutional affiliation, including, notably, film studios requiring larger buildings and sites (and lower land costs) than those commonly available in the metropolitan core, as well as new media firms associated with Simon Fraser University, the British Columbia Institute of Technology, and Discovery Park, all located in Burnaby, just to the east of the City of Vancouver. What follows is a description of three key industry aggregations comprising elements of Vancouver's new media sector within the City's metropolitan core: the East End artists cluster; computer services, 'core' new media and technical support services; and advertising and architecture.

(1) Clusters of artistic enterprise and new media production

Citing an extensive body of international research, Britton *et al.* observe that locational tendencies for new media indicate a preference 'for metropolitan centres, especially the central areas of those with significant artistic communities' (2005: 1). As in major centres of cultural production, such as London, New York and San Francisco, there are important interdependencies between artists and new media firms in Vancouver, as well as an element of tension, and at times pronounced dislocation tendencies. In London, artists have been displaced by the rent inflation ensuing from inflows of professional design firms and new media companies (as well as mainstream producer services) from areas such as Hoxton in

Shoreditch (Pratt in press). At the same time, the role of artists in new media production vividly illustrates the blurring of definitions, and the difficulty of establishing discrete industrial categories. Some artists work as freelancing subcontractors for new media companies; others are employed on the staff of larger concerns; notably within larger video game companies; while still others 'practice' as new media producers in their own right. There are also distinctions to be made between artists as practitioners of 'fine arts', as 'commercial artists', or as 'graphic artists' and 'graphic designers', the latter two groups tending to move freely within new media production systems in the city.

In Vancouver, artists are to some extent dispersed across the urban landscape, but are mainly clustered among particular districts, notably within the inner city and the City's East End. The East End artists' cluster (Figure 5a.2) can be positioned as a key element of the space-economy of cultural production in Vancouver, loosely articulated to other such sites and systems in the metropolitan core (Sacco 2006). Many of these artists occupy premises in old warehouse and other industrial buildings, residual features of Vancouver's resource processing, warehousing and distribution

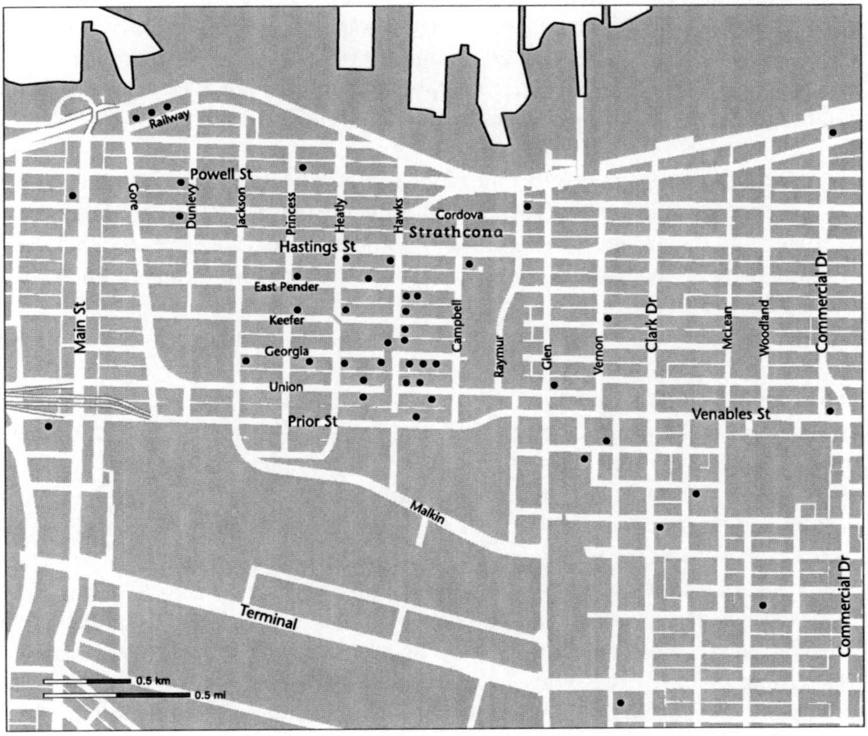

Figure 5a.2 Distribution of artists' studios and galleries in Strathcona and Grandview-Woodlands, Vancouver

Source: Sacco 2006

roles. Low rents thus comprise important attractions for many artists, while the proximity of the East End Artists Cluster to the edgy ambience and consumption amenities of Commercial Drive situated just to the east adds to the area's appeal.

The East End artists' district occupies an inner city terrain not yet subject to the full force of social upgrading and reconstruction, in contrast to the neighbourhoods proximate to the downtown proper, within which artists have found it increasingly difficult to maintain security of tenure. But as the comprehensive redevelopment of Vancouver's core proceeds further east, it seems likely that further pressures will be exerted on this East End cluster, following processes which have already been documented in East London (Pratt in press). The singular role of artists in the construction of aestheticized landscapes within the core confers no special privileges of tenure, as these examples vividly demonstrate.

The East End cluster comprises the most important concentration of artists within Vancouver's inner city, but many others are employed within 'core' multimedia firms, such as video game production, for which Vancouver is an important centre. Interviews with several of the major video game producers in Vancouver, notably Radical Entertainment and Electronic Arts (located on the western margins of the East End Artists District), confirmed that the key workers in these firms are artists and designers, rather than technology workers (or 'techies'). To elaborate, an interview with the VP of Radical Entertainment (located on the western margins of False Creek Flats), a major video game producer for Los Angeles publishers with about 250 employees, offered the following observation:

> Everyone seems to think that the video game business is about hiring the most advanced techies we can find. This is absolutely not true . . . we (and other companies in this business) are constantly on the lookout for talented artists and designers . . . I can train anyone to manage the technology side of things in a week, no problem.
>
> (Interview March 2004)

Thus for this enterprise (and for many firms within new media), art and design are the axial principles of development and leading aspects of competitive advantage within markets. Staff recruitment efforts tend to emphasize design and artistic *talent*, rather than more narrow technical skills. At the same time, high-level production and information technologies are critical to such functions as facilitating prototype development, accelerating image production, enhancing sales and marketing, and transmitting inputs, samples and finished products across space.

As a means of promoting synergies between the arts, design and technology, the Great Northern Way Campus (GNWC) has been established in the former industrial terrains of False Creek Flats, just to the west of the East End artists district, and to the south of Radical Entertainment. The GNWC comprises a consortium of the University of British Columbia, Simon Fraser University, the British Columbia Institute of Technology, and the Emily Carr Institute for Art, Design + Media, and has been established in part to promote a stronger articulation between artists and firms within the cultural production systems of Vancouver. To this end the GNWC will offer a Masters degree program in digital media commencing in 2007. (For details of the GNWC mission and program see: www.gnwc.ca)

(2) 'Core' new media: computer services, new media and design

Computer services and new media and design comprise core industries of Vancouver's new media sector. Since the late 1980s the development of these industries, together with complementary support industries, have emerged as important elements of specialized production systems within Vancouver's metropolitan core. Since the early 1990s several flagship new media enterprises and institutions have developed in Vancouver (Figure 5a.3), while a distinctive

Electronic Arts
Electronic Arts (EA), headquartered in Redwood, California, and established in 1982, is a leading interactive entertainment software company; its sites include downtown Vancouver, as well as an operation in the inner suburban municipality of Burnaby. EA develops, publishes and distributes interactive software worldwide for videogame systems, personal computers, and the Internet. EA posted sales of $3.1 billion in 2005.
Radical Entertainment
Radical Entertainment is one of North America's largest game developers, and operates from a 50,000 square foot facility in Vancouver's Main & Terminal area, on the eastern margins of False Creek Flats. Radical's specialties include real-time physics/animation hybrid simulation, next-gen console experience, and handheld wireless experience.
Blast Radius
Blast Radius (located in Yaletown) is a 'customer experience innovation' firm, established in 1996, and has over 350 employees in New York, San Francisco, Toronto, Vancouver and Amsterdam
Propaganda Games
Propaganda games is Buena Vista Games' new development studio in Vancouver, with a mandate to create innovative action/adventure games for the major video games consoles, focusing on developing original intellectual property
Mainframe Entertainment
Mainframe Entertainment, located in Vancouver, Burnaby and Los Angeles, is a Canadian computer animation company, producing children's computer animation TV series. Mainframe has over 300 full-time and contract employees
Great Northern Way Campus
The GNWC, located on False Creek Flats in Vancouver's inner city, is a consortium of the University of British Columbia, Simon Fraser University, the Emily Carr Institute of Art, Design + Media, and the British Columbia Institute of Technology, and offers (starting in 2007) a Masters program in Digital Media degree program

Source: New Media BC (2007)

Figure 5a.3 Examples of major new media firms and institutions in Vancouver space-economy of new media production has emerged within the reconstructed production spaces of the inner city.

Figure 5a.4 shows the location of firms grouped within each of these aggregates within Vancouver's Central Area, a terrain deployed for planning, land use and economic development purposes since 1988. (The current City Metropolitan Core Jobs, Economy and Land Use exercise takes in a somewhat larger territory, encompassing the East End Artists Cluster and a number of food and garment production

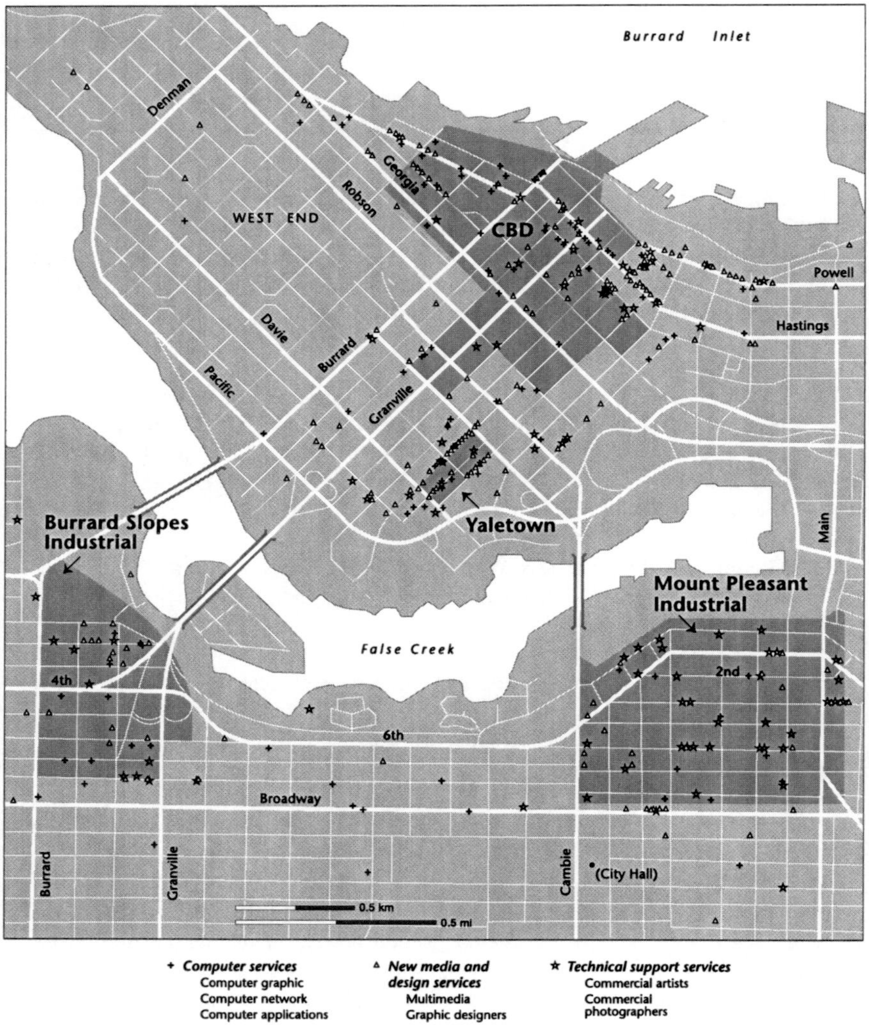

Figure 5a.4 Distribution of firms in computer services, new media and design services, and technical support services, Vancouver's central area

Source: author's survey, 2004

operations situated in the industrial zone between Hastings Street and the waterfront.) The largest cluster of computer services and new media is located in Yaletown, the epicentre site of Vancouver's New Economy, while other important concentrations are in Gastown and Victory Square on the Downtown Eastside, and in the Burrard Slopes Industrial District.

Yaletown functions as the most privileged space of cultural production in Vancouver's Central Area. Yaletown's brick warehouses and loading docks, each of which has been accorded official heritage designation by the City (1986), are acknowledged as high integrity features of the City's former resource processing warehouse and distribution built environment. The imprints of transformative episodes of the last twenty years are faithfully inscribed upon the heritage landscapes of Yaletown, including a small cohort of artists, a legacy of the district's 1980s revival from a prolonged period of industrial decline; a smattering of self-referenced 'dot.coms', reflecting its saliency during the tech-boom of the 1990s; and a larger ensemble of creative, technologically-intensive and knowledge-based firms representative of the 'New Economy' of the early twenty-first century inner city (Hutton 2008). Yaletown has been subject to processes of social upgrading as well as the 'industrial gentrification' experience described by Pratt in the Hoxton case (Pratt in press), driving a relentless filtering process favouring the most profitable, high-value new media producers, and squeezing lower-yield enterprises to the margins of the inner city and sometimes beyond. At the same time, Yaletown's cachet has attracted a rich mixture of high-end consumption amenities, which cater both to the area's enterprises and also to the 'loft-living' (Zukin 1989) residents of the area, as well as those of the nearby condominiums of the Downtown South and the Concord Pacific mega-project.

Victory Square and Gastown, on the western margins of the Downtown Eastside, present a grittier urban imagery than Yaletown, and share space on the CBD fringe with diverse social cohorts. These social groups include a sizeable contingent of the homeless, as well as sex-trade workers and drug dealers, reflecting the rough edges of urban life prevalent in this quarter of the city; but these also incorporate an expanding roster of professionals, managers and entrepreneurs, as the area is manifestly subject to insistent social upgrading. A panel of interviews with new media companies in 2004 supervised by the author disclosed that some of the creative workers ensconced within Victory Square and Gastown saw the mixed social space of the area as a positive environmental attribute, citing the distinctive edginess of street life and cultural references as complementary to their work. But other new media firms and workers found the somewhat conflictual spaces of the area as a nuisance, and expressed a hope that market success could eventually provide sufficient revenues to support relocation to Yaletown.

In Victory Square and Gastown we find a substantial element of Vancouver's film production and postproduction sector, as well as such crucial institutional supports as the Vancouver Film School (ranked as one of the world's top five post-secondary animation schools according to 3D World Magazine; Andrews 2007); technical programs of the British Columbia Institute of Technology; and an architecture studio of the University of British Columbia. The institutional platform for new media in the area will be substantially reinforced (as will the pressures of gentrification) by the comprehensive redevelopment of the former Woodwards Department store in the heart of the Victory Square-Gastown district. The Woodwards redevelopment project incorporates Simon Fraser University's Centre for the Contemporary Arts, as well as 700 hundred residential units. Postproduction firms in the area form part of what Coe has described as a 'neo-Marshallian' industrial district of film production in the Vancouver case, a branch plant industry with control and decision-making exercised largely in Los Angeles, but including a large, integrated sector of companies, labour, and production networks (Coe, 2001).

While the Yaletown and Victory Square/Gastown clusters occupy sites on the CBD fringe and inner city, Figure 5a.4 also shows a significant incursion of new media and computer graphics firms in the Central Business District proper, especially on the northern crescent closest to the port area. We can acknowledge here the influence of Vancouver's post-corporate trajectory, cited earlier as an influence on the reshaping of the core's economy, in which the relocation of corporate head offices and supportive business services has provided opportunity for creative industries, which might otherwise be located within the City's inner city clusters. A recent example is the location of a unit of Electronic Arts in the CBD.

Finally, Figure 5a.4 shows important distributions of technical support firms in Vancouver's Central Area, notably in Mount Pleasant and the Burrard Slopes. These technical services favour sites with lower rent costs than in the downtown peninsula proper, but which still enjoy easy access both to the creative industries and mainstream office firms of the CBD and CBD fringe. The panel of interviews conducted in 2003–2005, supplemented by recent survey work undertaken by the City's Central Area Division planning team, disclosed that these technical support firms comprise essential elements of the production networks underpinning Vancouver's creative economy, providing a traditional industrial district function, complemented by the increasing use of Internet and digital input sourcing. The elements of primary design firms and new media, together with the technical services located in mixed use areas on the margins of the core, suggest the integrative formation of a 'territorial innovation system', as described by Kevin Morgan (2004).

(3) New media in the producer services: advertising and architectural firms

Advertising and architecture are acknowledged as established creative industries, within which design and innovation are defining features of task specialization, product orientation, and competitive advantage at the level of the firm. Architecture has existed as a formal profession and practice since classical antiquity, while advertising has a later provenance, but was established as one of the mainstream business services in the early twentieth century. At the same time, traditional methods of production and marketing in both industries have been quite significantly modified by the introduction of computers, digital technologies and the Internet, legitimizing their inclusion within a broadly-defined new media sector. Research conducted in Singapore and London as well as Vancouver has disclosed that there is an appreciable blurring of industrial distinctions between advertising, corporate branding consultancies, and graphic designers specializing in business applications, as many firms in each sector present a self-defined 'creative design' identity.

Advertising and architecture have each represented important industries in Vancouver for a century. The emergence of advertising as a significant industry is associated with Vancouver's early service industry trajectory, and included major local firms with relatively long operating histories. Like other major industries in Vancouver, however, advertising has been subject to recurrent takeovers and mergers. These have included acquisitions of Vancouver firms by larger concerns in more highly-placed markets, as well as periodic consolidations and mergers of local advertising firms, undertaken with a view to achieving scale economies, new creative synergies, and expanded specialization portfolios. Recently, advertising has taken on a multimedia hue, as seen in the pervasive expansion of communication channels beyond the traditional print medium to include the Internet and digital technologies, and the diversification of telecommunications corporations (such as Telus) from telephone service to advertising and promotions. New media technologies are deployed by producer services firms as a means of expediting access to new markets and clients.

Architectural practice is not immune from the reconcentration of corporate power and market penetration by mega-scale firms characteristic of the global economy. But there is a remarkable history of robustness in Vancouver's architectural industry, although there have been to be sure some bleak years of greatly diminished sales and corporate retrenchment during Vancouver's periodic downturns. The city's relative geographical isolation stimulated the growth of a distinctive architectural idiom in the early years of the twentieth century, including creative inspiration derived from Vancouver's wilderness and environmental setting, followed by a local interpretation of modernism and the international style over the 1930s, 1940s and 1950s. The rapid physical growth of the city and region since the 1960s has also generated a sustained high demand for architectural services, and a corresponding rapid growth of firms over the past several decades. Relative to other industries, there has been relatively little penetration of the local market by foreign architectural firms, due in part to the somewhat cozy interweaving of actors and agencies in the urban development process, involving developers, architects, planning consultants, the property sector, and city planners.

The spectacular growth of mega-projects as well as smaller, unconsolidated development sites within Vancouver's urban core and in suburban locations has produced a local design vernacular of international significance (Punter 2003). Indeed, the high visibility and international acclaim for the 'Vancouver achievement' in architecture and urban design has allowed numerous Vancouver firms to successfully explore opportunities in the U.S., China, the Middle East, and elsewhere. In this industry the transnational orientation of the city's development should be acknowledged as a developmental influence, not only in the fusion of diverse design cultures in local architectural practice, but also in the complex connections of kinship and businesses which provide a conduit for leading Vancouver architects seeking to compete in distant foreign markets. Prominent

Vancouver-based Chinese-Canadian architects such as Bing Thom, James Cheng and Stanley Kwok produce work which incorporates design values intersecting the cultural worlds of East Asia and the Pacific North-West, reflecting the synergies of personal experience and professional practice which stimulate design innovation in the transnational city.

In seeking to position advertising and architecture as significant features of Vancouver's new media sector, we can identify important locational tendencies which lend support to our inclusion of these industries within the creative space-economy of the city. Apart from the introduction of digital technologies which represent the internal positioning of advertising and architecture as new media activities defined in terms of production processes and labour task specializations, the record of spatial shifts since the 1980s forcefully inserts these creative industries into the aestheticized landscapes of cultural production (Ley 2003).

During the growth of Vancouver's downtown corporate complex over the 1970s and 1980s, principally in response to the stimulus of demand for the city's corporate control, financial and business services generated by an expanding resource hinterland in British Columbia (Ley and Hutton 1987), advertising firms and architectural practices were securely embedded within the central office district. Each was integral to the complex patterns of input-output linkages characteristic of the 1970s and 1980s era office economy, even though a number of firms in each industry at times deviated somewhat from the segmented hierarchies of office work, presenting instead a more informal and 'flatter' organizational structure which anticipated the more fluid work styles of the New Economy. In part this central locational tendency was shaped by agglomeration dynamics. But the primacy of the CBD was also reinforced by the lack of alternative sites, as the inner city was still firmly entrenched within a disinvestment and decline trajectory, while more peripheral office centres in the region lacked the density of firms, imagery and amenities crucial to a viable commercial complex. That said, a few 'outlier' firms in the architecture, advertising and legal industries located themselves within the grittier inner city, in response to rent gradients, and, for some, lifestyle reasons.

But since the initial location of pioneering firms as precursors to the recent sequence of innovation, there has been since the 1990s a significant spatial shift in the clustering of advertising and architectural firms within the inner city external to the CBD. Figure 5a.4 shows distributions of architects and advertising firms in Vancouver's metropolitan core (2004). The patterns disclose a number of insights pertaining to the role of new media and creative industries in the changing space-economy of Vancouver's metropolitan core. First, the original tight clustering of firms within the confines of the CBD evident in earlier studies (Ley 1996) has been supplanted by multiple ensembles situated within the CBD fringe and inner city. These include, notably, a dense agglomeration of firms in Yaletown, as well as smaller but significant concentrations in the Burrard Slopes, Victory Square-Gastown, and the northern crescent of the CBD, as well as a linear strip along West Georgia Street. Second, the co-presence of advertising and architectural firms with computer graphics and 'core' new media firms (Figure 5a.5) in Yaletown underscores the epicentre status of this heritage district within the cultural

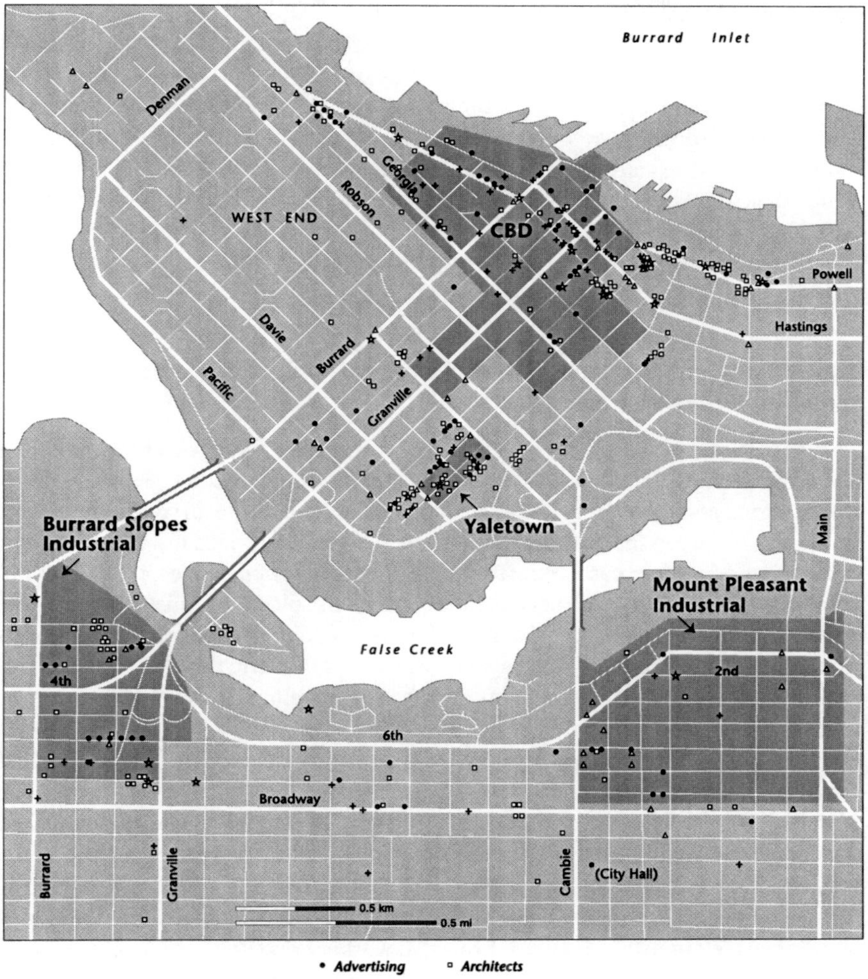

Figure 5a.5 Distribution of architects and advertising firms, Vancouver's central area

Source: author's survey, 2004

space-economy of Vancouver. Yaletown, with its dense concentrations of leading edge firms, upscale consumption amenities, and loft conversions and studios, represents one of the exemplary cultural quarters within international typologies of creative cities and sites, together with Hoxton, Soho and Clerkenwell in London, Lower Manhattan, Temple Bar in Dublin, Liberty Village in Toronto, and South Park in San Francisco's SOMA.

Third, the uniquely dense clustering of new media and other creative firms in Yaletown must be viewed principally as a product of preference rather than a forced locational choice reflecting the traditionally steep rent gradient between CBD and inner city. In fact, the post-corporate nature of the CBD, stripped of much of its corporate control through the workings of globalization, coupled with the sustained high demand for space within Yaletown as expressed by production firms, consumer services and residents, have combined to support Yaletown's ascendancy to the peak of the downtown's property market values. The expansion of new media industries and firms has helped shape a new landscape of production in the core in which the CBD is simply one of the available options for creative and knowledge-based industries and firms, rather than the uniquely privileged space of élite industries it represented at the apogee of the postindustrial era in the late twentieth century.

New media and the twenty-first-century city: observations from the Vancouver case

This case study of new media development in Vancouver suggests both pervasive and more distinctive features, following the mediating interactions between global restructuring and innovation processes, and the influence of local conditions. As K. C. Ho has observed in his forthcoming article, local conditions have the power to reshape, and in some cases transform, the globalizing tendencies of the cultural economy, underscoring the persistent resonance of 'place'. In this chapter I have attempted to depict a profile of new media development in Vancouver in conventional spatial terms, but also to suggest possibilities for enriching this genre of economic geography, first, by situating new media development within the broader trajectories of economic change in the metropolis, including the emergent space-economy of the core; second, by acknowledging local policy as an important local contingency in new media development, as represented in urban structure, land use planning and heritage programs, as well as in special-purpose agencies established to support new media and the cultural economy; and, third, to juxtapose the industrialization processes of the new economy of the inner city within a larger conceptual framework that acknowledges the (sometimes complementary, at other times conflictual) relationships between firms and workers, and those agencies (property firms, new categories of gentrifiers, and City council and planners) promoting the social reconstruction of the metropolitan core. Implicitly at least I am making an argument for an economic-geography approach which incorporates an urban studies inflection as a means of promoting a richer appreciation of the complex dynamics of innovation and restructuring in the metropolis.

A number of surveys and studies have established Vancouver as an important centre of new media activity, with high location quotients for cultural industries and creative industries in the national context (Vinodrai 2006). There is a substantial representation of new media firms in Vancouver's metropolitan core, including computer graphics and imaging, digital communications, and Internet services and web-design, including business and educational, as well as entertainment, applications. As in other cities, too, there is increasingly a more fully realized articulation between arts, design, new media technologies and business entrepreneurship evidenced in the generative process of new industry forms, disclosed in our sketches of emergent cultural production clusters in the inner city. The new Great Northern Way Campus has the potential to further promote these linkages and synergies through its digital arts and media program, exemplifying the institutional role in the development of the cultural economy, and in innovation processes among creative industries.

The Yaletown cluster, which has expanded beyond its original two-by-four block heritage site to encompass a larger terrain within the Downtown South, vividly illustrates the reterritorialization of economic and social space in the metropolis, with new media industries, generously defined, playing a central role in this transformative process. The expansion of professional, technical and scientific workers beyond the traditional bastion of the CBD to include the new industrial spaces of the inner city (Figure 5a.6) vividly demonstrates one salient aspect of this process in the Vancouver case. Vancouver encompasses a substantial base of new media, numbering approximately 600 firms in 2004, including a number of key specializations, principally video game production and digital media applications in education. Other distinguishing features include the fusion of cultures represented in an exemplary transnational city, particularly between Asian and western cultural symbols and practices. Vancouver's emergence as a site of creative industry formation includes an incipient role as a centre of inter-cultural fusion, production and dissemination, observed in architectural practice and graphic design, among other fields, and constituting a distinctive form of innovation in the cultural economy of the inner city.

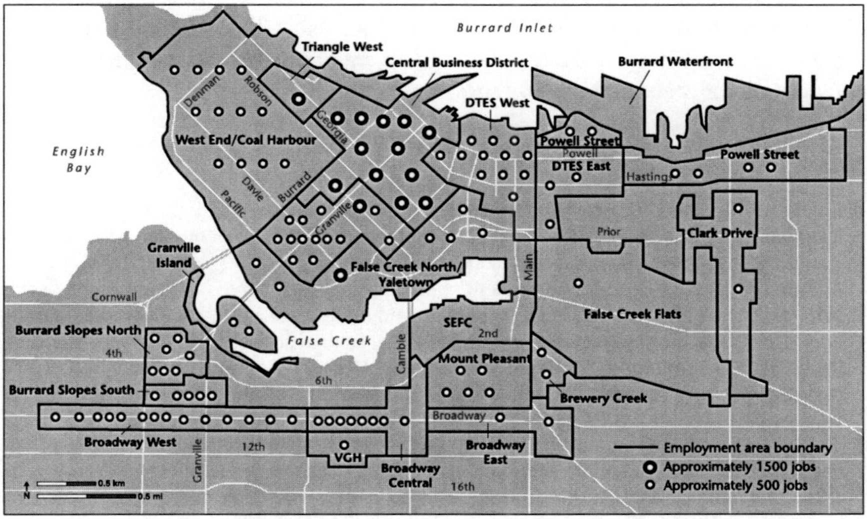

Figure 5a.6 Concentrations of workers in professional, scientific and technical occupations in Vancouver's metropolitan core

Source: City of Vancouver (2007) mapping of Census Canada data

That said, other contingencies of the Vancouver case, including a relatively weak corporate sector and lack of truly propulsive corporations, render new media firms vulnerable to acquisitions and takeovers, a syndrome observed in earlier phases of the city's development, notably in forest products and other staples sectors, as well as in telecommunications and biotechnology. Vancouver's peripheral location tends to create a branch-plant configuration of industry in terms of control functions, as seen in film and video production and postproduction, although this subordinate corporate status doesn't necessarily hinder the creativity of new media companies and the cultural labour force, nor constrain the dynamics of innovation in the new economy of the core.

A second local contingency concerns the momentum of the core's social reconstruction and the velocity of new residential development, including adaptive reuse (loft conversions, live-work and work-live studios) as well as the forest of high-rise condominiums which represent the 'new urban ecology' of Vancouver as a transnational metropolis. Two decades ago the defining planning problem was the rampant growth of offices in the CBD, and lack of downtown housing capacity. In the early years of the twenty-first century, this relationship has been reversed, with condominium development outstripping office development by orders of magnitude. The creation of new production spaces and employment zones in Yaletown and elsewhere in the core has offset this imbalance to an extent. But the City Planning Department is now conducting a strategic policy review in its 'Metropolitan Core Area Jobs, Economy and Land Use' exercise, a process designed to estimate the land use requirements of the city's economy, including those of new media and other creative, knowledge-based industries. The new policy discourse underscores the civic aspirations associated with this cultural trajectory of industrial innovation and development, as well as demonstrating the constant need to refine land use policies in an era of volatile industrialization and competition for space in the 'new inner city'.

Notes

1 I acknowledge here a research grant from the Social Sciences and Research Council of Canada, Grant No. 503 – 2001 – 0036, awarded under SSHRC's 'Initiative on the New Economy' program, which supported this field research. The field work included surveys of industry distributions and subsequent mapping; semi-structured interviews with firms, principally in Yaletown and Victory Square; and photography. I would like to acknowledge the invaluable assistance of my project RAs, Tanis Knowles and April Lawrence, of the School of Community & Regional Planning (Masters program); and also the expert cartographic advice and artwork of Eric Leinberger, of the UBC Department of Geography.

2 This project, the first comprehensive review of policies for Vancouver's metropolitan core since the approval of the seminal Central Area Plan was approved in 1991, has generated a wealth of data on the central area's economy, industries and employment. For access to these files, see: http://www.city.vancouver.bc.ca/commsvcs/planning/core-jobs/index.htm

3 See www.utoronto.ca/isrn/city-region_initiative

4 This study was undertaken by members of the University of Toronto-based ISRN project (see note 3 for web-site), conducted within an earlier program of work on clusters and

industrial innovation; the current work focuses on innovation and creativity within city-regions as the principal spatial unit of analysis.

5 I acknowledge insights generated (and generously shared) by graduate students participating within an extended series of Masters-level thesis studies on creative industries in Vancouver I have supervised at the School of Community and Regional Planning at the University of British Columbia, notably those prepared by Shauna Brail on Yaletown and Victory Square (1994); Naomi Pope on Yaletown and Belltown (in Seattle) (2002); François Dionne on the Cité Multimedia in Montreal (2002); Kevin Eng on the False Creek Flats High-Tech Zone (2003); Jennifer Johnston on the role of planning in developing the amenity base of Vancouver's Central Area (2003); and Helen Cain's study of institutional innovation in the cultural economy (2005).

References

Andrews, M. (2007) 'VFS named one of world's top five animation schools', *The Vancouver Sun.* Tuesday 20 November.

Asia Pacific Foundation of Canada (2007) *Leading the Way: Canadian Business Strategies in Asia.* Vancouver: APF.

Barnes, T., Edgington, D., Denike, K. and McGee, T. G. (1992) 'Vancouver, the Province, and the Pacific Rim', chapter 6 in: G. Wynn and T. Oke, *Vancouver and its Region.* Vancouver: UBC Press.

Bauman, C. (1997) *Multimedia in San Francisco.* San Francisco: San Francisco Planning Department (August).

Britton, J.N.H. (with R. Smith and D.-G. Tremblay) (2005) *Contrasts in clustering: the example of Canadian new media,* working paper, Toronto: Department of Geography, University of Toronto.

Christopherson, S. and van Jaarsveld, D. (2005) 'New media after the dot.com bust', *International Journal of Cultural Policy* 11: 77–93.

City of Vancouver (1991) *Central Area Plan.* City Planning Department, Central Area Division.

—— (1995) *Industry Land Policy Report.* Overall Planning Division.

—— (1999) *Council Report: False Creek Flats I-3 Zone.* City Planning Department and City Manager's Office, General Manager of Community Services.

—— (2006) *Metropolitan Core Area Jobs, Economy and Land Use Planning Process: Terms of Reference.* City Planning Department, Central Area Division.

Coe, N. M. (2000). 'On location: American capital and the local labour market in the Vancouver film industry', *International Journal of Urban and Regional Research,* 24(1): 79–94.

—— (2001) 'A hybrid agglomeration? The development of a satellite-Marshallian industrial district in Vancouver's film industry', *Urban Studies* 38: 1753–1775.

Costa, P. (2004) 'Milieu effects and sustainable development in a cultural quarter: the Bairo Alto-Chiada area in Lisbon', in: R. Camagni, D. Maillat and A. Matteaccioli (eds), *Resources Naturelles et Culturelles, Milieux et Developpement Local.* Neuchatel: EDES.

Gertler, M. S. (2003). 'Tacit knowledge and the economic geography of context, or: the undefinable tacitness of being (there)', *Journal of Economic Geography,* 3(1): 75–99.

—— (2006) Introduction to Meeting of 'Social Dynamics of Innovation and Creativity in City-Regions' Research Team: Kingbridge, Ontario

Hamnett, C. (2003) *Unequal City: London in the Global Arena.* London: Routledge.

Ho, K.C. (2005) 'Service industries and occupational change: implications for identity, citizenship and politics', chapter 5 in: P. W. Daniels, K.C. Ho and T. A. Hutton, *Service*

Industries and Asia-Pacific Cities: New Development Trajectories. London and New York: Routledge.

—— (forthcoming) 'The neighbourhood in the creative economy', special theme issue of *Urban Studies.*

Hutton, T. A. (2000). 'Reconstructed production landscapes in the postmodern city: applied design and creative services in the metropolitan core', *Urban Geography,* 21(4): 285–317.

—— (2004a) 'The new economy of the inner city', *Cities* 21: 89–108.

—— (2004b) 'Post-industrialism, post-modernism, and the reproduction of Vancouver's Central Area: retheorising the 21st century city', *Urban Studies* 41: 1953–1982.

—— (2006) 'Spatiality, built form and creative industry development in the inner city', *Environment and Planning A* 38: 1819–1841.

—— (2008) *The New Economy of the Inner City: Restructuring, Regeneration and Dislocation in the 21st Century Metropolis.* London: Routledge Studies in Economic Geography.

Indergaard, M. (2004) *Silicon Alley.* London and New York: Routledge.

Ley, D. F. (1996) *The New Middle Class and the Remaking of the Central City,* Oxford: Oxford University Press.

—— (2003). 'Artists, aestheticisation and the field of gentrification', *Urban Studies,* 40(12): 2527–2544.

Ley, D. F. and Hutton, T. A. (1987) 'Vancouver's corporate complex and producer services sector: linkages and divergence within a provincial staple economy', *Regional Studies* 21: 413–424.

Morgan, K. (2004) 'The Exaggerated Death of Geography: Learning, Proximity and Territorial Innovations Systems', *Journal of Economic Geography* 4: 3–21.

Olds, K. (2001) *Globalization and Urban Change: Capital, Culture and Pacific Rim Mega-Projects.* Oxford: Oxford University Press.

Peck, J. (2005) 'Struggling with the creative class', *Journal of International Urban and Regional Research* 29: 740–770.

Pratt, A. C. (2000) New media, the new economy and new spaces, *Geoforum* 31: 425–436.

—— (2005). 'Cultural industries and public policy: an oxymoron?', *International Journal of Cultural Policy,* 11(1): 31–44.

—— (in press) 'Urban regeneration: from the arts 'feel good' factor to the cultural economy. A case study of Hoxton, London', special theme issue of *Urban Studies.*

Punter, J. (2003) *The Vancouver Achievement: Urban Planning and Design.* Vancouver: UBC Press.

Sacco, P.-L. (with E. Del-Bianco and R. Williams) (2006) *The Time is Now: an Approach to Cultural Policy in Vancouver.* Vancouver: Vancity Foundation.

Scott, A. J. (2000) *The Cultural Economy of Cities.* London: Sage.

Short, J.R, Benton, L.M., Luce, W.B. and Walton, J. (1993) 'Reconstructing the image of the industrial city', *Annals of the Association of American Geographers* 83: 207–224.

Vinodrai, T. (2006) 'Overview of Canadian cities and the creative class', Presentation to Meeting of 'Social Dynamics of Innovation and Creativity in the City-Region' Research Team, Kingbridge, Ontario. May 2006.

Zukin, S. (1989)[1982 1st ed.] *Loft Living: Culture and Capital in Urban Change,* 2nd edn, Fredericksburg, PA: Rutgers University Press.

5b Creative biographies in new media

Social innovation in web work

Rosalind Gill

> It's all about innovation, everything I do. It's a constant learning process. I like that.
> (Stefan, male 50s)

> It's very important to me to be working on the cutting edge. It defines me. I lose interest in things that remain the same.
> (Elizabeth, female 40s)

Introduction: creativity and innovation in new media work

New media workers are innovators in multiple senses. In the first and most obvious sense they are creative workers whose work involves innovation on a regular basis. These workers create innovative products and services, from computer games to websites, to interactive programmes, designs or installations. They also work in a *field* that is entirely new – many of their job titles and work practices simply did not exist before the mid-1990s but are the outcome of the development of the World Wide Web, and the rapid technological transformations since then. But as well as innovating and creating new things in a novel field of activity, web workers are also innovating *new forms of work*: new career biographies, new practices of learning, new patterns of work organization across time, space and social relations. In this chapter it is these *social innovations* that are the focus, as I examine web workers' experiences of life in new media.

Until recently there was very little research on new media work or workers. The literature was dominated by geographical and economic perspectives concerned with place-based discussions of post-industrial urban spaces, with their familiar preoccupations with clustering, land use and economic development. These offered useful descriptions of the spatial dynamics of new media, usually focused on one city (Scott, 2000; Hutton, this volume) but rarely looked beyond the facade of the gentrified warehouses they observed to catch a glimpse of what was going on inside, let alone to explore the transformations of work happening within new media. To the extent that new media workers were the focus at all, they tended to be invoked in a way that conveniently fitted with the perspective of the theorist – usually called on to epitomize the dangers or benefits of the knowledge economy: on the one hand there is the image of 'net slaves', the 'precariat' or the 'cybertariat', which sees web workers as the victims of the move to more flexible, deregulated forms of working; on the other is the representation of the 'technobohemians' or 'digerati', a new information elite, at work in a web-based 'e-topia' (Lessard and Baldwin, 2000; Huws, 2003).

New media workers have been rhetorically conjured in a diverse range of contexts – yet they rarely appeared with their own agendas or speaking parts. In sociology, new media workers emerged as the poster boys and girls for the 'Brave New World of work' (Beck, 2000). They were the iconic exemplars of the move away from traditional notions of career (Flores and Gray, 1999; Leadbeter and Oakley,1999; Sennett, 2000) to more informal, insecure and discontinuous employment (Beck, 2000). They surfaced again in debates about the 'knowledge society' or the 'network society' – this time brought forth to wear the mantle of 'reprogrammable labor' (Castells, 1996), signifying a future in which the need to update skills and knowledge will be a constant requirement. And, more recently, they reappeared in debates about 'immaterial labor' and 'cognitive capitalism' (Hardt and Negri, 2005) or 'liquid modernity' (Bauman, 2005) with precariousness or precarity as the main focus here (Butler, 2004; Neilson and Rossiter, 2005).

Of late, however, there has been a growing interest in new media workers not as standard-bearers or exemplars of other phenomena, but – importantly – in their own right. This new attention is the result of the recognition of interesting and relatively distinctive organizational structures, working practices and 'career' biographies associated with new media: 'project based', 'freelance', 'entrepreneurial', 'informal', 'network based' and 'affective' are some of the key terms that circulate in attempts to capture the emerging forms of living and working within this field.

Two important pieces of scholarship which might be thought of as 'boundary texts' between the economic and geographical concerns of Hutton (2004; 2006) and Scott (2000) and the sociological concerns of this paper were the studies by Rosemary Batt, Susan Christopherson and colleagues (1999) and Mike Indergaard (2004). Both were firmly grounded in the spatial economy of a single city – New York – but also opened up a range of questions about the nature of new media work: the backgrounds, training and education of its protagonists, the available contractual statuses, the working conditions, the extent – or not – of unionisation, working hours, means of securing future work, and so on (see also Lloyd, 2006 on neo-bohemia). Andrew Ross's (2003) landmark ethnographic study of New York web companies Razorfish and 360hiphop made questions about working conditions central. In the last five years a small but significant body of empirical scholarship has looked carefully at a variety of features of new media work including its much vaunted 'flexibility' (Perrons, 1999; 2004a; 2007; Gottschall and Kroos, 2007; Deuze, 2007); the educational skills, trajectories and biographies of those who seek to work in the field (Gottschall and Heninger, 2004; Contu and Willmott, 2004; Damarin, 2006); its informal working cultures, with their links between the 'club' and 'company' (McRobbie, 2002; Oakley, 2007); its persistent inequalities despite claims to be a field of diversity and egalitarianism (Gill, 2002; Perrons, 2001; 2003; 2004a; Banks and Milestone, in press); the insecurities/difficulties it generates as a means of creating a livable life (Terranova, 2000; McRobbie, 2002; Mayerhofer and Mokre, 2006); and the passionate affiliation and affective ties it produces (Neff *et al.*, 2005; Ehrenstein, 2006; Kennedy, in press). The study reported here is a further contribution to this literature which is at once a critical sociology of work and an attempt to understand new media as a site of creativity and innovation.

The chapter is divided into 5 sections: first a brief introduction to the context of the research and the methods used. Second, I look at career trajectories in new media, noting the flexibility of work practices and employment statuses, as web workers build up entirely novel forms of career biography – that bear little resemblance to traditional linear notions. Third, the paper turns to issues of the knowledge economy, looking at new media workers as an example of knowledge workers who must constantly update their skills and knowledge, yet who do so, for the most part, outside of formal structures of education or training. Here the focus is on informal learning as an innovative technology of the social. The fourth section extends the focus on informality to consider the ways in which informal networks play a key role in new media workers lives, as both a source of work, knowledge, and support as well as providing the 'buzz' that makes new media an exciting field in which to work. Finally, the chapter turns to the central issue of how web workers manage various kinds of insecurity in their working lives.

Research context and methods

The research presented here is based on 34 interviews with web workers living and working in or around the city of Amsterdam in the Netherlands. The research was commissioned by the Institute of Network Cultures as a follow-up to an earlier cross-European research project on new media workers, which had challenged the myths of web work as 'cool, creative and egalitarian' and pointed to low pay, long hours and bulimic work patterns, as well as to the emergence of new and complex inequalities in the field (see Gill and Dodd, 2000; Gill, 2002). The present research was designed to update the original study for the moment 10 years after the development of the World Wide Web (2005), and to furnish qualitative rather than quantitative data to offer a richer and more nuanced understanding of new media workers' lives.

Thirty-four interviews were carried out with individuals in a range of different web-based professions. Random sampling was impossible because of the lack of a comprehensive list of web workers to serve as the sampling frame. Therefore the sample was constructed with heterogeneity in mind – to capture the experiences of people who had worked in the field for varying lengths of time, doing a range of different things, with a variety of kinds of contracts or employment statuses. The sample was also designed to include people of different genders, ages and ethnicities, as well as a mix of people with experiences in commercial and non-profit organizations. The research sample comprised 22 males and 12 females. Four people were under 30 and three over 50; the remainder were in their 30s and 40s. Seven of our interviewees were not Dutch, but lived and worked in Amsterdam, and we considered it important to include the experiences of ethnic minorities – whilst noting the overall whiteness of the field (an issue that I have discussed elsewhere – Gill, 2007).

Participants were invited to take part in an interview about 'work in new media' in which they were asked about a range of experiences of working in the field. Interviews took place in a variety of settings – workplaces, cafes or restaurants, or a hired room. In all cases they were carried out by one of two white female researchers in their late 30s (one Dutch, the other British) or, on some occasions, both researchers. Some interviews were conducted in English. Their duration was between 45 minutes and 2.5 hours, with the majority lasting between 1 and 1.5 hours. All interviews were recorded and transcribed, with the exception of one in which the respondent chose to send answers to questions over e-mail.

The interviews covered a range of different topics: the respondent's current work, their work biography and reasons for moving into new media, their education and training, both formal and informal, and their reflections on new media work – its pleasures, challenges, and so on. The final part of the interview was devoted to future plans. The tone of the interviews was pleasant and informal, and the topic guide was not adhered to rigidly. Rather, individuals were encouraged to talk about their own experiences, dilemmas, problems and hopes, and to tell us what it is like to be engaged in this kind of work in Amsterdam at this particular time. Most interviewees were happy to do this, and, as in much research, we had the impression that the interviews were experienced as enjoyable opportunities to talk, by the majority of people who took part.

Creative biographies in new media

The term 'new media work' covers an extraordinary diversity of different occupations. Rather than imposing our own definitions, interviewees were invited to tell us how they described their own work, and amongst the job titles we heard there was barely a single overlap. Self-described job titles included: programmer, interaction designer, editor, copywriter, business manager, artist, Flash illustrator, researcher, content manager, freelance concept maker, software document writer, consultant, project manager, website developer, and entrepreneur.

New media workers also fall into many different categories of employment. In constructing the sample we sought to include a mix of people who were in stable employment, people who were freelance, and others who had established their own business. Implicitly these categories were understood as discrete and as relatively stable. Both these assumptions, however, were challenged by the reality of new media workers' lives. Far from being fixed designations the statuses changed on an extraordinarily rapid and regular basis. Most people had experience of freelancing *and* of working on a steady contract for an employer. Many also had experience of establishing their own business and working in this for varying amounts of time. Moreover, as well as changing statuses *over time*, some people combined different statuses at the *same time* – working freelance in their own time, for example, but also in paid employment to 'pay the bills' or 'learn more skills'.

In short, work biographies in new media are extremely rich and complex. They bear little resemblance to traditional notions of the career with their expectations of linear development and progression up a hierarchy. Some short vignettes should help to illustrate this.

Margrit is a woman in her 30s, who worked for 10 years at three different new media companies, employed on what she understood as stable and secure contracts. However, in the last company she lost her job due to a restructuring, and subsequently decided to set up her own web design studio, with a partner. She now runs this, but is worried about its sustainability in the long term due to the extremely long hours she has to work.

Robert, male and also in his early 30s, set up a company with two friends, immediately after graduating with a specific and highly marketable set of skills. He was then asked to join a very successful agency, and opted to take a two-thirds contract with them, so that he could spend his remaining available time freelancing.

Paul is a web worker in his early 50s. He has worked freelance on ICT projects for 15 years now, but believes that he has finally found a niche and intends to set up his own business in the next year, though he is concerned about all the financial and legal aspects of running a company – for which he has had no training and has no experience.

Maria has been freelancing for 10 years, since her late 20s. She worries about keeping up with the field, and also worries about money. Ideally she would like to set up her own business, but is concerned about the responsibility of hiring other people.

Peter, a man in his late 20s, works for a company that employs 20 people. He has recently been promoted to a management role, though it is only on a six-month contract. Previously, he had his own web company, but wanted the financial security of employment, as well as the opportunities to take on bigger, more complex projects.

Martin is co-owner of a web agency. Although he is only in his mid-20s, this is his second business. He started his first business with two friends he made at college, but they went their separate ways, and he subsequently worked for a year as an employee in a web agency, before deciding to set up on his own again.

Compared to the reality of new media workers' lives, these tiny vignettes are artificially 'smoothed out' narratives, which capture little of the sense of 'making things up as one goes along' which emerged palpably from the interviews. In fact many interviewees spoke of their experience of having been able to turn a hobby or a passion into a means of earning money (McRobbie, 2002; Oakley, 2007; Banks and Milestone, in press). A fuller account, would capture more of the twists and turns and the serendipity that characterize web workers' lives – the sense of needing to be adaptable and ready to ' have a go ' at anything. One woman (Antonia) reflected humorously upon this:

> Well, I finished university, and I was really into music, and I helped out some friends doing video recordings of live gigs for a few months, and I was working in a bar to earn money. Then another friend who was in a theatre company needed someone at very short notice to help with the set design and to sew

> costumes – so I did that for a while, then I heard about this job doing web design for XX (record company) and because I'd had some experience of that and I knew someone who worked there I sent in my CV and they took me on, but it was only a short-term thing and it didn't last as after six months they decided they needed to set up a much bigger department, when they realised that the Web thing was really going to take off. But it was really good experience and I made some great contacts, and anyway I'd been planning to go with some friends to cycle around Central America so I did that for a year – it was amazing – and then when I got back I set up a company doing web sites for bands with two friends and we were able to get back in touch with (record company) and use the connections we have made there . . . .
>
> The story continued with many more short episodes of work until Antonia concluded: 'so, a typical new media biography, really!'

The detail and complexity of this account is not captured by the vignettes above. But despite their telescoped nature, the pen portraits do show how extraordinarily fluid and flexible new media workers' biographies are. This flexibility is, in itself, one of the novel features of this field of work. Two other sets of concerns also emerge very clearly from here: anxieties about money, and concerns about the long hours many workers felt they had to put in simply in order to survive in new media. Both these concerns help to account for some of the flexibility of career biographies, as workers balanced different anxieties, costs and pleasures – for example, offsetting job security against a loss of autonomy, or shorter hours against less innovative work.

Hours and pay in new media

Contrary to the myths of new media as a lucrative, highly paying field, in which there is much money to be made by eager young entrepreneurs, this study echoed earlier European research (Gill and Dodd, 2000) which points instead to the extremely low levels of pay received by web workers. Levels of earnings were highly correlated with employment status, with employees earning more than either freelancers or small-business owners. Indeed, in this research half were earning less than €20,000 per year. Freelancers pay rates might appear superficially to be reasonably high when quoted as hourly figures, yet such rates were not an accurate reflection of real pay – not least because of the pressures to 'pitch low' in order to get a piece of work, or because of the marked underestimation by freelancers of the time in which a project would take to complete. Respondents repeatedly told us that 'it always takes me three times longer than I think it will', with the effect that all the excess hours are unpaid. Time budgeting and other 'business' or self management skills were occasionally mentioned in interviews as desirable ones to learn, yet it is not clear that such training would actually help freelancers, given the competitive pressures on prices that most feel constrained by – that is, 'to win the contract, you sometimes have to quote it for less than it will actually cost you'. Without an intervention such as fixed union rates for the job – as exist in the highly unionised film industry, for example – it might be expected that the freelancer who pitched at the appropriate level would simply not get the job. Interviewees were painfully aware of this.

Perhaps the starkest disparity between the working lives of employed new media workers and their freelance counterparts, however, relates to the number of hours they worked. People employed on regular contracts almost uniformly worked between 35 and 40 hours per week. Indeed, if they worked longer, this was often classified as overtime for which they would be paid, or they would accrue 'time off in lieu'.

> I have a steady contract. I work 40 hours a week. I save up 4 hours each week and then I have a total of 10 weeks of holiday a year.
>
> (*Hugo*, male 40s)

Freelancers and company owners or directors, by contrast, tended to work between 55 and 80 hours per week, with the average working 65 hours.

> Int: How many hours a week do you work?
>
> Like 60 or so. Sometimes up to 80 when a project needs to be finished. In the last months they made three games a week and that means working day and night. Banners always have to be finished the next day. Websites take much longer.
>
> (*Joost*, male 30s)
>
> The last half-year I worked at six or seven days a week. After a while that gets nasty. Plus I worked 60 hours a week, there were just so many assignments and questions . . . . only then I am jealous of people with a steady job, they have those steady holidays.
>
> (*Karl*, male 50s)

One respondent told us exactly how he settled upon the length of his working week: he learned from others about the maximum number of hours it was possible to work over a long and sustained period without burning out, and he tried to keep to this number – 65 hours each week.

> Int: How many hours to you work a week?
>
> Oh 60 or 65. I don't want to work more because then I become burned out and my concentration lessens. We also have programmers who work 70 hours for two weeks and then they are not worth anything the week after.
>
> (*Thomas*, male 30s)

Many people regularly had to work through the night in order to finish projects, but then found themselves in other periods without any work at all; the pattern of working described by Andy Pratt (2000) as 'bulimic'.

> Well I think the hours that we make . . . It is sometimes really incredible. Working through the night happens regularly, and if you have kids as well . . . well I don't know. Plus you have to keep up and that takes time and energy as well.
>
> (*Alfred*, male 30s)

For some, like Alfred, such long hours and constant demands were experienced as exhausting and as potentially problematic when he projected himself into a future that might involve being a parent. But for others, working at night or through the night was part of the 'buzz' of the work:

> Sometimes I have to do research at night, but I'm always at home at night and at the weekends. I guess with my own company I'll put everything into it. But work can give you energy so that is no problem. That's when you are doing what you like.
>
> (*Jaap*, male 30s)

And sometimes working very long hours was almost a badge of commitment:

> Int: How does it fit in with the rest of your life?
>
> I don't do anything else. Well, some things. But it is creative and I put everything in there. And if you don't love what you do, you better stop.
>
> Int: So you work at home as well?
>
> Yes, but mostly I stay here that long that I'd better go to sleep when I get home!
>
> (*Joke*, female 30s)

Even this interviewee, however, did acknowledge that she might want to work for fewer hours as she grew older and 'to have some time for myself'.

Re-programmable labour? Informal learning in new media

Knowledge workers in contemporary society are required to continuously train and update their skills in order to take account of rapidly changing technologies. As Manuel Castells (1996) would have it, today's knowledge workers must be 're-programmable' – adept not simply in one set of skills or expertise, but able to adapt and learn continuously (Kotamraju, 2002; Sennett, 2000). In this sense, learning and flexibility and a set of technologies of the self become more important than core skills. As web workers are the apparent exemplars of re-programmable labour – a group of workers right at the cutting edge of technological change, as well as changing tastes, fashions and lifestyles – an important aim of this research was to discover something about their educational backgrounds, their learning, and the ways in which they coped with the necessity to keep up in a rapidly changing environment.

It is striking to note the extremely high level of educational qualifications amongst people who took part in this study. All but three were University graduates and approximately half of these also had a further qualification (sometimes a Masters degree). Without sufficient data about employment in new media in general, it is impossible to know whether this is representative of the field or an artefact of the sample. Nevertheless it does concur with an earlier study which concluded that European new media workers are amongst the most highly educated groups of workers in the world. Despite this, however, formal education was regarded by most (though not all) as having little relevance to their working lives. For many people, it is the speed of change that offers the challenge:

> It is all learning on the job. There is no course you can send me to where I can learn something. By the time I have finished that job 13 other things will have changed. There is not even a school course for this kind of job.
>
> (*Sebastiaan*, male 40s)

For the majority, learning is necessarily done informally alone or with others.

> I look around on the Internet. I don't have an official education in the field. There are some people who have helped me in the past, who have looked over my shoulder, but I don't need that any more now. Sometimes I just have to make do. For a DVD I was looking for software and I learned it in a night.
>
> (*Harrie*, male 30s)

Moreover, some people argue that courses are no substitute for teaching oneself in a hands-on manner.

> I took Microsoft Certified Engineer, I took TCP/IP and things like that because the company told you to do that. But they are only papers.
>
> (*Joke*, female 30s)

> Int: Do you prefer to learn it by yourself?
> I think it's the only way.
>
> (*Ralf*, male 40s)

Keeping up

In a field in which knowledge changes at an extraordinarily rapid pace, and new packages and standards proliferate, most people experience significant pressure to 'keep up' by staying abreast of current developments, and learning new skills. In this respect (as in others we have discussed already) people on relatively stable employment contracts usually occupied a position of advantage relative to freelancers or company directors. As noted already, such individuals were likely to be working significantly fewer hours each week, and also often received compensation for extra hours worked. In addition a number of interviewees told us that their employers paid for them to keep up-to-date in the field by taking courses.

> I just finished a course and you can take as many courses as you want. You have to take the initiative, that is clear, but then everything is possible. For instance I just took a course at XXX to get some more inspiration. And soon I will start a course in management.
>
> (*Liesbet*, female 30s)

For freelancers, though, learning and keeping up were almost always done at the individual's own expense in terms of both money and time.

> I have established for myself that I have to do them in order to understand them. That's my way of learning. Then you develop a sense for it. Only then.
>
> Int: And how many hours do you spend on it, on average?
>
> Not so much at the moment since I am so busy. And I have tight deadlines and I have to give them what they want . . . Say, 15 hours a week.
>
> (*Danielle*, female 30s)

Given that such large investments of time come on top of already very long working weeks, it is not surprising that some found this a source of anxiety.

> I do find the speed of change intimidating at times, I admit that. I find it difficult to keep my work in check. I used to take work home with me, in order to be able to read. And that has become a habit.
>
> Int: And do you think that is a good thing or a bad thing?
>
> Well it is a privilege to have a job which is also your hobby, but it shouldn't make you ill.
>
> (*Elisabeth*, female, 40s)

Even the thought of having to keep up and constantly keep learning new skills could sometimes be experienced as oppressive:

> A neighbor came by and he asked me whether I worked with Ajax yet. And I was like, oh my god I have to work with that and learn that now too. It's all a bit too much for me.
>
> (*Danielle*, female 30s)

Informality in new media work

Informal connections are the lifeblood of new media work. This is understood by many people as related to the 'coolness' of the industry (Gill, 2002; Neff *et al.*, 2003), which Andrew Ross (2003) has discussed in terms of the 'industrialisation of Bohemia'.

> It's very free and informal – maybe a little too cosy sometimes. But people like working here a lot. There's an excellent atmosphere.
>
> (*Liesbet*, female 30s)

It's friends club that got out of hand. It's very unpretentious.

(*Wilhelm*, male 30s)

For others, it is related to the opportunity to be autonomous and control one's own time:

I determine what I do, whenever I do it. Sometimes in the middle of the night, when there is a disturbance [I'll get up and work].

(*Ralf*, male 20s)

Most importantly, informal connections are the main mechanism of distributing work in new media. This could be seen vividly in Antonia's brief description of how she got into the field, as discussed earlier. In her story – described laughingly by herself as 'a typical new media biography' – all her work experiences came through friends and contacts. Such accounts were repeated – with slight variations – by all our participants.

How did you get the job?
Through a friend.

(*Kristoff*, male 50s)

One of my former students now works there and told the management about me.

(*Karl*, male 50s)

This assignment I got from somebody who worked in an advertising agency I worked for before . . . he remembered me from a job I had done.

(*BJ*, male 40s)

Well, from our network.

(*Joost*, male, 30s)

Well, my current boss knew somebody from the past and I ran into him at my brother's wedding and they wanted to have a talk with me. I was just starting another job so that didn't work out, but about a year and a half later I ran into him again at a reunion of my secondary school and I knew he had a multimedia agency and I liked the idea of it.

(*Wilhelm*, male 30s)

Informal connections, then, are central to life in new media. Friends, teachers, students, colleagues, clients – these are the conduits for finding work, regardless of whether one is a company director, freelancer or lands a stable job somewhere. Amongst our 34 respondents, only two reported ever having found work in new media through traditional means of job searching – namely responding to an advertisement. Given that each participant told us about three or four of their work experiences, this amounts to less than 2 per cent of the whole spectrum. In addition, company directors and freelancers were used to pitching for work, but in these cases informal connections could also play an important role, particularly through word-of-mouth recommendation.

> I usually know my clients and they know me. Then follows a briefing, sometimes there is a two week period to get to know the background, and then I dive into their product, the process and their documents and I start working with them.
>
> (*Sonia*, female 30s)

> It never hurts to network. That is true. I am friends with a lot of companies who do the same and I have established that the more people I know who do the same as I do, the more work I have.
>
> (*Danielle*, female 30s)

Fundamentally, finding work in new media – in whatever capacity or contractual status – is based on an amalgam between two commonplaces that circulated through our interviews. These were the phrases 'it's all down to who you know' and 'you are only as good as your last job' (see Blair, 2001). The two could sometimes be in tension, but often worked in concert – particularly in the absence of ' official accounts' of workers' achievements, such as employer references or formal qualifications (in a context in which, as we have seen, much learning is done informally or 'on the job') As the quotes above indicate, the entire economy of work opportunities operates through contacts – people you meet at conferences, parties, drinks evenings, friends of friends, ex-colleagues, etc.

The informality of the field raises some questions about fairness and equality; questions about how finding work in new media relies on knowing the right people, rather than on talent or merit per se. This is not to suggest that those who get work are not talented, but merely highlights the many others who may be excluded on the basis of not having the right contacts. There is, as yet, relatively little research about the significance of informal networks, yet that which exists points to their essentially conservative implications; that is, people tend to hire or give work to other people who are like them (Franks, 1999). Amongst the questions this generates are some that relate to the ongoing preponderance of men and white people in this field. In general, informal practices tend to reinforce, rather than challenge, existing inequalities, and do not serve equal opportunities practices well. The field is marked by the lack of constraints on institutionalized discrimination, though this is rendered invisible by the normalization of making work available on the basis of informal contracts.

For the field as a whole, questions need to be asked about how successful informal networking is as a way of distributing work opportunities. This is a significant unknown factor since, by definition, we did not get to interview those people who did not find work, who had not successfully networked, or built up an excellent database of useful contacts. Even within our successful group, however, some people did report that they found it excruciatingly difficult to pitch for work, and that, for example, shyness held them back. The intense self-discipline required by the independent new media worker who must bear all the risks and responsibilities for finding and keeping work, staying abreast of changes, attending to necessary insurances, and remaining vigilant to every opportunity, is captured perfectly by one of our respondents:

> Life is a pitch.
>
> (*Danielle*, female 30s)

The requirement to network and to build contacts also brings other pressures, named by Melissa Gregg (2006) as the 'compulsory sociality' of the neoliberal workplace, in which one can never really switch off or relax, and one is never totally away from work. Indeed, in this sense, the entire self is a work project that must be presented in all the right ways at all the right occasions. Angela McRobbie (2002) has written about the 'intimate geographies' of cultural industries work (including new media work) which are predicated on interpersonal exchange and bodily presence, despite the hype about 'virtuality' (see also Pratt 2002).

Several others told us how networking drinks had become a kind of necessity or obligation:

> Monday night is the only night I don't have networking drinks.
>
> (*Sonia*, female 30s)

> I belong to X and X networks. They organise a party every year. And seminars and conferences. There is a lot of informal stuff too. I like it, but sometimes when I walk around I think: do I belong to this? It's all very hyped. Maybe everybody thinks that.
>
> (*Liesbet*, female 30s)

The pressures associated with this work are, of course, unevenly distributed and impact mostly on those who are shy, those who do not drink, and those with other responsibilities (e.g. family responsibilities which made it difficult for them to attend evening drinks).

Precarious work and insecurity

For freelancers and some small business owners, insecurity and the precarious nature of work constituted major ongoing challenges.

> It is insecure. Maybe I will look for jobs two days a week to pay the rent. But really I'm too busy for that.
>
> (*Harrie*, male 30s)

For some, it related to particular periods, for example Christmas or summertime.

> It is important to have work in the summertime because that is traditionally a flat time. There is no social security for me. Not for unemployment or illness.

> I do have a pension so . . . But I understand that: that is the nature of freelancing, you take care of yourself. Maybe there should be something for people who are temporarily out of work. If or when there comes a time I cannot work anymore I won't have anything, so that's daunting. I'll have to go on basic welfare, that is really nothing. But that's the way it is.
>
> (*Kristoff*, male 50s)

As is clear in the above quote, this insecurity had far-reaching repercussions for many interviewees' lives. Lack of pensions, inability-to-work insurance, and other benefits impacted significantly on many participants – particularly those who were older and thus more able to imagine periods when they might not be able to work. In addition, as noted earlier in this report, an absence of paid holidays made it difficult for many freelancers to take any kind of a break.

> Int: Can you bridge the time between projects? Can you go on holiday?
>
> No I am in serious financial trouble. And I haven't been on holiday. People who work for TV get unemployment benefits in the summertime. We don't have that. We are independent. I got extra money from the tax office last year because I made so little money.
>
> (*Ralf*, male 40s)

A common feeling expressed by interviewees was the pressure of not being able to turn down work – in case other opportunities failed to materialize.

> It's very intensive and I don't have enough time to rest. Because it's always going on. And if you don't plan something for yourself, someone will call and say you have to be there and there. You can't say no to a job. Because you don't know when the next job is going to be.
>
> (*Liam*, male 40s)

Regulating the flow of work presented a challenge to many freelancers and small business directors, in a context in which there was a largely shared understanding that 'you can't say no to a job'.

> In an ideal situation I have two or three assignments at the same time. Lower than that is scary and higher than that is too busy. But two or three assignments is good.
>
> (*Geke*, female 20s)

But besides the anxiety about not having enough work, Geke highlighted another more subtle danger – the danger of commodifying one's time, of turning every hour into a billable entity:

> When you are a freelancer you have to be really careful that you don't make or turn every hour into money. If I surf for two hours on the Internet, then I did not

> make my money for today. On the other hand you also have days or whole months where you don't have a lot of work, so . . .
>
> (*Geke*, female 20s)

Insecurity and precarious work, then, were major issues for freelancers and people who had their own small companies. However, such problems could also affect people employed in larger organizations. One man we spoke to was on a zero hours contract, so could lose his employment/income with no notice whatsoever. It was striking to note the combination of high aspirations and large *potential* earnings, alongside employment contracts that were *actually* extraordinarily short and lacking in benefits. This seems part of a wider shift in what sociologist Ulrich Beck has called 'the Brave New World of work' in which workers are being forced to bear more and more of the risks associated with employment. This 'individualization of risk' could be heard, for example, on many occasions in which people told us that their 'steady' contract was actually for six months or less, yet in which they had a longer term expectation of owning shares in the company or participating in its profits.

> I have a half year contract. In my next contract I'll get part of the turnover, and in the long run I will probably get stocks in the company.
>
> (*Thomas*, male 30s)

In addition, many people experienced the familiar insecurity associated with being in companies that seemed to restructure on a regular basis. If companies keep their workers' contracts short, then making them redundant through restructuring, means that they incur few of the traditional costs associated with redundancy. The insecure, discontinuous, temporary and flexible style of future work discussed by sociologists appears already to be well established in the field of new media.

Conclusion

This chapter has considered the experiences of a group of creative workers in a rapidly changing field of new media. Here innovation and creativity take place against a backdrop of endemic insecurity, precariousness and individualization. Participants in the study diverged from popular stereotypes: they were neither 'bedroom millionaires' nor 'dot.com boomers', nor were they 'isolated geniuses' writing code in their attics or garrets. On the contrary, their earnings were modest – in many cases barely enough to live on – and their working lives were characterized not by isolation but intense sociality, with networking personal contacts as the key means of keeping up, staying in touch and finding work.

These new media workers had 'creative biographies' in at least two senses. Most straightforwardly they told stories of their lives as workers who constantly created and innovated in a rapidly changing creative industry in which nothing stayed still and they had to learn, change and innovate constantly. But in addition their biographies themselves were sites of innovation and creativity, as – in the absence of established scripts – they quite literally created ways of working and living in the emerging fields that constitute contemporary new media. These creative biographies are marked by passionate attachments or bonds of love to work in new media, by a strong preference for the informal over the formal (whether in learning/developing skills or finding work) and by 'compulsory socialities'; yet the increasing individualization of risk and responsibility was captured in phrases such as 'you are only as good as your last job' and 'life is a pitch' in which every sphere or occasion became a site of opportunity/discipline. Understanding what Angela McRobbie (2002) has called the 'pleasure-pain axis' of creative biographies such as these is central if we are to develop policies that will sustain creativity and innovation in new media and other areas of cultural work in years to come.

References

Banks, M and Milestone, K (in press) 'Individualization, gender and cultural work', *Gender Work & Organisation.*

Batt, R, Christopherson, S and Rightor, N (1999) 'Net-working: working life in a project based industry: a collaborative study of people working in new media in New York'. Working paper available from the authors.

Bauman, Z (2005) *Liquid Life*. Cambridge: Polity.

Beck, U (2000) *The Brave New World of Work.* Cambridge: Polity.

Blair, H (2001) '"You're only as good as your last job": the labour process and labour market in the British film industry', *Work Employment & Society*, vol. 15 no.1 pp. 149–169.

Butler, J (2004) *Precarious Life: The Powers of Mourning and Violence*. New York: Verso.

Castells, M (1996) *The Rise of the Network Society*. Oxford: Blackwell.

—— (2000) 'The institutions of the new economy', Keynote address to the Virtual Society Conference, London, 19th June.

Contu, A and Willmott, H (2004) 'Working and learning in a new media company', paper presented at the Workshop for 'Studying new forms of work: concepts and practices in the cultural industries and beyond', Berlin Free University, March.

Damarin, A K (2006) 'Rethinking occupational structure: the case of web site production work', *Work and Occupations*, vol.33 no.4 pp. 429–463.

Deuze, M (2007) *Media Work.* Cambridge: Polity.

Ehrenstein, A (2006) *Social Relationality and Affective Experience in Precarious Labour Conditions.* Unpublished Masters dissertation, University of Cardiff.

Flores, F and Gray, J (1999) *Entrepreneurship and the Wired Life: Work in the Wake of Careers.* London: Demos.

Franks, S (1999) *Having None Of It: Women, Men and the Future of Work.* London: Granta.

Gill, R (2002) 'Cool, creative and egalitarian? Exploring project-based new media in Europe *Information, Communication & Society*, vol.5 no.1 pp. 70–89.

—— (2007) *Technobohemians or the New Cybertariat? New Media Work in Amsterdam a Decade after the Web*. Amsterdam: Institute of Network Cultures.

Gill, R and Dodd, D (2000) *New Media: Working Practices in the Electronic Arts,* Final report submitted to DGV.

Gottschall, K and Henninger, A (2004) 'Freelancers in the German new media industry: beyond standard patterns of work and life', paper presented at the Workshop for 'Studying new forms of work: concepts and practices in the cultural industries and beyond', Berlin Free University, March.

Gottschall, K and Kroos, D (2007) 'Self-employment in comparative perspectives: general trends and the case of new media' in Fagan C, McDowell, L, Perrons, D, Ray, K and Ward, K (eds) *Gender Divisions in the New Economy: Changing Patterns of Work, Care and Public Policy in Europe and North America*. London: Edward Elgar.

Gregg, M (2006) 'On Friday night drinks: neoliberalism's compulsory friends', paper presented at the UnAustralia conference of the Cultural Studies Association of Australasia, December.

Hardt, M and Negri, A (2005) *Multitude*. London: Penguin.

Hutton, T A (2004). 'The new economy of the inner city', *Cities*, vol. 21 no. 2 pp. 89–108.

—— (2006) 'Spatiality, built form, and creative industry developemnt in the inner city', *Environment and Planning A*, vol. 38 no. 10 pp. 1819–1841.

Huws, U (2003) *The Making of a Cybertariat: Virtual Work in a Real-World*. New York: Monthly Review Press.

Indergaard, M (2004) *Silicon Alley: The Rise and Fall of a New Media District*. New York: Routledge.

Kennedy, H (in press) 'Emotional concerns, commercial imperatives and other complications in new media work'.

Kotamraju, N (2002) 'Keeping up: web design skill and the reinvented worker', *Information, Communication & Society*, vol. 5 no.1 pp. 1–26.

Leadbeter, C and Oakley, K (1999) *The Independents: Britain's New Cultural Entrepreneurs*. London: Demos.

Lessard, B and Baldwin, S (2000) *Net Slaves: True Tales of Working the Web*. New York: McGraw-Hill.

Lloyd, R (2006) *Neo-Bohemia: Art and Commerce in the Postindustrial City*. New York: Routledge.

McRobbie, A (2006) 'Creative London–Creative Berlin: notes on making a living in the new cultural economy', http://www.ateliereuropa.com/2.3_essay.php. (accessed October 28, 2008).

Mayer-Ahuja, N and Wolf, H (2004) 'Work and knowledge in the Internet industry: the German case' paper presented at the Workshop for 'Studying new forms of work: concepts and practices in the cultural industries and beyond', Berlin Free University, March.

Mayerhofer, E and Mokre, M (2006) 'The creative industries in Austria', paper presented at MyCreativity, Amsterdam, November.

Neff, G, Wissinger, E and Zukin, S (2005) 'Entrepreneurial labour among cultural producers: "cool" jobs in "hot" industries', *Social Semiotics*, vol. 15 no. 3 pp. 307–334.

Neilson, B and Rossiter, N (2005) 'From precarity to precariousness and back again: labour, life and unstable networks', Fibreculture issue 5 http://journal.fibreculture.org/issue5/neilson_rossiter print.html.

Oakley, K (2007) 'Better than working for a living? Skills and labour in the festivals economy', report produced for Celebrating Enterprise.

Perrons, D (1999) 'Flexible working patterns and equal opportunities in the European Union: conflict or compatibility?' *European Journal of Women's Studies*, vol. 6 no. 4 pp. 391–418

—— (2001) 'The new economy and the work–life balance: opportunities and constraints for women and men', paper presented at the Conference on Gross Domestic Product vs. Quality of Life, Ballagio, January.

—— (2003) 'The new economy and the work life balance. A case study of the new media sector in Brighton and Hove', *Gender work and organisation*, vol. 10 no. 1 pp. 65–93.

—— (2004a) 'Equity and representation in the new economy' in Kelly, J and Willman, P (eds) *Union Organization and Activity*. London: Routledge.
—— (2004b) 'Understanding social and spatial divisions in the new economy: new media clusters and the digital divide' *Economic Geography*, vol. 80 no. 1 pp. 45–61.
—— (2007) 'Living and working patterns in the new knowledge economy: new opportunities and old social divisions in the case of new media and care work' in Fagan, C, McDowell, L, Perrons, D, Ray, K and Ward, K (eds) *Gender Divisions in the New Economy: Changing Patterns of Work, Care and Public Policy in Europe and North America.* London: Edward Elgar.
Pratt, A (2000) 'New media, the new economy and new spaces', *Geoforum*, vol. 31 pp. 425–436.
—— (2002). 'Hot jobs in cool places. The material cultures of new media product spaces: the case of the south of market, San Francisco', *Information, communication and society*, vol. 5 no. 1 pp. 27–50.
Ross, A (2003) *No Collar: The Humane Workplace and Its Hidden Costs; Behind the Myth of a New Office Utopia.* New York: Basic Books.
Scott, A J (2000) *The Cultural Economy of Cities: Essays on the Geography of Image-Producing Industries*. London: Sage
Sennett, R (2000) *The Corrosion of Character*. New York: Norton.
Terranova, T (2000) 'Free labour: producing culture for the digital economy', *Social Text*, vol. 18 no. 2 pp. 33–57.

Part 6

Design

6a Fostering a culture of design

Insights from the case of Montréal, Canada

Deborah Leslie and Norma Rantisi

Introduction

Local economic development policymakers are increasingly interested in the relation between cultural industries and economic development. Design, in particular, has come to figure prominently in initiatives that seek to forge a unique identity for places and products within a global economy. Yet, little attention has been paid to regulating the complex activities – economic and cultural – implicated in design and developing a culture in which design is valued and encouraged. In this chapter, we provide an overview why it is a challenging sector through an examination of the case of the Montréal design economy. We assess the merits and the drawbacks of recent public and non-profit initiatives to promote design in the city, drawing attention to their top-down nature and to their privileging of the commercial dimensions of design. And we consider the lessons that the Montréal case offers for implementing sustainable, design-led development strategies.

Why Montréal? Within the last few years, the city of Montréal has become synonymous with design (Stolarick and Florida, 2006). In addition to being a UNESCO designated "design capital", it is presently the headquarters for the International Design Alliance.[1] Measured in terms of employment, the city is the sixth largest center of design in North America, following New York, Boston, Toronto, Chicago and Los Angeles (Design Industry Advisory Committee, 2004). The province of Québec estimates the economic impact of design to be $1.8 billion (City of Montréal, 2006). Seen in this light, design is the largest cultural sector in the province, accounting for 31,173 jobs (65.3 percent of which are in Montréal), and according to the City of Montréal, there has also been a 40 percent increase in the number of designers in the city in the last ten years (City of Montréal, 2006). The city has also become a world leader in design policy, exporting some of its more successful programs to other cities.[2] In 2004, the city hosted an international symposium, "New Design Cities", exploring the use of design in urban economic development initiatives and best practices in policy.[3] With a rich institutional nexus to support design, Montréal provides a unique case in which to assess the policy challenges associated with regulating this sector.

Divided into three main sections, the chapter begins with a review of different definitions of design as both a prominent sector and process, outlining the cultural and economic rationales underpinning practices of design. The second section maps out the key elements of a culture of design, and ways of forging it. The final section presents a historical overview of design policies in Montréal. We then highlight three contemporary institutions and initiatives to foster design. In particular, we argue that design policies have to engage with a variety of actors stretching across networks of production, distribution and consumption as well as supporting the economic and aesthetic rationales. The chapter draws upon 26 open-ended interviews with institutions involved in regulating design in Montréal, including key actors in local, provincial and federal government, professional associations, non-profit organizations, design schools, and museums.[4] The research also includes an analysis of government and institutional policy documents relating to design.

What is design?

As Bell and Jayne (2003: 121) note, design is a "fuzzy" concept. On the one hand, design is a sector in its own right, representing a number of fields such as fashion design, industrial design, graphic design, interior design, web design, landscape architecture, architecture, and urban design. These sectors produce tangible outputs or end products such as designed objects, services and landscapes. On the other hand, design also refers to a process, shaping the physical form, content and symbolic meanings of objects and landscapes. Defined in this way, design is a creative activity encompassing the redesign of current products or the development of entirely new products (von Stamm, 2004: 14). Alternatively, design may refer to a more gradual process of innovation, involving incremental changes to existing goods and landscapes.

Designers respond to a variety of stimuli, including changes in user needs, the formation of new markets and competing products. Products embodying principles of "good design", as defined by the design industry, are generally seen as higher quality, more accessible, better looking and longer lasting.

As a practice, design incorporates objective dimensions, which correspond to commercial and technical attributes, and subjective dimensions, which denote cultural attributes (Bryson *et al*., 2005). The objective aspects of design involve satisfying the business needs of clients in terms of costs, materials, and timing, while the subjective dimensions encompass an understanding of human behavior, fashion trends, taste, ethics and aesthetics (Bryson *et al.*, 2005: 4). Practices of design therefore require a hybrid skill set, as well as a willingness to take risks, challenge the status quo, and tolerate high levels of uncertainty. To some extent, designers are required to "think outside the box", developing imaginative solutions to contemporary problems (von Stamm, 2004: 13). However, designers are confronted with a paradox. While artistic worlds are governed by emotion, ambiguity and risk, the commercial worlds that designers often serve demand precise information about the financial contributions of design to a product's sales (Hertenstein *et al.*, 2001: 11). The value that design adds to a product or landscape ultimately evades such measures. As a result of these uncertainties and risks, and the multiple logics governing design, this sector requires particular attention by policy makers. The costs of design often need to be subsidized and the value of design actively promoted.

Design is also a highly place-specific practice. In particular, design tends to be localized in urban settings, where concentrations of specialized services, support institutions and skilled personnel cater to this activity and where aesthetic sensibilities are built up over time (Molotch, 2003). The construction of a unique set of histories and traditions means that a city's design culture cannot be easily replicated in other places. At the same time, design idioms are increasingly globalized, which makes it all the more important for a city to carve out a distinct identity. The localized nature of design poses further challenges for the regulation of this sector since local governments often lack the resources that are necessary to support such activity. As a result, design is a sector that requires the coordination of support and intervention from all levels of government, as well as from institutions outside the public sector.

How can a "culture of design" be fostered?

The complex nature of design has implications not only for which institutions play a role but for *how* those institutions can best cultivate an enabling environment (or broader "culture") for design activities. Following from Julier (2005) and Bell and Jayne (2003), a "culture of design" represents a set of shared sensibilities among key economic actors in and across design fields within a localized setting. Over time, these sensibilities are reinforced through established design practices and artifacts and can give rise to a place-based aesthetic consent, from which a distinctive identity (i.e. the Montréal-ness of Montréal) can be forged and reproduced.[5]

We suggest here that the development of a sustainable design culture demands a cultivation of aesthetic sensibilities at the industry, inter-industry and individual scales. First, design needs to be viewed as a *process* that entails the participation of different actors along an industry chain: producers, consumers and designers. The producers shape the process by establishing what is technically and commercially feasible, but in order for a design to be culturally legible, it must also be in tune with the preferences of the consumers. Designers are situated between these two key influences and must establish a vision that reconciles them. Thus, promoting the development of networks between actors within a particular field is essential for creating viable designs.

Second, design is not only subject to the participation of inter-related actors within a given field but as a place-based activity is also conditioned by the broader set of fields that constitute a local setting. A specific field such as apparel design, for example, can be influenced by furniture design or architecture (Leslie and Reimer, 2003), and the potential synergies between such fields are both direct and indirect. On the one hand, creative activities can directly feed off of one another, i.e. an apparel designer can be inspired by the fabric or color of a cushion. On the other hand, design fields can benefit from one another in indirect ways, as one field may forge a set of mental associations with the city in the minds of consumers (e.g. Gaudi's architecture in Barcelona), from which other fields can benefit (Scott, 1996). The symbiosis between fields suggests the need to promote the design process at multiple levels simultaneously; architecture, planning and product engineering all contribute to marking the image or reputation of a city.

Finally, as noted earlier, the individual designer faces the challenge of balancing aesthetic and commercial considerations and the inherent hybridity of design has implications for the kind of support that is required. A designer must translate ideas into commercially viable good and services; thus s/he is in need of services that can provide information on costing and the development of a business plan (interviews with designers). At the same time, a designer is still an artist and must be afforded the opportunity and spaces in which to experiment and explore. Financial support and networks with other creators can facilitate such practices by lowering the risks and costs of experimentation (Banks *et al.*, 2000).

In sum, a development strategy seeking to foster a design culture must enlist a range of actors and institutions – a feat which is not easy to implement in practice. Yet today a host of cities are embarking on initiatives to position themselves as design capitals. Cities as diverse as Stockholm, Barcelona, Glasgow and St. Etienne (in France) are sponsoring trade fairs, constructing design centers and appointing design advisors to oversee their design-related programs (see Power in this book; Julier, 1996; City of Montréal, 2005a). What these cities share in common is an industrial legacy, and the need to reorient their economic base and how that base is perceived by internal and external investors. Design-based regeneration is viewed as a linchpin for these transformations and for new place-identities in a post-industrial context.

In efforts to form new "identities" however, most policies remain centered on the commercialization, marketing and export of a distinctive "design aesthetic". In a context of market uncertainty and the downloading of fiscal responsibilities, activities where economic value is most readily realized are privileged, often at the expense of nurturing the aesthetic (or creative) dimensions of a localized design culture. As of yet, the promise of "design as development" is far from guaranteed and further analyses of the efficacy of policies are warranted. An evaluation of initiatives that have contributed to Montréal's international acclaim as a design capital, and of the broader political-economic context in which these initiatives have developed, can shed light on where policies have succeeded and where challenges remain for accommodating the diverse networks and logics – commercial and aesthetic – that constitute a sustainable design culture.

Evaluating Montréal's "culture of design"

Montréal's design economy and its policy context

> Why is Montréal interested in design? Because we in Montréal are convinced that design plays a key role in the city's social, cultural, and economic growth. Design, beauty and creativity are important elements that set Montréal apart from other cities of the world and attract tourists, new residents and businesses.

> Given the global competition among cities, the City of Montréal's design action plan will play a strategic role in enhancing the city's image and identity, making it more attractive, improving the performance of its economy, developing a sense of pride and improving its inhabitants' quality of life.
>
> (City of Montréal, 2006)

The emphasis placed on design in the City of Montréal relates to a historical project that Paul (2004: 574) has termed "imagineering". Since the 1950s, culture and design have been used by successive governments to assert Québec nationalism and construct Montréal as an "international city". In the 1970s and 80s, industrial decline, the rise of a francophone business class, and the growth of neoliberal governance regimes combined to force a reinterpretation of the world city project through the lens of jobs, tax revenue and economic growth. For Paul (2004: 586) the cultural dimensions of Montréal's "world class" status remained, but culture was supported for more instrumental and economic rationales. Against a backdrop of growing inter-urban competition, the city increasingly sought to brand itself as a "design metropole" in order to attract investment, talent and tourists. For Paul

> the new middle class became a follower behind Montréal business in a new cosmopolitan neoliberal alliance. The material foundation of the alliance lies in the 'cultural capital' (especially through participation in the education, art, leisure and entertainment industries) of the . . . growing interest in fostering a symbolic economy in the city to replace it's rapidly disappearing manufacturing base.
>
> (2004: 588)

The City of Montréal was thus early to recognize the value of design to urban-economic development. In 1985, a federal committee was established to study the economy of Montréal. The committee's report, known as the Picard Report, identified design as a key sector in the local economy, and a strategic resource to enhance the competitiveness of firms (Picard Report, 1986). In the aftermath of this report, the city established a Commissioner of Design in 1991, a position unique in the North American context (City of Montréal, 2006). For ten years, the Commissioner ran an annual design competition, Commerce Design Montréal. This competition was meant to stimulate investment in interior design in the private spaces in the city such as restaurants, hotels, and boutiques. Awards were given out to enterprises that hired a qualified interior designer to renovate their space. The main objective of this competition was to construct Montréal's identity as an international hub of design in order to attract visitors and provide manufacturers with a set of aesthetic associations that could be leveraged for/in their products.

By the early 2000s, however, the City sought to broaden its design mandate. In particular, there was a growing recognition that Commerce Design Montréal was confined to private establishments, and that there was a need to foster design innovation in all spaces of the city, including public environments. Design now forms a pivotal component of the plan launched in 2005: *Imagining – Building Montréal*

2025, A World of Creativity and Opportunities. This plan explicitly refers to the need to attract talent to the city through building quality of place: "Quality of place is one of the key factors in the success of leading 21st-century cities all over the world. Montréal's focus on those factors . . . will make it one of the most attractive cities on the international scene" (City of Montréal 2005b: 20). Under this new mandate, design has become a central objective in all municipal policies such as the City's Master Plan, the Economic Development Strategy, Heritage Policy, Cultural Development Policy, and the Strategic Plan for Sustainable Development (City of Montréal, 2006).

Most recently, the City of Montréal has unveiled an action plan, *Montréal, Design of the City/City of Design*, with two key objectives: to improve the design of the city itself, and to strengthen Montréal's position as a "city of design" (City of Montréal, 2006). In terms of the first aim, the city is sponsoring an economic development strategy that will support design innovation in public spaces in the city, as well as in urban planning and architecture. The City is investigating the possibilities for establishing a procurement policy for city projects that would encourage the use of Québec designers, and is developing an eco-sustainable design contest. To address the second aim, the City is creating a new expertise unit – the Design Montréal Action Group – that will be responsible for promoting design and hosting communication events. The City also aims to forge networks at the local, regional, national and international scales to promote best practices in design regulation.

While the City is a key actor in promoting design, the local government itself lacks the financial resources to adequately support the design sector. As a result, it has regularly had to leverage funding from other levels of the state for its projects. Moreover, other levels of government and non-governmental institutions have also instituted their own programs to regulate design. Montréal has a diverse array of programs aimed at the design sector, including a system of provincial tax credits subsidizing part of the costs of design among manufacturers (organized by the Government of Québec), as well as an Institute of Design (IDM), a non-profit organization which receives funding from multiple levels of government. There are dozens of education programs at four main universities and a number of colleges and Céjeps. The city is the headquarters of eleven professional associations in the design fields and boasts a number of permanent exhibition spaces (such as the Design Centre and the Canadian Centre for Architecture – CCA). Montréal also hosts a number of prominent international design trade shows such as SIDIM and Montréal Fashion Week. In 2006, the city launched a portal, "Creativité Montréal", for discussion and communication between designers and the public.

In the analysis that follows, we focus on three case studies to explore the innovative nature of the institutional initiatives that exist in the city. In particular, we examine Sensation Mode, the Salon International du Design (SIDIM) and the Institute of Design Montréal (IDM). Each of these cases represents an example of a non-profit organization working with support and funding from the City and other levels of government to re-brand Montréal. These cases have been chosen because of the unique way in which they promote the value of design, and encourage networks between key economic actors within the City's design fields. An assessment of the origins, mandate and key activities and programs of these institutions illustrates both the possibilities and continued challenges for fostering a sustainable design culture.

Fostering networks of design: three case studies

The first case that we highlight is the case of Sensation Mode, an events producer in the city focused on promoting Montréal fashion. With support from the municipal and provincial governments as well as private sponsors, Sensation Mode organizes two key events in the city: the Fashion & Design Festival and the Montréal Fashion Week. Each of these events is oriented to a different set of actors within the fashion design field but as the following discussion shows, both events contribute to the city's design culture by facilitating linkages within and between industries and by fostering a greater appreciation for fashion design.

The first event, the Fashion & Design Festival, is an annual fashion show that is oriented to consumers. It takes place over a five-day period and the venue is a section of a popular, downtown commercial street, which is closed off and turned into a giant catwalk. Initially established by Sensation Mode in 2001, this festival seeks to engage the broader public by developing a new concept for a fashion show, one with "a Montréal signature – with all this city's creativity" (Peruse 2002: A1). Most participants in the Festival are local designers, but the event also includes designers from other parts of Canada and abroad. In addition, it features dancers, singers and musicians in an effort to create a broader experience and spectacle around fashion. According to one of the organizers, "it is really [for] people that don't have access to the fashion world . . . it's really 'fashiontainment'" (interview). And not too coincidentally, the event is organized at the same time as the Grand Prix, so that designers (and by extension, their retailers) can capitalize on a large tourist market. By associating with the Grand Prix, the event not only sparks interest in fashion design among the local public, but also aims to position Montréal within the "global fashion world" by providing greater visibility to local talent (interview, Fashion Week director). And the visibility is clearly there, as more than 500,000 people attended the last festival (ibid.; Friede 2006a).

The public nature of the Festival is one feature that distinguishes it from other fashion events. Another distinctive feature is that the Festival is not juried; any designer who is willing to pay to use the stage can exhibit (interview with one of the co-directors 2006). The Festival also showcases the final-year projects by students from all the local fashion design schools, with each school being given one half-hour to present its designs on the catwalk (ibid.). This visibility can help design students link up with potential employers and can expose them to the marketing dimension of the field. It also helps generate a greater appreciation of the role that design schools play in training these fashion creators (interview, design school program coordinator).

The second event, Montréal Fashion Week, is a twice-yearly fashion show where local designers and manufacturers can present their collections to potential buyers and local, national and international media. The show takes place over a five-day period in a centralized, downtown location. And in the case where designers prefer to show off-site, the organizers still coordinate the presentations, so as to minimize conflict and maximize exposure. In contrast to the Festival, Fashion Week is more of a conventional fashion show; it is oriented to the industry and restricted to the media, buyers, industry executives and invited guests (interview, Fashion Week director). The orientation to the industry is evident by the fact that the organizers have space dedicated for a media lounge and a makeshift showroom, where a designer's sales agent can present samples to potential buyers (interview, Fashion Week director; Atkinson 2007).

Fashion Week was initially established in 2001 by the Montréal Fashion Network, a non-profit organization that provides an umbrella for sector associations in the industry. At the time, the organization was concerned about the survival of the local industry, as trade quotas were being removed by the World Trade Organization (WTO) and producers were facing heightened competition from abroad. According to a former director:

> By launching Montréal Fashion Week as a twice-yearly event, we intend not only to increase the visibility and renown of Québec fashion products and the industry that creates them, but also to position Montréal as one of the world's fashion capitals before the market opening set by the WTO for 2005.
>
> (Montréal Fashion Network Press Release 2001)

In earlier years, the event was mainly overseen or coordinated by board members of the Network, many of whom lacked experience in producing events and had a difficult time retaining sponsorships. Due to the success that Sensation Mode had with the Festival, both designers and government officials advised Montréal Fashion Network to let Sensation Mode run the Fashion Show and the group was signed on by mid-2005 (interview, city official).

As in the case with the Festival, Sensation Mode looks to blend fashion with other cultural sectors to foster a greater appreciation of the creative dimension of the industry.

The show is presently held in a performing arts theatre. And as part of the show's calendar, the organizers have included band performances and a play, where the performers wear creations by local designers, as well as a visit to Cirque de Soleil's costume design studio. According to one of the co-directors, "For us, there is a link between costume and fashion, and the creativity of Cirque de Soleil is international, so we can capitalize on that too" (interview).

A number of designers have noted the significance of Sensation Mode events to the industry and to their own visibility. According to one prominent designer,

> if you're just starting off and you're not the household name, the media is not really interested in you ... with the Fashion week in Montréal, they have a structure to bring in buyers from the States, the media ... If I was alone, somewhere else and not at the same time with the fashion week, I would never get that kind of coverage.
>
> (Interview)

The attention that these events have garnered and their potential for fostering networks and associations is evident in the growing number of visitors, buyers and journalists. Montréal Fashion Week now draws in 20 international buyers, including a large contingent from Asia (Atkinson 2007). Despite the benefits of these events in terms of their promoting and marketing functions, for young, independent designers, the costs remain prohibitive. While significantly less than the costs for showing at the New York shows, the cost for showing at Montréal Fashion Week is still CAN$2,000, plus the cost for models, stylists and any additional publicity. There are also the costs of creating the runway pieces, which often require expensive, luxurious fabrics (Friede 2006b). Thus, increasingly, there are more commercial designers and established manufacturers presenting on the runway rather than avant-garde designers. As one fashion promoter contends: " [the] City of Montréal is a 'design city' but they [the designers] don't get help . . . Montréal capitalizes on them, but they don't get back" (interview). One of the organizers laments the fact that talented designers are struggling to survive and find it too costly to participate in the shows. She even suggests that it threatens the whole industry: "its so important, because if we don't have these kinds of artists, at the end, the competition is so huge, we really have to keep the creativity alive" (interview). She suggests that more should be done in terms of identifying industry sponsors, and in sensitizing them to the value of design and why it is worth investing in and supporting (ibid.). This is a sentiment echoed by a number of designers who say they are in need of more support to remain creative, yet viable (interviews; Anon 2007).

The second program that we highlight is the Salon International du Design Interieur de Montréal (SIDIM) (Figure 6a.1). SIDIM is an international interior design show occupying over 200,000 square feet, which is held in May of every year and is funded by the local, provincial and federal levels of government as well as by corporate sponsors. It was initiated in 1989 by Ginette Gadoury, who had long been involved in promoting interior design as the founder of the magazine *Decormag* and who was approached by the local interior design industry and the association of interior designers to coordinate the show (Bernatchez 1989). As one of the early creators of SIDIM notes, the goal of this exhibition was "to act as a network between all the people involved" in interior design (interview, SIDIM official). And at present, it serves as the only annual event in Québec that brings together designers, architects, institutional managers, corporate buyers, retailers, manufacturers, business people, and distributors, as well as consumers – i.e. all the key actors in the interior design field – to one location.

To foster linkages between these actors, SIDIM is organized around a number of thematic spaces. Some of the thematic spaces focus on specific product categories such as furniture (Mobilier d'ici à demain). Other thematic exhibits are intended to promote design innovation around particular social issues such as the environment (Green Design) or in particular spaces such as the office (Office Environments). Still, another thematic cluster (which includes a meeting space and bar) is organized under the banner "Business Encounters". As with the other spaces, there is a strong emphasis on establishing ties between users and producers of design.

Figure 6a.1 SIDIM exhibit

However, the particular focus here is on business people, who constitute 30 percent of SIDIM's visitors and are viewed as increasingly influential actors in the industry: "when it comes to designing for office, business, institutional or residential space, this group represents a key link in the buying chain" (SIDIM, 2006). Designers appreciate this focus on business:

> My first project that went to SIDIM was an eco project and it was a chair . . . It was very comfortable adjustable chair and it was a really big success . . . To me SIDIM is business . . . I was really excited because I thought maybe I could sell my chair.
>
> (Interview, industrial designer)

In the process of developing industry linkages between industry actors, there are two unique features of SIDIM that contribute to a broader appreciation of design and the development of a design culture. First, the show profiles the *designers* themselves:

> the accent is [on] creativity . . . It is a show that gets designers involved as exhibitors, as much as visitors and buyers. That may be . . . the difference between us and the Toronto shows where most of the exhibitors are companies . . . so, we create a lot of projects within the show.
>
> (Interview, official, SIDIM)

To reinforce this focus, the "Tribune des designers" (Spotlight on Québec Designers) serves as the centre piece of SIDIM. This show presents work by Québec industrial and interior designers in business for at least one year. Designers present recently-launched products, as well as concepts and prototypes. In the latter case, the idea is to attract the interest of a local manufacturer/business person to nurture the product to development. Both established and new designers are profiled, and each year there is a retrospective of one Québec designer's work.

Moreover, the focus in SIDIM is not only restricted to commercially-oriented designers. Série Limitée, funded in part by the provincial government through the Société de développement des enterprises culturelles du Québec (SODEC), is a space that is oriented around artisans producing high-end creations (SIDIM, 2006). These works are meant to blur the boundaries between art and interior design fields and are typically one-off or limited-edition pieces. The explicit mandate behind the exhibit is to raise the profile of Québec artisanal designers among the consuming public and the media as well as to create a space where designers and artisans can meet agents, buyers and distributors and identify commercially viable markets for limited run products (interviews). Another goal of this initiative, however, is to promote networking and collaborations between craft-based artisans and professionally trained interior designers to make "design professionals better aware of the contributions that artisans bring to the execution of their design schemes" (SIDIM, 2006). In this way, Série Limitée works to encourage a dialogue between the mass and niche-oriented segments of the industry and nurtures the aesthetic elements of design through an exchange of ideas and techniques. There is thus a strong focus in Série Limitée in blurring the boundaries between design fields and creative sectors, and of trying to combine art and commercial rationales.

A second unique feature of SIDIM is that it is open to the public. Organizers stress the central importance of constructing an appreciation of design among the local citizenry as a means of completing the chain: "many of our exhibitors find sometimes that it is a hassle to give information to the public. We feel that the public needs to be informed and sensitized and that's what makes the whole community more open to design" (interview, SIDIM official). This official suggests that a culture of design is something that must be actively cultivated through policy initiatives:

> when we go around Montréal and see there is a natural sensitivity to fashion and to art . . . it is not something that you create out of nothing. It is something that exists and that you develop in one way or another, sometimes in a structured way and sometimes not in a structured way.
>
> (Interview, SIDIM official)

In addition to developing an appreciation of designers – and design – on the part of local producers, distributors and consumers, SIDIM aims to be an international trade show to build Montréal's reputation as an international design city and to foster global connections for its design sector. When SIDIM was first launched, the organizer even commented on the possibility of Montréal being part of a network of international design capitals, saying:

> We are mature enough for this. In my opinion, Montréal can already claim the title of capital of the arts in Canada because the artistic creation is blooming here as nowhere else, including Toronto. And we have the major designers in Montréal, designers who are recognized around the world.
>
> (Bernatchez 1989: C6; translated from French by the authors)

At SIDIM, space is set aside for international exhibitors from countries such as Italy, Spain, France and Belgium that "do not yet have business partners on the Québec, Canadian and U.S. markets to identify and meet targeted potential clients" (SIDIM, 2006). In this way, SIDIM aims to position Montréal as a node on a broader circuit of international design, a goal that is embraced by one of its primary funders as well. According to the Minister of Municipal and Regional Affairs, SIDIM has already made important steps in attracting foreign markets and in marking the reputation of the city:

> . . . the number of professional buyers coming to the show from outside Québec only increases each year. As well, SIDIM draws foreign exhibitors and media. Developing SIDIM's international appeal raises the visibility of Québec designers and their creations, which enhances Montréal's reputation as a hotbed of innovative design.
>
> (Government of Québec, 2006)

SIDIM constitutes an innovative policy intervention in the field of design, bringing together actors across the interior design chain, and emphasizing development, marketing, and distribution. The exhibition aims to create shared sensibilities and a unique place-based aesthetic, facilitating an exchange between creative fields as well as between avant-garde and mainstream design. There is also a recognition that designers need to translate works into commercially viable applications; to this end, business users, manufacturers, and investors are foregrounded within the trade show. Recently, the Québec government, arguing for continued support of SIDIM initiatives, said

> the potential of the design sector, which combines creativity and research, is growing steadily. Montréal can indeed be proud of the output of its designers, which warrants development and distribution. Indeed since Montréal is competing with other major urban centers, design is an ideal springboard.
>
> (Government of Québec, 2005)

While the exhibition is successful in enlisting a variety of actors and institutions and on branding Montréal as a design metropole, the exhibition remains focused on the commercialization of innovative interior design ideas and concepts, allowing relatively little space for artistic and social rationalities. Serié Limitée however offers an interesting exception and suggests that further platforms and bases for exchange between creators could be encouraged.

The final program we highlight is the Institute of Design Montréal (IDM), which was established in 1993 in response to the Picard Report with a mandate to "promote design as an economic value and to make Montréal a design center of international caliber" (IDM, 2001: 1). The founder and present head of IDM is a former federal civil servant with training in business, and someone who has long viewed design as means for value-added in Montréal's declining industries. Due to her long-standing ties with government, the Institute receives significant funding from multiple scales, including the federal level. And in comparison with the other institutions that we have examined, IDM is unique in that it governs a range of design fields, including industrial design, interior design, graphic design, new media, architecture, landscape and urban design.

IDM starts from the notion that Montréal possesses a number of strategic assets with respect to its design economy, including a large pool of design talent and strong design education programs. Montréal's design services are also seen as cost competitive (due to the lower value of the Canadian dollar). The city's multicultural diversity and the consumer's openness to novelty are viewed as broader aspects relating to the design culture of the city. A strong history of government support for design and the arts is also highlighted as a source of competitive advantage (IDM, 2001: 10). Among the main constraints facing the design sector, however, is the low recognition of the value of design on the part of business, and therefore the need to instill this culture in the private sector. The institute also acknowledges a lack of coordination among programs and a lack of consensus building among key stakeholders in design in the city (IDM, 2001: 10–11).

In light of these challenges, IDM aims to cultivate a design culture in multiple realms simultaneously, including business communities, government milieus, and the general public. To this end, it runs a number of programs aimed at linking designers with businesses, consumers, students and educators. One of these programs is the "idea laboratory". This program aims to stimulate the development of innovative products addressing important social needs such as those relating to the health of an aging population, transportation or sustainable design. The idea is to gather together "designers, business people, sociologists, anthropologists . . . and this group can get together and talk about how to promote design, how to develop it. So this is the observatory where the ideas come out" (interview, IDM). The main goal in the observatory is to develop opportunities that can be further exploited in a think tank, comprised of specialists. The think tank establishes terms of reference and methodologies to be used in the development of opportunity studies which are performed by consultants. Consultants, in turn, identify particular products that could be developed (IDM, 2001).

In addition to the networking that takes place in these settings, IDM runs a number of programs targeted specifically at manufacturing companies. One example is their design consultation service, which helps companies pay for the services of a designer (IDM, 2001). As an official with IDM notes:

> If there are companies interested in integrating design . . . they can consult a designer . . . I pay up to $500 for the visit provided that the president of the company is going to give his [sic] time. I want the president to go.
>
> (Interview, IDM)

The aim is to bring designers and manufacturers together for an initial consultation and to foster a recognition of design at the highest levels of an enterprise. The other program – Design Diagnosis – helps subsidize the cost of using design professionals. In this case, IDM will pay up to $10,000 to a company to integrate design into their existing products or to develop new products (interview).

Other IDM programs are more oriented around designers themselves, providing assistance at all stages of the design process, including conception and execution, as well as marketing and distribution. The Enterprise Liaison program, for example, provides financial support to help designers develop products to the prototype stage. The Marketing Support program provides financial assistance to designers to exhibit their designs at local, national and international trade shows, competitions, and exhibitions. Additional assistance is available to help create communication tools to be utilized at these events. One industrial designer acknowledged the assistance his office received from this program in order to develop a DVD, illustrating how to assemble his product. This promotional device could be easily shipped to international manufacturers (interview, Industrial Designer, Montréal). He notes that without IDM assistance it would be very difficult to interest larger, more commercially viable and mass production manufacturers (such as IKEA) located outside the local area. This was significant since his product required a significant investment in tooling, and there were unlikely to be local suppliers capable of producing it. In addition to these programs, IDM also has a billboard on its website to match designers with jobs and clients.

IDM also has programs that cater to design students. The student partnership program, for example, brings students together with private enterprise to develop concepts to the model stage. IDM also provides bursaries to students, and runs workshops on topics such as business start-up, managing a design firm, obtaining a patent and developing a portfolio. Programs such as these provide training in business skills that are often lacking in the design schools. They also serve to instill the value of business in designers at an early stage.

Like the other institutions we have examined, IDM also sees the integration of end-users as critical for cultivating a local design culture and mounts a variety of programs aimed at stimulating public awareness of design, such as an annual awards show and a Design Month.

Positioned in the Canadian context, IDM is a unique institution, leveraging funding across a variety of governmental scales, as well as from private sector interests and non-profit organizations. It intervenes across the network, bringing various stakeholders in the design community together such as designers, clients, consumers and students. Through its varied initiatives, there is a drive to ensure the commercialization of artistic concepts. IDM is relatively successful at blurring the boundaries between design sectors and in bringing together actors across creative fields. However, IDM is centrally oriented around the economic contributions of design. IDM's Strategic Action Plan emphasizes that design is an important component of the knowledge economy, and a key tool for differentiating products (IDM, 2001). It is thus the economic benefits of design which are given emphasis: "our vision implies the outcome of IDM's actions is above all of an *economic nature* and that its interventions are directed towards improving the competitiveness of enterprises" (IDM, 2001: 1). The director of the organization argues that the focus on commerce relates to the fact that,

> designers are a little bit artists. The economic value of things, they don't grasp it very well. They have a tendency . . . to have academic ideas . . . They are not pragmatic . . . But the thing is in this society, you have to be more grounded, particularly if you get financial assistance from the government. I cannot have the airy fairy . . . I have to get results.
>
> (Interview, IDM official)

Thus, while there is a strong emphasis on creating an economically sustainable design culture in IDM's projects, other aspects of sustainability such as artistic and social dimensions remain marginalized.

Designers express concern regarding the economic and industry-centered focus of IDM, as well as the arbitrary divides that are established between design and other artistic fields:

> Lots of designers of our [younger] generation, they just hate IDM. We all feel . . . they are not conscious of the actual reality of being a designer. Some of us have these eclectic backgrounds. We don't necessarily have to have a degree in industrial design . . . You will see some designers in Europe. They will be out of arts schools and they will be doing furniture and stuff like that and it is o.k. . . . But here it's different. The thing with IDM is they only promote industrial design. When we come in with this kind of material that we do, they say, 'What's that? Not our business.' It is not art and it is not design to their eye . . . It is design, but their notion of design is very strict and they haven't adapted themselves to the actual reality.
>
> (Interview, industrial designer)

More artistically-inspired design work thus falls outside of the mandate of IDM.

Another designer notes that IDM only really assists designers indirectly: "IDM is receiving money from the three governments: federal, provincial and municipal to help the industry in using design. So they are not necessarily helping designers. They are helping the industry using the designers" (interview, industrial designer). Frustration is therefore expressed by some designers who would like more direct support for designers themselves.

Conclusion: lessons from the Montréal case for understanding the nature and regulation of the design industry

Montréal's unique institutional heritage surrounding design relates in many ways to a historic discourse of nationalism in Québec and a desire to forge a distinct culture within Canada. However, since the 1970s, this discourse has more prominently focused on the economic foundations of nationhood. Under this rubric, culture and design are supported for more instrumental reasons, as vehicles of urban renewal, economic competitiveness, and talent attraction (Paul, 2004; Pratt, 1997). At all levels of government, design is seen to have important spillover effects on manufacturing and tourism. While a strong institutional base has emerged to foster design in the city, a key problem relates to the top-down nature of existing initiatives and the lack of coordination among them. The focus on economic rationalities in policy discourse has also hindered the development of a culture of design – one that embraces design's multi-faceted nature and accommodates the varied needs of designers. Designers, like artists, need affordable studio space to be able to forge their creations. They also need opportunities to learn from one another, to encourage and critique each other's work (Markusen, 2006). While design centers and trade fairs are important sites of networking and support, designers also need access to less instrumental sites of practice. As Markusen (2006) suggests, artists (as well as designers) need spaces of inspiration, where they can make art for their own satisfaction or to share with their own communities. Current design policies in Montréal emphasize economic sustainability at the expense of broader social and cultural imperatives and needs. Design has been prioritized in Montréal because of the contribution it makes to quality of place and economic competitiveness, rather than quality of life. Current policy initiatives in Montréal emphasize necessary linkages across the design network, but there could be greater direct support for designers themselves who struggle to make a living in the Montréal economy, and greater opportunities for engagement between designers. At the moment, designers tend to form a fairly fragmented community (interviews).

There is a need for better coordination between design initiatives and policies targeted at other cultural sectors in order to stimulate greater spill-across linkages in Montréal's creative economy (Stolarick and Florida, 2006). The initiatives that we have examined above go a long way in fostering a greater recognition on the part of policy makers, key industry stakeholders, and the public at large of the hybrid nature of design and the need to leverage support for this sector from multiple sources and levels (public and non-profit, local and non-local), but this recognition still needs to be translated into a coordinated policy.

Notes

1 The city became the headquarters of the International Design Alliance (IDA) in 2005. This organization includes members of both ICSID (the International Council of Societies of Industrial Design) and ICOGRADA (the International council of Graphic Design Associations). IDA includes 150 associations, industrialists, design offices, designers and universities in more than 50 countries.

2 The city recently entered into agreements with Saint Etienne, Lyon, and the Times Square Business Alliance in New York City to export its Commerce Design Montréal competition.
3 The proceedings of this conference were later published as a book, *Nouvelle villes de design/New design cities*, meant to foster the development of a network of design cities and greater cooperation and knowledge transfer between them.
4 In addition, we draw upon a number of additional interviews with industrial, graphic and fashion designers in Montréal.
5 In his analysis of the Los Angeles "aesthetic", Molotch (1996) is careful to suggest that the LA style is not necessarily defined by a particular "look" but rather by shared sensibilities about being renegade and yet versatile. We too suggest that an aesthetic consent can be constituted by more general shared traits.

References

Anon, 2006, Lets live up to city of design tag, *The Montréal Gazette*, Editorial, 22 May: A22.

Anon, 2007, L'état de santé de la mode a Montréal sur le podium, *Journal de Rosemont/ Petite-Petrie*, 12 March. Accessed online at http://www.journalderosemont.com/v4/article-83888-Letat-de-sante-de-la-mode-a-Montréal-sur-le-podium.html.

Atkinson, N, 2007, Le chic bilingue, *National Post*, March 24: WP.3.

Banks, M, Lovatt, A, O'Connor, J and Raffo, C, 2000, Risk and trust in the cultural industries, *Geoforum* 31 (4): pp. 453–464.

Bell, D and Jayne M, 2003, "Design-Led" urban regeneration: a critical perspective, *Local Economy* 18(2): pp. 121–134.

Bernatchez, R, 1989, Une étape dans le cheminement [de nos designers pour s'imposer localement et internationalement], *La Presse*, 7 December: C6.

Bryson, J, Daniels, P W and Rusten, G, 2005, Inside the "Industrial" design world: understanding the relationship between industrial design expertise, product development, and the manufacturing process, Paper presented at the Annual Meeting of the Association of American Geographers, Denver.

City of Montréal, 2006, *Montréal Ville Unesco de Design/Unesco City of Design*. http://ville.montréal.qu.ca/pls/portal/docs/page/design_mtl_en/media/documents/UNESCO_candidature_en.pdf.

——, 2005a, *Nouvelles villes de design/New Design Cities*, Montréal: Infopresse.

——, 2005b, *Imagining – building Montréal 2025, a world of creativity and opportunities*. http://ville.montréal.qu.ca/pls/portal/docs/page/mtl_2025_en/media/documents/imaginer_realiser_mtl2025_en.pdf.

——, 2003, *Framework, guiding principles and statement for a cultural policy*, Summary of the Report of the Advisory Group, 2 June, 2003.

Commerce Design Montréal, 2002/2003/2004, Guide Design Montréal, 2002/2003/2004.

Conlogue, R, 1993, Montréal launches design institute, *Globe and Mail*, 1 May: C21.

DIAC (Design Industry Advisory Committee), 2004, What can 40,000 designers do for Ontario? Executive Report, Toronto.

Donald, B and Morrow, D, 2003, *Competing for talent: implications for social and cultural policy in Canadian city-regions*, A Report Prepared for Strategic Research and Analysis (SRA), Strategic Planning and Coordination Department of the Department of Canadian Heritage, SRA-674.

Florida, R, 2005, *The flight of the creative class: the new global competition for talent*, New York: Collins.

——, 2004, *Cities and the creative class*, New York: Routledge.

——, 2002, *The rise of the creative class: and how it's transforming work, leisure, community and everyday life*, New York: Basic Books.

Friede, E, 2006a, Fashion draws crowds in grand style during F1 race week, *The Montréal Gazette*, 27 June: D1.

——, 2006b, Canadian designers want recognition, *The Vancouver Sun*, 24 October: C5.

Gertler, M and Vinodrai, T, 2004, *Designing the economy: a profile of Ontario's design workforce*, Report prepared for the Design Industry Advisory Committee, Toronto.

Gertler, M, Florida, R, Gates, G and Vinodrai, T, 2002, *Competing on creativity: placing Ontario's cities in North American context*, A report prepared for the Ontario Ministry of Enterprise, Opportunity and Innovation and the Institute for Competitiveness and Prosperity, November 2002.

Government of Québec, 2006, Government of Québec Grants $203,000 to the 18th SIDIM, Press Release, 25 May, 2006.

——, 2005, The Québec Government Grants $167,000 to the 17th SIDIM, Press Release, 26 May, 2005.

Hertenstein, J H, Platt, M B and Brown, D, 2001, Valuing design: enhancing corporate performance through design effectiveness, *Design Management Journal*, Summer, pp. 10–84.

ICSID (International Council of Societies of Industrial design), 2004, Montréal wins the bid to host the joint ICSID/ICOGRADA Secretariats, Posted on ICSID Website: http://www.icsid.org.

Institute of Design Montréal, 2001, *Strategic action plan: Institute of Design Montréal, Horizon*, 2005 summary report, Le Groupe Stragesult, 21 March.

Institute of Design Montréal, Website. www.idm.qc.ca.

Institute of Design Montréal. 2003, 2002, 2001, 2000, 1999. Les Prix de l'Institut de Design Montréal Edition. http://www.idm.qc.ca.

Jackson, P, 2002, Commercial cultures: transcending the cultural and the economic, *Progress in Human Geography* 26 (1): pp. 3–18.

Julier, G, 2005, Urban designscapes and the production of aesthetic consent, *Urban Studies* 42 (5/6): pp. 869–887.

——, 1996, Barcelona design, Catalonia's political economy, and the New Spain, 1980–1986, *Journal of Design History* 9(2): pp. 117–127.

Leslie, D and Rantisi, N M, 2006, Governing the design economy in Montréal, Canada, *Urban Affairs Review* 40(5): pp. 1–29.

Leslie, D and Reimer, S, 2003, Fashioning furniture: restructuring the furniture commodity chain, *Area* 35(4): pp. 427–437.

Markusen, A, 2006, Building the creative economy for Minnesota's artists and communities, *Cura Reporter*, Summer: pp. 16–25.

Molotch, H, 2003, *Where stuff comes from: how toasters, toilets, cars, computers, and many other things come to be as they are*, New York: Routledge.

——, 1996, L.A. as design product, in A J Scott and E W Soja (eds.) *The City: Los Angeles and urban theory at the end of the twentieth century*, Berkeley, CA: University of California Press, pp. 225–275.

Montréal Fashion Network Press Release, 2001 (July 12), http://www.furcommission.com/news/newsF03.h.html.

Paul, D E, 2004, World cities as hegemonic projects: the politics of global imagineering in Montréal, *Political Geography* 23: pp. 571–596.

Peck J, 2005, Struggling with the creative class, *International Journal of Urban and Regional Research* 29(4): pp. 740–770.

Perusse, B, 2002, Promoters always in fashion, *The Montréal Gazette*, 4 January: A1.

Picard Report, 1986, Report of the consultative committee to the ministerial committee on the development of the Montréal region, Minister of Supply and Services Canada, Cat No. C2–98/1986E.

Polese, M and Shearmur, R, 2004, Culture, language, and the location of high-order service functions: the case of Montréal and Toronto, *Economic Geography* 80 (4): pp. 329–350.

Pratt, A, 1997, Production values: from cultural industries to the governance of culture, *Environment and Planning A* 29: pp. 1911–1917.

Rochon, L, 2004, Montréal's designing woman: Montréal has something other Canadian cities lack – a design commissioner, *Globe and Mail*, 3 November:R1.

Rose, D, 1996, Made in Montréal: Institute aims to promote city as centre of Canadian design, *The Montréal Gazette*, 25 February:F1.

Santagata, W, 2004, Creativity, fashion and market behavior, in D Power and A J Scott (eds.) *Cultural industries and the production of culture*, London: Routledge, pp. 75–90.

Scott, A J, 2000, *The cultural economy of cities*, London: Sage.

——, 1996, The craft, fashion, and cultural products industries of Los Angeles: competitive dynamics and policy dilemmas in a multi-sectoral image-producing complex, *Annals of the Association of American Geographers* 86(2): pp. 306–323.

SIDIM, 2006, SIDIM Projects. http://www.sidim.com/2006/en/exposants/projects/index.php (accessed 28 October, 2008).

SODEC (Société de Développement des Entreprises Culturelles). Website: www.sodec.gouv.gc.ca.

Stolarick, K and Florida, R, 2006, Creativity, connections and innovation: a study of linkages in the Montréal region, *Environment and Planning* 38 (10): pp. 1799–1817.

von Stamm, B, 2004, Innovation – what's design got to do with it?, *Design Management Review*, Winter, pp. 10–19.

6b Creativity and innovation in the Scandinavian design industry

Designed in Stockholm

Dominic Power

In recent years design has become a hot topic. An ever growing list of firms and products has been marketing themselves as design-based, and 'designer' goods and lifestyles have become part of everyday consumption landscapes. Although, in general, it is hard to say whether it is the design of a product – rather than, for example, its price – that makes it successful, there is a greater recognition in the business world of the strategic value of design. This has meant that the market for design services has rapidly expanded in recent decades; and with it the design services industry. In national and regional policy circles design has also begun to be mainstreamed, and throughout the advanced world policymakers have started using design (and local design industries) as a symbol of progress and adaptation to new economic realities, as a tool in place marketing, and as a potential growth industry.

Beyond the hyperbole that surrounds design relatively little is known about the design business itself. Whilst there is an enormous literature on design objects, techniques and star designers there is a meagre literature on how industrial systems of firms that supply design services come to be innovative and competitive. Whilst designers are commonly assumed to be creative and innovative it is obvious that some will be more creative and innovative than others. Equally, whilst many places are home to concentrations of highly artistic and creative design people, there are far fewer places that are home to design industries that are not only creative but also innovative and internationally competitive. Economic geographers have a long history of analysing and theorizing such settings and characteristics and suggest that local characteristics are crucial to explaining why creative and innovative firms are seldom evenly spread geographically. Firms in all sorts of industries seem to be drawn together into agglomerations and the particularities of these agglomerations seem to help explain why and how these embedded firms become competitive, creative and innovative. In recent years cluster theory and research has been central to this type of work. In the rest of this chapter I will examine how certain hypotheses central to the cluster approach can help us understand why certain settings seem to support heightened levels of creativity and innovation in the Swedish design industry.

This chapter explores the case of Stockholm as a home to a creative, but also innovative and increasingly competitive, design services industry. The chapter draws on the aforementioned cluster approach and suggests that certain characteristics of the local industrial settings are indeed important to design firms' innovation and creativity. In particular, the chapter tests three hypotheses about how a cluster can support creativity and innovation: that creativity and innovation rest upon local inter-organizational collaborative interaction, competition and rivalry between local firms, and knowledge spill-over between firms that follows from the local mobility and sociability of individuals. I suggest that some evidence exists to support these hypotheses but that the Stockholm cluster indicates that creativity and innovation in the design industry are also shaped by processes not usually given much attention in cluster accounts: the role of (extra-local and/or temporary) events; and individuals' focus on their own, rather than their firms', careers.

Design?

There are significant difficulties defining design, and therein the industry, actors and competences that supply it. Defining design is difficult for a variety of reasons. First, 'design' has become synonymous not just with the aesthetic, etc. dimensions of products but also with a muddled set of lifestyle symbols and signifiers. This makes it difficult to distinguish the effect of design inputs into a product's value from the products other social, symbolic, brand, etc. value. In addition, design has increasingly been used by many firms and industries as a term synonymous with product progress, change and innovation. Thus a plethora of changes and progressive innovations to products are often labelled 'redesign'.

For the purposes of defining design and the design industry in this chapter I will focus on the process of design rather than its output: on the process of developing and designing a plan for a chair and not on the finished chair itself. The design process involves not just the planning and development of aesthetic aspects of a product but also their overall technological performance and character. The act of design involves not just shaping a product's appearance but also involves a range of inputs into the creation of the form and function of a product and its production, marketing and appeal to the consumer. This means that as a commercial product/service design exists in a variety of forms. A grossly oversimplified typology of commercial design appears in the list that follows. From this simple typology it can be seen that the current usage of the term includes commercial activities over and above the activities involved in developing the type of trendy objects lifestyle magazines tend to define as 'design'.

- Business-to-Business (B2B)
  - Design services: specialized design firms that supply design services to other businesses and organizations (e.g. designing a website for a supermarket; designing marketing or communications materials; designing components for a car maker)
- Business-to-Consumer (B2C)
  - Design products: where the entire value of the product is its design (e.g. designer ornaments and home decorations)

– Design*ed* products: where design is an important add-on or extra dimension that allows functional products to be sold at much higher prices (e.g. designer office furniture; high-end cars).

When thinking about design, it is also worth noting that it does not necessarily need to be integrated into the whole of the product's life story. Design can be used in many different phases or stages in the product's/service's life cycle. Design is commonly associated with the initial stages of developing (or redeveloping) a product – in the process of conceptualizing what is to be done or changed. Having established an aim or concept to operationalize, designers and design can prove invaluable to arriving at the right technical solutions to problems associated with production, storage and distribution. Finally design is increasingly being employed in commercialization phases. Here design plays a role in shaping the ways in which consumers find out about a product (differentiation, marketing and advertising), how it appears to them when they are making a decision (packaging, retail environments, etc.), and how their experience is in using the product (and therein the likelihood they will want to buy something more from the firm).

Thus it may be that a design firm is employed to develop a new concept for a product or service. Alternatively it may be that design and designers play an integral role in every stage from the birth of an idea all the way through to marketing and after-sales. Design then can be sold in different forms (as a B2B service, as a design product, etc.) and it can be involved in all stages of the business cycle: 'Design is a multifaceted concept which not only includes function and appearance, but which also suggests ease of manufacture and increasing the value of the product or providing features that make them sell at a profit' (Walsh *et al.* 1988: 202).

For the purposes of this article I will focus on the industry and firms that supply business-to-business design services. A wide range of producer services are included under such a broad category – so wide in fact that one might wonder if they should be classed as a category of services rather than as an 'industry' in their own right. I have classed them as an industry in this paper since those people working in design that I interviewed[1] viewed themselves not as service providers but as members of an industry with its own borders, practices, standards, industrial organizations/bodies, dedicated research and educational institutions. Those interviewed consciously saw themselves as being part of a growing industry that was, in their view, the creator of core competitive competences. In many cases they argued (rightly or wrongly) that it was ultimately the particular design, aesthetic, ergonomics, experience, symbolic value, etc. they gave chairs, cars, mobile phones, services etc. that was more important to people's choice than the material or functionality embedded in the product. The design people I talked to constantly stressed that they were not providers of add-on services but rather developers of core products that people bought, and as such they were an industry in their own right. In the rest of this chapter then the term industry is used to group these 'service providers' who share a developing set of institutions and a conscious collective identity. The Swedish design industry encapsulates a wide variety of design activities but presently it is graphic design, web design, industrial design and brand/communications design that dominate business-to-business design services in Sweden.

Design in Stockholm

Stockholm and Sweden have been closely associated with modern design for many decades. In particular, it has been long assumed that Stockholm is a central creative centre for 'Scandinavian design'. The term 'Scandinavian design' first appeared in 1951 as the title of an exhibition of home decorations and furniture – 'Scandinavian Design for Living' – at London's Heal's Department store. The exhibition was the first of a series of showcases for Nordic design, decoration and furniture. In 1954–1957 'Design in Scandinavia' toured Canada and America to great success and similar collaborative exhibitions in Milan during the 1950s and Paris in 1958 ('Formes Scandinaves') helped to form a globally recognized label that has been used to brand a wide variety of products. Despite Scandinavian designers' frequent pronouncements that the term is irrelevant, dead and buried, and despite the fact that very few of the most famous proponents of 'Scandinavian design' were Swedish, the label's international prestige has undoubtedly helped establish Stockholm's reputation as a high-quality design centre (Fiell and Fiell 2002).

Scandinavia and Sweden's reputations for design are not, of course, entirely unfounded. There is a deeply rooted tradition of design in these countries: both as an input into industrial production and as an everyday presence (Fiell and Fiell 2002). In Sweden design has long had a prominent place in society and has been supported by design conscious consumers and a set of supporting institutions; e.g. the Swedish Society of Crafts and Design (Svensk Form), founded in 1845, is the world's oldest design association. In addition, many of the countries' more successful companies have consciously used design in order to establish their competitive edges; e.g. IKEA, H&M.

However, design is not only a cultural phenomenon or a competitive edge to large firms, it is also a growing industry in its own right. Whilst accurate statistics on the design industry's size are notoriously difficult to obtain, a recent Nordic study (Power *et al.* 2004) found that in 2002 there were a total of 11,199 firms in the Swedish design industry: 5,631 graphic design firms, 2,740 architecture firms, and 2,828 'other design' firms (see Power *et al.* 2004 for details of the statistical definitions and databases used). Very small firm sizes dominate the industry. The industry was also growing quickly: 1993–2002 the total number of firms rose by 272 per cent and by 2003 the design industry had a turnover of 7,549 million SEK (around 838 million Euros). It is important to note that design firms are far from equally distributed across Sweden. Certain regions, and even city districts, show strong agglomeration tendencies. In Sweden, in 2003, 50 per cent of design firms and 52 per cent of industry turnover were in Stockholm; Västra Götaland (Göteborg region) had 15 per cent of firms and 23 per cent of turnover; Skåne (Malmö region) had 12 per cent of firms and 7 per cent of turnover. Evidence suggests that the strongest growth in design firm revenues is concentrated in the capital city. In 2002–2003 a total of 402 design firms had increases in turnover of over 10 per cent;

205 of these were based in Stockholm and 144 of these had increases of over 20 per cent.

The existence of such a strong urban focus is therefore an important issue that we need to deal with if we are to understand creativity and innovation in the Swedish design services industry.

There are many possible explanations for high levels of concentration. For instance, Scott suggests that service industries tend to be highly sensitive to distance effects and that co-localization tends to increase productivity through lowering transaction costs (Scott 1988; 2001). Where industrial activity is concentrated it is easier to meet clients and find new business. Concentration also makes it easier for firms and clients to source specialist services and labour. Moreover proximity to potential collaborators makes project-based working – a central way of organizing design work – easier and more flexible. The existence of a variety of small and flexible firms allows the design system to react quickly to new types of projects and new demands: networks of small firms that can quickly assemble project teams are increasingly a competitive strength of the Nordic design scene. Proximity to collaborators, competitors and innovators also means that firms located in agglomerations tend to be more innovative and up to date since they can see and meet new ideas and trends on a daily basis. In my research on design activities in Stockholm time and time again I came across designers that stated that informal social networks and 'just being there' helped them with their work, finding clients, and staying innovative and relevant. Lastly, we may wonder whether place-based reputational rents are accrued by firms in status locations like Stockholm, just as Molotch suggests happens for firms in the Los Angeles design industry (Molotch 1996).

Thus we can see that there are likely to be many dimensions to any explanation of why the design services industry is growing so strongly in Sweden and why it is so concentrated in certain local settings. The rest of this chapter focuses on two particular dimensions that may be of importance to such an explanation: first, the question of whether the local 'cluster' in Stockholm supports business-related innovation and creativity; second, how links to customers outside the cluster contribute to both the cluster and to firms' competitiveness and profitability.

Creativity and innovation in the Stockholm design industry

As already noted, design is an input into many types of products that combines a number of dimensions. In particular, design combines an aesthetic (even artistic) dimension with a problem solving dimension (for instance, increasing usability, bettering ergonomics, rationalizing production routines, etc.). Combining all these dimensions into competitive products is based on knowledge-based interactive processes – for instance, designers work in close dialogue with the clients and consumers. The creation of new, and adaptation to commercial purposes of, knowledge then is central to the competitiveness of design services and is likely to be supported by local networks and cluster dynamics.

The negotiation and co-creation of new business knowledge and innovations is, of course, not limited to design. A large number of studies have focused on how firms in 'clusters' create knowledge and innovation that result in increased economic value, etc. (Baptista 1998; OECD 2001; Malmberg and Power 2005; Malmberg and Power 2006). The godfather of cluster research, Michael Porter, defines a cluster as 'a geographically proximate group of interconnected companies and associated institutions in a particular field, linked by commonalities and complementarities' (Porter 2000: 254).

The cluster concept is a highly contested concept (Baptista and Swann 1998; Porter 1998; Martin and Sunley 2003; Malmberg and Power 2006) but it is also arguably a useful, and popular, concept for those interested in understanding why it seems that firms in many industries have a high tendency to agglomerate together. The cluster approach stresses the importance of the home base or local milieu in explaining why certain firms seem to be more competitive than others, and has been shown to have some use in explaining geographies of creativity and innovation in the cultural industries (Scott 2000; Bathelt 2002; Hallencreutz *et al.* 2003; Power and Scott 2004a; Hallencreutz and Power 2005; Pratt 2006).

Since the research this chapter is based upon found that the creativity and innovation of the Stockholm design services industry seems to rely heavily upon local networks and locally rooted capabilities and interactions, it is fitting then that we try and see if the cluster concept can help us understand the place and its industry. If design services rest upon being rooted in milieus that are good at supporting knowledge creation it is interesting to examine how exactly the Stockholm design cluster supports knowledge creation.

Why the Stockholm design cluster might support knowledge and creativity: three hypotheses

Malmberg and Power (2006) suggest that the literature on knowledge and innovation in agglomerations currently rests upon three main hypotheses (or ideal types). First is the hypothesis that knowledge in industrial clusters is created through various forms of local inter-organizational collaborative interaction. This proposition is grounded in the idea that firms that collaborate more with other firms in the local milieu will innovate more, and in the idea that firms that meet sophisticated demands from demanding customers in the local milieu will be forced to innovate at a higher pace than other firms.

The second hypothesis commonly found in the literature in this field is that the increased competition and intensified rivalry, which one is likely to find in dense proximate networks of firms, speeds up knowledge and innovation processes. The idea here is that rivalry between similar firms in local milieus will be more intense and will create pressure to innovate in order to outsmart the local rival. In part, this is related to the fact that geographically proximate firms are more visible to each other, which makes observation, monitoring and benchmarking easier and more efficient. Therefore, firms with nearby rivals will be more innovative than firms whose main competitors are located elsewhere.

The third hypothesis is that knowledge in clusters is created through spill-over effects following from the local mobility and sociability of individuals. A key notion behind this is the idea that knowledge diffusion will be more rapid among local firms than among globally dispersed firms, due to the intensity of informal interaction in the local milieu as well as through flows of people in the local labour market. This type of spill-over is based upon and added to by local labour market processes: it is through people moving jobs and firms that most new ideas, contacts, etc. come to firms.

However, just as Malmberg and Power (2006) suggest, it seems that if we look at the Stockholm design services 'cluster' these three hypotheses are only partially true.

How the Stockholm design cluster supports knowledge and creativity: three hypotheses tested

1. Does local inter-organizational collaborative interaction support knowledge and creativity?

If we take the first of these hypotheses we find that there is some degree of local inter-firm collaboration. Firms do work together occasionally but in general Stockholm design firms' focus is not on jointly developing new ideas or products with other design firms. Their focus is on developing new knowledge with the specific clients they have at the time. The majority of firms interviewed suggested that the last thing they really wanted to do was share their ideas and knowledge with other design firms. Nonetheless all firms suggested that they do occasionally work together with firms from other design specialities: for instance, industrial designers reported that they often collaborated with architects and communications designers. Many of these relationships were contract based and involved buying additional services in order to get the job done rather than sharing knowledge or jointly developing new ideas with other firms.

It appears then that just as in other knowledge-based industries (Angel and Engstrom 1995; Hendry *et al.* 2000) intense collaborative interaction with similar and related firms in the localized cluster does not come out as a major knowledge creating mechanism in the Stockholm design industry. In other industries firms commonly link up with other types of local organizations, such as universities or research institutes, to create new products and ideas; there is virtually no evidence of this happening in the design industry. The only relations between firms and design schools seem to be in staff recruitment (most Stockholm firms recruit almost exclusively from local design schools) or when professional designers give guest lectures at local design schools.

2. Do local competition and rivalry support knowledge and creativity?

If then there is limited evidence of formal collaborative interaction in Stockholm, perhaps increased local competition and rivalry – the second hypothesis – can help us explain creativity and innovation in the cluster. Whilst non-altruistic motives are seldom studied by regional scientists and economic geographers there is some evidence (Sakakibara and Porter 2001; Power and Hallencreutz 2002; Boari *et al.* 2003; King *et al.* 2003; Power and Hallencreutz 2005) that local rivalry effects knowledge creation. Talking to designers in Stockholm quickly reinforced the idea that they saw themselves as in direct competition with their peers. Although the demand for design services has been consistently increasing, the margins on most projects are still relatively small and competition is intense both for smaller jobs and for the custom of large organizations that understand, and pay for, high quality design services. Many large Swedish firms – especially those in automotives or consumer durables – have begun to outsource large parts of their design needs and tend to favour relatively long-term supplier relationships. Getting their foot in the door of these large firms was viewed as especially important for Stockholm's industrial and graphic designers. Interviewees suggested that intense competition and indeed dirty tricks were used by small firms trying to get a start.

Competition is not only intense for large clients but also for high profile clients. Working for certain high profile clients – such as Ericsson the mobile phone manufacturer – was deemed especially important in the long term. Though these clients do not always pay the best, design firms garner significant reputational capital from working for profile clients. In a business where the work process is hard to quantify or value and the product is almost entirely immaterial/intangible, the firm's past clients and reputation is in essence their only asset. Firms then compete aggressively for profile clients as well as for day-to-day business.

Competition for business was said, by all firms interviewed, to directly result in a constant pressure to innovate and develop new approaches and ideas. That the industry is dominated by very small – most often one or two person – and young firms helps increase competitive pressures. Small design firms in Stockholm reported that their size makes every job crucial to their vulnerable finances but also that the growth of the industry and the design education sector means that there is a constant stream of new entrants into the marketplace; new entrants with new ideas and lower costs.

All these competitive pressures are, many interviewees said, made more immediate and intense by proximity to their peers and competitors. Simply being able to see competitors, ex-colleagues, student friends, etc. on the street and at events meant that members of the industry were constantly in touch with how everyone else was doing. It is not surprising then that the combination of a highly competitive marketplace and constant reminders of how well others seem to be doing leads to often intense personal rivalries. Designers frequently pointed to personal rivalries (and resentments) as an explanation for why certain individuals were particularly driven to succeed and indeed for many firm level mergers, splits and acquisitions. It seems then that in the case of Stockholm (usually relatively friendly) rivalry is a more important booster of knowledge creation than various forms of collaboration.

3. Does knowledge spill-over follow from the local mobility and sociability of individuals?

The third hypothesis about why clusters support knowledge creation is that in various ways the sociability and mobility of individuals is thought to lead to spill-over effects. In other words, knowledge that should rest in one firm spills over to other firms when individuals meet each other or change jobs. A range of studies of other industries suggest that informal knowledge exchanges do seem to occur across groups of professionals and specialized individuals in clusters (Thrift and Leyshon 1994; Coe 2000; Bennett *et al.* 2001; Grabher 2001; Lissoni 2001; Grabher 2002; Benner 2003; Welz 2003). The Stockholm design cluster also seems to confirm this hypothesis.

The most important forms of interaction in the cluster seem to spring from the sociability of individuals and from labour mobility. Designers constantly referred to the importance they attach to the networks of friends and contacts they have developed in the local area over years of schooling, freelancing and different jobs. Early career experiences were often said to have long-lasting effects and that the friends/contacts made in design education and in the first one to two years of professional life were vital for the rest of their professional careers. Indeed the majority of small new firms interviewed were set up by two to three friends from one of the main design schools found in Stockholm. Designers were not merely tied to the old school of course and they frequently said that they actively courted new contacts and friendships within the profession and that this was an important part of their search for new opportunities and also important for learning new things.

These social networks are constantly worked upon in a series of informal spaces and meeting places. Designers placed strong emphasis on after-hours and informal meeting places and events. Many younger designers suggested that certain bars and meeting places were important to getting to know new people and maintaining old contacts and that even late at night they found inspiration and new ideas through conversations with other design professionals. In a recent study of the New York digital media industry, Neff also found that social events and night time activities were a central focus for people working in creative industries (Neff 2005).

Beyond the firm-centric local cluster? Events and individuals' careers

To varying degrees then there do seem to be some sort of 'cluster' dynamics operating to support creativity and innovation in the Stockholm design services industry. Cooperation, rivalry, competition, labour mobility and sociability all seem to play roles; though not necessarily in the proportions or ways that cluster accounts typically wish them to. If economic geographers often rely on three main hypotheses to account for an industry's creativity and innovation, it must be noted that these hypotheses are typically underpinned by an implicit set of (normative) assumptions about privileged actors, time and space.

In particular, my research in the design sector has led me to notice various difficulties and limitations imposed by two normative assumptions commonly held by cluster theorists (and enacted by policymakers). First, industrial knowledge and innovation processes that are supportive of a local cluster need to happen locally (ideally in some sort of creative industries version of an industrial estate or science park) with some regularity or frequency (ideally daily). Second, that there is seldom any mention of individuals in these accounts of creativity and innovation processes: it is primarily the development of the firm/system of firms that creativity and innovation processes are constructed around and towards. These observations have led me to suggest (on the basis of the Stockholm case) two additional hypotheses:

- That clustered firms will often find specific (extra-local and temporary) events as important complements to the day-to-day dynamics supporting creativity and innovation.
- That social contact networks within a cluster are most likely to be motivated by individuals more concerned about developing their careers than the careers of their employers.

The role of events in creativity and innovation

Whilst informal spaces and events were deemed the most important for sharing ideas and getting new contacts, a series of other temporary spaces have begun to be important for Stockholm designers. Two local events – the Stockholm International Furniture Fair, and Future Design Days – and one international one – the Milan International Furniture Fair/Milan Design Week – were repeatedly mentioned.

The Stockholm International Furniture Fair is essentially a trade fair dedicated to the sale of various furniture, lighting and interiors products, but has in recent years developed into a fair that is also the focus for designers and design firms who do not directly work with interiors. Swedish designers said that the Stockholm event was their primary annual focus (since the majority of their clients are from the Nordic region) but as they built reputations or tried to expand further abroad, the Milan International Furniture Fair/Milan Design Week became another crucial set of dates and deadlines in their year. Many designers suggested that as the industry has grown and become increasingly specialized/niched large numbers of Swedish designers have been forced to seek clients abroad. International trade fairs like Milan (and to a lesser extent Stockholm) offer one of the only spaces within which they can efficiently meet potential clients from a variety of far-off places. In addition, high status foreign events like Milan (but also the design fairs in London, Cologne, and New York) were said to be often used not to reach foreign markets but to market themselves as international to domestic clients.

Participation in international and domestic trade fairs occurs for a variety of reasons (Power and Jansson 2008). Those designers that attend trade fairs, by and large, do so in order to reap some sort of economic or business benefit. Participation involves personnel and other costs, and firms that exhibit also incur significant costs for their stand, prototypes, exhibition materials, public relations, entertainment, etc. Exhibiting at Milan involved a much higher level of costs and was considered both a badge of honour and also a major capital investment. The smaller Swedish firms we interviewed who exhibited in Milan reported average spending of €50,000 for the stand alone – a substantial amount for the firms in question. This figure does not include costs for manufacturing prototypes to exhibit, personnel, travel and hotels. For larger and more prestigious firms, it is not uncommon to spend up to €200,000 on the design of the stands only (Power and Jansson 2008). For small firms these costs represent often a large part of their annual expenditure and indicate both how important firms view trade fairs and why the firms interviewed viewed trade fair attendance (and especially exhibition) as primarily a capital investment that must be matched by increased sales. Few firms could afford to view these events as simply information gathering or informal networking events. Nonetheless, Stockholm International Furniture Fair was attended even by designers with no direct products to sell to the furniture and interiors industry. These designers suggested that attendance was important for: networking, marketing, knowledge flows/creation, and for recruitment/job hunting. Lastly, the Fair has also become an important focus for the various design associations and representative bodies who now actively use the event (in conjunction with Stockholm city authorities) to market Swedish design to an international audience.

Respondents also pointed to conferences and networking events as being a regular feature of how they manage social/business networks and as spaces in which they learn new things. One such event is an annual design 'festival' and conference called The Future Design Days that is now held in Stockholm. This event invites speakers from around the world, and has grown rapidly into a major focus for the Stockholm and Swedish design industry. Unlike trade fairs such events offer firms and individuals more freedom to just sit and listen to new perspectives. The designers we interviewed suggested that the combination of intense social interaction (e.g. during the coffee breaks and evening events) combined with the chance to listen to lectures and seminars was useful; especially since they were not expected to sell anything at this type of event. It seems important then for designers to have meeting places and spaces (whether permanent or temporary) in order to engage in the latest trends, techniques, business models and ideas.

Building careers rather than clusters

There seems to be a strong case that local sociability helps spread knowledge, skills and contacts in the local milieu. However, it can be misleading to concentrate attention on the role of networks and sociability in designers' creativity and innovation. There is considerable evidence from Stockholm that designers primarily see the city as an arena for their careers and a platform for forming different working constellations to deal with new projects; and that they seldom see networks and interaction as central to creativity or learning. In this it can be said that Grabher's (Grabher 2001) idea of project-based ecologies can be seen to exist in the

Stockholm design industry. As Vinodrai (Vinodrai 2006) notes in relation to the Toronto design industry, dense social networks and intersecting career paths in the local area help designers get new work, coordinate new projects 'across a wide variety of industrial and organizational contexts' (Vinodrai 2006: 251).

Designers in Stockholm seemed to accept the idea that their careers were almost guaranteed to be a muddled combination of project-working, employment, freelancing, entrepreneurship and perhaps unemployment. By staying in the local area and constraining their labour mobility to a relatively limited scene it becomes easier for designers to build the reputations and contact networks they need to build careers with. Designers suggested that in recent years the speed at which people change job or work form (in a firm, freelance, start-up, etc.) has dramatically increased and that an oversupply of newly qualified designers from the expanding design education sector has allowed firms to rapidly replace employees and to take in (often short-term) workers to match the skills and staffing levels their workloads demand. In other industries there is considerable evidence that local labour mobility plays an important role in rates of innovation and that localized clusters that are relatively successful tend to have higher rates of labour mobility into the cluster, within the cluster, and within the cluster firms (Angel 1991; Almeida and Kogut 1999; Gilson 1999; Cooper 2001; Fosfuri *et al.* 2001; Dahl 2002; Madsen *et al.* 2003; Song *et al.* 2003; Power and Lundmark 2004).

Of course what is good for individuals' careers and for the cluster's overall knowledge creation and spreading might not be good for all firms, and there is evidence suggesting that firms in clusters with high labour mobility view such 'dynamism' as a considerable cost (Almeida and Kogut 1999; Dahl 2002) and even a potential threat to the trade secrets or styles they hope to commercialize (Ronde 2001; Fosfuri and Ronde 2004). For an industry where many of the 'secrets' they are selling are entirely subjective or stylistic and extremely difficult to copyright/patent, labour mobility may negatively affect firms. In fact designers said that were constantly worried that people would copy or steal their ideas and that this was an explanation of why they often did not want to share ideas or work with other people.

It would be wrong then to see the milieu as primarily a place where organizational change and coordination was made possible: as many firm-centred accounts of local milieus often suggest. Designers suggested time and again that it was less a platform for short-term collaboration/projects and more an arena within which long-term careers could be built. They were aware that at certain points in their working lives they would be working more or less freelance or in short-lived 'project ecologies' (Grabher 2001). However, they were also likely to spend significant parts of their lives employed full-time in a firm or organization or likely to maintain very long relationships with certain clients. This means that although the organizational capacities and potentialities the milieu offers the industry is important to firms, for individual design workers it is the long-term career possibilities the place seems to offer that attract them and keep them there. It is also important to recognize that there may be a life cycle element to individuals' attraction and attachment to place. Many of the design workers interviewed had spent significant periods abroad but had moved back 'home' to Sweden. Equally many suggested that they would prefer to live elsewhere but that friends and family kept them in place. It seems then that we should be careful not to ignore individuals' perspectives when trying to explain why so many creative and innovative design firms agglomerate in places like Stockholm.

Conclusion

In the introduction to this chapter I suggested that we need to focus more attention on understanding design as an industry or a business; and to look at how different places support it in different ways. Work in economic geography suggests that explanations of firms' innovation and creativity are likely to lie in the characteristics of local industrial settings; and that the cluster approach may help us do this. Evidence from Sweden's dominant design centre, Stockholm, seems to support the idea that the local industrial setting does indeed have very important consequences for creativity and innovation in the design industry. It seems that the cluster approach's suggestion that phenomena such as local inter-firm competition and rivalry as well as knowledge spill-over following from individuals' local sociability do support creativity and innovation. However, though the local industrial setting in Stockholm is crucial to explaining firms' creativity and innovation, it is not necessarily in the ways that standard accounts of clusters' effects may have us believe.

In the Stockholm case there was little evidence to support all aspects of the three hypotheses most often used to explain clustering and clusters' role in industrial creativity and innovation. First, there was little to support the idea that knowledge or innovation was created through local inter-organizational collaborative interaction. Even though firms often worked together, they did not tend to collaborate formally or to share much when they did work together. However, there was considerable evidence to suggest that the drive to be creative and innovative was often underpinned by the competitive dynamics of the rapidly changing and growing industry. Furthermore it seems that whilst there was little collaborative interaction aimed at sharing knowledge, there was plenty of personal rivalry between designers and that this rivalry (combined with close proximity to competitors) did motivate many to continually innovate and upgrade. Personal rivalries born out of social proximity are undoubtedly just a part of a wider phenomenon apparent in Stockholm. All the designers interviewed actively sought to bind themselves into local social networks; networks they believed to be important not just for their knowledge of what is going on but mainly for their fight to secure long-term careers. It seems that knowledge spill-over from individuals' sociability does occur, though it is the nature of the career structure in an industry characterized by a high degree of labour mobility that seems to best explain the importance individuals attach to this local sociability.

Whilst the initial three hypotheses only partly helped explain the Stockholm case two additional hypotheses emerged from the research. These were that creativity and innovation were likely to be effected by the role of (extra-local and/or temporary) events, and by individuals' focus on forwarding their own, rather than their firms', careers. Individual designers and design workers worked hard to build up social networks and contacts. But this work was said to be primarily motivated by the desire to secure a career in a difficult and ever changing industry. Networks may have involved knowledge spill-over, etc. that helps firms but they are built and maintained by individuals who seemed relatively confident in their creative abilities but very concerned about securing their own livelihood.

Second, if networking, rivalry, competition, sociability and labour mobility happen on a regular basis within the confines of central Stockholm they also happen in events or spaces that are far from permanent or geographically concentrated. Designers in Stockholm placed especial importance on intense, short-lived and temporary events: such as trade fairs, conferences and industry gatherings. They were willing to incur considerable costs to travel to foreign events in the hope of finding new clients and new inspiration. It is not surprising perhaps that in an industry where the 'product' itself is relatively easy to export and which is based upon techniques and creative styles that come from around the world that designers are not necessarily looking for permanence or stable spatial fix when they seek out inspiration, innovations or new knowledge. The creative and innovative core of the Stockholm design industry then seems to rest upon a complex set of local networks and relations within the local cluster. However, if we are to understand creativity and innovation in design services we must be open to the idea that designers cannot get everything they need from the local arena, and that openness to wider sets of creative and knowledge flows and geographies is an important part of how they work and innovate.

The case of the Stockholm design industry points to the idea that creativity and innovation in the cultural economy is highly linked to the particularities of place. The patterns and processes apparent in design services are likely to be mirrored in other industries that rest upon knowledge-based and intangible products and services. In such activities, firms will commonly try to compete through the pursuit of monopolistic competition (Chamberlin 1933; Power and Scott 2004b) and by constantly differentiating themselves (Levitt 1975 [1960]; Levitt 1981) from what they view as the competition. The way in which they use their local setting is shaped by these competitive dynamics and is a likely explanation to why rivalry rather than collaboration is prominent in many cultural economy hotspots. Equally the rapidly changing industrial landscape, where firms are most often small and flexible, may explain why many cultural economy workers invest so much time in their networks and sociability. Rather than trying to share knowledge they are trying to build networks that will find them the next job or project. The patterns and processes apparent in Stockholm are also likely to be shared by other agglomerations/clusters of cultural industry firms located in areas with limited local demand or on the periphery. What happens locally on a regular basis is important but for highly specialized cultural activities limited local markets means individuals and firms alike invest heavily in events that can help them reach new markets and new people. We must therefore complement our understandings of what happens locally with an appreciation of the complex events and circuits that link local cultural economies to their customers.

Acknowledgements

This chapter draws upon many sources and a long series of empirical projects on the design industry. In particular, it draws upon a series of articles and book chapters written by the author together with Anders Malmberg and on empirical work conducted jointly with Johan Jansson and by the pan-Nordic research project *The Future in Design.*

Notes

1 This research has been funded by various organisations, spanned several years and involved a total of over 100 interviews in Sweden and the Nordic countries. Around 60 of these interviews were carried out in the Stockholm region.

References

Almeida, P. and B. Kogut (1999). 'Localization of knowledge and the mobility of engineers in regional networks.' *Management Science* 45(7): 905–917.

Angel, D. P. (1991). 'High-technology agglomeration and the labor market: the case of Silicon Valley.' *Environment and Planning A* 23(10): 1501–1516.

Angel, D. P. and J. Engstrom (1995). 'Manufacturing systems and technological change: the US personal computer industry.' *Economic Geography* 71(1): 79–102.

Baptista, R. (1998). 'Clusters, innovation and growth: a survey of the literature.' *The Dynamics of Industrial Clustering: International Comparisons in Computing and Biotechnology*, (eds) P. Swann, M. Prevezer and D. Stout. Oxford, Oxford University Press.

Baptista, R. and P. Swann (1998). 'Do firms in clusters innovate more?' *Research Policy* 27: 527–542.

Bathelt, H. (2002). 'The re-emergence of a media industry cluster in Leipzig.' *European Planning Studies* 10(5): 583–611.

Benner, C. (2003). 'Learning communities in a learning region: the soft infrastructure of cross-firm learning networks in Silicon Valley.' *Environment and Planning A* 35(10): 1809–1830.

Bennett, R., P. Robson and W. Bratton (2001). 'The influence of location on the use by SMEs of external advice and collaboration.' *Urban Studies* 38(9): 1531–1557.

Boari, C., V. Odorici and M. Zamarian (2003). 'Clusters and rivalry: does localization really matter?' *Scandinavian Journal of Management* 19(4): 467–489.

Chamberlin, E. (1933). *The Theory of Monopoly Competition.* Cambridge MA, Harvard University Press.

Coe, N. (2000). 'The view from out West: embeddedness, inter-personal relations and the development of an indigenous film industry in Vancouver.' *Geoforum* 31(4): 391–407.

Cooper, D. (2001). 'Innovation and reciprocal externalities: information transmission via job mobility.' *Journal of Economic Behavior and Organization* 45(4): 403–425.

Dahl, M. (2002). *Embedded knowledge flows through labor mobility in regional clusters in Denmark.* DRUID's New Economy Conference, Copenhagen.

Fiell, C. and P. Fiell (2002). *Scandinavian Design.* Köln, Taschen.

Fosfuri, A., M. Motta and T. Ronde (2001). 'Foreign direct investment and spillovers through workers' mobility.' *Journal of International Economics* 51(1): 204–222.

Fosfuri, A. and T. Ronde (2004). 'High-tech clusters, technology spillovers, and trade secret laws.' *International Journal of Industrial Organization* 22(1): 45–65.

Gilson, R. J. (1999). 'The legal infrastructure of high technology industrial districts: Silicon Valley, Route 128, and covenants not to compete.' *New York University Law Review* 74(3): 575–629.

Grabher, G. (2001). 'Ecologies of creativity: the Village, the Group, and the heterarchic organisation of the British advertising industry.' *Environment and Planning A* 33(2): 351–374.

—— (2002). 'The project ecology of advertising: tasks, talents and teams.' *Regional Studies* 36(3): 245–262.

Hallencreutz, D., P. Lundequist and A. Malmberg (2003). 'Local embeddedness and international competitiveness: the case of the Swedish music cluster.' *The Institutions of Local Development*, (ed.) F. Sforzi. Aldershot, Ashgate.

Hallencreutz, D. and D. Power (2005). 'Cultural industry cluster building.' *Proximity, Distance and Diversity: Issues on Economic Interaction and Local Development*, (eds) P. Oinis and A. Lagendijk. London, Ashgate.

Hendry, C., J. Brown and R. Defillippi (2000). 'Regional clustering of high technology-based firms: opto- electronics in three countries.' *Regional Studies* 34(2): 129–144.

King, C., A. Silk and N. Ketelhohn (2003). 'Knowledge spillovers and growth in the disagglomeration of the US advertising-agency industry.' *Journal of Economics and Management Strategy* 12(3): 327–362.

Levitt, T. (1975 [1960]). 'Marketing myopia.' *Harvard Business Review* 53(5): 26–42.

—— (1981). 'Marketing intangible products and product intangibles.' *Harvard Business Review* 59(3): 94–103.

Lissoni, F. (2001). 'Knowledge codification and the geography of innovation: the case of Brescia mechanical cluster.' *Research Policy* 30(9): 1479–1500.

Madsen, T., E. Mosakowski and S. Zaheer (2003). 'Knowledge retention and personnel mobility: the nondisruptive effects of inflows of experience.' *Organization Science* 14(2): 173–191.

Malmberg, A. and D. Power (2005). '(How) Do (firms in) clusters create knowledge?' *Industry and Innovation* 12(4): 409–431.

—— (2006). 'True clusters / A severe case of conceptual headache.' *Clusters in Regional Development*, (eds) B. Asheim, P. Cooke and R. Martin. Oxon., Routledge.

Martin, R. and P. Sunley (2003). 'Deconstructing clusters: chaotic concept or policy panacea?' *Journal of Economic Geography* 3(1): 5–35.

Molotch, H. (1996). 'LA as product: how design works in a regional economy.' *The City: Los Angeles and Urban Theory at the End of the Twentieth Century*, (eds) A. Scott and E. Soja. Berkeley, University of California Press.

Neff, G. (2005). 'The changing place of cultural production: the location of social networks in a digital media industry.' *Annals of the American Academy of Political and Social Sciences* 597(1): 134–152.

OECD (Organisation for Economic Co-operation and Development) (2001). *Innovative clusters: drivers of national innovation systems*. Paris, OECD.

Porter, M. (1998). 'Clusters and the new economics of competition.' *Harvard Business Review* Nov-Dec: 77–90.

—— (2000). 'Locations, clusters and company strategies.' *The Oxford Handbook of Economic Geography*, (eds) G. Clark, M. Feldman and M. Gertler. Oxford, Oxford University Press.

Power, D. and D. Hallencreutz (2002). 'Profiting from creativity? The music industry in

Stockholm, Sweden and Kingston, Jamaica.' *Environment and Planning A* 34(10): 1833–1854.

—— (2005). 'Music and creative profits.' *Popular Music Studies Reader*, (eds) A. Bennett, B. Shank and J. Toynbee. Oxon., Routledge.

Power, D. and J. Jansson (2008). 'Cyclical Clusters in Global Circuits: Overlapping Spaces and Furniture Industry Trade Fairs.' *Economic Geography* 84(4): 423–448.

Power, D. and M. Lundmark (2004). 'Working through knowledge pools: labour market dynamics, the transferase of knowledge and ideas, and industrial clusters.' *Urban Studies* 41(5–6): 1025–1044.

Power, D. and A. Scott (2004a). *Cultural Industries and the Production of Culture*. London, Routledge.

—— (2004b). 'A prelude to cultural industries and the production of culture.' Power and Scott 2004a.

Power, D., J. Lindström and D. Hallencreutz (2004). *The Future in Design – Country Report: The Swedish Design Industry*. Oslo, The Nordic Innovation Centre.

Pratt, A. (2006). 'Advertising and creativity, a governance approach: a case study of creative agencies in London.' *Environment and Planning A* 38(10): 1883–1899.

Ronde, T. (2001). 'Trade secrets and information sharing.' *Journal of Economics and Management Strategy* 10(3): 391–417.

Sakakibara, M. and M. Porter (2001). 'Competing at home to win abroad: evidence from Japanese industry.' *Review of Economics and Statistics* 83(2): 310–322.

Scott, A. (1988). *Metropolis: From the Division of Labor to the Urban Form*. Berkeley and Los Angeles, University of California Press.

—— (2000). *The Cultural Economy of Cities: Essays on the Geography of Image-Producing Industries*. London, Sage.

—— (2001). 'Globalization and the rise of city-regions.' *European Planning Studies* 9(7): 813–826.

Song, J., P. Almeida and G. Wu (2003). 'Learning-by-hiring: when is mobility more likely to facilitate interfirm knowledge transfer?' *Management Science* 49(4): 351–365.

Thrift, N. and A. Leyshon (1994). 'A phantom state? The de-traditionalisation of money, the international financial system and international financial centres.' *Political Geography* 13: 299–327.

Vinodrai, T. (2006). 'Reproducing Toronto's design ecology: career paths, intermediaries, and local labor markets.' *Economic Geography* 82(3): 237–263.

Walsh, V., R. Roy and M. Bruce (1988). 'Competitive by design.' *Journal of Marketing Management* 4(2): 201–216.

Welz, G. (2003). 'The cultural swirl: anthropological perspectives on innovation.' *Global networks – A Journal of Transnational Affairs* 3(3): 255–270.

Part 7

Museums/Visual Arts/Performance

7a Creativity and innovation in the cultural economy

Museums, galleries and the visual arts

Sara Selwood

Arts Council England (ACE) regards the contemporary visual arts as fundamental to the creative industries. Having been 'nurtured through creative innovation' and 'entrepreneurial risk' (Jackson and Jordan, 2006. Part 1:1), they have – it asserts – 'come to drive the creative industries' (ACE, 2006a:7).

However, the ACE's advocacy is, arguably, shaped as much by the desires of the Department for Culture, Media and Sport (DCMS), as it is by the visual arts' own performance (Selwood, 2007). While notionally operating at arm's length from it, ACE, along with a number of other agencies, is formally responsible for delivering the government's cultural policy. This means that the subsidised sector in general is expected to contribute to the creative economy and, more specifically, is thought of as 'incubating' the creativity and innovation considered vital to the success of the creative industries. But, as this chapter reveals, neither DCMS nor ACE are fully convinced of the efficacy of the relationship. Indeed, according to Peter Hewitt, Chief Executive, ACE, the arts still need 'a new enterprise personality and [to] skill up so as to be able to capitalise on new partnerships with the commercial creative industries and with government across Whitehall' (Hewitt, 2006). Such tensions between rhetoric and the realities set the tone for this chapter.

Neither of DCMS's two mapping documents, which track the contribution that the creative industries made to the economy treat the contemporary visual arts as 'core' to the creative industries (DCMS, 1998c; 2001). They are, thus, distinguished from craft production, the live performance of music and the performing arts – which are explicitly described as core to the creative industries.[1] At best, the visual artists are regarded as suppliers to the art trade, which functions purely as a commercial distributor. Their formal exclusion from the art and antiquities market (one of the so-called creative industries) is presumably predicated on their perceived lack of any immediate 'potential for wealth and job creation through the generation and exploitation of intellectual property' (DCMS, 1998c: 3).

DCMS's perceptions of the relationship between publicly funded museums and galleries are similarly damning. It regards them as quite separate from the creative industries – at best having a non-specific although 'close economic inter-relationship' with them (DCMS, 1998c:3).

Museums and galleries' perceived exclusion from matters of wealth and job creation appears to have been reinforced by a number of factors. Publicly funded organisations' apparent lack of commercial acumen in selling works which they originally commissioned has also been called into question. The National Audit Office (which scrutinises public spending on behalf of the Parliament) recently investigated two instances of apparent profligacy by the Baltic:[2] one related to the gallery's failure to recover £100,000 initial production costs of *Tyne Bridge* which it had commissioned from Chris Burden; the other to the lack of evidence that Antony Gormley (subsequently appointed to be one of the gallery's trustees) could be expected to reimburse the £175,000 cost of *Domain Field* should it be sold (Bailey, 2006; Varley, 2005a; 20005b). As the second example implies, publicly funded institutions are not supposed to contribute to the relative wealth of those with whom they have a formal relationship. The Tate's purchase of works by one of its artist trustees, Chris Offili, for example, prompted the Charity Commission to criticise the gallery's acquisitions policies and procedures and its processes for managing conflicts of interests.[3]

As the Accounting Standards Board has acknowledged (2006), there are considerable problems with current accounting requirements for heritage assets, including museums' collections – which are often deemed 'priceless'. Museums and galleries rarely consider exploiting the market value of such assets as their permanent collections. When they do have to sell items, it is usually under duress. The *Code of Ethics* promoted by the Museums Association, which represents the people and institutions constituting Britain's museums and galleries, insists that collections should be treated as 'non-negotiable assets in financial affairs'. It advises museum professionals to 'refuse to mortgage collections or offer them as security for a loan' and 'sustain the financial viability of the museum irrespective of any valuation placed on items in its collections' (Museums Association, 2002: para 1.4). The sale of works from public collections intended 'to plug a hole' in museums and galleries' finances is generally considered beyond the pale (see, for instance, Museums Association, 2006; Jenkins, 2006; Davies, 2006). However, the tide may be turning (AEA Consulting, 2003; Museums Association, 2005) – not least because museums may only remain sustainable if their rates of acquisitions are managed in relation to disposals (Merriman, 2006).

Perhaps, even more strikingly, museums and galleries appear not to regard increased attendances as necessarily contributing to their financial sustainability. As the House of Commons' Culture, Media and Sport Committee found, museums experienced a number of financial costs arising from free admission, including increased wear and tear, higher cleaning costs and in some cases the need to increase staffing levels (House of Commons, 2002: Ev 45)

But, despite their apparent detachment with commerce at one level, at another level the government's interest in the cultural economy has evidently touched a nerve in the subsidised cultural sector. Over the past decade, the visual arts, museums and galleries have sought to boost, if not promote, their income generating capacity and economic impact (AEA, 1999). It was is not by chance that Tate Modern celebrated its first and fifth birthdays by publishing economic impact studies (Tate, 2001; 2005), nor that the National Museums Directors' Conference (NMDC) published a major report on the economic impact of national museums in anticipation of the 2004 Spending Review (Travers and Glaister, 2004) and another in anticipation of the 2007 Comprehensive Spending Review (Travers, 2006). At base, these efforts constitute a public relations exercise and, as such, are intended to contribute to the construction of institutions' reputations (Selwood, 2004). They also indicate the sectors' willingness to comply with DCMS's own aspiration 'to be viewed more seriously as an economic department' (Jowell, 2005a), while simultaneously justifying its subsidies on the grounds that its mission is to promote the 'value of culture' (Jowell, 2004).

The visual arts' commercial success partly depends on the long-standing, and mutually beneficial, relationship between art dealers and subsidised visual arts organisations. However, the precise contribution that the public sector makes to the art market and the pricing of artists' work has not been explored in detail by ACE.[4] Its efforts to promote the economic value of the visual arts tend to be rather more parochial. These include its promotion of particular initiatives, such as its support of the Frieze Art Fair.[5] It has also attempted to develop the market for contemporary visual arts and craft (Morris Hargreaves McIntyre, 2004; 2006) not least by promoting an interest-free loan scheme, Own Art, intended to encourage people to purchase works of contemporary art.[6] It also proposes to invest in developing the market for art outside London (ACE, 2006b: 30).

But, if – despite its best efforts – the subsidised visual arts, museums and galleries are still not assumed to contribute to wealth creation, are they considered to be either 'creative' or 'innovative'? And, if so, what do they understand by 'creativity' and 'innovation' and how are these qualities manifest within their operations?

This chapter examines how 'creativity' and 'innovation' are considered to pertain to museums, galleries and the visual arts. It considers the government's expectations of these sectors, and how the sectors themselves describe their own 'creativity' and 'innovation'. It draws on the grey literature[7] (including online publications), and on a set of elite interviews with museum, gallery and visual arts specialists.

This chapter is constructed in three parts:

Part 1 considers DCMS's use of the terms 'creativity' and 'innovation' and their applicability to museums, galleries and the visual arts;
Part 2 considers those sectors' efforts to be recognised as contributing to 'creativity' and 'innovation'; and,
Part 3 pulls together some observations on the basis of the above.

DCMS

Under New Labour, much of what characterises, if not determines, the interests of subsidised cultural sector bodies cascades down from central government through its polices; the content of its funding agreements, their targets and performance indicators; and earmarked funding and related initiatives (Selwood, 2004). DCMS describes much of its work in relation to 'creativity', not least as it applies to individuals, communities, education and the economy.

The cultural strategy that the Labour Party published prior to its May 1997 election victory, identified the importance of what it then referred to as 'the cultural industries', (Labour Party, 1997).[8] Once in power, it renamed the Department of National Heritage as the Department for Culture, Media and Sport. The new Department's most striking feature was its explicit association with what it now referred to as the 'creative industries'. The Department explicitly sought to carve out a role for itself in 'looking beyond subsidy, in encouraging links between publicly supported and privately financed initiatives, and in promoting the wider sectors.' By Autumn 1998, DCMS had already taken what it called a 'broader view' – 'encouraging the breakdown of barriers between the subsidised, commercial and voluntary activity' (DCMS, 1998b: para 7). Whether or not it was intended to do so, this strategy established a stark comparison between what was subsidised and what was 'beyond subsidy', between the creative industries and the rest of the department's cultural portfolio.

The level of attention paid to the creative industries by the Department over the years has fluctuated (Purnell, 2005). But, the Prime Minister's letter to the Secretary of State for Culture, Media and Sport reappointing her after Labour's third successive election victory in May 2006[9], left her in no doubt that these were to be prioritised again:

> I want you to continue to give a high priority to the creative economy. You will need to look at the regulatory environment within which the industries work and whether there are incentives that could increase productivity. You will also want to plan to ensure that the industries have access to the right skills.
>
> (DCMS, 2006a)

Various initiatives by other government departments had served to foreground 'creativity' by this time, including the review of *Creativity in business: building on the UK's strength* (Cox, 2005). Commissioned by the Chancellor of the Exchequer and published by the Treasury, this considered how best to strengthen the relationship between businesses (particularly SMEs) and creative professionals in a range of design, arts and related disciplines. A DTI (Department of Trade and Industry) report of the same date described the current state of knowledge on the economics of creativity and design and their role in driving business performance and productivity. Indeed, the Prime Minister specifically reminded the Secretary of State for Culture, Media and Sport to collaborate with the DTI in respect of creative industries.[10]

DCMS's engagement with the 'creative' appears relatively detached in its Annual Report 2006, where it restricted its use of the word 'creative' to the creative industries. One aspect of the Department's overall mission is described as being to 'champion the tourism, *creative* and leisure industries'. The report also refers to the rate of growth in the *creative* industries compared to that of the economy as a whole; and it looks forward to the launch of the Creative Economy Programme – 'the first step towards our goal of making the UK the world's *creative* hub'. This programme, which focuses on 'key productivity levers' for the creative industries, appears to have had little to do with museums, galleries and the visual arts.[11]

But, in practice, DCMS employs the terms 'creative' and 'creativity' considerably more than its 2006 Annual Report suggests. 'Creativity', for instance, determines parts of the department's organisational structure, which features a Director General, Culture, Creativity and Economy; a Minister for Creative Industries and Tourism; and a Creative Industries unit.[12] It also has what it refers to as a 'culture and creativity website'. A text-based search on DCMS website for the words, 'creative' and 'creativity' produced some 472 html results.[13] Predictably, the vast majority of these specifically refer to the creative industries and the Creative Economy Programme.[14] Other results contain references to creative business; creative exports and to such initiatives as the Creative Industries Forum; a Creativity Advisory Forum for the Cultural Olympiad (tasked with demonstrating 'energy, creativity and vitality').

Strikingly, the Department's use of the words 'creative' and 'creativity' are far from being restricted to the creative industries' profit-making capacity. DCMS freely applies these terms to activities which are both loss-making and consume subsidies (Heartfield, 2006: 76). Its references to 'creative talent', 'creative success', creative workshops' and people engaging 'creatively with media' abound. It associates 'creativity' with management procedures , such as 'creative decision-making', not to mention the reinterpretation of DCMS's own intentions. Thus, tax relief is construed as intended to 'maintain the industries' creative and technical skills', and the lighter regulation of the lottery is described as being to encourage 'creativity'.

Whilst its definition of the 'creative industries' is readily available (for example, DCMS, 1998c: 3), the Department is less explicit about defining 'creativity' per se. Drawing on the National Advisory Committee for Creative and Cultural Education 1999 report, *All Our Futures: Creativity, Culture & Education*, and work produced by the Qualifications and Curriculum Authority, the Department (DCMS, 2006b: 4) proposes that young people's 'creativity' involves 'thinking or behaving imaginatively'; that such 'activity is purposeful: that is, it is directed to achieving an objective'; that these 'processes must generate something original' and that

> the outcome must be of value in relation to the objective. Creativity is not limited to the arts but should be embedded across the whole curriculum. Creativity is not at odds with raising standards or an end in itself but should produce outcomes of real value.
>
> (DCMS, 20006b: 4)

While DCMS wants to be taken more seriously as an economic department, it also wants to be regarded equally seriously as an education department. However the relationship between education and 'creativity' is not at all clear cut, as a report commissioned by Creative Partnerships – *Rhetorics of Creativity* (Banaji and Burn, 2007) suggests.

'Creativity' is regarded as a feature of particular bodies which DCMS subsidises. However, as the following examples, suggest it is unclear how meaningfully the term is applied. The BBC licence fee, for instance, is described as representing a form of 'venture capital for the whole of the nation's creativity' (Jowell 2006) and the Corporation's process of tendering and commissioning becomes 'a window of creative competition'. The limitations of BBC3's target audience created a 'creative straightjacket', (Barwise 2004:5) whereas the BBC Trust's Purpose Plan has been specifically designed to stimulate creativity and cultural excellence. Another of DCMS's agencies, MLA (Museums, Libraries and Archives Council) seeks 'to improve people's lives by building knowledge, supporting learning, inspiring creativity and celebrating identity' (HOC, 2006: Col 328W). For their part, libraries are envisaged as being able to 'harness and deploy creativity to inspire and change lives' (Burnham, 2008).

Not surprisingly, 'creative approaches' are regarded as delivered daily by the creative hubs – partnerships between cultural organisations and schools. DCMS is keen to encourage children to 'explore their creativity' and 'creative potential'. In a report of 1999 for the Department, the National Advisory Committee for Creative and Cultural Education had emphasised the importance of 'developing the creative abilities of young people' and the power of culture to deliver on this. Both qualities were re-emphasised in Paul Roberts' report, *Nurturing Creativity in Young People* (2006), commissioned as part of the Cultural Economy programme. In arguing for a more coherent 'creativity offer', Roberts proposes a framework for administering 'creativity' which starts with early years and develops through mainstream education into the creative industries. The government's response sets out what more it can do to nurture young people's 'creativity' (DCMS, 2006b). Neither museums, galleries nor the visual arts are held up as paradigms, although they are acknowledged as contributing to a number of initiatives which are cited as examples of good practice including the £100million DfES/DCMS flagship programme, Creative Partnerships.[15]

This might be taken to imply that the Department's doesn't particularly associate museums, galleries or the visual arts with 'creativity'. But, according to the Secretary of State for Culture, Media and Sport, DCMS's increase in arts funding specifically constituted an investment in '*creativity* and quality' (Lammy, 2006). It follows that works of art saved for the nation are perceived as connecting people to 'knowledge, information, *creativity* and inspiration' (DCMS, 2004); and in that DCMS perceives museums as 'centres of knowledge, with a clear – and growing – role as educators' (DCMS, 2005a: 6), their capacity to 'excite and inspire us and encourage us to develop our imagination' (ibid.: 10) is central. In short, museums and galleries are regarded as 'feeding' the creative industries (ibid.: 11).

A search of DCMS's website for 'innovation' and 'innovative' produces broadly similar findings. An analysis of the 271 html results,[16] suggests that the Department's use of 'innovation' broadly focuses on the creative economy, even though it is applied to cultural organisations more generally. Estelle Morris, a former arts minister, regarded 'innovation' as fundamental across the board: The arts and creativity are more important now than they have ever been. The arguments for creativity and innovation are more urgent . . . The reason one company thrives and another doesn't is its ability to innovate (Morris, 2003).

For DCMS, 'innovation' is fundamental to economic growth: and competition.

The majority of creative industry firms are classed as necessarily 'innovation active'. Evidence of broadcasting's 'ability to innovate' is critical: the BBC is expected to 'innovate continually' (DCMS, 2003a). The Department even applies the terms to gambling which it describes as an 'innovative industry' (DCMS, 2003b) – presumably referring to something that might be new in particular circumstances.

Like 'creativity', 'innovation' is perceived to function as a management tool. DCMS considers it desirable for cultural organisations to be imaginative – to have an 'innovation action plan', 'innovative packaging', 'innovative ways of selling', 'innovative approaches'. Historic innovation, is one of the criteria against which DCMS makes decisions about listings and export deferrals. The department expects programmes and projects to display evidence of both. Thus 'innovation' (like 'creativity') is about organisations' approaches, modes of operation, ideas. 'Innovative ways to involve the public' are particularly commonly referred to – but are rarely specified.

Such rhetorics are not just applied to DCMS's funded organisations: the Department applies it to itself. It describes what it does as 'policy innovation' and credits its own initiative, Culture Online, as having been an 'innovative way to give access', 'encourage mass participation and inspire people to interact with arts, heritage and cultural organisation in an innovative way'.

DCMS also regards 'innovation' as one of the objectives of funding, if not its fundamental rationale. Certain funds are allocated to the creative industries and the non-profit sector specifically to encourage 'innovation'.[17] Grants are awarded to museums specifically for 'imaginative and innovative schemes' to boost access (DCMS, 2002); lottery funding gives distributors 'the confidence and indeed legitimacy to innovate, take risks, and be creative . . .'; and DCMS's £6million Challenge Fund, set to be launched in 2007, is intended 'to boost innovation in the arts' (DCMS, 2005b). Indeed, the Secretary of State views the increase in government investment in culture and the arts since 1997 as having produced 'a genuine renaissance in creativity and imagination across the country' (ibid.) – although the difference made is not specified.

Local authority websites provide other examples of the excessive use of 'creativity'. A search of the LGA's (Local Government Association) website,[18] for instance, produces results which show the use of 'creativity' attached to cultural projects. Essex County Council's *Creative consequences: understanding the value of arts in Essex 1999/2000–2004/2005* (2006) is one such example. But the same website also carries numerous links to reports in which 'creative' is applied to a range of activities which are not particularly cultural. Results include 'creative solutions to . . . complex and difficult problems', 'creative usages of current community sentence options', 'creative procurement', 'creative collaborations', 'creative ways of supporting families with anti-social behaviour'; 'creative links'; and 'innovative and creative space'. 'Creative' was not always used in this way. Pick's idiosyncratic, *Weasel Words. A Beginner's Dictionary for Ambitions Arts Bureaucrats* of 1980, which set out to describe 'the curious and loathsome cant' of the time, 'affected by politicians and rumour-mongers of the arts', for instance, contains no reference whatsoever to the words 'creative', 'creativity', or 'innovation'.

But 20 years on not only has the use of the term 'creativity' 'become ubiquitous, it has become essential'. As such it 'is now both an economic imperative and an unquestioned social good, it is both what drives change and what protects us from its harmful effects' (Oakley, forthcoming). Banaji and Buer (2007) describe its omnipresence as related to politics, education, social good and economic imperative. It is, they assert, 'democratic in its formulation' and fits neatly with liberal pedagogies.

> It connects with everyday life in ways that other rhetorics do not, investing people's mundane actions and choices with a potentially romantic edge. However pro-social models of creativity . . . tend to depend to a large degree on socially-endorsed notions of adequacy, acceptability and wise choices . . . It has no clear relation to culture, especially popular culture and the arts, and thus removes the term from its historical context.
>
> (Banaji and Burn, 2007: 22)

Museums, galleries and the visual arts

It follows that DCMS associates museums and galleries, in some capacity, with 'creativity' and 'innovation', and – by association – with the creative industries. But, how 'creative' or 'innovative' are they considered to be? DCMS appears to be in two minds about it. Although the Minister for Culture has described the cultural sector as 'more creative, innovative and popular than ever before' (Lammy, 2006), the Department itself evidently regards museums as having still more potential to fulfil. 'For their contributions to be recognised – socially, economically, politically, and culturally – the sector needs to demonstrate that it is cohesive, innovative and visionary' (DCMS, 2005b: 30).

Museums, galleries and the visual arts agencies' own accounts suggest that they have consciously risen to the challenge of deliberately promoting their creative credentials. They have no hesitation in describing themselves as 'creative', 'innovative', and as fundamental to the creative industries and creative economy, particularly in documents intended for DCMS's consumption.

For example, the report of the Task Force on Regional Museums, *Renaissance in the Regions* (2001) set out what major regional museums and galleries would have to do if they were to make a full contribution to meeting local, regional and national social- and economic-policy goals. Its strategy was so successful that since 2002 nearly £150million has been allocated to regional museums (Lammy, 2005). This depended, in part, on responding to the wider policy context informed by an emphasis on 'creativity', manifest in the need for creative industries strategies to integrate with other related strategies (Regional Museums Task Force, 2001: 28), the experience of Creative Partnerships programme and Culture Online (ibid.: 52–53). *Renaissance* sought to encourage museums to work together in a 'creative way'; to forge creative partnerships with external bodies; to 'open up their collections and spaces for all to use in a creative way for learning, inspiration and enjoyment' (ibid.: 5); and to encourage the development of skills which can contribute to the creative economy in a number of ways (ibid.: 53).[19]

Other lobbying documents produced by the museums sector articulated similar enthusiasms using much the same language. *Museums and Galleries: Creative Engagement* (Enterprise LSE. 2004:2), for instance, was one of several reports commissioned by the National Museums Directors' Conference in anticipation of the 2004 Spending Review. As its title suggests, it presented a case for the 'creative' output of NMDC institutions, collectively one of the world's biggest repositories of art, culture, science and natural history.[20] This rested on those institutions' 'innovative thinking and practice', and ability

> to create social capital, educating and empowering individuals and groups alike, creating networks and stimulating dialogue . . . they also inspire creativity in their audiences, thereby enhancing both individual and, through their contributions to the creative industries and broader economy, the well being of the nation.
>
> (Enterprise LSE, 2004: 2)

While arguing that museums' 'creativity' is virtually impossible to catalogue or measure, the report lists numerous instances of institutions 'making links', 'changing perspectives', undertaking 'research development and consulting' and contributing to, and creating, 'places and spaces'. This suggests that creativity constitutes a management style.

Two years on, MLA's response to the 2006 Creative Economy Programme consultation, also focused on the 'significant contribution that museums, libraries and archives make to enabling "creativity" and the creative industries', despite traditionally having been seen as being 'beyond' them (MLA, 2006: paras 1.1–1.2).[21]Drawing on advocacy commissioned from Demos, it assumes that by dint of housing, preserving and presenting artefacts and information, museums and galleries constitute 'the natural resources of a creative age' (Holden and Jones, 2006: 7, cited in MLA, 2006: para 2.1). They are, thus, 'crucial in inspiring creativity' (Holden and Jones, 2006: 23).

> The Creative industries require people with imagination and an entrepreneurial attitude. Investment in children and young people for longer term gain is essential. The Creative Economy will also require people to be able to learn independently long after they exit the formal education system. Through their work with children and young people museums, libraries and archives are helping them build the skills and motivation they will need to succeed in the creative economy. Museums, libraries and archives hold legacy collections that have a new potential when exploited for creative purposes.
>
> (MLA, 2006: para 2.4)

ACE's response to the DCMS consultation on its Creative Economy Programme was broadly similar. It described the arts as 'a crucial part of the ecology within which the creative economy sits', and as 'crucial to achieving the Cultural Economy Programme's stated aim of establishing Britain as the world's creative hub' (ACE, 2006a). As 'a vital part of the creative economy', a focused attempt by Government to develop this sector will, logically, benefit many individual artists and creative businesses (ibid.) But if, as in the case of museums and galleries, government fails to maintain, if not increase, its subsidises, ACE warns, the creative industries will ultimately suffer.

ACE's desire to associate itself with the creative industries is also apparent in its core planning documents, which make the same points. In its *Agenda for the Arts, 2006–8*,[22] for example, ACE not only states that it intends making artists more entrepreneurial, but that the Council itself positively contributes to the country's long-term aspirations as a creative economy by providing opportunities for children and young people to participate in arts and 'creativity'. 'At a time of intense international competitiveness, arts and creativity will continue to play a significant part in injecting innovation and enterprise into the economy'. It intends to

> keep engaging with DCMS's Creative Economy programme, to create a framework to support innovation, growth and productivity; . . . incorporate the programme's findings into our action plans, which prioritise risk investment in new talent; . . . find new ways of developing creativity in all levels of education; . . . identify sustained ways of improving cultural leadership performance.[23]
>
> (ACE, 2006a)

ACE's putative visual arts strategy, *Turning Point* (ACE, 2006b) echoes many of these points. It regards it as a 'paradox that visual artists are not included in the current de?nition of the creative industries. This masks the overall contribution that they make both in economic and social terms' (ibid.: 33). It asserts that contemporary visual art 'drives the creative industries' as well as 'popular culture' (ibid.: 7). But, it singles out the visual arts' particular brand of 'creativity' as requiring special treatment, regarding the 'drain' from the public to commercial galleries where the rewards are not only financial but also creative and supportive, offering focused and unencumbered working with artists as problematic. This is because of the 'implications for widening participation and for the vitality and sustainability of the visual arts and the creative industries in England' (ibid.: 36)

Conclusions: the rhetoric and the reality

This chapter has considered the circumstances within which museums, galleries and the visual arts have had to justify themselves as 'creative' and 'innovative' and as contributing to the cultural economy. Their agencies' very general use of the rhetorics of 'creative', 'creativity' and 'innovation' suggest that – as a matter of principle – museums, galleries and the visual arts in the subsidised, if not the not-for-profit, sectors wish to associate themselves with the creative industries by default. Such emulation blatantly appeals to, and appropriates, the political cachet of the creative industries. Their lobbying may be defensive – but, the last thing that museums, galleries and the visual arts aspire to is the lack of subsidy which typifies DCMS's treatment of the creative industries. But, to what extent are the paradigms of 'creativity' and 'innovation' as applicable to the creative industries, fit for museums, galleries and the visual arts' purposes? Will their use of them ultimately invite accusations of failure? These issues were put to a handful of museums and visual arts specialists who were interviewed for this chapter. Their responses are considered below.

Museums, galleries and the visual arts as inspirational

In advocating for sustained, if not increased, funding museums, galleries and the visual arts' case for 'creativity' rests on a simple point. They present themselves as the guardians of creative capital and, as such, crucial to its development. Their core work is, by definition, intended to encourage 'interest, even passion, in particular creative abilities and skills of a high order', and to inspire 'creativity' in their visitors and, thus contribute to the creative industries and the economy albeit indirectly. Perhaps, not surprisingly, given its origins in promoting British design, the V&A has, perhaps, been the most concerned, if not consistent, in referring to its impact on the creative industries.[24] While they have always implicitly been concerned with inspiring 'creativity' they do not have a monopoly on it. Moreover, any attempts to prove, if not quantify, their contribution to the development of the creative industries are beset by methodological conundrums. As one of the interviewees put it: 'None of the advocacy produced points to a body of empirical evidence which demonstrates that "creative play" in museums and galleries, for example, increases the chances of our directly inspiring someone to make the next great technological breakthrough.'

But, should such institutions need to justify themselves as catalysts for others' 'creativity'? Quite apart from the demands of advocacy, how do they describe their own 'creativity', and what conditions do they regard as necessary for it to thrive?

Defining creativity in museums

Even within the very small sample of interviewees referred to, there were considerable differences in defining 'creativity', identifying where it resides, or what contributes to its flourishing. One interviewee, for instance, described 'creativity in museums [as residing] in the machinery of conversion – raw information or collections, and converting them into something different that can be understood by non-specialists.'

This might embrace what another interviewee identified as museums, galleries and the visual arts' creation of 'public value'.[25] Cultural organisations' creation of public value is, arguably, dependent on their ability to change. Although one interviewee insisted that 'change and creativity are not same thing', another effectively regarded them as, in some respect, synonymous:

> In the past, the differences between museums and galleries were rather extreme ... museums were the kind of places which were far from having any creativity. They were static and fixed in the past, rather than in the present. They didn't focus on creativity or have any interest in it, and were uninterested in change and development. In contrast, museums of contemporary art seemed very different.

Current notions of 'best practice' suggest that museums and galleries should be applying 'the most creative kind of ideas about the management and administration of organisations, because we believe that you get the best public value out of that.' They should do their best to respond to the public, on behalf of whom they are enacted. This may involve their working with

> artists and the public in ways that are genuinely collaborative, and offer opportunities to make things happen which wouldn't happen otherwise ... There's been a huge change. I often joke about the worst excesses of bureaucracies that existed when I first joined museums in a period that was so unbearably non-creative that I can't bear to look back to it.

As Sandy Nairne, Director of the National Portrait Gallery, said in his Keynote address to the 2006, Museums Association Conference: 'creative risk-taking encourages displays that are controversial, publications that stimulate responses, activities that stretch and challenge the participants, and appropriate acquisitions and exhibitions that will generate public debate.'

Arguments which militate against creativity and innovation

Paradoxically, there may be a downside to subsidised organisations working 'creatively', especially when they have to account to government for their effectiveness. As one interviewee put it, 'I might think that a very creatively managed organisation is a good thing ... but it might not sit very easily with the greater degree of accountability and the regimes in and around government.' Another interviewee suggested that some methods of accountability or accountability poorly applied might have a potentially dampening effect on creativity and could even encourage risk-averseness. 'The culture of targets encourages the use of tried and tested approaches. There's less risk taking, which runs counter to creativity in some cases.' Is it 'creativity' per se that institutions should be aspiring to, or should it be the capacity to keep changing? 'How long can something remain innovative for? Mainstreaming inevitably detracts from what was once innovative and creative. The issue isn't just about being great at innovation, but about being good at exploiting it.'

For one interviewee, museums and galleries need to function as 'enterprises' across the board, was generally understated. They regarded enterprise as embracing both creativity and innovation:

> I often talk about wanting the . . . gallery to be involved in enterprise and wanting there to be a tremendous continuity between enterprise at one end

(commercial things – are we good at producing really nice products for the shop?) through to public and social enterprise at the other – are we good at designing programmes which will really excite people, interest them and engage them – particularly when they may be new audiences?

In my mind, that notion of enterprise unites, or stands over, what I otherwise find an unhelpful divisiveness between . . . work done to raise money through sponsorship, for example, and the work done by curators in knowing things, understanding and interpreting things, we now have a situation where we need curators to talk to sponsors and take part in the process of raising funds. Equally, the people who work in development and communications have to know more than the basics, without being specialists, about the works of art and working with artists. So, I see enterprise (and I might, or might not use the term 'creative enterprise') for public benefit as being a way that an organisation can work together.

Nurturing and frustrating creativity

What conditions might be necessary for this, or other forms of 'creativity' to flourish? Some interviewees considered initiatives, such as *Renaissance in the Regions*, or the Arts Council of Great Britain's earlier, *Glory of the Garden* strategy,[26] vital – not least as being 'good for workforce development', and as being 'a way of preventing the dust from settling.'

But, a number of factors were identified which might militate against institutions' 'creativity'. These included funding streams being tailored to the delivery of government objectives; conditions of employment; and the lack of a culture of criticism within museums and galleries:

Education and diversity might, conceivably, be where most interesting work is being done. But a general shortage of resources, and the earmarking of project funding, means that many other activities appear to have been curtailed – exhibitions, publishing, creating events etc. These days, curators spend much more of their time doing routine admin and supporting the work of freelancers (curators, exhibition designers, writers) rather than actually doing creative things themselves.

The lack of a culture of communication and criticism was also considered crucial:

I'm always surprised that the basic tools of the trade aren't a bigger focus of museum studies courses or of museum evaluation. Great exhibitions (permanent or temporary) are one the main ways in which visitors interact with museums. The same goes for things like websites ...

No one seems to talk about what makes a good one or a bad one in terms of design or content, or how much of a pleasure they are to use. If you worked in TV, or on a magazine, you'd constantly be having debriefs or criticisms afterwards to help you improve next time.[27]

A lack of time and space were also considered to frustrate 'creativity':

> The lack of career progression, and peoples' inability to move on, means that there is often a feeling that there is a great weight of people above new entrants which will never shift. People think that that they'll have to have been doing something for a long time to be allowed to assume any responsibility. Only yesterday, someone at the Museum of London said to me . . . . that museums are over-professionalised, that they exaggerate the amount of qualifications and experience you need to do particular tasks . . . and that that's a bit stifling.

Museums and galleries are now, as someone else suggested, 'virtually a postgraduate-entry "profession"'.

Opinions varied about short-term appointments being made in *Renaissance*'s regional hubs. The scheme was intended to create 'new blood' appointments to strengthen, or create capacity, in regional museums and 'enable them to make their full contribution to society' (Regional Museums Task Force, 2001: 129). From a traditional perspective, such appointments are regarded as essentially 'peripheral', because they provide new appointees with insufficient time to be 'creative'. Post holders need more time and greater security to fulfil their potential – conditions which are conventionally regarded as restricted to 'core' workers'. But, changes in legislation mean that those new employees have equal rights under the law.[28] As one interviewee put it, the short-termism of new jobs in regional hub museums is purely 'an illusion, created by MLA's caution'. Moreover, 'a great many people who've been working on museums for a long time have never done anything remotely creative'.

> There does seem to be a lack of vision among many senior museum people. They're reactive, following whatever line government or MLA is putting forward as today's 'big thing', rather than leading the way. Many seem rather demoralised: they're doing a lot of admin, or trying to find money etc. ... rather than encouraging staff to be ambitious. Several people feel that they've ended up in management, and aren't doing the things that interested them in the first place.

Indeed, the combination of low pay and long-term contracts might even detract from creativity:

> A job needs to be very exciting to make you happy with £20,000 after years of study and experience. I suspect that quite a lot of people who would be good in museums go elsewhere, once they realise you spend a very long time waiting in the foothills.

Observations

There is, it appears, a gap between the rhetorics of 'creativity' and 'innovation' and the pragmatic realities of subsidised museums, galleries and the visual arts. In aspiring to be regarded 'more seriously as an economic department', DCMS has promoted the notion of there being a close financial relationship between its subsidised bodies and the creative industries. In advocating for their sectors, NMDC, MLA and ACE, necessarily comply. However, the responsibility of justifying, if not delivering on, such pronouncements inevitably comes down to individual organisations. Pressure to function as economic catalysts, if not create economic impact, sits uncomfortably, although perhaps not incompatibly, with the fact that they are subsidised because, as the Department's former Chief Economist put it, they constitute 'market failures' (Creigh-Tyte and Stiven, 2001: 174ff). Moreover, 'creativity' and 'innovation' in museums, galleries and the visual arts pertain to a number of things including changes in institutions' outlooks and management, if not the transformation of their profit-making capacity. Perhaps the semantics, used to describe museums, galleries and the visual arts' relationship to the creative industries, could do with being a little less creative.

Acknowledgements

I should like to thank Andy Pratt and Paul Jeffcutt for inviting me to write this chapter. It draws on some ideas initially explored in a conference paper, 'The collection and use of creative industries' data in the context of UK cultural policy', presented to the Association of Cultural Economists International (ACEI) conference, Vienna, 2006. I'm particularly grateful to those people whom I interviewed in the course of writing this chapter, not least for opening my eyes to things I would otherwise have been unaware of: Sandy Nairne, Director, National Portrait Gallery; Nick Dodd, Chief Executive, Sheffield Galleries & Museums Trust; Jane Morris, freelance journalist; and Professor Stuart Davies, Bournemouth University. I'm also grateful to my colleagues at City University, especially Chris Naylor; Kate Oakley for sight of her forthcoming papers and her insights into the Creative Economy Programme; and Stephen Holt, for advising me about employment law. Finally, I'd like to thank all those who were generous enough to comment on the draft of this paper, which has benefited considerably from their perceptions.

Glossary

ACE Arts Council England, the national development agency for the arts in England, which distributes public money from government and the National Lottery.

BBC British Broadcasting Corporation, a public service broadcaster, financed by a TV license paid by households and regulated by BBC Trust.

Creative Partnerships The government's flagship programme in the cultural education field, launched in 2002. The intention is to give school children aged 5–18 and their teachers the opportunity to explore their creativity by working on sustained projects with creative organisations and individuals. Creative Partnerships operates in 36 areas of the country and is primarily concentrated in areas of economic and cultural deprivation and areas which suffer from rural isolation.

Culture Online A programme intended to build a digital bridge between learning and culture which ran between 2002–2007.

DCMS Department for Culture, Media and Sport, government department responsible for policy on the arts, sport, the National Lottery, tourism, libraries, museums and galleries, broadcasting, creative industries including film and the music industry, press freedom and regulation, licensing, gambling and the historic environment.

DfES Department for Education and Skills, government department responsible for children's services, education and lifelong learning in England.

DTI Department of Trade and Industry, government department responsible for trade, business, employees, consumers, science and energy.

LGA Local Government Association promotes the interests of English and Welsh local authorities – a total of just under 500 authorities.

MLA Museums, Libraries and Archives Council is the lead strategic agency for museums, libraries and archives in England.

NMDC National Museums Directors' Conference represents the leaders of the UK's national museums and galleries. These comprise the national museums and galleries in England, Scotland, Wales and Northern Ireland, the three national libraries, and the National Archives.

Renaissance in the Regions A government funded programme intended to transform England's regional museums, making them 'world class and fit for the 21st century'.

SME Small and Medium-sized Enterprise

V&A Victoria and Albert Museum

Notes

1 The creation and production of crafts are regarded as 'core activities', as is the production of film and video; production of sound recording and live performance of music; content origination and performance production of the performing arts (DCMS, 2001). Visual artists' exclusion from the value chain considered to be 'creative industries' is not unique: whereas publishers are included, for example, writers are not.

2 Despite being originally funded with £41million ACE lottery funding, with an annual subsidy of over £1.3million supplemented by support from Gateshead Council and with an expendable endowment from ACE, in 2006 the Baltic was reported to be facing a 'funding shortfall' (Bailey, 2006).

3 'Tate welcomes Charity Commission decision on acquisition of works by Artist Trustees', press release, 19 July 2006, http://213.121.208.204/about/pressoffice/pressreleases/2006/trustees_acquisitions.htm. (retrieved 6.12.2006). The gallery is beginning to disclose sales prices, which were formally confidential. This is doubtless also associated with the impact of the Freedom of Information Act 2000, which gave everyone the right to access information held by the public sector: http://www.direct.gov.uk/RightsAndResponsibilities/RightsAndResponsibilitiesArticles/fs/en?CONTENT_ID=4003239&chk=xi42h7&cids=Google_PPC&cre=Rights_and_Responsibilities&gclid=ClnywoSh4IgCFSFMXgodVD7J0Q (retrieved 6.12.2006).

4 That relationship underlies the *KunstKompass* rankings, initiated in 1970 by the German

economist, Willy Bongard. These are published annually in the German business magazine, *Capital*, and assess artists' rankings, their fame and market value on the basis of a series of indicators. These include the presence of their work in large private and public collections, acquisitions by large museums, participation in major fairs and biennale exhibitions, sales on the international market, and so on.

5 Frieze Projects are commissioned under the auspices of Frieze Foundation, a not-for-profit organisation supported by Arts Council England and the Culture 2000 programme of the European Union (2005–07). They comprise an annual curatorial programme presented at Frieze Art Fair: Frieze Commissions, Frieze Talks and The Cartier Award. See http://www.friezeartfair.com/projects/ (retrieved 6.12.2006). The October 2006 fair generated some £30 million sales of contemporary art in the space of a single week. The profitability of contemporary art is underlined by the fact that, in November 2006, New York Sotheby's sold 70 contemporary paintings and three-dimensional works for a total $125.1 million. This was the second most successful auction in this field ever held at Sotheby's, falling shy of the May 2006 total by $3 million (Melikian, 2006).

6 http://www.artscouncil.org.uk/ownart/index.html (retrieved 19.10.04).

7 Defined as that 'produced on all levels of government, academics, business and industry in print and electronic formats, but which is not controlled by commercial publishers' (The Fourth International Conference on Grey Literature, Washington, DC, 1999, cited on http://www.nyam.org/library/greywhat.shtml (retrieved 19.10.04).

8 This may have been inspired by *Creative Nation* (Commonwealth of Australia, 1994) and/or Gorham & Partners' (1996) *Briefing Paper on the Export Potential of the Cultural Industries* for the British Council.

9 Other priorities included the 2012 Olympics; BBC charter, digital switchover; porting fitness and participation; stewardship of cultural sector; terrorism.

10 See Blair's letter (pp. 2–3) attached to DCMS (2006a).

11 Representatives from museums, galleries and the visual arts were involved, mostly as part of the Infrastructure working group. This was charged with considering the relationship between the subsidised cultural sectors and the creative industries. The thematic approach adopted by the recent consultation focused on infrastructure; competition and intellectual property; access to finance and business support, education and skills; diversity; technology; evidence and analysis. http://headshift.com/dcms/index.cfm?fuseaction=main.viewSection&intSectionID=506 (retrieved 12.12.2006). Oakley has suggested (personal correspondence, 20.12.2006) that this thematic approach may have militated against those sectors' engagement with the Creative Economy Programme being given a higher profile.

12 For DCMS's organisational structure at October/November 2006, see http://www.culture.gov.uk/about_us/our_structure/ (retrieved 6.12.2006).

13 http://www.culture.gov.uk/global/siteSearch/SearchResults.htm?_SRH_DB=SiteIndex&_SRH_STYPE=SIMPLE&_SRH_SearchString=creativ (retrieved 6.12.2006).

14 Including, for instance, the Creativity Towers – a new model for establishing concentrations of specialist creative workspaces in new developments.

15 Creative Partnerships, which began in 2002, aims to develop:

- the creativity of young people, raising their aspirations and achievements;
- the skills of teachers and their ability to work with creative practitioners;
- schools' approaches to culture, creativity and partnership working; and
- the skills, capacity and sustainability of the creative industries.

It focuses on the most deprived communities in England. http://www.creative-partnerships.com/ (retrieved 6.12.2006).

16 http://www.culture.gov.uk/global/siteSearch/SearchResults.htm?_SRH_DB=SiteIndex&_SRH_STYPE=SIMPLE&_SRH_SearchString=innovation (retrieved 6.12.2006).

17 NESTA (the National Endowment for Science, Technology and the Arts), for instance, endowed over £300million from the National Lottery in 2005/6 specifically to foster innovation in the UK. Its mission is 'to transform the UK's capacity for innovation', http://www.nesta.org.uk/index.aspx (retrieved 6.12.2006).
18 Searches for 'creative' and 'creativity' produced 134 results, http://www.lga.gov.uk/ (retrieved 6.12.2006).
19 These include inspiring creative people and designers; providing reference material for art and production design in television and film; presenting stories and context for radio, television, publishing, film and video; creating interactive online learning resources and leisure software.
20 These comprise the national museums in England, Scotland, Wales and Northern Ireland, the British Library, National Library of Scotland, and the National Archives.
21 It also describes its own contributions to each of the Cultural Economy Programme's working party themes: infrastructure; competition and intellectual property; education and skills; diversity; technology.
22 Its priorities include taking part in the arts; children and young people; the creative economy; vibrant communities; internationalism and celebrating diversity.
23 ACE's response to the Creative Economy Programme consultation focuses on its own role and interest in the creative economy – its commitment to fostering creativity and the role of the arts; supporting small business, innovation and growth and the contribution of the individual artist; international positioning and global market-making; the importance of culturally vibrant communities in the creative economy; and the need for more robust evidence, analysis and 'next practice'. This plays to the notion that ACE acts as an R&D agency for the arts sector in the UK, initiating, supporting, incubating and developing new ideas from artists that have become fuel for the creative economy (ACE, 2006a).
24 The origins of the V&A go back to a 1835 Select Committee charged to look into the failures of British design in respect to domestic and overseas trade (comparable to the later Industrial Hall, Birmingham, 1885). In that sense, it represented an early intervention by the government to promote the economics of 'creativity' (Selwood, 1999). In relation to the V&A's more recent attempts to set out its relationship to the creative industries, see Travers and Glaister (2004: 30) and Johnson and Thomas's 1995 colloquium paper referred to by Anderson (1999: 142).
25 See, for instance, Holden (2006; 2004) Hewison (2006); Lee, Naylor and Oakley (2006); ACE (2006d).
26 This ten-year development strategy (ACGB, 1984) put forward a case for regional development and the need to strengthen partnerships in funding, particularly in conjunction with local authorities. It offered a £5million package, including £2million of new money from local authorities. It was particularly significant in relation to the development of regional museums which were encouraged to promote contemporary art.
27 This is precisely the object of Serrell (2006).
28 According to Incomes Data Services:

> Traditionally, employment protection legislation has been geared towards individuals with regular full-time jobs working under open-ended contracts of employment. However, working patterns have changed significantly in recent years, and there has been a marked increase in the number of individuals whose working arrangements are 'atypical'. One such arrangement involves the use of fixed-term contracts.
>
> The Fixed-term Employees (Prevention of Less Favourable Treatment) Regulations come into force on 1 October 2002. The regulations, which implement the EC Fixed-Term Work Directive (No.99/70), give fixed-term employees the right in principle not to be treated less favourably than permanent employees of the same employer doing similar work. The right, which is exercisable by complaint to an employment tribunal, applies where the less favourable treatment is on the ground that the employee is

employed on a fixed-term contract, and is not justified on objective grounds. http://www.incomesdata.co.uk/brief/fixed-termsupp.htm (retrieved 6.12.2006).

References

Accounting Standards Board (2006) 'Heritage assets: can accounting do better?', Discussion Paper. http://www.frc.org.uk/images/uploaded/documents/Heritage%20Assets%20DP%20web %20optimised.pdf. (retrieved 02.11.2008).

ACE (2006a) Department for Culture, Media and Sport. Creativity Economy Programme – public consultation. http://www.cep.culture.gov.uk/index.cfm?fuseaction=search.show SearchResults&vcSearchString=ACE (retrieved 10.11.2006).

—— (2006b) *Turning Point, Arts Council England: A strategy for the contemporary visual arts in England.* London: Arts Council England.

—— (2006c) *Our agenda for the arts, 2006–8.* http://www.artscouncil.org.uk/downloads/our_agenda_2006.rtf. (retrieved 10.11.2006).

—— (2006d) 'Arts Council England launches its first-ever public value inquiry,' Press release, 7 November 2006. http://www.artscouncil.org.uk/pressnews/press_detail.php?browse=recent&id=741 (retrieved 10.12.2006).

ACGB (1984) *The glory of the garden: The development of the arts in England. A strategy for a decade.* London: Arts Council of Great Britain.

AEA Consulting (1999) *Creative industry: generating income for museums and galleries,* London: Museums and Galleries Commission.

—— (2003) *Too much stuff? Disposals from national museums.* London: National Museums Directors' Conference.

Anderson D (1999) *A common wealth, museums in the Learning Age.* London: Department for Culture, Media and Sport.

Bailey M (2006) 'Baltic Gallery in Gateshead investigated by National Audit Office. Major commissions by Chris Burden and Antony Gormley examined', *The Art Newspaper*, 11 June 2006. http://www.theartnewspaper.com/article01.asp?id=306 (retrieved 22.10. 2006).

Banaji S and Burn A (2007) *Rhetorics of creativity: A review of the literature* for the Institute of Education. London: Creative Partnerships and Arts Council of England.

Commonwealth of Australia (1994) *Creative nation: Commonwealth cultural policy.* Canberra: Commonwealth of Australia.

Cox G (2005) *Cox review of creativity in business: building on the UK's strengths.* http://www.hm-treasury.gov.uk/cox_review_creativity_business.htm

Creigh-Tyte S and Stiven G (2001) 'Why does government fund the cultural sector?' in Selwood S (ed.) *The UK cultural sector. Profile and policy issues.* London: Policy Studies Institute, pp. 173–188.

Davies S (2006) 'Disposals', *Museum News: The Journal of National Heritage*, issue 79, p. 9.

DCMS (1998a) *A new cultural framework.* London: Department for Culture, Media and Sport.

—— (1998b) *The DCMS comprehensive spending review: A new approach to investment in culture* (mimeo).

—— (2001) *Creative industries mapping document 2001.* London: Department for Culture, Media and Sport.

—— (2002) 'Tessa Blackstone announces £5.2 million grants for 49 museums around the country', press release, July 2002. http://www.culture.gov.uk/Reference_library/Press_notices/archive_2002/dcms151_2002.htm (retrieved 22.10. 2006).

—— (2005a) *Understanding the future: Museums and 21st-century life. The value of museums*. (http://www.culture.gov.uk/Reference_library/Consultations/2005_closed_consultations/21_centuary_museums.htm (retrieved 22.10. 2006).

—— (2005b) 'Tessa Jowell unveils £6 million challenge fund to boost innovation in the arts and culture', press release, April 2005. http://www.culture.gov.uk/Reference_library/Press_notices/archive_2005/dcms057_05.htm (retrieved 22.10. 2006).

—— (2006a) 'Tessa Jowell welcomes Prime Minister's appointment letter', press release, 079/06. http://www.culture.gov.uk/Reference_library/Press_notices/archive_2006/dcms079_06.htm (retrieved 22.10. 2006).

—— (2006b) 'Government response to Paul Roberts', Report on nurturing creativity in young people, press release. http://www.culture.gov.uk/Reference_library/Publications/archive_2006/govtresponse_nurturingcreativity.htm?contextId={E35EF5B5-B3A4-4205-9E77-ECC01B82666F} (retrieved 22.10. 2006).

—— (2006c) *Understanding the future: Priorities for England's museums*. London: Department for Culture, Media and Sport.

DTI (2005) *DTI economics paper no.15: Creativity, design and business performance of the role of creativity and design*. http://64.233.183.104/search?q=cache:1hEAJBwC-xgJ:www.dti.gov.uk/files/file13654.pdf+DTI+Economics+Paper+No.15:&hl=en&ct=clnk&cd=1&client=safari (retrieved 22.10. 2006).

Enterprise LSE Cities Project Team (2004) *Museums and galleries: Creative engagement*. London: National Museums Directors' Conference.

Gorham & Partners (1996) *Briefing paper on the export potential of the cultural industries for the British Council* (mimeo).

Heartfield J (2006) 'A business solution for creativity, not a creativity solution for business' in Mirza, 2006: pp. 71–92.

Hewison R (2006) *Not a sideshow: Leadership and cultural value – a matrix for change*. London: Demos.

Hewitt P (2006) 'Arts in the core script – writing ourselves in'. The Smith Instituite Arts Lecture, 12 July 2006, *New Statesman* and http://www.artscouncil.org.uk/pressnews/press_detail.php?rid=0&sid=&browse=recent&id=685 (retrieved 22.10.06).

Holden J (2004) *Capturing cultural value: How culture has become a tool of government policy*. London: Demos.

—— (2006) *Cultural value and the crisis of legitimacy: Why culture needs a democratic mandate*. London: Demos.

Holden J and Jones S (2006) *Knowledge and inspiration: The democratic face of culture. Evidence in making the case for museums, libraries and archives*. London : MLA, (on behalf of Demos).

House of Commons (Culture, Media and Sport Committee) (2002) *National museums and galleries: Funding and free admission*. First report of Session 2002–03. HC 85. London: Stationery Office.

HM Treasury (2005) *Cox review of creativity in business: building on the UK's strengths*. http://www.hm-treasury.gov.uk./independent_reviews/cox_review/coxreview_index.cfm (retrieved 21.11.2006).

Jackson T and Jordan M (2006) *Review of the presentation of the contemporary visual arts. Part 1: Analysis & recommendations; Part 2: Surveys of the Sector & Appendices*. http://www.artscouncil.org.uk/aboutus/project_detail.php?browse=recent&id=517. (retrieved 27.05.08).

Jenkins S (2006) 'The disgrace is not that this Lowry is being sold but the reason why' *The Guardian* 27 October 2006. http://arts.guardian.co.uk/comment/story/0,,1933256,00.html (retrieved 21.11.2006).

Jowell T (2004) *Government and the value of culture*. London: Department for Culture, Media and Sport

—— (2005) SoS speech to the city, 14 March, Bloomberg (mimeo).

Lammy D (2005) Keynote address to Museums Association Conference. 26 October 2006. http://www.culture.gov.uk/Reference_library/Press_notices/archive_2005/lammy_ma_speech.htm (retrieved 21.11.2006).

—— (2006) Speech at the launch of Demos 'Cultural value and the crisis of legitimacy' publication, 29 March 2006. http://www.culture.gov.uk/Reference_library/Press_notices/archive_2006/lammy_demos_speech.htm (retrieved 21.11.2006).

Labour Party (1997) *Create the future: A strategy for cultural policy, arts and the creative economy*. London: Labour Party.

Lee D, Naylor R and Oakley K (2006) Giving them what they want: the construction of the public in 'public value'. Unpublished paper given at the conference, *CRESC Media and Social Change*.

Melikian S (2006) 'Sotheby's contemporary art sale reaches $125.1 million', *International Herald Tribune*, 15 November 2006. http://www.iht.com/articles/2006/11/15/features/contemp.php.

Merriman N (2006) 'Disposal: sustaining the future', *Arts Industry* 3 November 2006 :10.

Mirza M (ed.) (2006) *Cultural vultures: Is UK arts policy damaging the arts?* London: Policy Exchange.

MLA (2006) Creative Economy Programme Consultation. Response from the MLA Partnership. http://www.cep.culture.gov.uk/index.cfm?fuseaction=search.showSearchResults&vcSearchString=MLA (retrieved 10.11.2006).

Morris E (2003) Speech to Cheltenham Festival of Literature, 16 October 2003. http://www.culture. gov.uk/cgi-bin/MsmGo.exe?grab_id=50&page_id=3804416&query=cheltenhamfestival &hiword=cheltenham+festival+FESTIVALS+ (retrieved 10.08.04).

Morris Hargreaves McIntyre (2004) *Taste buds: How to cultivate the art market*. London: Arts Council England.

—— (2006) *Making it to market: Developing the market for contemporary craft. Executive Summary*. London: Arts Council England.

Museums Association (2002) *Code of ethics for museums*. London: Museums Association.

—— (2005) *Collections for the future: Report of a museums association inquiry*. London: Museums Association.

—— (2006) 'Dismayed by Bury's decision to auction Lowry', 20 September 2006, http://www.museumsassociation.org/12949 (retrieved 21.11.2006).

Nairne S (2006) 'Who gets the right to culture? Enterprise and diversity in the 21st-century museum'. Unpublished keynote address, Museums Association Conference Bournemouth (23 October 2006).

National Advisory Committee for Creative and Cultural Education (1999) *All our futures: Creativity, culture & education*. Sudbury: DfEE Publications.

Oakley K (forthcoming) 'Creating a mess – Disentangling policy and research from "creativity". Paper presented at the Royal Geographic Society Conference, to be published in a special issue of *Geografiska Annaler: Human Geography*.

Pick J (1983) *Weasel words: A beginner's dictionary for ambitious arts bureaucrats*. Eastbourne: Offord Publications.

Purnell J (2005) 'Making Britain the world's creative hub', Speech to ippr, 16 June 2005. http://www.culture.gov.uk/global/siteSearch/SearchResults.htm?_SRH_DB=Culture_Internet&_SRH_STYPE=ADVANCED&ORQUERY=purnell&PHRASEQUERY=ippr (retrieved 10.12.2006).

Regional Museums Task Force (2001) *Renaissance in the regions: A new vision for England's museums*. London: Resource.

Roberts P (2006) *Nurturing creativity in young people. A report to Government to inform future policy.* http://www.culture.gov.uk/Reference_library/Publications/archive_2006/nurturing_creativity.htm (retrieved 2.11.08).

Serrell B (2006) *Judging exhibitions : A framework for assessing excellence*. Walnut Creek, CA: Left Coast Press.

Selwood S (1999) 'The Applied Art Museums' commercial role: Intervening in the creative economy'. Unpublished paper given at the *Museums of Applied Art Re-Apprised* conference. London: V&A.

—— (2004) 'The politics of data collection: Gathering, analysing and using data in the subsidised cultural sector in England', *Cultural Trends*, No. 47, pp. 13–84.

—— (2007) 'Future uncertain: Art Council England's vision for the future of the contemporary visual arts', *Futures*, 39: pp. 1201–1222.

Tate (2001) *Economic impact of Tate Modern*. Press information. http://www.tate.org.uk/home/news/110501_3.htm (retrieved 31.07.05).

—— (2005) *Tate Modern: The first five years.* London: Tate.

Taylor C (2006) 'Beyond advocacy; developing an evidence base for regional creative industry strategies', *Cultural Trends*, 57: pp. 3–18.

Travers T (2006) 'Museums are key to Britain's success as a creative economy', http://www.nationalmuseums.org.uk/Travers_Report.html. (retrived 2.11.08).

Travers T and Glaister S (2004) *Valuing museums. Impact and innovation among national museums*. London: National Museums Directors' Conference.

Varley W (2005a) 'Trouble at t'mill, melt down at Newcastle's Baltic?' *State of Art*, Autumn 2005: pp. 4–5.

Varley W (2005b) 'Trouble at t'mill, Part 2', *State of Art*, Winter 2005: pp. 3–5.

7b Does Hamlet have to be naked?

Art between tradition and innovation in German theatres

Doris Ruth Eikhof

In 2002, the conservative party's spokesman for cultural politics in Hamburg, Germany, and self-acclaimed supporter of the art of theatre demanded to stop funding one of the countries' most renowned public theatres. He claimed the theatre's avant-garde productions featured the same content as the shows in the nearby red-light district, but were aesthetically less pleasing. Thus, he argued, neither form nor substance of this cultural production were worthy of public money (Hamburger Abendblatt 2002). At the same time, the vice president of the German parliament launched a campaign to have the German-speaking theatre industries put on to the UNESCO world's cultural heritage list to help preserve this unique and art-friendly field of cultural production (Laudenbach 2003a). Far from being extreme attitudes towards the state of German theatre, these two initiatives illustrate the discussion and conflict arising around tradition and innovation in the industry.

As for the vice president of the parliament's campaign, the theatre industry in German-speaking countries has indeed developed unique features, inherited from hundreds of years of artistic performance. Theatres stage a different play every night, and the organisational structures in which these plays are produced have barely changed over the past 300 years. Nor, in many cases, have the buildings and names of the theatres. Each theatre employs a group of actors on temporary contracts, the ensemble, who work together for a relatively long time and draw on the tradition of touring theatre companies. Public funding of up to 95 per cent of their annual budgets relieves German theatres of commercial pressures and allows them to focus on producing art. From early days onwards, this system of cultural production was designed to advance art and artistic innovation. Hence the vice president's claim to preserve it as a rare biotope of *l'art pour l'art*.

As for the senator, he also called on the long-standing tradition of German theatre for justification. In a manner representative for a significant part of theatregoers and politicians, he claimed that in the land of Goethe and Schiller, tax payers deserved better value for their money than plays which frequently feature naked protagonists, blood or excrements. Theatre directors' interpretations of plays, their use (or abuse) of the human body, religious symbols, strong language, violent and sexist scenes have been the subject of an ongoing public debate for decades. More formal aspects of stage performances, such as the use of video screens, microphones or music have been disputed as well. The discussion of nudity on stage is one of the most typical debates around artistic innovation. Conservative critics and audiences complain that nudity on stage is unnecessary and appalling, a 'cheap shocker' and of little artistic value. Theatre artists, on the other hand, claim that literally undressing a figure enables them to express aspects such as human vulnerability in a novel way – for them, Hamlet has to be naked sometimes.

Debates on the other aforementioned aspects of stage performance follow similar lines: what are new forms of artistic expression to some are aesthetical impertinences to others. While directors and theatre managers call on the freedom of the arts granted by the German constitution, their opponents deny untraditional work the status of art in the first place. The conflict between tradition and artistic innovation in theatre results from a special deal between art and politics in Germany. Art of whatever kind is believed to educate a person's character and mind. Since the state is responsible for educating its citizens, not only schools and universities, but also theatres, museums, operas, ballets and orchestras are fully, or at least extensively, funded from public sources. In return, the cultural system has to fulfil two requirements: to produce art as well as to educate and entertain the local community. The first criterion is assessed via a theatre's success in the cultural field, which in turn is significantly influenced by the opinion of theatre critics and fellow theatre artists. The second criterion is measured in audience turn-outs. But since the masses tend to favour traditional play interpretations whereas the critics appreciate artistic innovation and avant-garde art, achieving both goals at the same time is a difficult task for theatres. The need to follow both imperatives of tradition and innovation crucially impacts artistic production in German theatres. Producing art which is recognised within the cultural field as well as education and entertainment which are recognised by the political field poses challenges for the way in which creative talent and artistic production are organised and managed.

Artistic innovation and the conflicts surrounding it have been one of the focal points of creative industries research. However, most studies analyse the relationship between quality, novelty and dynamics of creative production and the industry or production structures it is embedded in (see, for instance, Jeffcutt and Pratt 2002; Lampel *et al.* 2000; Strandgaard *et al.* 2006). Studies of industries such as film, advertising, music or new media have analysed which structures and mechanisms are particularly beneficial for stimulating artistic creativity and thus artistic innovation (see, for example Alvarez *et al.* 2005; Caves 2000; Davis and Scase 2000; Monthoux 2004; Pratt 2002; see also Bilton and Lorenzen in this collection). Other authors have approached the issue of stimulating creativity and innovation from a (human resource) management perspective and have outlined principles of dealing with creative individuals (for example Howkins 2001; Sutton 2001).

The analysis of the German theatre industry presented in this chapter bridges these two approaches. By analysing the conflicts around artistic innovation, it identifies structures and mechanisms on the levels of the individual, organisation and industry, and links them to their broader societal and historical context. In so doing, it becomes clear that artistic innovation in German theatre is tied into a potentially conflicting relationship with longstanding traditions of cultural production. This chapter draws on qualitative empirical data and secondary data both collected in a series of studies by the author and Axel Haunschild between 2000 and 2003 (see also Haunschild 2003; 2004; Eikhof and Haunschild 2006; 2007). The overall aim of this research project was to describe the German theatre industry as a production and employment system and to analyse various aspects of cultural production and artistic work in theatre on individual, organisational and industry level. Such research has not been undertaken before. It invokes very personal aspects of work and identity on the one hand and intangible constructs such as reputation and understanding of art on the other. It therefore requires both diverse empirical approaches and an integrative theoretical framework (see annex).

The chapter's first section has discussed general tensions and problems in the field, and has outlined how traditional structures and contemporary innovations seek to resolve the dilemmas of stability and change. The next section outlines the roots of the theatre industry and the role tradition plays in today's theatre in Germany. The third section analyses the theatre industry as a cultural field and explains how artistic innovation is crucial for gaining reputation in this field. The fourth section analyses how creative work and cultural production are organised to meet the demands of both tradition and innovation. The final section provides a concluding discussion of the relationship between tradition and artistic innovation in theatre and in the cultural field in general.

Behind the scenes: the roots of the German theatre industry

In order to understand the influence of tradition on artistic production in German theatres, one needs to look into the history of theatre. From the Middle Ages until well into the sixteenth and seventeenth centuries, European theatre was organised in touring companies. These groups of actors were led by a managing director/actor, who was responsible for commercial as well as artistic aspects. The actors staged plays they often wrote themselves and undertook all related activities such as stage design and ticket sales as well. In the United Kingdom, touring companies settled down to found permanent theatres as early as the sixteenth century, with Philip Henslowe's 'The Admiral's Men' at the *Rose Theatre* and William Shakespeare's 'The King's Men' at the *Fortune Theatre* being the most prominent examples. Despite their names, these theatre companies were not funded by any admiral or king, but were economically independent and bore the risk of business themselves (Waidelich 1991a: 20).

On the European mainland, it took until the end of the seventeenth century for touring companies to settle down (for example see Simhandl 2001: 133–140; Waidelich 1991a: 19–38). But more important than the time lag was the organisational form of these newly founded theatres. Central European theatre companies either resided as royal theatre groups with one of the many princedoms' courts (with their shows open to the general public as well) or they ran publicly funded theatres in free cities. By the end of the nineteenth century, every city in what was to become today's Germany, Austria and Switzerland had a city theatre (*Stadttheater*), which was funded by external sources rather than ticket sales. Most of these new theatres' managers were concerned with artistic production only, and financial aspects were dealt with by civil or royal accountants in the respective government's administration. Theatre and art in general were believed to advance a person's character and mind, and as such were regarded as part of the education a state had to provide for its citizens (see, for example, Schiller 2000; Simhandl 2001: 149–148). In addition, a strong belief in art for art's sake supported the advancement of theatre as a superior good of its own right. This attitude is best summed up in a letter from the Prussian secretary Duke von Hardenberg to the manager of the Royal Prussian Theatre, Count von Brühl in 1815: 'We want you to produce the best theatre in Germany! Afterwards, tell us how much it was' (quoted in Waidelich 1991a: 34).

Today, the German theatre industry consists of 150 public theatres. Private theatres exist, but in terms of artistic quality and reputation, the public theatres account for what is recognised as the German theatre industry. Public theatres today face slightly tighter budget restrictions than their nineteenth century counterparts, but the respective cities or local states still finance up to 95 per cent of their local theatre's annual budget (Pitz and Köhn 2001). These budgets are paid for by income tax raised at city or local state level. Total subsidiaries for all German theatres, some of which also house opera and ballet, amounted to 2,144 billion Euros in 2002/3, compared to 387 million Euros earned by the theatres themselves via ticket sales and merchandising. The most commercially successful public theatre of that financial year, the *Thalia Theater Hamburg*, still earned as little as 23.4 per cent of its annual budget itself. A good 75 per cent of all theatres' aggregated spending was personnel costs, paying wages for a total of just over 39,000 employees (all figures Deutscher Bühnenverein 2004). The system of financing theatres via income tax relieves German theatres from market pressures faced by privately run theatre enterprises such as those in the UK or US. The production of theatre shows on Broadway and in London's West End is much more market-oriented, with marketability as the constraint on artistic innovation (Caves 2000: 116–120; Daves and Scase 2000: 46, 70). German theatres, on the contrary, are able to first and foremost focus on the artistic content of their production (Eikhof and Haunschild 2007). However, since income tax is collected and spent at *Länder*-level, the resources available to public theatres in Germany vary considerably with size and wealth of the respective *Land* (Briegleb 2005).

What had been a mere belief in art for art's sake and its educational benefits in nineteenth-century princedoms and empires was made a constitutional right after the Second World War. Critically, Article 5 (3) of the German constitution guarantees freedom in the production of art and establishes the state's obligation to publicly fund the production of art. This article contains potentially explosive material for the creative industries. The constitutional right to artistic freedom results in a central principle for cultural production, called '*Kunstfreiheit*' (literally: freedom of the arts). *Kunstfreiheit* means that unless he or she violates another constitutional right (such as, for instance, human dignity), an artist can produce any artistic content he or she chooses to produce. This right stands irrespectively of whether the artist works independently or is employed. Translated into the practices of cultural politics and artistic production, this constitutional right means that the state has to pay for the production of art (for example by providing budgets to cultural institutions and signing employment contracts with managers of theatres, operas, museum or orchestras), but may not interfere with the content produced. In theatre, the person responsible for the artistic content of the production is the theatre manager, and he or she only. Theatre managers decide which plays to stage and in which interpretation. They are employed by the local city or state government, but due to the constitutionally guaranteed freedom of the arts, the respective government's influence on the artistic product of its theatre is strictly limited and, as a result, rarely exercised.

Since the nineteenth century, the most significant changes in the German theatre industry were brought about by various attempts to codify established practice in union contracts and founding charters of industry bodies (see Waidelich 1991a: 48–58). In 1846, the employers' association *Deutscher Bühnenverein* was founded (see also Lennartz 1996). This network of theatres was set up to enforce good practice, especially by preventing dealings between theatres and dubious actors' agents. It also strived to benefit actors, for instance by setting up a pension fund and initiating the use of standard employment contracts. Nevertheless, in 1871 the *Genossenschaft Deutscher Bühnen-Angehöriger* was founded as a trade union for all theatre-related professions (see also Genossenschaft Deutscher Bühnen-Angehöriger 2004: 785). Since 1874, the *Deutscher Bühnenverein* and *Genossenschaft Deutscher Bühnen-Angehöriger* are partners to an industry-wide union contract. Their first agreement already regulated industry-wide terms of contract termination, working hours and breaks, job categories, paid sick leave and maternity leave as well as an actor's right to be cast for a certain number of roles per season. In 1919, the trade union and the employers' association set up a special court for labour law cases. It was hoped that this court would be able to provide immediate settlement of conflicts while taking into account the special needs of artistic production. The quartet of employers' association, trade union, industry-wide union contract and labour law court still constitutes the back bone of the German theatre industry today.

From the beginning of the twentieth century onwards, acting, directing and playwriting became established degrees at German universities. Until then, private teachers had dominated the education of actors and directors, while playwrights either graduated in general literature studies or were autodidacts. The institutionalisation of drama studies in universities, essentially influenced by the theoretical schools of Russian Konstantin Stanislawski and Austrian Max Reinhardt, resulted in a relatively homogenous curriculum for drama students. Students graduating from today's 20 German-speaking state drama schools enter the labour market with a set of standard qualifications. On this market, they either meet potential employers directly or via a central agency, the *Zentrale Bühnen-, Fernseh- und Filmvermittlung*. This state-run agency mediates contracts between all stage- and film/TV-related professions and potential employers, thus opening a wider field of employment to drama school graduates (Waidelich 1991b: 51–53).

The second half of the twentieth century saw few changes in the German theatre industry. In the German Democratic Republic, theatres were run by the state as well, the major difference being that actors had permanent contracts. After the reunification, most east-German theatres were vastly overspent and faced financial difficulties, some of them had to close or merge (Briegleb 2005). At the same time, the integration of East and West Germany into one capitalist economy, followed by economic recession at the turn of the century, diminished public spending and thus public budgets available for theatres, operas, orchestras and museums. Across all cities and local states, theatres faced (sometimes severe) budget cuts and, following a more neo-liberal political spirit, were asked to account for their efficiency and effectiveness (Briegleb 2003; Herdlein 2004; Laudenbach 2003a, 2003b). Theatre managers had to reduce personnel costs and find more cost-efficient ways of using their productive resources. The results of these efforts included, for example, an increasing use of freelance labour, changes in the rehearsal systems, cuts in equipment budgets or the relocation of equipment depots from rent-intensive city-centre locations to suburban storehouses (Briegleb 2005; Laudenbach 2003b; von Otting 2001). In 2001, the union contract was revised and restructured. This reform gave the theatres more discretion in applying the regulation and improved some of the actors' rights, especially with respect to paid leave during the season. Nevertheless, the reform of the union contract was mainly a formal exercise and had little impact on the day-to-day work on stage.

Overall, the German theatre industry has been fairly stable with respect to its industry and production structures. Effectively, the union contract and court rulings codified not only employment practices, but also production processes. Given the framework of nightly shows and daily rehearsals, industry-wide regulations allow(ed) for little deviation in the way theatre was and is produced. As a result, the German theatre industry has been characterised by homogenous, traditional production structures from the first employers' association guidelines until today. In addition, the ideological superstructure, the paradigms of art for art's sake and of arts educational value, have a long-standing history. From the daily plights of artistic work to plays and philosophical ideas, tradition plays a dominant role in German theatre.

Centre stage: the ambivalence of innovation

The historical perspective employed in the previous section introduced traditions of the German theatre industry which strongly influence the production of theatre today, but which often stand in conflicting relationships with the imperative of artistic innovation. This section will examine the role of innovation in theatre and analyse the theatre industry as a cultural field. A theoretical framework of special value for the analysis of artistic work and production is the Theory of Praxis by Pierre Bourdieu (e.g. 1990; 1993). Bourdieuian conceptualisation allows research of the drivers behind individual practices, such as the desire to produce art for art's sake. Bourdieu's theory also offers rich descriptions of different fields of social action (i.e. the business field or the art field). Based on and verified in extensive empirical analyses, Bourdieu points out different logics that govern individual and organisational action within these fields. For this chapter, Bourdieu's approach helped to identify two central logics within the field of theatre, i.e. tradition and *l'art pour l'art*, and how they influence individual and organisational practice (for a complementing analysis of the logics of art and business in theatre see Eikhof and Haunschild 2007). The advantage of the theory of practice is that it links analysis of macro and meso structures (such as field logics, industry dynamics, financing structures or contract types) to individual action (such as artistic work practices or marketing one's creative self). In so doing, practice theory helps to identify how abstract ideas of tradition and artistic innovation are translated into individual action and concrete practices of producing art. For instance, individuals adhere to the idea of being part of a bohemian milieu and artistically innovative avant-garde (macro level), which motivates their artistic practice (individual level) and at the same time helps to cope with uncertainties arising from their employment contract (meso level) (Eikhof and Haunschild 2006). Such interdependencies are invisible to theoretical approaches focusing solely on the labour process or economic measures of industry performance.

Bourdieu analyses certain fields or subsectors of society according to the 'rules of the game' which influence individual action and collective structures within a field (see, for example, Bourdieu 1984; 1990; 1993). Individuals seek to secure or advance their position in such fields by (inter-)acting in specific ways. Whether they achieve these aims depends on whether the rules in the given field promote their doings. These rules of the game, or logics, are distinctive for each field, and while some practices may be rewarded in one field, they will be less successful in others. For instance, altruistic behaviour may earn merits within the religious field, whereas it may lead to financial loss in the economic field.

In a practice-theory perspective, the cultural industries constitute the field of cultural production or cultural field. Drawing on empirical research, Bourdieu (1984; 1993; 1999) characterises the respective field logic as one referring to the idea of art as a greater good, as a transcendental phenomenon represented in humankind's doings and accounting for more than the sum of all works of art. In short, the field of cultural production is characterized by the logic of *l'art pour l'art* (Bourdieu 1998: 182; 1993; 1999). This logic is fairly vague and continuously contested, and it is up to each individual artist to justify their actions as works of art. This process of recognition within the cultural field has to take both tradition and innovation into account. On the one hand, a common understanding has developed in the cultural field and its subfields such as theatre, music, sculpture or painting, as to what is (traditionally) regarded as art and what is not. On the other hand, since humanism, the mere reproduction of art has been denied the status of 'true' art. The idea of artistic innovation is central to the cultural field. Established cultural canons are frequently challenged by new, avant-garde movements, which, if successful, become acknowledged as (a new form of) art and are taken onto the canon. Artistic innovation can invoke an unlimited number of possibilities such as the use of new materials, techniques and forms, the production of new content, new subjects, new methods of assembling 'traditional' components, or new ways of presenting or contextualising artistic production. The key issue is whether one's innovative endeavour is recognised as art by other actors in the cultural field. A homogenous, 'objective' understanding of art to which everyone could relate is absent (see also Hesmondhalgh 2007; Throsby 2001). Dense networks of critics, curators, art managers, agents, fellow artists, art-lovers and last but not least audiences and politicians continuously evaluate artistic production. Appreciation is expressed by awarding prizes, writing favourable reviews, inviting artists to a festival or exhibition or, on the side of the more direct consumption, attending an exhibition or show and buying a book or painting. Negative reviews and explicit ignorance, but also the sheer lack of the aforementioned positive signs testify disapproval within the cultural field.

In the German field of cultural production, artistic innovation will earn artistic reputation, and artistic reputation will earn funding. For a deeper understanding of these relationships, two aspects need to be looked at: the ways in which artistic reputation can be gained and the different kinds of artistic reputation that can be earned. The following two subsections analyse both aspects for the German theatre industry.

Gaining artistic reputation

A person's or an organisation's artistic reputation is intangible and hard to measure. It consists of the collectively shared perception of this person's or organisation's artistic capability and capacity for artistic innovation. In German theatre, artistic reputation is ascribed mainly to theatre managers, directors and actors, and to a lesser extent to the theatres themselves or to stage designers and costume designers. Indicators of artistic reputation can be divided into two categories:

1 *Publicised announcements such as positive reviews, prizes and invitations to theatre festivals.* Reviews in national newspapers such as *DIE ZEIT, Frankfurter Allgemeine Zeitung* or *Süddeutsche Zeitung* represent the most influential and regular public assessment of cultural production in theatre, since these newspapers will review every new premiere of artistic relevance. On an annual basis, prizes give important information on theatres' and individual artists' standing. The German-speaking theatre industry knows a number of prizes for actors, actresses, directors or playwrights. One of the most influential journals, *Theater heute*, also votes the Theatre of the Year, to honour the overall artistic output of an organisation. Depending on how renowned the prizes themselves are, for instance on whether it is a local or national competition, being a laureate can significantly improve a person's or organisation's standing in the cultural field. Finally, invitations to present a play at the leading theatre festival are regarded as indicators of a person's or theatre's artistic reputation. Theatre festivals, especially the *Theatertreffen* in Berlin, *Autorentheatertage* in Hamburg, *Theatertage* in Mülheim and *Stückemarkt* in Heidelberg, bring together the season's allegedly best productions. The festival directors are either theatre managers or other renowned individuals, and an invitation from such a major player in the industry is a reliable indicator of the industry's favourable rating of a director's, author's or theatre manager's

work. Partaking in a festival also gives the opportunity to reach a wider audience and to network.

2 *Artistic partners, who have a good reputation themselves.* Theatres as organisations can earn artistic reputation by contracting prestigious managers, directors or actors. The individuals themselves can advance their status within the community by working with renowned partners, for instance with a director whose play has just been voted Play of the Year or with an actor or actress who have previously been recognised for their artistic work. Similarly, working at an established theatre can advance an individual's artistic reputation – although this depends on which theatre manager runs the theatre. The constellation of partners an individual or a theatre works with is crucial for assessing their position within the cultural field.

Indicators of both kinds are regarded as signs of artistic quality and thus capacity for artistic innovation. Although the accreditation of artistic reputation is often obscure, never objective and always debatable, the German theatre industry is characterised by a fairly unanimous hierarchy. Despite all differences in detailed assessments, individuals throughout the industry mostly agree on who belongs to the top group in each category, who constitutes the midfield and who is of lesser artistic importance. This informal yet highly effective ranking system of artistic inputs was described by Richard Caves as the A-list/B-list property indicative of creative industries in general (Caves 2000).[1] It directly influences staffing decisions and interpersonal relationships. Overall, both theatres as organisations and individual theatre actors will strive to acquire the described indicators of artistic reputation, since they will not only enable them to participate in cultural production, but will increase the chances of getting funding or employment, respectively. Furthermore, artistic reputation is crucial for acquiring renowned partners for collaboration. However, the fact that indicators of artistic reputation are acquired does not guarantee funding or access to desired human resources either. The kind of reputation gained plays a crucial role.

Differences in artistic reputation

Artistic reputation is earned by producing, but not simply reproducing art. The kind of artistic reputation gained depends on the degree of innovation inherent in the work. The innovative content of a new theatrical production can differ widely; it can take any form on a continuum from developing a traditional style to negating traditional forms or contents to taking an exactly opposed, anti-traditional artistic position. For instance, in traditional theatre, words are clearly attributed to individual figures and are essential ingredients for portraying characters and developing the storyline of the play. Producing an innovative, yet traditional interpretation of a play might mean adapting the context to a modern setting, for example staging 'Romeo and Juliet' as a love-story between a Jew and an Arab in present day Israel. In radical opposition to such traditional approaches, modern playwrights prioritise the text and deconstruct protagonists by allocating the spoken text equally to a number of actors, who then act as spokespeople for the words, not as distinguishable figures.

Either approach can stimulate praise or condemnation, depending on the artistic understanding and education of the critic or theatre-goer. While mainstream critics prefer traditional approaches, critics in favour of more radical artistic innovation dismiss those as too conformist and opt for avant-garde works. As a rule of thumb, critics writing for specialist theatre journals and liberal, upper-class newspapers, left-wing politicians, theatre artists themselves and theatre-goers with cultural-educational rather than entertainment interests (typically professionals in research and education, social care or cultural production) will favour avant-garde theatre (see also Schulze 1992; Vester 2005). Traditional interpretations are preferred by critics writing for conservative upper-class or boulevard newspapers, conservative politicians and theatre-goers seeking entertainment rather than catharsis (typically professionals in conservative industries such as banking, trade and finance or clerical workers in business and technical professions (ibid.).

Whether reputation for traditional or innovative approaches to theatre is more likely to secure funding depends essentially on the respective government and the party and cultural politics agenda of the minister or senator in charge for the local theatre. At two of the theatres studied, the managers had to renegotiate their contracts. In order to give the government sufficient time to appoint potential replacements, renegotiations were held 18 months before the contracts ran out. Both managers negotiated with the same city government represented by a conservative senator for cultural politics. Manager A had run his theatre with a balanced mix of avant-garde productions, which had been highly praised by the theatre community and the more adventurous critics, and entertaining plays of high quality, but little artistic innovation. As a result, he had increased the theatre's reputation within the cultural field, won the prize for Theatre of the Year, and had also performed well in economic terms. Consequently, manager A had no problems renegotiating a follow-on contract with a slightly increased budget for the theatre as well as himself personally. Theatre manager B had deliberately focused on avant-garde productions by young directors and playwrights, staged by a cast of young, extravagant actors. Mainstream productions had been taken off the repertoire. While his experimental and very political approach to theatre worked well for a young, alternative audience and like-minded critics, the established audience of subscribers and the local conservative press were appalled. Influenced by a public campaign against this allegedly 'wrong understanding of art', the senator for cultural affairs did not prolong manager B's contract, but appointed a more mainstream manager instead. Ironically, by the time manager B had to leave, the theatre community agreed that in the 18 months since renegotiations it had actually been manager A, who was running the overall more innovative and provocative repertoire.

The analysis of the theatre industry as a field with *l'art pour l'art* as its main logic points to the relevance of artistic innovation in German theatre. Innovation is crucial for gaining artistic reputation and thus also for receiving public funding, which also depends on a theatre's artistic reputation. However, the example of the two theatre managers highlights the ambivalent role of innovation. Artistic innovation as such does not necessarily guarantee the reputation one needs to survive in the cultural field. In depends on the context of artistic production; whether artistic innovation is perceived positively and as a contribution to the advancement of art in general – and whether it is recognised as artistic innovation in the first place.

Ongoing drama: can tradition and innovation be reconciled in creative production?

As outlined in the previous sections, tradition and innovation both play vital roles in the German theatre industry. Long-standing traditions of organising and funding theatrical production provide the framework in which theatre art is produced today. The key elements of these structures are publicly funded theatres with a fairly stable core group of actors. Private theatre companies and temporary projects, which sometimes contribute significantly to the artistic development in the industry, do exist, but receive very little funding, if any, and can thus effectively not compete with the established main actors in the industry, the *Stadttheater*. In other cultural industries such as film or music artistic innovation may be stimulated by setting up a new company or group or using new location. The funding structure of German theatre in effect locks theatrical production into the set organisational structures of a publicly owned body and into the real estate of century-old venues for artistic performance. In terms of content, traditional interpretations of plays which are hundreds of years old themselves have a strong influence on what is perceived as art and what is not. Nevertheless, producing artistic innovation is the central means of earning artistic reputation in the cultural field. Being perceived as producing *l'art pour l'art* is crucial for attracting renowned collaborators and for obtaining public funding.

As a result of this special setting in the German theatre industry, theatres have to fulfil requirements of tradition and innovation alike. They have to use the traditional structures for producing art and they have to produce plays which are of educational and entertaining value to a number of crowds and thus attract substantial audiences. At the same time, they have to be artistically innovative to earn a reputation within the cultural field and with more adventurous audiences. Over the years, a number of mechanisms and structural characteristics have evolved which enable theatres to reconcile tradition and art – or at least to keep conflicts between them at a viable level. Five of these mechanisms, the repertoire system, the ensemble, the theatre manager's position, the use of alternative venues and of freelance directing teams, stand out in particular.

The repertoire system

The central mechanism for reconciling tradition and innovation is the repertoire system. In this system of production, theatres produce a number of plays simultaneously and then choose a different play to stage every night. Each play is produced by a team of actors, directors, stage and costume designers and other support staff. Typically, directors, stage and costume designers will be freelancers hired for one play, while actors and support staff are on temporary contracts for a year. For directors, stage and costume designers, work ends on the day of the premiere. Actors and most support staff keep working on the production until it is finally taken off the repertoire. Up to four teams simultaneously rehearse a new play each, the current premieres. Rehearsals take place during the day; and at night, actors stage the scheduled show. This production process is clearly marked by the time flies property and motley crew property outlined by Caves (2000),[2] with the idiosyncrasy that motley crews work simultaneously and artists fluctuate between different motley crews on a daily basis. A season's repertoire consists of successful productions from the previous season(s) and of new plays produced in that season. An average theatre in Germany will stage 10–20 premieres per season and have between 15 and 30 plays 'on the repertoire'. This system has three main consequences:

1 Theatres can satisfy different interests in theatre throughout the week. The repertoire programme offers the opportunity to, for instance, stage a fairly traditional play on Thursday, an avant-garde production on Friday, and a more entertaining play on Saturday. Typically, weekday shows include a traditional interpretation which attracts school classes. Saturday and Sunday nights often feature crowd pleasers for a geographically wider target group that would not travel into town after work on a weekday. Premieres are usually scheduled Thursday to Saturday, so that reviews can make it into the weekend newspapers. This way, theatres can stage artistically innovative plays and attract substantial crowds in the same week. The repertoire system of alternating plays is a crucial means for reconciling imperatives of tradition and innovation, since it allows using the same resources to produce art of very different content.
2 Actors work in more than one team per day; usually they will be in a rehearsing team during the day and work with a show team at night. Depending on rehearsal schedules, even working with three different teams per day is not uncommon, for instance when, in addition to current premiere rehearsals and nightly show, a play from a previous season is given an afternoon/late night run-through after a longer period of stage absence. Due to the highly personal nature of acting, actors perceive this team-hopping as quite demanding. However, all theatre artists interviewed also said the constant change of project teams stimulates artistic creativity and innovation. Actors, directors and managers alike reported that working with different partners, being exposed to new ideas and new personal relationships on a regular basis boosts the development of art as well as of personalities and careers.
3 The repertoire system only works if the team that produced a play in the previous season(s) is still around in the following season. If actors had to be replaced and new actors trained for the roles, resources would be diverted from current premier production and keeping old plays on repertoire would become too costly. The *ensemble* mode of employment (see further) grants this flexibility. Actors usually stay with a theatre for longer than just one season, so they will be able to stage last season's plays with the original cast in the following

season. In addition, contracts usually require freelance directors to conduct run-throughs in later seasons to maintain the standards of the original productions.

The repertoire system is much more challenging in terms of planning and organising than the en-suite system in which the same play is staged every night until public attention and ticket sales wane. Staff work on multiple teams and have to be coordinated with freelancers whose availability is determined by their work at other theatres. Scheduling daily rehearsals and nightly shows and allocating resources such as rehearsal rooms or technicians in a way that takes account of all individual availabilities is a complex task. But despite its complexity, this production system gives German theatres the flexibility needed to attend substantially different crowds in the same house by producing a variety of artistic contents.

The ensemble

The repertoire system of production corresponds with a specific mode of employment, the ensemble. An average German theatre employs a core group of 25–40 actors on temporary contracts. Contracts run for one year and are automatically prolonged unless one of the parties to the contracts cancels them. This system enables the theatres to keep a mix of different actors which they need to staff a number of plays, and at the same time grants the flexibility to adjust staff qualifications to current productions by not prolonging contracts and hiring new actors.

Together with the production mode of different teams, the ensemble employment mode combines the advantages of a stable group (for instance the familiarity with each other's strengths and weaknesses or financial security to back up artistic experiments) with the advantages of project work (continuous change and development and circulation of ideas). In so doing, it is as essential for the German theatre industry as the repertoire system. Albeit less obviously connected with the reconciliation of tradition and innovation, an ensemble which is well-staffed in terms of its actors' and actresses' personalities and qualifications crucially provides the pool of resources necessary for producing the variety of plays that constitute the repertoire.

The ensemble mode of employment is also closely connected to the traditional industry structures described above (see also Haunschild 2003, 2004). As a result of the standardised education drama students receive at university, employers can trust graduates to be able to play not only specific types of characters, but a broader variety of roles – a qualification essential for an ensemble actor. A middle aged ensemble actress, for instance, has to be able to play a glamorous Shakespearean elfin queen as well as Ibsen's Nora and a run-down heroin addict in a contemporary play – often within the course of 36 hours. Memorising the scripts and more crucially being able to bring complex characters alive and to metamorphose into them at any given time requires excellent acting skills acquired in years of training. Drama schools also develop the social skills actors need for adapting to constantly changing teams and to directors' different styles and interpretations. The repertoire system depends on such adequately educated ensemble actors.

Temporary contracts, short contract duration and nation-wide careers connected with the ensemble system also ask a considerable amount of flexibility and spatial mobility of the actors and result in significant employment insecurity (Haunschild and Eikhof 2009). The industry-wide union contract, well-established industrial relations and the special labour law court combine to reduce this insecurity to a viable level (Haunschild 2004). Paradoxically, union contract and court rulings grant flexibility because of their rigidity: given the set context of nightly shows, the detailed rules of union contract and court rulings leave little room for idiosyncrasies in the production process. As a result, production processes in any two theatres are almost identical. This increases the flexible use of labour and the creativity-enhancing constant rearrangement of teams, since it does not take long for any theatre artist to adapt to a new employer's production system. Training costs, which can be substantial in other industries, are nearly zero in theatre.

The idiosyncratic position of the theatre managers

The third important feature to be discussed here was not designed to reconcile tradition and innovation, but ultimately helps to do so: the theatre manager's idiosyncratic position.[3] As outlined above, theatre managers enjoy freedom of art, *Kunstfreiheit*, to run the theatre according to their artistic beliefs. They will have a temporary contract, typically for five years, which may then be prolonged. During the duration of the contract, theatre managers are basically free to produce the theatre they choose to, according to their understanding of art. Such protected artistic beliefs also include a personal opinion of to what extent tradition and innovation should influence theatre. The theatre manager's personal take on theatre as art will influence the plays chosen, the ensemble hired, and most crucially, the freelance directors contracted to direct the plays. The government has no direct influence on artistic or economic decisions. The prolongation of the manager's contract usually depends on (1) whether the local government assesses the theatre manager's work positively, i.e. it believes his or her theatre fulfils both functions of producing art and educating and entertaining the public and (2) whether the theatre manager is interested in a renewal.

This way of appointing and dismissing theatre managers means that theatre managers are given a five-year period to produce art according to their own ideas and afterwards the government decides whether it approves of the produce. Thus, art is judged with a mid- to long-term perspective, which can crucially influence the outcome of the assessment. Within five years, an initially innovative and disputed approach to theatre may have become renowned and established. While a shorter period of judgement might have prompted a government into dismissing a theatre manager for lack of artistic reputation, mid-term developments can lead to more favourable assessments – for instance if the innovation earned the theatre manager a prize or high attendance numbers after initially being ignored. On the other hand, five years may also see changes in the government and in the agenda for cultural politics, which in turn may influence the judgement of a theatre manager's work. Temporary contracts for theatre managers in combination with the constitutionally granted freedom of art set the framework for theatre managers' work and relieve them from the pressures of achieving goals – crucially, the reconciliation of tradition and innovation – on a day-to-day basis.

Alternative venues

More recently, larger theatres in particular have found another way of reconciling tradition and innovation: spatial separation. Traditionally, theatres presented plays only on their main stage, which was mostly situated in a prominent building in the city centre. Many of these buildings are architectonic testaments of the bourgeoisie's cultural achievements and evoke associations of Goethe, Shakespeare and audiences in frocks rather than of alternative, avant-garde theatre. In recent decades, a good deal of artistic innovation has indeed taken place outside these temples of Thalia and Melpomene. Theatres have increasingly used their rehearsal stages and other alternative locations like cafeterias as public venues. These stages are usually smaller and less well equipped than the main stage and are often situated in off-city centre, semi-industrial areas lending them a rougher, more 'authentic' feel. They are typically used to stage plays with a smaller cast and less stage design, which is mostly the case for avant-garde productions and plays by contemporary authors. In some cases, theatre's off-main stage venues have become well established as a local core of artistic innovation.

Thus, by simply dedicating a different venue to the production of avant-garde art, theatres are able to integrate imperatives of both tradition and innovation even on the same night. For one of the theatres researched, the commercial use of the rehearsal stage also substantially increased ticket earnings. Furthermore, a number of interviewees reported they preferred working on the small stages because the projects staged there were 'real theatre art' and the audiences (usually young, alternative, urban people) more the kind of people they want to play for. Like theatre organisations, actors themselves are often torn between the lure of the main stage in a traditional representative theatre building with a big audience and the more old-style bohemian aura of intimate, small-scale productions for art's sake. Thus, the opportunity to play in different venues allows reconciling traditional and innovative imperatives on the individual level as well as on the organisational level.

Freelance directing teams

As mentioned earlier, directors, stage designers and costume designers are usually hired as freelancers. They frequently form directing teams which earn themselves a distinctive reputation for the theatre by styling the production (Blair [2001] observed a similar form of semi-permanent work groups in the film industry). Directing teams or individual directors are hired by a theatre manager to produce one play. If the cooperation is successful, the team or the respective individuals will be hired again. Theatre managers usually have a network of directors or directing teams whose style of producing they like and whom they invite to work at their theatre. Ties between theatre managers and directors or directing teams are usually stable and outlast a manager's change of positions.

Hiring freelance directors or directing teams enables theatres to staff key positions of the production process with artists of different approaches. By appointing directors with radically different preferences in producing theatre, plays of heterogeneous artistic character can be produced sequentially and simultaneously. The result is a repertoire which represents a broader variety of theatre art and thus increases the chances of successfully reconciling the imperatives of innovation and tradition.

In combination, repertoire system, ensemble and freelance directors, the idiosyncratic position of the theatre manager and the use of alternative venues provide ample opportunity to reconcile tradition and innovation in the German theatre. Most of these features have a long-standing history. The roots of the ensemble can be traced back to early touring companies with fairly stable teams of actors. Once these theatre companies settled down at royal courts, they had to play different plays to prevent boredom, hence the development of the repertoire system. Throughout the eighteenth and nineteenth centuries, the position of a state-funded, artistically independent theatre manager evolved. Yet, it is difficult to say which features were prerequisites and which ones were results. Taking into account the complex interdependencies of historical developments it is probably most adequate to conclude that today's characteristics of the German theatre industry co-evolved as a set of structures that has proved viable given the peculiar nature of the cultural field and the specific imperatives of tradition and innovation in German theatre in particular. More recent developments like the use of alternative venues indicate that there is room for innovation in the system itself. And although the future of the state-funded ensemble theatres is frequently debated amongst experts, there is little indication that the system itself will cease to exist too soon (Brieglеb 2005; Deetje 2003; Deutscher Bühnenverein 2003; Herdlein 2004; Schmidt 2005; Waidelich 1991b: 108). The existing mechanisms for reconciling tradition and innovation are flexible enough to enable theatres to satisfy their different stakeholders.

Conclusion

This chapter has outlined the roles that tradition and innovation play in German theatre. Theatrical traditions and the roots of the German-speaking theatre industry are central to industry structures and the organisation of artistic production as well as the criteria against which artistic output is judged. Innovation plays a central role not despite, but because of tradition: traditionally, theatres have to justify their doings by gaining reputation in the cultural field, which in turn is gained by artistic innovation. Nevertheless, the imperatives of tradition and innovation translate into goals which often contradict rather than complement each other. These potential clashes have to be circumvented on a daily basis. The chapter has outlined a number of mechanisms and structures within the theatre industry which help doing so:

the repertoire system, the ensemble, the idiosyncratic position of the theatre manager, hiring freelance directing teams and using alternative venues.

In the terminology of organisation theory, cultural production in the German theatre industry is essentially based on a production and employment system which grants flexibility in the content of production as well as numerical flexibility and flexible specialisation with respect to labour use. The traditional production system enables theatres to adapt the content of their artistic production to the current circumstances, especially to critics' and audiences' responses, at fairly short notice. This would not be possible without (1) a workforce which is not only specialised enough to produce various contents, but can also produce these in high quality and (2) an employment system which allows the flexible use of labour. The combination of repertoire system and ensemble contracts provides flexibility in all those aspects. Features such as the use of freelance workers, which effectively make the employment system a crossover between the core-periphery model and flexible specialisation, and of multiple outlets such as rehearsal stage or canteens support this system and increase flexibility in creative production even further. This flexibility can then be used to follow the imperatives of tradition and innovation, despite theatres being locked into the organisational form of static, state-funded bodies. Overall, these structures and mechanisms can be regarded as highly successful. Even though in 2004 the number of new plays per theatre varied from one in some smaller theatres to a maximum of 23 in one of the largest theatres, the overall output was 1,724 premieres. On average, this equals 11 premieres per theatre; that is more than one new play per month of the season (Deutscher Bühnenverein 2004). In sum, this can be regarded as an indicator for considerable artistically innovative activity. However, the success of this system depends on other industry structures such as the education system and the industry-wide union contract (see also Haunschild 2004) or the bohemian lifestyle of theatre actors, which backs up their high involvement with work (Eikhof and Haunschild 2006).

Nevertheless, it would be misleading to conclude that the mechanisms and structures outlined in the previous section could erase all tensions between tradition and innovation. Tradition and innovation exist as different referent points, and it is likely that they will continue to do so for at least two reasons.

First, the degree up to which tradition and innovation are reconciled at a specific theatre and the manner in which this is done depends very much on the individuals involved, most importantly on the theatre manager and the local politicians. Individual actors within the cultural field define their standing not exclusively, but to a considerable extent by positioning themselves on the continuum between traditional and innovative approaches to theatre art. Some theatre managers have a reputation for producing mainstream theatre, some are perceived as avant-gardist. Some politicians favour experimental approaches on stage, some advocate traditional interpretations. The same holds true for dramatists, actors, stage and costume designers and, most importantly, directors. This focus on the individual artist is typical for the cultural field as such; modern understanding of art concentrates very much on the individual genius and embraces the idea of idiosyncrasy as a central paradigm (see also Alvarez *et al.* 2005; Svejenova *et al.* 2007). Depending on their own understanding of the tradition-innovation relation, actors in the cultural field will produce mainstream or avant-garde theatre (or a mix thereof) or will ask their respective appointees to do so. Thus, while the structures of the theatre industry described earlier provide the opportunity to reconcile tradition and innovation, it depends on the individual whether these opportunities are taken and if so, in what way.

Second, and on a more abstract level, the ambivalent relationship of tradition and innovation is an essential element of the cultural field itself. The whole field with *l'art pour l'art* as its dominant logic is based on the ideas of constant development, of the dynamics of creativity and artistic worldviews and of constant changes of forms and subjects. The very essence of cultural production is challenging established ways by bringing about artistic innovation. Evening out all tensions between tradition and innovation would effectively mean halting the field to a standstill and eventually eradicating its *raison d'être* and heartbeat. Using the German theatre industry as an example, this chapter has pointed out how tensions between tradition and innovation can be channelled, their imperatives reconciled and viable ways of accounting for both of them found. But the basic antipodes of tradition and innovation will remain characteristics not only of the German theatre industry, but also of the field of cultural production in general. For some, Hamlet will have to continue being naked in moments of vulnerability while others would prefer him hiding under the sheets.

Annex

The chapter is based on primary and secondary data collected in a series of studies. Primary data includes 45 semi-structured in-depth interviews. A first set of 10 interviews was carried out in a public theatre situated in a city with approximately 500,000 inhabitants. Interview partners included both members of the theatre's management group and actors. A second set of 5 interviews was conducted with representatives of intermediary organisations: the national employers' and employees' associations, the state-run work agency for actors, and a state-run theatre school. Based on these first 15 interviews, a more detailed study of the individual aspects of employment was carried out. For this, a third set of qualitative interviews (30 interviews) was conducted with theatre actors, theatre students, directors and a theatre manager in two public theatres situated in a city with approximately 2 million inhabitants. Additional insight was gained by partaking in industry events such as premieres and readings and by informally meeting up with theatre artists, for instance after shows. Secondary data used includes interviews with theatre artists in newspapers and practitioner journals, statistical reports and information given on theatres' and intermediary organisations' websites.

Acknowledgements

The author would like to thank Axel Haunschild for the enjoyable and productive collaboration on the research project *Arbeitswelt Theater*. Thanks are also extended to Paul Jeffcutt, Andy Pratt and Chris Warhurst for their comments and support.

Notes

1 Caves (2000: 7) emphasises that creative inputs are vertically differentiated. Differences in talent, skill, originality or proficiency result in industry-wide ratings of artists, for instance in the categorisation of A-list and B-list actors in the film industry.
2 As further characteristics of the creative industries, Caves (2000: 5–8) points out that in most creative productions (i) temporal coordination of input factors is crucial in order to meet project deadlines such as premieres or exhibition dates and to realise revenues (*time flies property*) and (ii) project teams combine different skills and work ethos of specialised workers (*motley crew property*).
3 In German, the theatre manager is called *Intendant*, which does not translate into English. The word *Intendant* does not carry managerialist connotations. On the contrary, the position of an *Intendant* has traditionally been held by persons of foremost artistic reputation.

References

Alvarez, J. L., Mazza, C., Strandgaard Pedersen, J. and Svejenova, S. (2005) 'Shielding idiosyncrasy from isomorphic pressures: Towards optimal distinctiveness in European film making', *Organization* Vol. 12(6): 863–888.

Blair, H. (2001) 'You're only as good as your last job: The labour process and labour market in the British film industry', *Work, Employment & Society* Vol. 15(1): 149–169.

Bourdieu, P. (1984) *Distinction: A Social Critique of the Judgement of Taste*, Routledge and Kegan Paul, London.

—— (1990) *The Logic of Practice*, Polity Press, Cambridge.

—— (1993) *The Field of Cultural Production: Essays on Art and Literature*, Columbia University Press, New York.

—— (1998) *Praktische Vernunft. Zur Theorie des Handelns*, Suhrkamp, Frankfurt/M.

—— (1999) *Die Regeln der Kunst. Genese und Struktur des literarischen Feldes*, Suhrkamp, Frankfurt/M.

Briegleb, T. (2003) 'Ein Sommernachts-Alptraum', *brand eins* Vol. 2: 100–102.

—— (2005) 'Wer A ist, muss auch B sagen', *Theater heute. Die neue Klassengesellschaft? Jahrbuch 2005*, Sondernummer 2005: 4–18.

Caves, R.E. (2000) *Creative Industries: Contracts between Art and Commerce*, Harvard University Press, Cambridge/Mass.

Davis, H. and Scase, R. (2000) *Managing Creativity: The Dynamics of Work and Organization*, Open University Press, Buckingham/Philadelphia.

Deetje, R. (2003) 'Als aus Berlin Las Vegas wurde', *Die Zeit* 27:37.

Deutscher Bühnenverein (ed.) (2004) *Theaterstatistik 2002/2003* Vol. 38, Köln.

—— (ed.) (2003) *Muss Theater sein? Theaterbrevier* Deutscher Bühnenverein Bundesverband deutscher Theater e.V., Köln.

Eikhof, D.R. and Haunschild, A. (2006) 'Lifestyle meets market: Bohemian entrepreneurs in creative industries', *Creativity and Innovation Management* Vol. 13 (3): 234–241.

—— (2007) 'For art's sake! Artistic and economic logics in creative production', *Journal of Organizational Behavior* Vol. 28(5): forthcoming.

Genossenschaft Deutscher Bühnen-Angehöriger (2004) *Deutsches Bühnenjahrbuch 2004*, Vol. 22, Hamburg.

Hamburger Abendblatt (2002) '*Schlachten, diesmal nicht auf der Bühne*', 03.12.02: 7.

Haunschild, A. (2003) 'Managing employment relationships in flexible labour markets: The case of German repertory theatres', *Human Relations* Vol. 56(8): 899–929.

—— (2004) 'Employment rules in German theatres: An application and evaluation of the theory of employment systems', *British Journal of Industrial Relations* Vol. 42: 685–703.

Haunschild, A. and Eikhof, D.R. (2009) 'Bringing creativity to market: Actors as self-employed employees', in C. Smith, and A. McKinlay (eds) *The Labour Process in Creative Industries*, Palgrave, Houndmills Basingstoke.

Herdlein, H. (2004) 'Das Wasser steigt und steigt', *bühnengenossenschaft. Fachblatt der Genossenschaft Deutscher Bühnen-Angehöriger* No 3.

Hesmondhalgh, D. (2007) *The Cultural Industries*, 2nd edn, Sage, London.

Howkins, G. (2001) *The Creative Economy: How People Make Money From Ideas*, Penguin, London.

Jeffcutt, P. and Pratt, A.C. (2002) 'Managing creativity in the cultural industries', *Creativity and Innovation Management* Vol. 11(4): 225–233.

Laudenbach, P. (2003a) 'Wir können auch anders', *brand eins* No 10.

—— (2003b) 'Das McKinsey-Theater des Jahres', *Theater heute. Das unbequeme Erbe. Jahrbuch 2003* Sondernummer 2003:35–44.

Lampel, J., Lant, T. and Shamsie, J. (2000) 'Balancing act: Learning from organizational practices in cultural industries', *Organization Science* Vol. 25(3): 541–574.

Lennartz, K. (1996) *Theater, Künstler und die Politik. 150 Jahre Deutscher Bühnenverein*, Henschel Verlag, Berlin.

Monthoux, P. de (2004) *The Art Firm: Aesthetic Management and Metaphysical Marketing from Wagner to Wilson*, Stanford University Press, Standford CA.

Pitz, C. and Köhn, M. (2001) 'Öffentliche Trägerschaft – aber wie?', *Die Deutsche Bühne*, Heft 7: 26–29.

Pratt, A.C. (2002) 'Hot jobs in cool places: The material cultures of new media product spaces; the case of the South of the Market, San Francisco', *Information, Communication and Society* 5(1): 27–50.

Schiller, F. (2000) *Über die ästhetische Erziehung des Menschen in einer Reihe von Briefen* Reclam, Stuttgart.

Schmidt, T. (2005) 'Den Vorhang hoch und alle Säle offen!' *Die Zeit*, No. 31: 37.

Schulze, G. (1992) *Die Erlebnisgesellschaft. Kultursoziologie der Gegenwart*, Campus, Frankfurt/M. and New York.

Simhandl, O. (2001) *Theatergeschichte in einem Band*, Henschel Verlag, Berlin.

Strandgaard, J., Svejenova, S., Jones, C. and de Weerd-Nederhof, P. (2006) 'Editorial', *Creativity and Innovation Management* Vol. 15(3): 221–223.

Sutton, R. I. (2001) 'The weird rules of creativity', *Harvard Business Review* Vol. 79(8): 94–103.

Svejenova, S., Mazza, C. and Planellas, M. (2007) 'Cooking up change in haute cuisine: Ferran Adrià as an institutional entrepreneur', *Journal of Organizational Behavior* Vol. 28(5): forthcoming.

Throsby, D (2001) *Economics and culture*, Cambridge University Press, Cambridge.

Vester, M. (2005) 'Class and culture in Germany', in F. Devine, M. Savage, J. Scott and R. Crompton (eds) *Rethinking Class: Culture, Identities and Lifestyles*, Palgrave, Houndmills Basingstoke, pp. 69–94.

von Otting, L. (2001) 'Wer sparen will, muss investieren', *Die Deutsche Bühne*, 7: 36–37.
Waidelich, J.-D. (1991a) *Theatermanagement/Theaterorganisation. Teil I: Problemaufriß und Geschichte des Theatermanagements bis zur Gegenwart,* Fernuniversität, Hagen.
—— (1991b) *Theatermanagement/Theaterorganisation. Teil II: Strukturen und Rezepturen der gegenwärtigen Theaterarbeit,* Fernuniversität, Hagen.

Part 8

Conclusion

Conclusion

Andy C. Pratt and Paul Jeffcutt

Warning: context sensitive

The aim of this book has been to interrogate the relationship between creativity and innovation, and the cultural and creative industries. The main part of the book has been taken up with industry/practice-specific case studies; we see this as a necessary part of grounding, on the one hand, the theoretical work, and on the other more generalised assertions. Our aim is to achieve more than a sum of the parts of the collection, by seeking to make the introduction and conclusion of the book articulate with the case study material. In sum, we have been pursuing two main lines of investigation.

First, we have examined the nature of, and any similarity or differences between, a range of cultural and creative industries. This line is valuable because, depending upon the evidence, one may be able to discuss, or advocate for, the cultural economy in a generic sense (this is, of course, the general assumption that lies behind much policy and academic research). Moreover, there is an additional point that these case studies may help to underline. That is if, and in what ways, the cultural and creative industries are different to the 'rest of the economy'.

The second line of investigation has concerned innovation and creativity, specifically to examine whether it is valid to see the cultural and creative industries as the 'poster children' of innovation and/or creativity, or are they as innovative and creative as the rest of the economy? Again, much policy and recent management interest has been generated by the hope that the creative and cultural industries may 'deliver' innovation and creativity, and thereby competitive advantage to particular locations.

Hence, our cautious approach, as demonstrated in chapter one of this book, where we sought to survey carefully the notions that underpin creativity and innovation, as well as those of the cultural economy. We pointed to the need to be careful about these central concepts as well as the tendency to generalise about all industries, or all of the cultural economy. If anything, the abiding message of this book is to be sensitive to context; that is, a context that is potentially an equal player in the construction of outcomes. In this concluding chapter we review these initial propositions, and consider whether, in the light of the foregoing case studies, they hold good; this accounts for the first two sections of this chapter. The third section considers what our case studies tell us about the cultural and creative industries, especially their differences and similarities, and what innovation and creativity 'look like' in them. Finally, we round off this chapter, and the book, with some pointers to the routes that need to be pursued in future research work to furnish a robust evidence base for both understanding, and for policy making in the field.

Revisiting the key concepts

In this part of the chapter we will review some of the core ideas, and responses to them, that we introduced in chapter one and which constitute the main argument around which this book is constructed: creativity and innovation, the knowledge economy, and the cultural economy.

Innovation and creativity

We outlined in chapter one the common elision of innovation and creativity; we accepted that in their own terms they are different, however, with respect to process they shared much in common. Many resist such a formulation as it seems to reduce creativity to innovation: this generates three reactions.

First, and perhaps the most simple and straightforward, it has been argued that the creative and cultural industries are all about creativity and innovation; they quite literally trade on novelty (a much derided version of innovation). Therefore, whatever the creative industries do is – by definition – creative. There is a good deal of circular argument here, but also blind assertion (to which one is always tempted to respond, 'well, name an uncreative industry?'). However, the notion has common currency and it has been taken by many to justify the importation of business or managerial practices found in cultural industries into non-cultural industries in the anticipation that this will make these industries creative too. We argue that this position is ill-founded.

Second, that creativity is bound up with an idealistic and humanistic conception, whilst innovation is more closely aligned to the rational and scientific. In effect, for those who see creativity as special, aligning it with (commercial) innovation draws the 'sacred (art)' to the 'profane'. Moreover, a central problem common to many accounts of innovation and creativity is the neglect of process in favour of a concern with outputs ('killer' products or great art) as 'evidence' of creativity or innovation. A point that we stress strongly is that outputs cannot be independently valued and measured, but that they are context dependent. The common measure (or, properly, a proxy) of innovation is a 'patent'; however, the gap between know-how and the application of that knowledge can be critical; moreover, an elegant or efficient solution to a problem may not be regarded so by users (or potential users). As we noted in the introduction, in the cultural economy virtually every product is an 'innovation', but this does not guarantee success in the market place or with the audience. A whole structure of differentiation and taste making, or market and audience preparation, has to take place to accommodate any product to a new market. All of which we take to signal the need for a far more nuanced interpretation of innovation and creativity; a step that arguably brings innovation closer to the traditional value qualification of creativity, and which brings production closer to consumption.

A third category of problem for scholars of innovation or creativity is whether to consider them as fundamentally the product of individuals, or of societies/systems. Thus, there is a strong model of the creative genius, or the innovative lone entrepreneur who has a flash of insight – the Eureka moment – and thenceforward is a success. Such notions also rely upon ideas such as genius being born rather than developed. Clearly, these notions play well with atomistic concepts of human nature and human action, also with accounts that are normative and non-critical (an interesting point as scholars highlight the innovative nature of critical thinking!). Often, such atomistic notions of innovation and creativity are countered by a strongly structural approach such that it is social and market structures and regulation that shape innovations, and creativity, and their success or failure. Much work has been carried out in the middle-ground of institutional and network analyses of innovation, and to a lesser extent creativity. Our discussion in chapter one sought to follow this middle ground, not only stressing the iterative and heuristic nature of innovation and creativity, but also by highlighting their socially embedded character (in time and place, as well as in industry).

However, in our resolution of this tension we argued for a somewhat unusual point, namely that innovation and creativity should not be seen as inputs, outputs nor processes, but as effects. Innovation and creativity are not discrete processes that can be simply 'inserted' into an existing organisational structure. By this we mean that what is or is not considered to be innovative or creative can only be determined in contexts. Of course, this is why the activities that we label innovation and creativity are so risky – there is no perfect knowledge about what will or will not 'work'. We are prepared to accept that there is a range of more or less stable[1] innovation and creativity effects; where there is strong regulation and highly rule bound interactions, and innovations are small (in Kuhn's [1962] terms: normal science), the future is commonly close to the past. However, arguably, such conditions apply in the least innovative and creative activities. The most radical and significant changes are not accounted for by such explanations. An argument that is strongly supported by empirical evidence is that the cultural and creative economy is at the extreme end of innovation and creativity. So, for this reason alone we can justify the need to take a radical starting point on innovation and creativity; however, we would like to suggest that other activities may also benefit from such analyses. Of course, based upon our stress on contextuality, we would expect the processes and forms of innovation and creativity to look quite different in various activities. It is this point that underpins the selection of the creative and cultural industries, and in particular a range of creative and cultural industries, for investigation in this book.

The knowledge economy

The notion of the knowledge economy, or sometimes the new economy, or simply aspects of the service sector are commonly put forward as the leading edges of economic growth. Most accounts of this variety share a common lineage with the work of writers such as Rostow (1971), who elaborated a model of modernisation and development, combined with the Fisher–Clark three-sector model of the economy (Fisher, 1952; Clark, 1940) and Kondratieff business cycles (see Marshall, 1987). In the latter sense authors often point to the 'next cycle' as that being characterised not by coal or oil, but by learning/knowledge, or even 'creativity'. Perhaps the most influential – but deeply flawed – work in this field is that of Bell (1973) on the post-industrial society. Critically, two of the most cited writers of the information and creative economy deploy Daniel Bell's thesis (Castells, 1996; Florida, 2002). To a large extent both agree that the value added to products is knowledge, or perhaps culture as a specific form of knowledge, and thus the division of labour/labour market/occupation that adds that value is critical to success. In Bell's thesis it is massive state investment in education and culture for the scientific class, and for Florida it is the need to attract the 'creative class' because these workers will attract economic activity in the form of 'high-tech' activities. For both technology is the source of all value.

We take quite a different tack here; we accept the point that the creative added value (termed the culturalisation of the economy by some) is a key to competitive success in crowded and competitive markets (where value and form of expression, rather than simple price point, is a differentiator).[2] Thus, the development and incorporation of creativity and innovation are 'core business'. In our studies, and those of our contributors to this volume, we have sought to uncover how creativity and innovation take place in the 'hottest' businesses (the creative and cultural industries). It is clearly a complex picture, but if we were to sum it up we'd refer to it as the *mediation of knowledges*. Thus the so-called knowledge economy – in our view – is not simply one of quantity but one of quality. If there is one clear lesson of the information age then it is that quantity does not lead to quality. In fact it commonly results in quite the opposite! So, the challenge is how to both seek out and scan as much knowledge as possible, and how to filter it (using which terms), and how to incorporate knowledge produced in different 'registers'.

The mediation role and the embodiment of this in people, networks and institutions as intermediaries is, we consider, the defining element of the knowledge economy. Thus, the interpretative knowledge of any player, and the mediation and translation of ideas and information is their 'value added'. However, we must go further as the way that these ideas and knowledeges find their way to others is also critical. One mode, characterised by the Fordist firm (for example the BBC, pre-1990s) is to create a huge organisational box that contains everyone, and within which you create bureaucratic structures that you hope will distribute innovations and recruit those who have already learned creative practices (for a discussion of this process more generally, see Chandler, 1977). The mode we see more often today is the network of project-based, short-life enterprises and individuals where the network, in a semi-public domain, is the 'cloud' through which users interact (Grabher, 2004). Many of the studies in this book have sought to examine the dynamics of this emergent network form (i.e. 'the cloud') in physical, social, economic and governance terms.

Lest it be imagined that a semi-public emergent network with many freelancers sounds like a neo-liberal fantasy we should also point out the dark side, namely that the 'semi-public' nature of this form is conditional on complex membership rules and reputation, the result being that the new knowledge economy is at least as closed to wider society as before. This ensues despite what Gill (2002) provocatively terms the 'Benetton image' that new media companies commonly try to project (and by default much of the creative economy). The myth of rags to riches is one that has driven industries such as popular music for many years; however, a careful examination of the socio-economic backgrounds of participants reveals a distinct bias to the mainly young, white, male, middle classes. In the UK, and it is likely in other nations for which we do not have direct data, the creative and cultural industries are particularly poorly representative of diversity.

Thus, our point about existing concepts of the knowledge economy reinforces our statement on innovation and creativity, namely that of context dependency, or context construction, as a point of departure. That dependency, or construct, is constituted through knowledge and information. Drawing upon the ideas of Latour (1988), we suggest that the critical aspect of comprehending innovation and creativity is to understand how knowledge and information are sustained, mediated and translated, and 'packaged' to appear as 'an innovation'. This takes us a step further, namely that such knowledges are not the sole preserve of individuals, or of collectives, but they are about a negotiation and reputation process – this forces us to consider the role that not only 'artists' play in the processes, but also that of managers, marketeers, editors, journalists, manufacturers, and even consumers. It is this point that many authors have been trying to capture through the re-conceptualisation of the creative and cultural industries as comprising the whole 'cycle', or chain, of production.

The cultural economy

In the introduction to this book we provided a limited definition of the cultural economy (the creative industries) that has been in common use by policy makers and academics in recent years, based upon the definition produced by the UK Department of Culture Media and Sport. However, we also noted that policy and academic debate had moved on to a more systemic definition – one that encapsulates the whole production chain. We can summarise such work as a 'depth definition' of the cultural industries (Pratt, 1997). A more traditional starting point is a 'breadth definition', which lists activities, or more normally art or cultural forms, that should be included under culture or creativity. Looking from this perspective alone we can highlight the problems of the common usage of 'creative industries'. If the taxonomic principle is 'creativity' then it is difficult not to include the whole economy; which, if any, activities are not creative, or for that matter not innovative? More properly, common usage would perhaps point to the product rather than the process, as no process can be unequivocally 'creative' (our contextual point). What then is a creative product (aside from one produced by a creative industry)? This definition must be constituted with reference to context; what do users and society consider 'cultural' as opposed to perhaps utilitarian, or social or economic?

Thus the shift to a production chain conceptualisation is to be welcomed. Moreover, it is one that resonates with our discussion of one trajectory of work on innovation that seeks to examine the whole production process. Recent empirical work on the cultural economy has reinforced this point, perhaps stressing – more than much innovation literature – the role of interaction between markets/ audiences and producers.

We can underline how a contextual/embedded definition of the cultural economy focuses our attention to the whole production process; consumption and production, as well as the society it is situated in. Likewise innovation and creativity can be defined in relation to this. So far, so good, but when we define the outliers of the cultural economy we can recognise, as we have done explicitly in this book, that there are significant differences *within* the cultural economy. Is such difference greater than the differences with the rest of the economy, and to what degree? The response to such a question may be a spur to policy debates, or analysis that explores either the more specific, or the generic. As we have noted, we find in favour of specificity. However, this does not go far enough; for what is the particular character of the different industries, what do they share and what is different? As we outlined in our introductory chapter, the uniqueness of the creative economy is one of its apparent characteristics (See chapter one, Box 1.3). What this book has shown further is that the character of innovation and creativity is both shaped by this uniqueness, and characterises it. So, innovation and creativity do not appear the same in each industry, although there may be some common ways of thinking about the problem in all of the creative economy; and we are open to whether this is due to the 'extreme' nature of the industries, and their markets, or something fundamental (although we are not sure what this could be). Accordingly, we are more in favour of conceptualising the cultural economy as a continuum rather than one that simply breaks neatly along industry specific lines.

If we accept this, then we can pursue a radical interpretation and make a claim that the cultural economy may not be different in principle from the rest of the economy.[3] Perhaps the difference to be stressed here concerns our conceptualisation of the process of production. We have been arguing for a fine-grained analysis that pays particular attention to what are normally regarded as the 'residuals' of economic calculation; processes that are not visible to normative and quantitative techniques of measurement. Arguably, such processes are dominant in the cultural economy, and it benefits explanation to investigate them with appropriate tools. It may well be the case that such an approach could reveal the significance of these residual factors throughout the rest of the economy. However, this is a speculative statement and will require more research.

We are also keen to point out that innovation and creativity are integral to the cultural economy and they are valorised within and under particular circumstances – their users do seldom see them as separate or as a potential add-on but rather as integral to it. In the following section we can reflect upon what the internal differences are, in terms of innovation and creativity, within the cultural economy. We stress issues of organisation, labour process, and of markets, as well as the emotional labour process.

Reflections on the industry case studies

As discussed in the introductory chapter to this collection we chose to make the contributions 'work' by articulating them in two ways. First, we placed two different perspectives on innovation and creativity together in each of the separate industry studies. Overall, we were seeking to explore the degree and nature of variations between the various cultural industries covered here. Second, we hoped to some extent to control for variations inherent in authors' interpretations of creativity and innovation (and their relationship) which single case studies may have obscured. More significantly, we hoped that the contrasting perspectives might add to the richness of analysis that we anticipated would be needed to begin to pick up nuances in practices.

We believe that the collection more than meets our expectation that variation would be demonstrated across the cultural industries. It is a fair assumption that one would find further variance across other cultural industries not included in our case studies as well. This is a simple point, but an important one for policy makers and business strategists and points to the need to attend to differences in response and regulation. The more subtle point is how and why does innovation and creativity occur in these industries, and is it so different to non-cultural industries? As we outlined in our introductory chapter, many writers assume that because industries are producing cultural or creative industry products then their practices must be creative or innovative. We have sought to challenge this. However, we have pointed to other reasons for considering the cultural and creative industries as having a stronger tendency to creativity and innovation, that of the peculiar, or extreme market and regulatory conditions that they exist within. We believe that this collection provides us with several insights into how and why different cultural industries respond to such conditions. In part the responses are associated with the various ways and means of mediating, filtering and valuing knowledge in a timely and effective way; hence our previous discussion of the significance of subtle analysis of knowledge formation, use and exchange. However, albeit in a variety of ways, issues of organisation also play a role. We feel that it is clear that innovation and creativity cannot be isolated and simply inserted or extracted and replicated, 'magic bullet' style, into existing processes. The nature of embeddedness and interdependency between all aspects of the production process leads us to support the notion of a 'field of innovation and creativity', one that is articulated in each industry, in a particular time and place. This does not mean that we are saying that everything is unique, rather that we can identify a framework for analysis, but that the empirical manifestations are particular in most cases.

In conclusion, we have identified six salient themes that emerge from this collection. The first significant point that we feel should be made concerns the theme of clusters: whether styled cultural or creative. Policy makers and planners have been much taken by the notion that a cluster of creative businesses will be a sustainable and growth medium for firms. Generally, this is either based upon the idea of co-consumption spaces (retail 'honey pots'), or of agglomeration economies. The former can be criticised on the basis that it does not add to cultural production directly; it is instrumental. The problem with the latter is twofold. First, that agglomeration economies often refer to transport costs; costs which are generally small in the creative industries. Second, that agglomeration economies are about the minimisation of transactions costs/business costs. There is little evidence to sustain such notions of cost minimisation due to co-location in the case of the creative industries. However, it does seem that a significant opportunity is afforded by co-location for collective learning, knowledge exchange and validation of ideas, as well as recruitment of staff. Ironically, those advocates of creative clusters primarily focus on infrastructure provision and not on the facilitation of knowledge exchange. Our work does suggest that this later tactic would be more effective – albeit if differently configured in each industry. The key to this difference is the variations between industries. The spatial aspect of 'clustering' is real, and very marked – but it is also distinctive in that the cultural industries are not ubiquitous, but very selective in their locational preferences; this highlights the massive and subtle role that social and cultural milieux and history play in the embedding of the cultural industries (see chapters by Andy Pratt and Galina Gornostaeva, and Deborah Leslie and Norma Rantisi, as well as Jeffcutt 2004). Moreover, it stresses a path dependency that will not come as welcome news to those seeking to jump on the 'cultural bandwagon'.

Second, it was interesting to note that some creative industries and their workers had a very strong self-image of themselves as 'creative', and to some extents, notably in the advertising industry, had constructed an organisational form and labour markets/ workers to reproduce it. This leads to a point on creative identity, it the construction of creative subjects is enmeshed in the structures within which they are located. These issues are discussed extensively by Sean Nixon and also strongly resonate with both Rosalind Gill's and Dominic Power's discussion of the creative identity of workers. For these workers we can see further examples of what in her study of the fashion industry Angela McRobbie (2002) calls the 'pain–pleasure axis'. The emotional labour of work in the cultural industries, and the precariousness of work itself are further examined in Gill and Pratt (2008).

A third theme articulates the tension between individual and structure in a different manner, that of the distribution of rights. Chapters by both David Hesmondhalgh, and Andy Pratt and Galina Gornostaeva pointed to issues associated with intellectual property rights and the challenge to industry norms that digitisation can afford. The core point here concerns the demarcation of ownership and copying; how copying may itself be a creative resource; and how, it may undermine profitability. Large corporate bodies have sought to protect their rights positions and in effect stifle small companies. Likewise, current World Trade Organisation negotiations on intellectual property rights are tending in the direction of ceding the intellectual property rights of individuals to those of corporations. This has led to discussion of a 'tragedy of the intellectual property commons' where, those opposing it argue, that free ideas are the life blood of innovation (Pratt and Kretschmer, in press).

Fourth, is the issue of public–private funding. Despite a priori expectations we found very little difference in terms of the commercial or non-commercial industries/practices. There was always a tension between profit and art, but what is critical is the mode of governance of this boundary. The examples from the arenas of theatre and museums illustrate well how the commercial field interpenetrates the artistic one. We also find the same tensions being managed in the film industry.

Fifth, the nature of innovations. As we have noted, normative studies of innovation tend to use patents as proxies, or even direct evidence, of innovation; we discussed the way in which such measures ignore the differential take up and marketisation of innovations. In the creative and cultural industries this is much more of a problem, as in effect every new product is an innovation, and product turnover is so rapid. Moreover, there is little relationship between success in take up and adoption and technological or functional 'fit': with fashions, markets, or audiences. First, this exposes the need to examine the complex interactions that lead to the take up and adoption of cultural products and services, something that several of our contributors point to. Second, it highlights the 'winner takes all' character of cultural markets as expressed through monopoly control or supply of products, a 'chart monopoly' (where one product dominates consumption), or through a critical monopoly (the market/audience shaping power of the education and the media).

Finally, we can highlight a set of issues associated with institutional heritage, and institutional 'lock in'. Sara Selwood very clearly outlines the tensions within the museum sector between traditional ways of operating and those of new public management targets. Doris Eikof's study highlights a similar terrain – albeit from an opposite starting point – in her study of innovation in German theatre companies.

Beyond this book: the wider implications

Policy and academic

A number of implications follow on from the discussion and consideration of the studies collected in this volume. First, in terms of theories of innovation and creativity and their specificity, or otherwise, in relation to the cultural economy. We have not found normative, or even institutional, theories of innovation and creativity to be that useful. Analyses of our selection of case studies has pointed to the ways in which apparently key processes slip 'under the radar' and others are given undue import from conventional perspectives. The examples of patents and spatial proximity/clustering are cases in point.

We did not conclude however, that one should simply propose a unique innovation and creativity theory for the cultural economy; rather, that we consider such accounts to be placed on a continuum; or, perhaps more accurately based upon a number of key processes that will be variously manifest under local conditions (time, space, and industry). Accordingly, we found that expressing this as a 'field of innovation' gives a more satisfactory and workable account. Following from this it should be clear that we would underline the necessity of paying particular attention to the differences between cultural industries (audiences, markets, investment, production process, distribution, etc.), and underpinning this with the ways in which knowledge is modified and exchanged, and evaluated. In this sense we found the division between commercial and non-commercial, informal as well as formal, activities in this process less salient. Indeed it pointed to the need to examine *both* sides of these dualisms: to view them as dualities. Allied to both points was our experience of the combination of qualitative and quantitative data. The available quantitative data that are commonly used simply measure co-location and proximity, not interaction (economic or social): we found this to be unhelpful, and particularly valued the insights into the nuances of processes provided by qualitative analyses. It is also clear that protagonists seldom see what they are doing as innovative and are seldom good informants for social scientists asking them about 'innovation'; in this sense – for the protagonists – innovation and creativity is business as usual, it is what/how they do (Oakley *et al.* 2008). They may see, or fashion themselves, as creative; however, we would caution against the notion that there are unproblematic categories of 'creative individuals' (that one might identify by industry or occupation), but that creativity is an effect of the particular construct or field of innovation, Sean Nixon's chapter illustrates this very well.

Whilst the objective and scope of the book is not primarily focused on policy making or policy advice it should be seen as a contribution to the evidence base out of which policy can be developed. As we have noted, this evidence base is – at best – patchy. The implications for thinking about policy in this domain are quite significant. First, we would argue for specific policies rather than simply a blanket or generic policy (either for all industries, or for all creative industries). Second, we would caution against the use of output measures on their own, or physical proximity; rather we would stress the need to examine the potential role in supporting and enabling local–global eco-systems of production and the knowledge arbitrage that is woven around them.

Future directions

One message that this book was founded upon, and which the findings have reinforced, is that detailed accounts of particular cultural industries are of considerable value. In fact, we would argue that they are essential to understand creativity and innovation and by extension all aspects of the cultural economy. Clearly, the wave of statistical mapping documents, starting with that of DCMS (1998), have helped to open the door to research and policy making in this field; if nothing else, showing the relative importance of the cultural economy in traditional output and employment measures. However, as this book and others have shown, this exercise can only scratch the surface of understanding the processes involved, and, what might be the best indicators or proxies of them. It should be clear by now that co-location, and even employment and output data, is quite inadequate for this task.[4] Interaction is the key, but interaction that cuts across the conventional boundaries of this field (e.g. commercial/non, formal/non, arts/cultural etc.). Furthermore, such interaction should be viewed in a very subtle manner that gives full consideration to aspects of knowledge formation and learning; as well as the process of filtering, scanning and sorting, both individual and collective.

Despite the significant policy, political and academic interest in innovation and creativity, our critique has highlighted the low priority given to the understanding of the processes by which they happen, and are understood, in practice. As such our account might stand as an immanent critique of quantitative and normative accounts that deploy an a priori notion of knowledge as a fixed item and quota. Our account has shown how the exchange of knowledge is a process of translation and interpretation. Crucially this process is about mediation and utilisation *in situ*; it is embedded in the social and economic practices, and local and regulatory structure, and the historical or institutional structures. We might hypothesise that those activities that are best organised (and it will be a different form of organisation in each case) to scan, filter, and strategically deploy information will be the most successful.

Moreover, in the nature of incomplete and unknowable knowledge the role of reputation formation and regard also plays a significant part (as does the sheer economic power to shape markets). The activities of the cultural economy are by their nature some of the most risky businesses around. Despite this, protagonists manage to (on the whole) make money, or are successful in their terms. Certainly, the creative and cultural industries sector has outperformed most others in terms of growth at an international level (KEA European Affairs, 2006; UNCTAD 2008). In this collection our co-authors have focused their attention to the how's and the why's of this change. It is clearly not a matter of simply setting the right price for the best product. Growth is rooted in the high spend of the population on cultural economy products but mediated by subtle shifts in justification or qualification that affect demand and are further destabilised by rapid technological change. The responses characterised by novel forms of organisation, and of the access to knowledge mediated by reputation, are critical in rebalancing the knowledge-risk dialectic[5]. Finally, the role of those outside the firm (in other firms, freelancers, and those in the informal sector, and consumers) who act as intermediaries and sounding boards are critical (as audiences, and/or brokers). These are the actors who shape translations[6] – sometimes faithfully, sometimes not, sometimes normatively, sometimes radically so. This too is an important field for future research. We hope that this book has both established the case, and stimulated further interest in the need, for systematic and sustained research on the cultural economy.

Notes

1 In the sense that this term is used in debates about Social Studies of Technology (see MacKenzie and Wajcman, 1999).
2 An indicative discussion of the importance of value(s) can be found in Callon *et al.* (2002).
3 This is a double manoeuvre: that the cultural economy is not the same as the rest of the economy, but, that the rest of the economy is similar to the cultural economy.
4 Most trade data is of physical goods, invisible or digital trade; or the trade in intellectual property rights is simply not counted. This lead to a massive under-representation of the cultural economy.
5 This is the idea that increased knowledge of a situation reduces the risk of uncertainty, and vice versa. Banks who are used to normative decision making tend to charge higher rates

of interest to business they identify as being in 'high risk' activities (high risk should be read as non-normative, or, colloquially, something that we don't know about).

6 Commonly invisible to academic and policy analyses.

References

Clark C, 1940, *The conditions of economic progress* (Macmillan and Co., limited, London)

Bell D, 1973, *The coming of post-industrial society* (Basic Books, New York)

Callon M, Meadel C, Rabeharisoa V, 2002, "The economy of qualities" *Economy and Society* 31 194–217

Castells M, 1996, *The rise of the network society* (Blackwell Publishers, Cambridge, MA)

Chandler A D, 1977, *The visible hand : the managerial revolution in American business* (Harvard University Press, Cambridge, MA; London)

DCMS, 1998, "Creative industries mapping document", (Department of Culture, Media and Sport, UK, London)

Fisher G B A, 1952, "A note on tertiary production" *Economic Journal* 62 820–834

Florida R L, 2002, *The rise of the creative class : and how it's transforming work, leisure, community and everyday life* (Basic Books, New York, NY)

Gill R, 2002, "Cool creative and egalitarian? Exploring gender in project-based new media work in Europe" *Information, communication and society* 5 70–89

Gill R C, Pratt A, C, 2008, "In the social factory? Immaterial labour, precariousness and cultural work" *Theory Culture & Society* 25

Grabher G, 2004, "Learning in projects, remembering in networks? Communality, sociality, and connectivity in project ecologies" *European Urban and Regional Studies* 11 103–123

Jeffcutt P, 2004, 'Knowledge Relationships and Transactions in a Cultural Economy' *Media International Australia* 112 67–82

KEA European Affairs, 2006, "The economy of culture in Europe", (European Commission DG5, Brussels)

Kuhn T S, 1962, *The structure of scientific revolutions* (University of Chicago Press, Chicago; London)

Latour B, 1988, *The Pasteurization of France* (Harvard University Press, Harvard)

MacKenzie D A, Wajcman J, 1999, *The social shaping of technology* (Open University Press, Buckingham England ; Philadelphia)

Marshall M, 1987, *Long waves of regional development* (Macmillan, London)

McRobbie A, 2002, "From Holloway to Hollywood: Happiness at work in the new cultural economy", in *Cultural Economy* (eds). P du Gay, M Pryke (Sage, London) 97–114

Oakley K, Sperry B, Pratt A C, 2008, "The art of innovation: Fine arts in the UK economy", (NESTA, London)

Pratt A C, 1997, "The cultural industries production system: a case study of employment change in Britain, 1984–91" *Environment and Planning A* 29 1953–1974

Pratt A C, Kretschmer M, in press, "Breaking out of the box: The production of music and copyright" *Information, Communication & Society* 12.2

Rostow W W, 1971, *The stages of economic growth : a non-communist manifesto* (Cambridge University Press, Cambridge)

UNCTAD, 2008, "The creative economy report" (UNCTAD/ UNDP, Geneva/New York)

Index